TExES

TEXAS EXAMINATIONS OF EDUCATOR STANDARDS

PPR: Pedagogy and Professional Responsibilities

2ND EDITION

Frances van Tassell, Ed.D.
Associate Professor
Department of Teacher Education
and Administration
University of North Texas
Denton, Texas

Betty Crocker, Ed.D.
Associate Professor
Department of Teacher Education
and Administration
University of North Texas
Denton, Texas

BARRON'S

About the Authors

Frances van Tassell and Betty Crocker are professors in the Department of Teacher Education and Administration at the University of North Texas. Both have written many books and articles in the field of education.

Acknowledgments

Learner Centered Schools for Texas: A Vision for Texas Educators and the teacher competencies for the PPR examinations for EC–6, 4–8, 8–12, and EC–12 are reprinted with the kind permission of the Texas Education Agency (TEA).

© 2010. Texas Education Agency. All Rights Reserved.

Permission to use, copy, and distribute these documents for educational, research, and non-profit purposes, without fee, and without a written agreement is hereby granted.

Permission to incorporate these documents into commercial products may be obtained by contacting the Texas Education Agency.

The documents are supplied "as is," without any accompanying services from the TEA. The TEA makes no representations or warranties of any kind regarding the documents, including the implied warranties of merchantability and fitness for a particular purpose.

Further, the end-user of these documents agrees to indemnify and hold harmless the TEA and its governing board, officers, employees, and representatives from liability or any injury and/or damages to persons or property that may result from any negligent or intentional act or omission when using these documents.

All inquiries should be addressed to:
Barron's Educational Series, Inc.
250 Wireless Boulevard
Hauppauge, New York 11788
www.barronseduc.com

ISBN-13: 978-0-7641-4380-9
ISBN-10: 0-7641-4380-8

ISSN 2154-0411

Printed in the United States of America
9 8 7 6 5 4 3 2 1

FSC
Mixed Sources
Product group from well-managed forests and other controlled sources
Cert no. SW-COC-002507
www.fsc.org
© 1996 Forest Stewardship Council

Contents

PART I

INTRODUCTION AND
EXPLANATION OF
CERTIFICATION IN TEXAS

State and National Testing Requirements

> As of this printing, the Texas Assessment of Knowledge and Skills (TAKS) is the official test for K–12 students. In the 2011–2012 school year, it is scheduled to be replaced by the State of Texas Assessments of Academic Readiness (STAAR).

North American society requires that teachers in public and private schools be well educated. Historically, two types of knowledge and skills have been considered necessary to be a highly qualified, effective, and long-time teacher. These two elements are the science of teaching and the art of teaching. The science of teaching typically refers to the teacher's extensive knowledge of content domains and competencies in the certification area(s). For example, a highly qualified teacher might have completed 18–24 credit hours of history to be successful as a middle school history teacher in Texas. Another example is a person who earned a minimum of 24 credit hours in science who is highly qualified to teach eighth-grade integrated science. A third example is someone who earned 24 credit hours in biology and who teaches high school biology. These college credit hours are generally considered evidence that a subject area teacher is qualified to teach that content area.

The second element, the art of teaching, typically refers to the teacher's ability to plan, design, deliver, assess, and provide continuous feedback. A strong teacher has well-defined skills. He or she motivates students while skillfully managing and disciplining the class. A strong teacher involves parents and the community in the school life of students. He or she also has effective communication skills that encourage the community to be more interested and involved in student learning. A strong teacher is knowledgeable about assessments, lesson planning, and technology. Teachers in Texas must be skillful in both the science and art of teaching to be effective and face the challenges found in today's classrooms.

Today's teachers must be competent in and knowledgeable about both general and content pedagogy. Teachers must know more than just the content of the subject they teach. They must know how to teach effectively so that students learn to the best of their abilities. Teachers must also know the pedagogy that is directly related to that content (content pedagogy). The art of teaching includes knowing culturally sensitive instructional practices so that students from all backgrounds are academically successful. Teachers must also know how to align the curriculum, both horizontally and vertically. With this knowledge, teachers can identify gaps in the curriculum that might cause students to fall behind in their academic development. The TExES PPR tests include both general pedagogy and content pedagogy competencies.

Often, citizens, politicians, government officials, and even some educators claim that the art of teaching is not a necessary component. They suggest that if a teacher knows the subject that she or he is assigned to teach, the teacher will be effective. They claim the teacher will be able to guide students toward the knowledge and skills necessary for today's workplace. Interestingly, however, the state of Texas requires any person who wishes to obtain Texas teacher certification to pass the pedagogy certification examination as well as the content test(s) for the targeted subject area(s). Both content and pedagogy tests are included in the gamut of Texas certification tests referred to as Texas Examinations of Educator Standards (TExES).

LICENSING OF TEACHERS

You might ask if all states require testing for licensing or certification. States do require some type of testing to verify that the candidate has the requisite knowledge for teaching. States look to national boards and professional specialty organizations for standards that guide the development of a certification or license examination. Based on these external standards and those of the given state, a testing company is usually contracted to develop the state test. Several states employ a more universal test, such as the PRAXIS (Professional Assessments for Beginning Teachers). Typically, educators at all levels participate in the final determination of appropriate tests. They make decisions and recommendations about the appropriateness of the items on a given test. States also employ strategies to affirm that test items are free of bias in order to protect the rights of all candidates to take a fair and unbiased examination. Title II of the Elementary and Secondary Education Act (federal law) requires that states report the mandated testing success of candidates who graduate from educator preparation programs. This requirement is intended to ensure that all children and youths have highly qualified teachers in their classrooms.

TEACHER SHORTAGE

As states face an increasing shortage of well-prepared and qualified teachers, the demand will continue to increase for highly qualified teachers. This means that teachers who have academically successful students, who are competent in content areas, and who are capable of effectively engaging all learners in a supportive environment will be in high demand. The more you learn as a teacher, through staff development programs and/or continued graduate studies, the more capable you will become as a teacher. You will have more stamina and motivation to remain in the classroom until retirement age.

Unfortunately, statistics show that about 50 percent of new teachers leave the classroom during or soon after the first five years. That fact leads to a shortage of teachers in some fields and in some geographic areas. If new teachers had the support of mentors, desirable teaching assignments, and confidence in their abilities, they would probably remain as teachers for many years. No doubt, when you decided to become a teacher, you believed that this would be a lifelong profession. However, without knowledge of content, pedagogy, and content pedagogy, you may face the same challenges that others face in their first year and that cause them to leave the teaching profession.

Who Takes the TExES and Why

At the present time, any person who wishes to obtain initial certification in Texas must take the TExES tests. Whether a person completes a higher-education teacher preparation program, a Texas Education Service Center or School District Alternative Certification program, or any other program in a venue that focuses on the preparation of teachers, that person must both sit for and pass the state pedagogy test. He or she must also meet the content-area requirements (usually through a state content-area test). The content-area test determines the certificate and its grade levels.

The pedagogy and professional responsibilities (PPR) test (the focus of this study guide) should be taken at the grade level grouping for the certification area sought (i.e., EC–6, 4–8, 8–12, or all-level EC–12). However, it is possible for a candidate who has taken the 4–8 or EC–12 PPR test along with the 4–8 generalist content-area test to be certified for grades 4–8. The content generalist test determines the grade levels of certification. Tests within the PPR set are obviously designed to measure the teacher candidate's knowledge of pedagogy at the grade level cluster.

In addition to the PPR test, all candidates for initial certification in Texas must take and pass a specific content test designed to measure knowledge of the content of the subject(s) in which certification is sought. This means that all persons seeking Texas certification must take and pass at least two certification examinations before receiving a certificate to teach as a highly qualified teacher in Texas. These two exams are the PPR and the specific content test or tests. (*Note:* In addition to obtaining passing scores on the two required certification tests, each candidate for certification must also be fingerprinted as part of a national criminal background check.)

Under the Texas Education Agency (TEA), the Texas State Board for Educator Certification (SBEC) contracts with a testing company to develop and maintain examinations. These tests ascertain teacher candidates' knowledge of pedagogy and their ability to demonstrate whether or not they are highly qualified teachers in the state of Texas. Any person seeking initial certification in Texas at one of the existing grade level clusters must, as mandated by the Texas Administrative Code, 230.5 (b), take both the PPR and the content tests in the area(s) for which certification is sought.

PASSING THE EXAMINATIONS

All state certification tests are based on the state-mandated curriculum, the Texas Essential Knowledge and Skills (TEKS). All certification tests are administered at sites across the state and sometimes in neighboring states. In addition, some of the TExES exams are also offered via computer testing at specific test centers. All of the TExES exams are criterion referenced rather than norm referenced. That means your scores will be compared with the knowledge identified in the criteria (the TEKS) rather than compared with all other test takers. Each test is based on a set of competencies that all teachers are required to have knowledge of and the ability to implement. The practice tests in this study guide are based on those test frameworks. You will receive a score for the overall test plus scores for the domains and the competencies. These scores will help you identify areas where you need to increase your knowledge or improve your skills. Your score is based on how many items you answer correctly, which means that you are not penalized for incorrect answers. Do not anticipate receiving actual raw scores on your tests. Instead, the state uses a formula that generates scaled scores. At present, the minimum passing scale score is 240 out of 300.

Persons who have previously achieved passing scores on required certification examinations and who hold current Texas certificates are not required to pass an additional pedagogy test in order to add certification at a different grade level. If you are interested in adding an area of certification, contract SBEC to learn the process for adding additional certifications.

In summary, all persons wishing to become initially certified in the state of Texas must take and pass, at the designated standard level, two state certification examinations. Once you are certified in Texas, if you wish to add another level or area of certification, you can do so through the state (SBEC). For more information on this route to additional certification, contact the staff at the office of the SBEC. Of course, to add any other level or area of certification, the candidate must pass the requisite certification test.

Effective Use of This Study Guide

The following chapters of this study guide are developed in line with the standards and the descriptors deemed by the TEA and SBEC to be critical for teaching. The focus of this text is the set of pedagogy examinations required of all persons seeking initial certification in the state of Texas.

At each of the grade level clusters are four standards for the PPR examination. Knowledge and application descriptors vary by grade level clusters. Therefore, the chapters that define and describe the standards pay particular attention to each of the grade level clusters. This ensures that all readers can find the appropriate information for the particular certification area. Even though readers will be focused on one of the grade level clusters for certification, they should review the entire text. It covers all grade levels. It also offers extensive test items for practice and developing competence in the domains, competencies, and constructs of the PPR examinations. Table 1 indicates the four domains covered on each grade level group test, with the percentage of items covered for that domain.

TABLE 1

Domains and Percentage of Test by Grade Level Group

Domains	EC–6	4–8	8–12	EC–12
I: Designing Instruction and Assessment	4 competencies 31% of test	4 competencies 31% of test	4 competencies 31% of test	4 competencies 31% of test
II: Creating a Positive Classroom Environment	2 competencies 15% of test	2 competencies 15% of test	2 competencies 15% of test	2 competencies 15% of test
III. Implementing Instruction and Assessment	4 competencies 31% of test	4 competencies 31% of test	4 competencies 31% of test	4 competencies 31% of test
IV. Professional Roles and Responsibilities	3 competencies 23% of test	3 competencies 23% of test	3 competencies 23% of test	3 competencies 23% of test

As the table indicates, the focus in each grade level group is the same. As a result, the percentage of the test by domain is common across groups.

This book lists, describes, and explains each standard in an overall framework. The four standards are dispersed across four domains. In Domain III, Standards I and III are addressed along with Standards I–V of the Technology Applications Standards. Table 2 identifies the domains and related standards.

TABLE 2

Domains and Standards

Domains	Standards
I: Designing Instruction and Assessment	PPR Standard I
II: Creating a Positive Classroom Environment	PPR Standard II
III: Implementing Instruction and Assessment	PPR Standards I and III Technology Applications Standards I–V
IV: Professional Roles and Responsibilities	PPR Standard IV

Note that Technology Application Standards are intentionally integrated into the PPR test in each of the grade level groups. Candidates must know about the applications of technology. They must also be able to design, develop, implement, and assess appropriate technological skills throughout the curriculum. The goal is to ensure that all students have contemporary technological skills.

HOW THIS BOOK IS ORGANIZED

Following an introductory description of each standard, the knowledge and application competencies identified by the SBEC as critical for beginning teachers are discussed. These include terms, concepts, and research data related to the area. In no way is this study guide intended to teach all the knowledge needed to become a highly qualified teacher. Rather, it provides a cluster of concepts that might serve as a reminder of the knowledge and skills learned in a teacher preparation program. It also provides test-taking strategies along with diagnostic and sample test questions.

The diagnostic and sample tests are developed by one of the authors. The format is similar to that on the SBEC website. The author of the test items has not developed test frameworks or test items for the SBEC and therefore does not have explicit knowledge of actual test items. Readers of this text (candidates for initial Texas teacher certification) are encouraged to combine these test items with those found in the diagnostic test examples, taken from the SBEC website (www.sbec.state.tx.us/standards). By using both, candidates should succeed on the pedagogy tests.

You can use the questions in this study guide and on the SBEC website in five different ways. Each way will help you develop confidence and competence in your test-taking skills. First, these questions will help you practice test-taking strategies. Second, they will help you understand how PPR tests are structured. Third, you can use your results to analyze your strengths and weaknesses. Use that information to determine which competencies you understand and which you need to study more. Fourth, reading the answers will help you analyze why a particular response is the acceptable answer. Remember that you must always choose the best answer. Fifth, these questions will help you develop confidence. You will increase your knowledge and understanding of the test frameworks and measured competencies.

Readers must be aware of current scientific and descriptive studies conducted by nationally and/or internationally recognized researchers in the areas covered by the competencies. The research and resources mentioned in this text are in no way exhaustive. You can find many high-quality research reports just by searching professional journals or the Internet. Readers should go beyond the resources cited in this book. They should become more fully apprised of the latest findings related to teaching and learning, particularly in the areas of content, learning, and instruction.

The glossary follows the appendices. Words and phrases appearing in bold type throughout Chapters 1–10 of this guide can be found in the glossary (Appendix F) along with other important educational words and phrases. Candidates should study these terms and their definitions thoroughly. Doing so will ensure confidence when sitting for the test(s) and will integrate this knowledge into the conceptual frameworks necessary for effective teaching.

PART II

TEST-TAKING STRATEGIES
AND
SELF-ASSESSMENT GUIDE

Preparing for the Test

Think of the last time you were highly stressed. What caused your stress? How did you react to that stress? To what degree did the stress cause you to function at a level lower than your optimal performance? Were you at your best mentally? What about your physical condition? What about your emotional status?

As you prepare for the PPR exam, you can help yourself succeed. In order to perform at an optimal mental capacity, our physical and emotional selves need to be as strong as possible. For many people, taking a high stakes examination like the TExES PPR creates a lot of stress. If you are one of those people, now is the time to prepare yourself mentally and emotionally. These aspects will be discussed in later chapters. Make sure you are at your best physically. Let's talk about ways to ensure that you are as physically ready for the TExES as possible.

Think about Abraham Maslow's hierarchy of human needs. Remember how he stated that at the lowest level are the basic human needs? Proper diet, sufficient sleep, sufficient rest or relaxation, and a comfortable and safe environment are basic to the welfare of human beings. Take the next 15 minutes to walk around your residence and assess the elements of your living space. Determine if you could improve the setting to increase your physical health.

What did you find? Did you find an ergonomically correct workstation where you study, read, do homework, or take care of routine daily business? Did you find a room where sleep is assured, with low to no lighting, with few or no sounds, and with comfortable bedding? Did you find healthy food in your refrigerator, cabinets, pantry, or other storage areas? How can you improve these? Do some things that need your attention now in order to be prepared by the week before the tests.

PHYSICALLY

The following strategies are suggestions for preparing physically for the test. Think about these strategies, and analyze whether or not they would be helpful to you. Sometimes if the body is rested, the mind is more confident and the emotions are more stable. If the body is healthy, the brain tends to process more effectively.

1. For at least three days before the TExES test, arrange your surroundings and your schedule so that you have a minimum of six to eight hours of sleep each night. Each person's body operates on its own clock. Although six hours of

sleep are sufficient for some people, others need a full eight hours. For several weeks before the test, monitor your body and see how much sleep results in optimal brain activity and physical stamina. Sleep-deprived bodies are less effective and less efficient than fully rested bodies.

2. Start exercising so that you are actively engaged one or two days before taking the test. This will help increase your stamina, particularly if you choose to or need to take two examinations in one day. If you have time for nothing more than 15 minutes of walking each day, do it to help your body maintain stamina.

3. On the day of the examination, dress in layers. It is impossible to know in advance what the test setting will be like on the day you take the test. To be prepared for either a cool room or one that is uncomfortably warm, wear removable layers of comfortable clothing. For some people, being cold causes a slowing of the brain's processing because the body focuses on getting warmer. For some people, being too warm causes frustration. The resulting stress might create a less-than-optimal thinking situation.

4. In addition to layering, wear comfortable clothing. Keep in mind that few people in the testing environment will even remember that you were present, much less remember what you wore that day. Because the TExES are high-stakes examinations, people taking these tests will be focused on themselves and their optimal performance. If loose clothing such as a sweat suit makes you more comfortable, wear it. If dressing in more professional clothing helps you to think more actively, wear it. The type of shoes you wear could also impact your test performance. If you have problems sitting for lengthy periods of time, you may need to put your legs or feet up in the chair. So wearing comfortable, soft shoes might be a good idea. Slipping your shoes off could be distracting to other test takers. You would not appreciate someone else doing that, so do not plan to do it yourself.

5. You will be sitting in a chair for two to five hours at a time. Think about how this might impact your back, your legs, your shoulders, and so on. You might obtain permission to take a soft pillow into the testing environment. If you have lower-back problems, take a small pillow into the registration area and ask permission to use it. Just be sure to arrive early enough to ask for this permission and to return the pillow to your car if your request is not granted. Providing a doctor's note that you need a cushion might be a good idea, just in case.

6. Several days before the test, put yourself into a noisy environment and see if you can concentrate on a challenging task without being distracted. If you are at all distracted, bring well-fitting earplugs to the test. Test takers have often commented that this strategy alone helped them perform much better on the test. Often, auditory learners are distracted by extraneous noises. In the testing environment, someone may be coughing, tapping a pencil, rattling paper, or creating other noises that might at other times seem insignificant but will be distracting during the test.

7. Be sure to eat and drink properly the night before the examinations and especially on the morning of the test. Even if you do not usually eat breakfast, definitely eat some food that morning. Think about what foods give you the most energy and stamina. For some people, this means a sugar-based food. For others, it is carbohydrates. Protein works effectively for some people. Before the day of the test, figure out what foods work most effectively for you in a high-stress situation.

8. If you are a coffee drinker, drink your regular amount of coffee. Do not think, though, that more caffeine will be good for you on the test date. For many people, increased caffeine causes anxiety. You certainly do not want to put your body in that situation. Likewise, if you are not a coffee drinker, do not consume caffeine, thinking it might help to startle your body into action. If you need to remain in the testing environment for five hours, the effects of the caffeine might wear off and your body might go into a lull just when you need to be thinking at your best. There is also the issue of too many trips to the restroom caused by drinking too much caffeine or other liquid. Research shows that the brain needs to remain hydrated at all times to think optimally. So be sure that you drink plenty of water the day before and the morning of the test.

9. If you register to take two examinations on the same date, bring a packed lunch. Be sure that the food is nonperishable, does not need refrigeration, and is nutritious. Do not bring junk food. Although fast-food restaurants might be near the testing site, you might not know this in advance. You might not have time to purchase your food and eat it within a comfortable time frame, and you might not be able to buy healthy food.

10. Although you will not be allowed to take food and drink into the testing environment, it works for some people have hard candy in a pocket and then discretely slip it into their mouth to help them concentrate. Of course, you want to avoid rattling candy wrappers. A good idea is to put unwrapped candy in a ziplock plastic bag that can be slipped into your pocket. Since test sites have assigned test administrators, be respectful if the administrator asks you not to eat the candy.

11. If you are taking two tests on the same date, try to find some time between the two sittings to get some exercise. If the administration site is in a safe area, take a short walk. If not, walk within the building and/or do some stretching exercises. This will be especially helpful if you were not able to get sufficient sleep the night before.

12. For some people, finding a hotel near the testing site is a good idea. If you have small children at home or face some other potential interruption to your sleep, this might be even more important. Some test takers get together with others to share the cost of such a room.

In summary, be sure that you recognize the impact of your physical health and stamina on your brain's processing potential. Think about all the ways you can prepare yourself physically for optimal mental performance. Each person's body has its own unique needs. Know yours, and respond appropriately.

MENTALLY

Previously, we talked about analyzing yourself in a stressful situation. What did you discover about your mental capacity and brain functioning when you did that brief analysis? Now ask yourself the following questions.

- Do you consider yourself a "poor" test taker?
- Do you think you have more knowledge in some areas than in others?
- Do you think more linearly than randomly?
- Is it easy for you to apply basic knowledge in a context situation?
- After narrowing down multiple-choice answers to two, is it easy for you to select the better of the two or do you doubt yourself?
- Do you tend to overanalyze when faced with limited choices?
- Do you tend to add additional information to a test item scenario, thinking that more information is logical and could impact the right answer?
- Do you tend to overanalyze the information in a test item scenario, thinking of exceptions and unique situations that would influence your answer selection rather than using only the information provided on the test?
- Is it easy for you to make clear connections between questions and answer choices in a multiple-choice test?

Think about the term **metacognition**. Persons who can analyze their thinking processes, who can monitor their own thinking and learning, and who can effectively adjust their thinking to varying contexts have the skill of metacognition. As you prepare for the Texas certification examinations, you should spend several weeks before the test monitoring your learning pattern. Ask yourself if you know the most effective strategies for you to solve problems. Ask yourself what adjustments you need to make to most efficiently learn what is needed for the accountability tests. Think like an outsider who is analyzing your brain to determine if particular thinking strategies work more effectively for you. For example, some people learn and think more effectively in an inductive mode, whereas others find more success in a deductive mode. Inductive thinkers prefer knowing the elements of a given task before looking at the big picture. In contrast, deductive thinkers understand better by looking at the big picture first. Apply this to the certification tests. You might be most effective by looking at the question before reading the information provided as background (e.g., in a scenario) or in the stem of the question. Others perform more efficiently by looking at the background information or question stem before looking at the question itself and all possible responses. Some people even find it effective to look at all possible responses before reviewing either the background information or the question itself. By applying metacogition skills, you become adept at understanding what works best for your own mental constructs.

Another important aspect of how the brain processes information is **schemata**. Remember what Jean Piaget said about **assimilation** and **accommodation**. If your brain has preexisting schemata (building blocks of knowledge or understanding), then you can readily learn new information. However, if these schemata (**prior knowledge**) are not present, your brain will attempt to adjust the schemata you do possess in order to accommodate the new information. This knowledge should be helpful to you as you consider each item on the certification test. This learning concept also confirms the absolute necessity of knowing the domains and competencies, the content and pedagogy that support each competency, and the ways your brain most effectively processes information.

Think about the following questions as they relate to your mental preparedness for optimal success on the TExES. Ask yourself these questions.

- Have you read and studied the Texas standards?
- Have you read and studied the TExES domains and competencies?
- Have you taken the complete practice test on the SBEC website?
- How might you ensure that you are as mentally ready as possible to score well on the TExES you will be taking?

STRATEGIES TO PREPARE MENTALLY

These questions should help you identify potential problems you will face with the multiple-choice items on the TExES PPR. You must know in advance what mental strategies you should employ to avoid putting unnecessary stress on yourself while taking the test. Read the following comments and strategies. See how they might guide you when responding to the questions above.

1. The most important mental preparation will occur before you arrive at the test site. Cramming the night before the test will likely be futile and will certainly take away from the rest you will need. A better approach is to plan ahead and schedule study time each day for at least two weeks before the testing time. Do your best to forget about the test the day and the evening before. Instead, relax, do something fun, and be confident in your preparation and knowledge. Schedule a block of time each day that fits within your schedule so that nothing interferes with your study and preparation for the test(s).

2. Organize small study groups to review the competencies and take the practice tests together. You can then discuss why certain choices are good or not so good. Analyze the reasons why each possible response is right or wrong. Look for connections between words or phrases in each response and those in the background information, test question, or question stem. Learn how to identify critical elements so you can make logical connections for each of the possible responses. Get your study groups together at least six weeks before the test. This strategy will help you develop more confidence in your understanding of the format and the concepts of the test. The more confidence you have about taking the test, the more likely that your performance will be high.

3. Make flash cards or note cards, and keep them with you at all times during the week or two weeks before the test. Whenever you find a few moments, take out the cards and review the critical elements you have recorded on them. The more you know about the content and pedagogy of the test, the more likely you are to perform well. The more you practice answering test items, the more confident you will be about your knowledge.

4. Know the vocabulary terms that are pertinent to the PPR test. Refer to the glossary at the end of this guide for terms you need to know. Use the card

and small study group strategies to practice these words. Learn their meanings and how to use them during the test. You might be able to answer some test items simply by knowing the vocabulary/language of the profession.

5. As you take the sample tests in this text or the extended diagnostic/practice test on the SBEC website (www.sbec.state.tx.us), think about how you choose each answer. Is it easy for you to determine the best of the four? Is it easy for you to narrow your answer to the best two? Do you have problems when choosing between the best two? Can you understand why one response is the best answer and not the others, which may be distracters? Once you select what seems to be the best two answers, go back to the question to see which one is most directly linked to the focus of the question. Do not imagine, invent, or assume extra data or variables. These may have little to do with the question and will certainly distract you from choosing the most appropriate answer. Use only the information actually given in the question rather than thinking about all the other possible variations that might fit. Do not assume any information that is not given in the stem or in the background information. Doing so is dangerous. However, you must use inference to read between the lines. Do not go beyond the words and add information that is not given. Taking the TExES tests is a balancing act. You should focus on words like "*best*," "*first*," "*most*" in the question. These words are clues that will guide you when you have narrowed down your options to two responses.

6. Spend sufficient time before the test to learn how to "think like the test." This will help you become comfortable with narrowing down choices and then analyzing why one of the two answers is correct.

7. Look for logical responses to the test items. The TExES were developed to determine if you know pedagogy and content pedagogy best practice as well as content. Ask yourself what the best teacher would do in the situation described in the background information or in the stem of the test item. This may or may not be what you have seen teachers do. To score well on the test, rely more on what you have learned about best practice than on what you might have seen in field experiences or in teaching settings. Sometimes extenuating circumstances create learning situations where teachers must make decisions that are not always based on best practice. For this reason, you may have seen teacher practices that are not directly in line with best practice as identified in current research. Do not discount these observations. However, do recognize that your answer choice may be negatively impacted by such experiences. Your own teacher choices should be confirmed primarily by your knowledge of best practice.

8. Develop a strong sense of self-confidence in your ability to perform well on the test. One way to help you create this sense of self-efficacy is to be fully prepared. Review your notes from education studies. Take the diagnostic and sample tests in this book as well as the complete diagnostic test on the SBEC website. Look for the best practice responses to the test items.

9. Most importantly, use common sense. Items on the TExES PPR test(s) are written to depict a somewhat *perfect teaching and learning environment* where teachers have students/learners of all types. In these perfect scenarios, the

teachers know best practice and employ the most effective teaching strategies. Such a classroom has a teacher who creates a learning environment clearly focused on students' engagement and learning. The teacher assesses learning in meaningful ways. The teacher also builds on students' knowledge and experience to ensure that all have an optimal opportunity to learn and thrive. Think of yourself as a first-year teacher in this type of setting. Decide what would be the *right* or the *best* thing to do. This setting does not include perfect children or youth. It is simply a typical classroom that has a teacher who is truly current on research-documented best practice and who believes all learners can be successful.

Your state of mind and mental stamina may well be the critical elements impacting your success on the TExES. Just as your mental preparation is critical to your preparation for the TExES, so are your background knowledge base and your belief in yourself as a teacher candidate and as a test taker. Consider the suggestions for emotional preparedness that follow.

EMOTIONALLY

Earlier, we talked about preparing your whole self. Think now about how your physical and mental states are impacted by your emotional state. What emotional status do you want on the day of the TExES? What can you do now to prepare for that day? Read the following questions to think about your attitude.

- How do you see yourself as a test taker?
- Do you consider yourself weak in certain knowledge or ability areas?
- How much value do you place on preparing for a given task?
- Why is it important for you to perform at your best on the TExES?

The answers to these questions may let you know your emotional readiness for scoring well on the certification examination(s). Now read the following statements and suggestions. They might effectively guide you in improving your emotional readiness for the test.

STRATEGIES TO PREPARE EMOTIONALLY

Perhaps one of the most important elements of preparing mentally and emotionally is to believe in yourself and your abilities to do well on the test. Some people display a picture of themselves as highly successful at the given task. For example, people who wish to lose significant weight sometimes post a picture of a much slimmer body on the refrigerator. Others who wish to own and drive a red sports car post a picture of such a car in a strategic place in their home or office. You might try this strategy by finding a photograph of a person who is highly successful in business or education to whom you might relate when thinking about passing the certification exam. Look at this picture frequently. Tell yourself that this is what you will look like when, *not if,* you are successful in obtaining certification. According to motivational theorists, such visualization is a major component of preparing yourself mentally.

Another idea is to talk about yourself as being "good" in a given area rather than using negative language such as "I'm just not good in … [math, writing, and so on]."

Sometimes if we believe strongly enough that we are good at something, our self-talk helps us become more capable in that area. Ask yourself if getting together with friends, peers, classmates, and so on would help you build confidence in yourself as a test taker. If it would, commit to this strategy. Keep away from people who have negative attitudes about education and especially those who talk negatively about the certification tests. Especially avoid individuals who state that the test is based on an unrealistic ideal teaching setting rather than on best practice. Focus your study group's energies on building a positive approach to the competencies and on understanding the reason the state requires verification of knowledge and skills. The purpose of the study group is to learn together how to select the best answers to test items and to build a deep understanding of the competencies.

A word of warning might be appropriate at this point. Taking a negative attitude toward the state certification examinations will do you no good as you prepare for these high-stakes tests. Educators at all levels and from all areas of Texas have participated in preparing these mandated tests. It is not as though some group of persons from an unknown place created a test for Texas teachers. Parents, politicians, legislators, and business and industry leaders demanded some measure of teacher preparedness and accountability. Thus the TExES were created. Develop a mind-set that takes you to the test site with a positive attitude, where you believe in yourself as a highly qualified teacher.

Avoid anything or anyone that might result in an emotional upheaval the day of the test. The state has banned the use of cell phones at all testing sites. Absolutely no cell phones of any type will be allowed in the test center. The same is true for PDAs or any photographic-type devices. If you forget to leave your phone in your car and have it with you when you enter the test site, you put yourself at great risk of being dismissed without your test fees being refunded. Rushing to take your cell phone back to your car might cause you to be late when returning. Once the test site doors are closed, no one will be permitted to enter, even if you were in the testing area before. If someone drops you off, you must leave your phone with that person. You will have no other place to deposit it outside the test site. If you are late entering the test site for any reason, you will not be admitted. Your scores will be canceled, although you haven't taken the test.

To summarize, each individual has unique ways of thinking, learning, processing information, and problem solving. You must clearly understand how you mentally process information. Incorporate this knowledge while preparing to take the high-stakes TExES test(s). Only after you understand your own thinking processes will you be able to teach your students to do the same. By teaching them these skills, you will help your students become **self-directed** and **self-monitoring** learners. Similarly, only when you know how your own brain works will you be able to employ strategies that ensure your emotional preparedness for first-time success on the Texas certification examinations.

Understanding Test Structure

The state's educational leaders believe in the right of every child or youth to have a qualified teacher. This teacher must know content (the subject matter) and pedagogy (how to teach). They also believe all students should be able to learn in an educational environment focused on student learning. As a result, certain overarching concepts flow throughout the PPR examinations. Generally speaking, almost all test items are written in a scenario format that describes teacher X in classroom Y with students Z. You must read literally and inferentially, but not make assumptions. Read the background scenario information, the test items/questions, and all possible responses before selecting an answer. Always choose the best answer. Do not make assumptions about the passages or test questions. If you do, you might choose the wrong response.

As mentioned previously, some test takers work better by reading the question first and then scanning the background information for data needed to make a decision. Others work effectively by reviewing the background information first and then reading the question and possible responses. The key is to carefully pair the background information with what the question is asking for *exactly*.

Test takers often ask whether or not they should change an answer after marking it. Many believe that first choices tend to be accurate and are often changed from a right answer to a wrong one. No evidence proves that this common perception is wrong because no research has been conducted on what happens with individuals who keep their first choices. However, when Nicholas Skinner, a psychologist and educator at King's College in Ontario, conducted an analysis of the research on changing answers, he found that approximately 50 percent of the changes made shifted from a wrong to a right answer, 25 percent went from a right to a wrong answer, and 25 percent went from a wrong to a different wrong answer. Skinner's research revealed that more women than men changed answers and that women were more likely than men to go from a right to a wrong answer. You should always have a valid reason for choosing each answer you select and also for changing any answer. Read the item and the possible responses carefully. Focus on the information given in the question. Afterward, only if you are positive that you have chosen the wrong answer should you change your mark.

One serious concern about changing an answer is that you might not be able to erase the smudge from your answer sheet completely. If the electronic machine that scores the answer sheet detects that you have made two marks for a given item, you will automatically lose credit for that item even if one of your marks is the right one. For this reason, it is imperative that you take several pencils with quality erasers to the test administration site. Some test takers mark their choices in the test booklet first and then transfer them to the score sheet. You must be cautious when doing this, however. You must mark the line on the answer sheet that corresponds with the item in the test booklet. Be very careful not to get off the line and mark your response to item 15 on line 16.

Know what strategy works best for you. Employ that strategy when changing answers or deciding whether to mark the answers in the test booklet or on the answer sheet.

Self-analysis Rubric

Use Table 3 as a guide to preparing for the Texas PPR examination. Think about how this table/rubric could help you determine your success potential. Read each competency listed in the table, and then mark your degree of knowledge and/or understanding in this area. Be brutally honest with yourself as you indicate your level of readiness. Only you (or possibly members of your study group) will see these scores. Your goal is not overconfidence. Do not inflate your scores. If your score is 1 or 2, you should be prepared for these competencies. A quick review of these competencies a day or two before the test should be sufficient for you. If your score is a 3, 4, or 5, you obviously need to research information to develop your knowledge base in these areas. Focus on these areas when you establish small study groups or when you intensify your personal preparation in the weeks before the test.

This table is *not* exhaustive. It does not show every area you must know about to be successful on the PPR test. The items included in the table are to inform you of the depth of knowledge teachers must have. Teachers must know more than just the basics. The table should help you prepare for the domains and competencies included on the PPR examination. As you read the chapters that identify domains and competencies, think of this short assessment.

Use a scale of 1–5 (see below) to ascertain your level of prior knowledge and understanding (thus preparedness) for the knowledge needed across the domains and competencies of the PPR examinations.

> **(1) Highly competent**
> **(2) Competent**
> **(3) Somewhat competent**
> **(4) Little knowledge/competency**
> **(5) No knowledge/competency**

TABLE 3

Rubric for Determining Prior Knowledge and Skill for the Texas PPR Test	
Competency	Your Score
Human development cognitive characteristics (Piaget)	
Human development psychosocial characteristics (Erikson)	
Human development moral reasoning characteristics (Kohlberg)	
Human development physical characteristics	
Human development language characteristics	
Strategies for assessing learners' readiness for learning	
Strategies for designing developmentally appropriate instruction	
Skills in instructional task analysis	
Skills in developing appropriate student-centered learner outcomes	
Skills in determining appropriate instructional materials and supplies	
Strategies for delivering effective, developmentally appropriate instruction	
Field-dependent and field-independent approaches to learning	
Visual, auditory, kinesthetic, and tactile modalities of learning	
Deductive and inductive approaches to learning	
Convergent and divergent approaches to learning	
Strategies for building and/or activating learners' prior knowledge/schemata	
Strategies for overcoming lack of prior knowledge and experiences	
Strategies for developing skills of metacognition	
Environmental variables that impact student learning	
Effective techniques for grouping learners	
Various strategies for cooperative learning	
The effect of teacher expectations on student learning	
Indicators of and effects of stress on student learning	
Characteristics of students who are experiencing depression	
Indicators of child abuse/responsibilities in reporting child abuse	
Characteristics of culture and impact on student learning	
Impact of social and economic status on student learning	
Effect of peer influence on student learning	
Strategies for working with English language learners	
Impact of second-language acquisition on student learning	
Approaches to bilingual and ESL (English as a Second Language) instruction	
Expository instructional strategies (direct instruction)	

TABLE 3 (continued)

Rubric for Determining Prior Knowledge and Skill for the Texas PPR Test	
Competency	Your Score
Inquiry instructional strategies (scientific approach)	
Demonstration/modeling of instructional strategies	
Strategies for employing students' extrinsic and intrinsic motivation	
Strategies for leading learners toward becoming self-motivated	
Strategies for guiding learners toward becoming self-directed	
Strategies for increasing learners' self-esteem and self-efficacy	
Strategies for engaging parents in school activities and student learning	
Communication skills for working with parents and the community	
Impact of verbal and nonverbal tools of communication	
Cultural characteristics of communication and impact on student learning	
Technological skills for effective and efficient communication	
Strategies for effective conferencing with parents	
Laws and regulations for addressing needs of special-needs learners	
Approaches to working with parents of special-needs learners	
Skills for conducting ARD (Admission, Review, Dismissal) meetings with colleagues and parents	
Strategies for efficient teacher-student conferencing activities	
Strategies for mentoring and being mentored	
Skills for effective use of time, space, and resources	
Skills for establishing long- and short-term instructional goals	
Skills for writing appropriate daily lesson plans and instructional units	
Skills in selecting useful themes for designing effective instruction	
Skills in developing appropriate assessment techniques	
Knowledge of standardized assessments (norm/criterion-referenced tests)	
Use of descriptive interpretation of standardized tests (mean, median, and so on)	
Skills in writing and evaluating teacher-made tests	
Skills in utilizing and evaluating textbook published tests	
Knowledge of innovative means of assessment and evaluation	
Use of portfolios and rubrics for assessment	
Employment of performance tasks and related assessments	
Knowledge of diagnostic/readiness measures and when to use them	
Assessment-related issues (bias, reliability, validity, grading, and so on)	

TABLE 3 (continued)

Rubric for Determining Prior Knowledge and Skill for the Texas PPR Test	
Competency	Your Score
Strategies for reflective thinking and learning	
Questioning techniques (levels of questions, cuing, probing, and so on)	
Issues of wait time when employing instructional questioning	
Skills of selecting appropriate and effective instructional strategies	
Strategies for monitoring student learning	
Skills in adjusting instruction to meet identified needs of learners	
Levels of cognition (Bloom's taxonomy)	
Homogeneous and heterogeneous grouping strategies	
Strategies for developing rapport with students	
Strategies for ensuring a positive social and emotional classroom climate	
Strategies for effective and efficient discipline management	
Skills in establishing routines and procedures for the classroom	
Skills in including students in establishing of rules and procedures	
Strategies for classroom management (time, space, routines, resources, and so on)	
Effective means of delivering quality lessons (models of instruction)	
Skills in establishing smooth transitions	
Strategies for addressing students' off-task behaviors	
Skills for establishing safe and appropriate physical classroom characteristics	
Ability to employ teacher self-reflection and self-evaluation	
Understanding of how personal factors influence teaching	
Strategies for and skills in working with a teaching team	
Strategies for working with special-areas teachers (inclusion, arts, and so on)	
Skills in developing professional goals	
Skills in accessing opportunities for professional growth	
Laws and rules related to teaching in Texas	
Strategies for engaging in site-based decision making	
Knowledge of legal and ethical constraints related to teaching in Texas	
Texas Code of Ethics and Standards for Teachers	
Knowledge of students' rights in educational settings	
Knowledge of teachers' rights in educational settings	
Knowledge of national educational laws (civil rights, due process, gender equity)	
Knowledge of laws regarding student confidentiality	

TABLE 3 (continued)

Rubric for Determining Prior Knowledge and Skill for the Texas PPR Test	
Competency	Your Score
Knowledge of laws related to parents' rights related to education	
Components of federal laws related to inclusion (IDEA/Individuals with Disabilities Act, ARD, IEP/Individualized Education Plan)	
Skills in ensuring a least restrictive learning environment	
Knowledge of types of and sources of authority in educational settings	

PART III

STANDARDS AND DESCRIPTORS OF KNOWLEDGE AND APPLICATION OF THE TExES PPR

Standard I: Designing Instruction and Assessment to Promote Student Learning

> **The teacher designs instruction appropriate for all students that reflects an understanding of relevant content and is based on continuous and appropriate assessment.**

> Note to EC–12 candidates: Read this chapter in its entirety because test items will cover all the competencies for each of the three grade level clusters.

The critical elements of this standard include the declarative and procedural knowledge necessary to design, develop, and deliver developmentally appropriate instruction, as well as to design, develop, and apply appropriate assessments that inform the learning community of the success of students under the teacher's care. To design appropriate instruction, teachers must first be knowledgeable of the developmental characteristics of learners across the grade level cluster of the required TExES PPR. The teacher must also be current on educational research that describes best practice for teaching and learning. Part of the success of a teacher's development of instruction is the manner in which the teacher works collaboratively and cooperatively with colleagues, specialists, parents, and administrators. Of course, it is imperative that teachers include students as learners in the decisions made about effective activities that provide avenues for learning the concepts inherent in the stated goals of instruction.

In order to ensure that each student learns to the greatest extent possible, all teachers must be knowledgeable of the characteristics of special-needs learners, including those who have physical or mental disabilities as well as those who exhibit characteristics of gifted or talented learners. Teachers in Texas must be prepared to work in inclusive settings where it may be possible that learners with various abilities or disabilities will be present in the day-to-day instructional setting. In addition, teachers in Texas will likely face a classroom of learners whose home environments may collectively represent as many as five to ten different languages.

KNOWLEDGE AND APPLICATION COMPONENTS FOR GRADES EC–6

At the initial level, Texas teachers must know and understand the intellectual, social, physical, and emotional developmental characteristics of students in grades EC–6. This knowledge base includes an understanding of factors that affect growth in the physical, cognitive, social, and emotional domains and how growth in one domain affects growth in one or all of the other domains. Teachers must also be knowledgeable about the physical growth and health of students (nutrition, sleep, prenatal exposure to drugs, abuse).

Social and Emotional Development

Teachers must know about and understand other factors that impact learning, such as characteristics of social and emotional development. This includes the potential effects of a lack of affection and attention, a limited opportunity for verbal interactions, changes in family structure, and so on. In addition, teachers must have a firm understanding of the stages of play development and the importance of the role of play in young children's learning and development. Part of this knowledge base is an ability to apply knowledge of the developmental stages of play, from solitary play to parallel play to cooperative engagement with others. Furthermore, teachers must have knowledge of the developmental changes in children's thinking as young learners move from primarily concrete thinking to the ability to reason and think logically, to understand cause and effect, and to organize information systematically. Finally, as part of this knowledge base on developmental characteristics, teachers must be able to demonstrate knowledge and skills related to how development in one domain can positively or negatively impact development in one or more of the other domains. It is imperative that beginning teachers have the knowledge and skills necessary to plan lessons that reflect an understanding of students' developmental characteristics and needs. (See explanatory information related to this conceptual framework at the end of this chapter.)

Developmental Differences

A second knowledge component of Standard I relates to how students' developmental characteristics have implications for planning appropriate instruction. Beginning teachers must recognize the lifelong impact that experiences in grades EC–6 have on a young learner's individual development and thus on society. In addition, teachers must know the wide range of individual developmental differences that characterize students in these grades, which includes understanding how different rates of development affect learning in each domain, and be able to demonstrate knowledge of the implications of possible developmental variances when planning instruction. Teachers must know how developmental characteristics impact learning and performance, such as varying levels of attention span and the need for physical activity and movement. Part of this knowledge component includes an understanding of the importance of helping young learners apply decision-making, organizational, and goal-setting skills, such as choosing learning centers, putting materials away, or completing a self-initiated project. How young children rely on concrete thinking, motor and sensory input, and direct experience is knowledge that beginning teachers must have in order to design, develop, and implement appropriate instruction and assessment. As children in grades EC–6 mature, teachers must know how to help students make smooth transitions between concrete and abstract thinking. Finally, teachers must know how to use a knowledge of the developmental characteristics and needs of learners at these ages in order to plan meaningful, integrated, active learning and self-directed experiences that promote development of the whole child. Effective teachers demonstrate an ability to adapt lessons that address students' varied backgrounds, skills, interests, and learning needs, including the needs of English language learners.

Varied Needs

The third component of Standard I is related to the characteristics and instructional needs of students with varied backgrounds, skills, interests, and learning needs. Teachers must be able to use effective approaches that address varied learning needs and preferences, which include having the ability to use spontaneous activities that promote quality learning. Teachers must also know how to use observations of children at these ages in order to determine the growth and development that result from effective teaching.

A fourth area of Standard I is related to different approaches to learning that may be exhibited by young learners. Teachers must know what motivates students at these ages to become active, engaged learners. Knowledgeable teachers must be able to plan instruction that effectively motivates learners to want to learn and achieve. To enhance this motivation, teachers must be aware of and be able to use various motivational strategies, including extrinsic as well as intrinsic motivators. Teachers must be able to adapt and adjust to teachable moments when learners exhibit excitement about learning or bring their own personal experiences to the learning setting in an appropriate way that will lead to making connections by activating prior knowledge and capitalizing on prior experiences.

Cultural Differences

The final elements of EC–6 Standard I relate to cultural and socioeconomic differences and the significance of such differences when designing and delivering instruction. Teachers must acknowledge and respect the cultural and socioeconomic differences of students when determining appropriate learning activities, goals, and learning outcomes. Teachers must also be able to communicate and work effectively with parents from all socioeconomic levels, including how to initiate and encourage parent-teacher communications. Teachers must know about nonverbal language patterns inherent in the communication practices of the various cultural groups represented in their classroom. They must also know appropriate strategies for instructing English language learners. As the state of Texas becomes more and more diverse and as more languages are represented in Texas classrooms, it is imperative that all teachers have the knowledge and skills that allow them to address the needs of English language learners rather than leaving this solely to bilingual or English-as-a-second-language (ESL) teachers. While it is logical to expect support from teachers who have specialized in helping learners acquire the English language, it is not enough to expect them to meet all the needs of language learners. All teachers must possess the knowledge and skills required to assist learning in students from all cultural, socioeconomic, and language backgrounds.

Competencies: Domain I, EC–6

COMPETENCY 001

The teacher understands human developmental processes and applies this knowledge to plan instruction and ongoing assessment that motivate students and are responsive to their developmental characteristics and needs.

The following are the stated characteristics of a beginning teacher who meets the expectations of this competency.

- Understands the life long impact of experiences provided in grades EC–6 on individual development and on society.
- Recognizes that positive and productive environments for students involve creating a culture of high academic expectations, equity throughout the learning community, and developmental responsiveness.
- Knows the typical stages of cognitive, social, physical, and emotional development of students in grades EC–6.
- Recognizes the wide range of individual developmental differences that characterize students in grades EC–6 and the implications of developmental variation for instructional planning.
- Recognizes factors affecting the physical growth and health of students in grades EC–6 (nutrition, sleep, prenatal exposure to drugs, abuse) and knows that students' physical growth and health impact development in other domains (cognitive, social, emotional).
- Recognizes factors that affect the social and emotional development of students in grades EC–6 (lack of affection and attention, limited opportunity for verbal interactions, changes in family structure) and knows that these factors impact development in other domains.
- Knows the stages of play development (from solitary to cooperative) and the importance of the role of play in young children's learning and development.

- Recognizes challenges for students during later childhood and early adolescence (self-image, physical appearance, eating disorders, feelings of rebelliousness) and effective ways to help students address these challenges.
- Demonstrates knowledge of developmental changes in students' thinking (from primarily concrete thinking to the ability to reason and think logically, then to understand cause and effect, and then to organize information systematically).
- Uses knowledge of cognitive changes in students (emergence and refinement of abstract thinking and reasoning, reflective thinking, and increased focus on the world beyond the school setting) to plan instruction and assessment that promote learning and development.
- Understands that student involvement in risky behaviors (use of tobacco, alcohol, and other drugs; gang involvement; misuse of technology) impacts development and learning.
- Analyzes how developmental characteristics of students in grades EC–6 impact learning and performance, and applies knowledge of students' developmental characteristics and needs when planning effective learning experiences and assessments.
- Demonstrates knowledge of the importance of peers, peer acceptance, and conformity to peer group norms and expectations for students, understands the significance of peer-related issues for teaching and learning.
- Recognizes the importance of helping students in grades EC–6 apply the skills of decision making, organization, and goal setting (selective learning centers, putting away materials, completing a self-initiated project).
- Uses knowledge of the developmental characteristics and needs of students in grades EC–6 to plan meaningful, integrated and active learning, and play experiences that promote development of the whole child.
- Understands how development in any one domain (cognitive, social, physical, or emotional) impacts development in other domains.

IN SUMMARY

Table 4 presents general developmental information for children aged 3–10 in order to provide the necessary knowledge for teachers of EC–6 students. Readers are encouraged to access child development textbooks, articles in early childhood journals, or websites that provide information related to children of these ages in order to acquire further and fully developed knowledge of their developmental characteristics.

TABLE 4

Developmental Characteristics of EC–6 Learners

Domain	Pre-K—Kindergarten	Grades 1–4	Grades 5–6
Physical	Active, motor development, need frequent rest breaks, developing large muscles, developing eye-hand coordination, may experience difficulty in focusing eyes	Tend to be active, need to move about often, need frequent breaks, need rest periods, better large muscle control, may be farsighted, may be prone to accidents	The beginning of noticeable differences in height between sexes, able to maintain focus for longer periods of time, less restless, more control of both fine and large muscles, the beginning signs of sexual maturation
Cognitive	Preoperational, short attention span, self-regulating patterns of language	Move from preoperational to concrete, need variety of activities, ready to learn	Beginning to move from concrete to abstract thinking, still rely on hands-on learning to understand concept optimally
Social	Initiative versus guilt, frequent changes in friends, parallel play (beside, not with), enjoys sharing time, need explorations and investigations, developing skills of choice and independence	Industry versus inferiority, more selective in choosing friends, prefers organized games, focuses on rules, may argue frequently, enjoys talking, may tattletale	Interested in peer groups, still in industry versus inferiority stage
Emotional	Preconventional, frequent but brief disagreements, awareness of sex roles, emotions readily shown, tend to be teacher pleasers, need firm limits with consistency	Sensitive to criticism and rejection, eager to please, sensitive to others	More sensitive to opinion of peer group, the beginning stages of infatuation, less reliance on parents

Piaget's Stages

Children in grades EC–6 are at two to three stages of cognition as described by Piaget. During the **preoperational stage**, **schemata** are formed, yet children are typically unable to mentally reverse actions and events. They are acquiring the ability to conserve and to de-center. They rely on symbolic and representational models for understanding concepts, and they use intuitive thinking to explore ideas. As EC–6 children progress to the next stage, **concrete operations**, they become more capable of mentally reversing actions. However they generalize only from concrete experiences. They are not yet able to manipulate conditions mentally without experiencing related events and concepts. As students begin to develop abstract thinking skills, they more readily understand the needs of others and are less focused on themselves. They still need concrete hands-on experiences. However, they begin to think abstractly, without concrete examples, and begin to understand ideas from an abstract viewpoint. **Prior knowledge** and experience must be incorporated into the learning environment, as young learners need the support of previously developed schemata so that they can **assimilate** new learning into old. Otherwise, teachers must provide the support and scaffolding necessary to assist the learner's attempts to make mental **accommodations** in order to effectively process and comprehend the new knowledge. According to Piaget, it is normally at the point of mental **disequilibrium** that learning takes place, when sufficient cognitive conflict produces confusion that compels the learner to seek equilibrium. Young learners are often **egocentric**. They have difficulty seeing others' points of view if those points of view differ from their own. As students grow older and more mature, they lose some of the egocentric tendencies and begin to understand ideas and events through the eyes and experiences of others.

Erikson's Stages

Another domain of development is the **psychosocial**, as described by Erik Erikson. He believes that children in the age range of 4–5 experience conflict between initiative and guilt. At this stage, the child learns to acquire direction and purpose in activities. According to Erikson, it is critical that both the positive and the negative aspects are experienced in each crisis stage in order to develop and move forward through the stages. From about age 6 to the onset of puberty, children experience **industry versus inferiority**. To successfully progress through this stage, they acquire a sense of mastery and competence.

Kohlberg's Stages

Correlated with the cognitive and social domains is the domain of **moral development**, as proposed by Lawrence Kohlberg. It is in this domain that emotional development occurs. Kohlberg suggests that individuals must progress through four stages in order to develop to the highest level of reasoning. At the first stage, there is no sense of responsibility and no idea of right or wrong. Obviously, most children in grades EC–6 have progressed far beyond this stage. At the second stage, there is an obedience/punishment orientation. At this stage, one considers the personal consequences of actions before determining whether to act or not. The authority figure (the teacher) determines the standards and rules that must be obeyed. At the third stage, typical of young learners, there is an instrumental orientation, so that an "eye for an eye" standard is adopted. At this stage, an egotistical attitude develops that focuses on satisfying one's own needs first. The next stage is the "good boy/good girl" orientation, where being nice and pleasing are important. Children at this stage are considerate of the feelings of others and can put themselves in others' shoes. Intentions are important, and the behavior of the majority is considered correct. Dependent on their prior experiences and environments, children at EC–6 ages typically fall within these early stages. Note, though, that some may be entering the later stages of moral understanding.

Maslow's Stages

Another educational psychologist who offered insight into environmental factors that affect learning was Abraham Maslow, who proposed a **hierarchy of human needs**, suggesting that each level in the hierarchy must be satisfied for successful advancement to the next level. Young children must have their **basic human needs** met in order to function cognitively, socially, emotionally, and physically. These needs include sufficient and nutritious food, appropriate shelter, environmentally safe water and air, and adequate sleep. Often, young children experience family or environmental influences that disallow satisfactory meeting of these needs. So they are challenged when in the learning environment of the school. If the basic physical needs are not met, young children may be preoccupied with their survival and/or their physical suffering. It is at this and the next stage that the issue of child abuse is prominent.

In Texas, failure to report **reasonable suspicion** of child abuse is a misdemeanor and may be punishable by a stiff fine. Teachers must be cautious about what constitutes reasonable suspicion. Simultaneously, they must be on guard as they observe children's physical, social, and emotional behaviors. Any sign of child abuse, if within reasonable suspicion, must be reported to the appropriate authorities (the Child Protective Service) within 48 hours of the event resulting in reasonable suspicion (Chapter 34, Section 34.03 of the Texas Family Code). Teachers must be careful to inform the principal, the school nurse, and the school counselor of such action so that campus leaders are aware of the suspicion of abuse and of the report to the authorities. However, the primary responsibility is to report the suspicion to the state authorities.

To continue with Maslow's hierarchy, next are **safety needs** that must be met. Young children need order, structure, and limits in order to feel safe. Too much or too little boundary setting on the part of the teacher may negatively impact the feeling of safety children need in order to successfully engage in cognitive experiences. If safety needs are not met, young children will likely experience feelings of fear that result from environmental chaos and/or disorganization. Obviously, young learners need to feel safe in their home environments. However, a sense of safety in the school setting is also crucial. In fact, at times, students feel safer in school than they do at home.

Next in Maslow's hierarchy is a **sense of belonging**. Young children need to be able to risk reaching out for affection, exploring and developing friendships, and experiencing being accepted by peers and adults. This is the stage where upper-elementary students begin to be drawn into gang membership if they are not experiencing a feeling of belonging at home or within a supportive group at school. Students at this age may also be enticed into using tobacco or drugs to feel that they are accepted by their peers.

Progressing forward, children need to develop a **sense of self-worth** so that they have confidence in themselves to master their world. They need to experience achievement and competence, as well as recognition of their status by others. These needs, if unmet, may result in feelings of insecurity and inferiority that cause anxiety about personal worth. Teachers must plan curriculum and learning activities that will ensure student success as often as possible. Teachers must also give students frequent feedback. This allows students the opportunity to improve and to achieve their personal goals.

In general, teachers must be aware of the theory of self-fulfilling prophecy when working with EC–6 children. Learners at these ages must believe that the teacher recognizes their abilities, believes in their potential for success, and is vitally interested in their well-being. If learners frequently experience defeat in their endeavors, they will likely cease to experience motivation sufficient to learn effectively and will soon decline in academic growth.

COMPETENCY 002

The teacher understands student diversity and knows how to plan learning experiences and design assessments that are responsive to differences among students and that promote all students' learning.

The following are the stated characteristics of a beginning teacher who meets the expectations of this competency.

- Demonstrates knowledge of students with diverse personal and social characteristics (ethnicity, gender, language, background, exceptionality) and the significance of student diversity for teaching, learning, and assessment.
- Accepts and respects students with diverse backgrounds and needs.
- Knows how to use diversity in the classroom and the community to enrich all students' learning experiences.
- Knows strategies for enhancing their own understanding of students' diverse backgrounds and needs.
- Knows how to plan and adapt lessons to address students' varied backgrounds, skills, interests, and learning needs, including the needs of English language learners and students with disabilities.
- Understands cultural and socioeconomic differences (including differential access to technology) and knows how to plan instruction that is responsive to cultural and socioeconomic differences among students.
- Understands the instructional significance of varied student learning needs and preferences.

IN SUMMARY

Diversity among students is a major influence in today's classrooms. Teachers must be fully aware of the social characteristics of each of their learners. Ruby Payne's (2003) work on understanding poverty is an important resource for teachers. Payne discusses the characteristics of generational and situational poverty. She describes the registers of language and how they impact students' success in the classroom. She also describes environmental characteristics that might be found in the homes of children who live in poverty settings and discusses how these factors might translate into classroom behaviors. There are also texts written for teachers and business people that describe the verbal and nonverbal characteristics of cultural groups around the world. This knowledge could be very beneficial for teachers who face as many as 15 languages being spoken across the grade levels on any given campus.

Significant in this competency are concepts about family. Teachers must learn about the families and home environments of the students in their classrooms. If the school district supports such, a home visit before the beginning of, or during, the school year can inform teachers about experiences children are accustomed to and can possibly indicate how families direct children to behave in educational settings.

Diverse Backgrounds

Wise teachers capitalize on the diverse backgrounds and abilities of the students in their classrooms. An example is when teachers find ways to celebrate the diversity among their students. If you have a student from a Middle Eastern culture, you might ask that student's parent to speak to the class about the geography of that region of the world. Such an experience might build a sense of belonging and confidence for the student. Children in grades EC–6 who speak languages other than English might be asked to tell stories in their native languages. Parents might be asked to contribute to instructional units by preparing foods depicting the culture of the family. Art prints or music from cultures around the world might be used in the classroom to encourage conversations about those cultures or to motivate students to explore the cultures represented.

When planning and adapting lessons for children from diverse backgrounds, the teacher may find it challenging to know all that is necessary for optimal learning for all the students. Calling on specialists can provide the scaffolding a teacher may need in order to learn about inclusion strategies, second-language acquisition strategies, and cultural characteristics. Integration of the curriculum and partnering with other teachers provide means for adapting to the needs of various learners. Another strategy is to use cooperative and collaborative group activities. Children from different backgrounds learn from one another as they play or work together to complete tasks. The infusion of other languages into day-to-day activities could help young learners value other languages and get to know their classmates in a nonthreatening environment. Developing in students a sense that the classroom is a learning community is vital to the development of diverse perspectives and to an appreciation of social justice.

Learning Methods

An additional aspect of this competency involves how people learn. Numerous studies have been conducted to learn about the brain. Howard Gardner's (2000) work on **multiple intelligences** informs teachers that in developing intelligence learners may use ways other than the traditional logical sequential or verbal approach. Learners vary across modality strengths, such as verbal, auditory, kinesthetic, and tactile. From all we know about the development of young children, it is clear that learners in grades EC–6 benefit from hands-on, manipulative-oriented, concrete learning activities prior to moving to abstract thinking. The teacher is responsible for knowing the latest research on how people learn, for ideas to engage learners in various contextual settings, and for using assessment tools that provide knowledge of how learners in the classroom may best be served.

There are numerous ways teachers can employ strategies that help students from various ethnic, cultural, environmental, or experiential backgrounds to feel more a part of the learning community. The critical aspect of this competency is that the teacher not only recognizes diversity in the classroom but also goes to great lengths to demonstrate and model respect for, appreciation of, and recognition of the value of diversity.

COMPETENCY 003

The teacher understands procedures for designing effective and coherent instruction and assessment based on appropriate learning goals and objects.

The following are the stated characteristics of a beginning teacher who meets the expectations of this competency.

- Understands the significance of the Texas Essential Knowledge and Skills (TEKS) and of prerequisite knowledge and skills in determining instructional goals and objectives.
- Uses appropriate criteria to evaluate the appropriateness of learning goals and objectives (clarity; relevance; significance; age appropriateness; ability to be assessed; responsiveness to students' current skills and knowledge, background, needs, and interests; alignment with campus and district goals).
- Uses assessment to analyze students' strengths and needs, evaluate teacher effectiveness, and guide instructional planning for individuals and groups.
- Understands the connections among various components of the Texas statewide assessment program, the TEKS, and instruction; analyzes data from state and other assessments using common statistical measures to help identify students' strengths and needs.
- Demonstrates knowledge of various types of materials and resources (including technological resources and resources outside the school) that may be used to enhance student learning and engagement, and evaluates the appropriateness of specific materials and resources for use in particular situations, to address specific purposes, and to meet varied student needs.
- Plans lessons and structures units so that activities progress in a logical sequence and support stated instructional goals.
- Plans learning experiences that provide students with opportunities to explore content from integrated and varied perspectives (providing an integrated curriculum including thematic units, providing multicultural learning experiences, employing play as a learning mode, permitting student choice, involving students in projects, designing instruction that supports students' cooperative work and ability to reflect on other points of view).
- Allocates time appropriately within the lessons and the unit, including providing adequate opportunities for students to engage in reflection, self-assessment, and closure.

IN SUMMARY

The state of Texas has a mandated set of knowledge, skills, and dispositions that must be addressed in all classrooms across the state. This mandated curriculum framework is referred to as the Texas Essential Knowledge and Skills, the TEKS. Each teacher at each grade level is responsible for effectively teaching these TEKS so that all learners leave that grade level with the expected knowledge and skills. It is not enough to verify that you have *taught* the TEKS. Teachers must make sure that their students have *learned* the TEKS.

Teachers in grades EC–6 should employ a variety of assessment strategies for determining the appropriateness of learning objectives. Teacher observation is a confirmed assessment tool for knowing what young children are able to do and even what they have learned. As students demonstrate academic, social, and emotional growth, teachers may logically annotate their observations of learning and growth. The important thing is that teachers use some tool of documentation, such as a rubric or a checklist, that will provide verification that the child has learned the intended objective and has been successful in demonstrating the expected learning outcome.

TAKS/STAAR

As of publication of this book, the TEKS are measured by the Texas Assessment of Knowledge and Skills (TAKS) and will be referred to as such throughout the book. However, in the 2011–2012 academic/school year, the TAKS will be replaced by the next generation of Texas testing of K–12 standards. This new test, the State of Texas Assessments of Academic Readiness (STAAR), includes the 12 end-of-course assessments and the required grades 3–8 assessments (see www.tea.state.tx.us). This new version of state assessments will be more rigorous as it measures student performance and academic growth.

TAKS is a statewide standardized measure of student learning and is a criterion-referenced test that judges whether or not a student has the knowledge and skills identified in the required curriculum (the TEKS). Effective instruction should focus on the curriculum standards of the TEKS; thus, when these standards are measured by the TAKS, there should be a one-to-one correlation among the state curriculum, instruction, and assessment. Teachers should have the ability to identify students' strengths and weaknesses so that all learners have optimal opportunity to learn the required essentials of the curriculum. One way to ensure that there are no gaps in teaching and learning is to align the curriculum vertically and horizontally. Another way is to work cooperatively with other teachers to deliver integrated curriculum-learning strategies.

Teacher Resources

To plan appropriate instruction and learning activities, teachers must use effective resources and materials. For teachers of grades EC–6, these may include community resource persons, community sites that can be used for field trips, parents and caregivers, and businesses. Materials include **manipulatives** for science and mathematics; play center materials such as dress-up clothes, blocks, and art supplies; technology resources such as educational software and graphics software; maps and globes for social studies understandings; and so on. Keep in mind that the resource or material should be directly aligned with the teaching objective and expected learning outcomes. Students in grades EC–6 need frequent hands-on experiences and activities that involve the whole body and mind. So teachers must carefully analyze what is the most appropriate and effective resource or material.

Teacher Planning

The scope and sequence of the curriculum are important elements that guide in the effectiveness of learning. **Scaffolding** of learning is vital to successful progression to the next grade level. Teachers must first determine at what stage the young learner operates and then plan lessons and units that fit within the "window of learning" described in the scaffolding process. The sequencing of learning events must be logical while staying within the framework of the state-required curriculum. Employing thematic units of instruction helps to integrate content knowledge and skills. It also motivates students to learn.

Perhaps the most important element of teacher planning is matching goals and objectives with student learning outcomes and assessment techniques. Little is gained by selecting a fun activity that has little or no relationship to the intended outcome or teaching objective. Careful attention must be given to the selection of learning activities and/or strategies that are carefully aligned with the TEKS goals. Such activities/learning experiences should ensure that learners are engaged in inquiry and exploration. Young children have creative minds that need to be developed. Problem solving is a welcome challenge to young learners if provided in a developmentally appropriate context. Teachers who integrate the curriculum help learners see clear connections and make learning fun and applicable to real-life experiences. Additionally, teachers should employ strategies that allow learners to understand curriculum concepts from more than one perspective. Role playing is an excellent way to help children see how others react or respond. For example, having a group of second-graders act out how children would solve a problem on the playground helps the children see various strategies for solving problems.

Finally, the management of time is important in this competency. If the teacher notices/observes that learners are not grasping the concept of a lesson, that teacher must monitor and adjust the strategies to allow for reteaching or for clarifying misconceptions about the concept. Students must be given time to reflect on their learning, to engage in self-assessment, and to share their learning with their peers. An effectively delivered lesson brings closure for students so that they leave the lesson with a confirmed understanding of what was learned. Having children complete a K-W-L (What I Know (K), What I Want to Know (W), What I Learned (L)) chart, write a summary paragraph, draw a picture depicting the lesson, orally state what was learned, or complete one of various other closure activities helps confirm the goal of the lesson.

COMPETENCY 004

The teacher understands learning processes and factors that impact student learning and demonstrates this knowledge by planning effective, engaging instruction and appropriate assessments.

The following are the stated characteristics of a beginning teacher who meets the expectations of this competency.

- Understands the role of learning theory in the instructional process; uses instructional strategies and appropriate technologies to facilitate student learning by connecting new information and ideas to prior knowledge, making learning meaningful and relevant.

- Understands that young children think concretely and rely primarily on motor and sensory input and direct experience for the development of skills and knowledge and uses this understanding to plan effective, developmentally appropriate learning experiences and assessments.
- Understands that the middle-level years are a transitional stage in which students may exhibit characteristics of both older and younger children; understands that these are critical years for developing important skills and attitudes (working and getting along with others, appreciating diversity, making a commitment to continued schooling).
- Recognizes how social and emotional characteristics of students (attention span, need for physical activity, interacting with peers, searching for identity, questioning principles and expectations) impact teaching and learning.
- Applies knowledge of the implications for learning and instruction of students' wide range of thinking abilities.
- Teaches, models, and monitors organizational skills at an age-appropriate level (establishing regular places for materials, sorting blocks by shape and size during cleanup).
- Teaches, models, and monitors age-appropriate study skills (using graphic organizers, outlining, note taking, summarizing, test taking) and structures research projects appropriately (teaches steps in research, establishes checkpoints during research projects, helps students use time management).
- Stimulates reflection, critical thinking, and inquiry among students (provides opportunities to manipulate materials and to test ideas and hypotheses, provides repetition for increased conceptual understanding, encourages exploration and positive risk-taking, creates a learning community that promotes positive contributions, effective communication, and the respectful exchange of ideas).
- Enhances learning by providing instruction that encourages the use of refinement of higher-order thinking skills (prompting students to explore ideas from diverse perspectives; structuring active-learning experiences involving cooperative learning, problem solving, open-ended questioning, and inquiry; promoting students' development of research skills).
- Teaches, models, and monitors organizational and time-management skills at an age-appropriate level (keeping related materials together, using organizational tools).
- Analyzes ways in which teachers' behaviors (teacher expectations, student-grouping practices, teacher-student interactions) impact student learning and plans instruction and assessment that minimize the effects of negative factors and enhance all students' learning.
- Analyzes ways in which factors in the home and community (parent expectations, availability of community resources, community problems) impact student learning; plans instruction and assessment with awareness of social and cultural factors to enhance all students' learning.
- Understands the importance of self-directed learning and plans instruction and assessment that promote students' motivation and their sense of ownership of and responsibility for their own learning.

- Analyzes ways in which various teacher roles (facilitator, lecturer) and student roles (active learning, observer, group participant) impact student learning.
- Incorporates students' different approaches to learning (auditory, visual, tacticle, kinesthetic) into instructional practices.

IN SUMMARY

This competency includes many elements. As aleady stated, teachers must have a full understanding of the impact of learning theory on classroom practice. The teacher must address the varying ways that learners acquire knowledge and skills. Styles and modalities of learning are factors that positively or negatively affect student learning depending on how the teacher recognizes and addresses these variances within the classroom. It is not only possible but often likely that a beginning teacher may be faced with a wide range of ability levels within the assigned grade level classroom. Teachers must have a wealth of instructional strategies and a clear understanding of how children learn in order to provide all children an equal opportunity to learn.

Because young children most often learn concretely, the teacher must provide concrete, hands-on learning activities, materials, and resources. As EC-6 learners develop and begin to move out of the concrete into the abstract stage of learning, teachers must help students by employing effective strategies that ensure learning. Children in grades EC–6 rely heavily on input from motor engagement and sensory experiences. Teachers of children of these ages should plan for frequent movement and involvement of the whole body in learning activities. Sensory strategies should be employed to develop the senses of touch, smell, taste, and hearing. Placing objects of varying textures in a paper bag and having children reach into the bag to feel the textures is a strategy for developing their sense of touch. Older EC-6 learners need to be involved in peer-learning settings, such as cooperative learning groups or research study teams. Problem solving and community engagement activities are good strategies for developing older EC-6 knowledge and skills.

Teachers must guide young learners in developing and strengthening skills in organization and planning. Assigning students job titles such as supply handler, floor monitor, materials distributor, and so on, helps them learn responsibility while seeing the benefits of organization and planning. Teacher modeling is critical for the development of these skills. Research by Bandura (1986) and others indicates that learning often occurs through observation. Therefore, the teacher is a vital link in modeling for students appropriate skills of organization and responsibility. Teacher behaviors certainly impact student learning. Teachers must monitor negative behaviors or experiences that could detract from optimal student learning.

Teachers must also guide students toward becoming reflective thinkers, self-directed learners, and self-assessors. Motivational strategies should be employed at all times so that children will want to learn and to see learning as fun as often as possible. Young learners need to experience freedom and fun within the context of the educational setting. Thus it is the role of the teacher to provide stimulating and motivating learning experiences. Older EC-6 students can monitor their own learning, can work collaboratively to solve problems, and can manage their own materials and supplies.

KNOWLEDGE AND APPLICATION COMPONENTS FOR GRADES 4–8

Texas teachers must know and understand the intellectual, social, physical, and emotional developmental characteristics of students in the middle grades. This includes an understanding of factors that affect growth in the physical, cognitive, social, and emotional domains and how growth in one domain affects growth in one or all of the other domains. Teachers must be knowledgeable about the physical growth and health of students at this age level (nutrition, sleep, exercise).

Social and Emotional Development

Other factors that impact learning at these ages include social and emotional development. This includes the positive or negative effects of guidance by parents or caregivers, attention from peers, opportunities for extended verbal interactions, changes in family structure, and so on. Teachers must have knowledge and understanding of the important role of peer influence at these ages, especially in the upper middle grades. Part of this knowledge base is an ability to apply knowledge of the stages of cognitive, social, emotional, and moral reasoning development. Teachers must understand the developmental changes in the thinking of 10- to 14-year-old children as they move from concrete thinking to formal thinking and develop the ability to reason and think logically, understand cause and effect, and organize information systematically. Finally, teachers must be able to demonstrate knowledge and skills related to how development in one domain can positively or negatively impact development in one or more of the other domains. It is imperative that beginning teachers have the knowledge and skills necessary to plan lessons that reflect an understanding of students' developmental characteristics and needs.

Developmental Differences

A second knowledge component of Standard I relates to how students' developmental characteristics have implications for planning appropriate instruction. Beginning teachers must recognize the impact that experiences in early grades have on a middle learner's development. Teachers must know the wide range of developmental differences that characterize students in the middle grades and how these differences affect learning and performance. This includes understanding how varying rates of development impact growth in each domain and being able to demonstrate knowledge of these implications when planning instruction. The importance of helping middle level learners apply decision-making, organizational, and goal-setting skills learned in the earlier grades is seen as 10- to 14-year-old youth explore what it means to be an adult. Teachers must be able to design, develop, and implement developmentally appropriate instruction and assessment strategies for grades 4–8 in order to ensure that knowledge and skills learned in previous grades are carried forward into the more complex learning experiences typical of grades 4–8. Effective teachers demonstrate an ability to adapt lessons that address students' varied backgrounds, skills, interests, and learning needs, including the needs of English language learners.

Varied Needs

The third component of this standard is related to the characteristics and instructional needs of students with varied backgrounds, skills, interests, and learning needs. Teachers must be able to use effective management and instructional approaches that address the learning needs and preferences of all students in order to promote expected growth and development.

A fourth area of Standard I is related to different approaches to learning that may be exhibited by middle level learners. Teachers must know what motivates students at these ages to be actively engaged learners who want to learn and achieve. To acquire this motivation, teachers must be aware of and able to use various motivational strategies, including extrinsic as well as intrinsic motivators. Teachers must be able to adapt and adjust to teachable moments when learners exhibit excitement about learning or bring their own personal experiences to the learning setting. Such a focus on the student is an appropriate way to help middle level learners make connections. Activating prior knowledge and capitalizing on prior experiences assist learners in seeing the relevance of their learning. It is important to know enough about students at these ages so that learning strategies can be selected to promote optimal learning in a student-centered setting.

Cultural Differences

The final element of Standard I relates to cultural and socioeconomic differences and their significance when designing and delivering instruction. Teachers must acknowledge and respect the cultural and socioeconomic differences of students when determining appropriate learning activities, goals, and learning outcomes. This is especially important for middle level learners. Peer and family influences are major factors in these learners' commitment to and attention to learning. Teachers must know appropriate strategies for instructing English language learners. As the state of Texas becomes more and more diverse, and as more languages are represented in Texas classrooms across the state, it is imperative that all teachers have the knowledge and skills that allow them to address the needs of English language learners rather than leaving this solely to the bilingual or ESL teacher. School is especially challenging for children who immigrate to this country during these age periods. Often, children of other nationalities do not have fluency in the English language; thus, they are challenged not only by the academic part of school but also by the social aspect. While it is logical to expect support from teachers who have specialized in helping learners acquire the English language, it is not enough to expect these specialists to meet all the needs of language learners. All teachers must possess the knowledge and skills required to assist learning by students from all cultural, socioeconomic, and language backgrounds.

Readers are encouraged to review the explanatory notes for Domain I competencies presented in the EC–6 section. Although not all characteristics of learners are the same, many of the elements of the various competencies cross all grade levels, so rather than lengthen this study guide, you are asked to preview "In Summary" in the EC–6 section of this chapter.

Competencies: Domain I, 4–8

COMPETENCY 001

The teacher understands human developmental processes and applies this knowledge to plan instruction and ongoing assessment that motivate students and are responsive to their developmental characteristics and needs.

The following are the stated characteristics of a beginning teacher who meets the expectations of this competency.

- Recognizes that positive and productive environments for middle-level students involves creating a culture of high academic expectations, equity throughout the learning community, and developmental responsiveness.
- Knows the rationale for appropriate middle-level education and how middle-level schools are structured to address the characteristics and needs of young adolescents.
- Knows the typical stages of cognitive, social, physical, and emotional development of middle-level students.
- Recognizes the wide range of individual developmental differences that characterizes middle-level students and the implications of this developmental variation for instructional planning.
- Demonstrates an understanding of physical changes associated with later childhood and adolescence and ways in which these changes impact development in other domains (cognitive, social, emotional).
- Recognizes the challenges for students during later childhood and early adolescence (self-image, physical appearance, eating disorders, feelings of rebelliousness) and effective ways to help students address these challenges.
- Understands that student involvement in risky behaviors (drug and alcohol use, gang involvement) impacts development and learning.
- Demonstrates knowledge of the importance of peers, peer acceptance, and conformity to peer group norms and expectations for middle-level students and understands the significance of peer-related issues in teaching and learning.
- Recognizes that social and emotional factors in the family (parental divorce, homelessness) impact the development of middle-level students in different domains.
- Uses knowledge of cognitive changes in middle-level students (emergence and refinement of abstract thinking and reasoning, reflective thinking, and increased focus on the world beyond the school setting) to plan instruction and assessment that promote learning and development.
- Analyzes ways in which developmental characteristics of middle-level students impact learning and performance and applies knowledge of students' developmental characteristics and needs to plan effective learning experiences and assessments.
- Recognizes the importance of helping middle-level students apply decision-making, organizational, and goal-setting skills.

- Understands that development in any one domain (cognitive, social, physical) impacts development in other domains.

IN SUMMARY

Students in grades 4–8 are much different than those in the early grades. Because of the rapidly changing physiological, social, and emotional stages of youth at these ages, it is typical that they test their boundaries often. Teachers should establish clearly defined expectations and classroom rules that are understood and accepted by all. If students participate in setting rules, establishing routines and procedures, and deciding on consequences for misbehaving, they will be much more likely to self-monitor and peer-monitor behaviors. Youth of these ages need clearly defined limits to guide their rapid growth in all developmental areas. Of course, rigid rules and excessive limits reduce the freedom and sense of power that these youths greatly need. Excessive rules, limits, and structure serve only to invite students' hostility, resentment, rebellion, and lack of attention to the curriculum.

Social Needs

Positive social interactions are critical during this period. As peers become more influential than family, teachers should encourage peer interaction by employing small-group learning activities. A wise teacher will also provide small-area venues where youth can meet in informal groups. Paired with social peer exchanges, youth at these ages need positive relationships with teachers and parents. Teachers can develop adviser-advisee arrangements, possibly with business mentors, teachers at other grade levels, or family members who have time to serve in this capacity. Many teachers schedule their personal time so that they can attend athletic or arts (fine or performing) activities in which their students participate.

Establishing Identity

Students at these ages need a strong sense of competence as they try to compete with others and establish their own identities. An emphasis on academics and the setting of high standards may help them accept the challenges of cognitive development. Teachers should set high expectations for all students while adjusting to the particular needs of individual students. Much scaffolding may be needed at these ages, as students often turn their energies more toward social activities than toward the school curriculum. Because youth of these ages are often very sensitive to the criticism of peers and adults, a well-developed system of immediate and positive feedback can be very helpful to self-esteem at this time.

Physical Activity and Sleep

At these ages, physical activity is vital to the overall health of the individual. It is recognized that this nation has an increasing problem with obesity, even among youth, and there is no reason why schools cannot offer students opportunities for developing stamina, flexibility, power, and strength. Teachers who collaborate with the physical education staff can find ways to incorporate such physical engagement into the mandated curriculum. Noncompetitive physical activity should be included as often as possible, but particularly during breaks and during lunchtime. At these ages, students need more sleep than at other times, and if they are not given an opportunity for physical engagement during the day, teachers may find them sleeping during academic assignments.

Student Involvement

Student councils or committees, grade level or classroom newspapers and reporters, and service learning projects help students become more connected with their communities (school and greater communities) during this period. Involvement in civic-type activities helps students see their roles in the community and develops their competence in taking leadership roles in the future.

It may be more of a challenge to engage parents of middle-level learners than those of young children. To encourage parent involvement, teachers should send home frequent communications in the form of a note to parents, a newsletter, or an e-mail message. Teachers can plan curriculum units that offer opportunities for parents to become involved. Obviously, athletic and arts performances are good draws to get parents of middle graders to the school. An open house might be paired with a band concert.

Review Table 5 for a quick reminder of the developmental characteristics of learners at ages 10–14. Remember that these are generalized characteristics and may not always be indicative of exactly where you will find middle-level learners.

TABLE 5

Developmental Characteristics of 4–8 Learners		
Domain	Ages 10–14	Grades 4–8
Physical	Growing steadily; differences between girls and boys regarding height and weight gains; good motor coordination; sexual characteristics evident in girls at about age 11	Need a variety of activities; may be awkward at times; may have poor eating habits
Cognitive	Developed perception of time, space, number; enjoy challenging intellectual problems; learning to reason; very curious and inquisitive	Moving into understanding of symbolism; attention span of 15–20 minutes; may set unrealistic standards; enjoy open-ended questions; concrete operational moving into formal
Social	Highly affected by peer pressure; enjoy competition; may enjoy hero worship; may develop crushes; developing boy/girl relationships	Less influence by parents; industry versus inferiority; moving into identity versus role confusion; more considerate of others
Emotional	Concerned about rules and fairness; broader view of right and wrong; faced with more difficult choices	Vary between impulsive and reflective thinking and acting; development of personal values; may have a "law-and-order" orientation

COMPETENCY 002

The teacher understands student diversity and knows how to plan learning experiences and design assessments that are responsive to differences among students and that promote all students' learning.

The following are the stated characteristics of a beginning teacher who meets the expectations of this competency.

- Demonstrates knowledge of students with diverse personal and social characteristics (those related to ethnicity, gender, language background, exceptionality) and the significance of student diversity for teaching, learning, and assessment.
- Accepts and respects students with diverse backgrounds and needs.
- Knows how to use diversity in the classroom and the community to enrich all students' learning experiences.
- Knows strategies for enhancing one's own understanding of students' diverse backgrounds and needs.
- Knows how to plan and adapt lessons to address students' varied backgrounds, skills, interests, and learning needs, including the needs of English language learners and students with disabilities.
- Understands cultural and socioeconomic differences (including differential access to technology) and knows how to plan instruction that is responsive to cultural and socioeconomic differences among students.
- Understands the instructional significance of varied student learning needs and preferences.

IN SUMMARY

An effective means for developing middle-level learners' sense of self-definition is to plan activities that offer opportunities to be creative and expressive. Personal journals, simulated journals, diaries, art portfolios, Internet searches and monitored chats, and academic portfolios can help youth of these ages develop a strong sense of identity, which is vital to their progress toward adulthood. Students of these ages must be frequently engaged in learning and social activities that will develop their sense of self-efficacy, self-esteem, and self-directed learning.

Frequent opportunities for independence are needed to develop learners who are self-directed and capable of monitoring their growth and development. Assigning responsibilities is helpful in classroom settings during this period. Cooperative grouping that provides each member a role of responsibility and accountability helps develop skills that will be needed in the senior grades and beyond.

As middle-level learners expand their social horizons, they encounter diversity in many areas of their lives. It is imperative that teachers recognize the need for students to appreciate diversity and understand events through the perspectives of others. Pairing of students in cooperative groups is one effective strategy for exposing learners to a wide array of cultural and ability variances as they learn to appreciate others who may not be like them.

Teachers who plan activities that provide opportunities for speakers of other languages or students with disabilities to be highlighted recognize the value of inclusion and engagement in learning. Students from other countries have much to offer during geography and history lessons, language experiences, or cultural idea exchanges. As the teacher demonstrates a disposition of valuing other cultures and abilities, middle-level learners benefit from this modeling as they explore ways to address their own biases.

COMPETENCY 003

The teacher understands procedures for designing effective and coherent instruction and assessment based on appropriate learning goals and objectives.

The following are the stated characteristics of a beginning teacher who meets the expectations of this competency.

- Understands the significance of the Texas Essential Knowledge and Skills (TEKS) and of prerequisite knowledge and skills in determining instructional goals and objectives.
- Uses appropriate criteria to evaluate the appropriateness of learning goals and objectives (clarity; relevance; significance; age-appropriateness; ability to be assessed; responsiveness to students' current skills and knowledge, backgrounds, needs, and interests; alignment with campus and school district goals).
- Uses assessment to analyze students' strengths and needs, evaluate teacher effectiveness, and guide instructional planning for individuals and groups.
- Understands the connections among various components of the Texas statewide assessment program, the TEKS, and instruction; analyzes data from state and other assessments, using common statistical measures to help identify students' strengths and needs.
- Demonstrates a knowledge of various types of materials and resources (including technological resources and resources outside the school) that may be used to enhance student learning and engagement; evaluates the appropriateness of specific materials and resources for use in particular situations, to address specific purposes, and to meet varied student needs.
- Plans lessons and structures units so that activities progress in a logical sequence and support stated instructional goals.
- Plans learning experiences that provide students with opportunities to explore content from integrated and varied perspectives (by presenting thematic units that incorporate different disciplines, grouping students in study teams, providing multicultural learning experiences, prompting students to consider ideas from multiple viewpoints).
- Allocates time appropriately within the lessons and units, including providing adequate opportunities for students to engage in reflection, self-assessment, and closure.

IN SUMMARY

Teachers should employ a variety of teaching methods to keep the attention of and to motivate students in grades 4–8. Too much focus on direct instruction (lectures) may turn students off and may possibly create behavior challenges. Instructional approaches such as teacher modeling, demonstrations, small groups, peer tutoring, and independent learning are helpful in keeping youth actively engaged and motivated. Students need frequent opportunities to explore, hypothesize, and try their hands at innovative ways to solve problems. An inquiry approach to teaching and learning is motivational at these ages. Frequent inclusion of technological tools is a must in today's classroom. At these ages, students are accustomed to electronic games, fast-moving movies/videos, and high-tech entertainment. If they are forced to sit in a boring classroom, there will be a high potential for lack of interest, poor motivation, and discipline problems.

Retaining Information

The curriculum for these grades is intense. Teachers must ensure that prior concepts have been attained and are retained through implementation of appropriate diagnostic measures and observations of student growth. It is not sufficient to claim that you have *taught* the curriculum; what is important is whether or not the students *learned* the curriculum. In addition to a motivating and extending academic curriculum, students of these ages are often highly engaged in extracurricular activities.

Student and Parent Participation

Assessment procedures should be carefully matched with the ways students learn and with how the curriculum has been delivered. Monitoring of student progress is vital for middle-level learners, as they may often be drawn away from academics into a more peer-oriented focus. Frequent feedback is important at these ages. Clarifying of misconceptions and positive feedback on progress are important assessment tools in these grades. Families should be encouraged to be part of the learning and assessment process, such as logging time when students read at home, assisting with Internet searches, and helping to build models.

A significant part of assessment is the Texas accountability test, the TAKS. Parents should be involved in the preparation for these high-stakes tests, especially during the middle years. Sending home packets for study two weeks before the test is helpful for showing middle-level learners that parents are concerned and interested in their academic progress. Teachers must also be competent in discussing with parents what the test results mean.

Summative assessments, at the end of units or at the end of the grading period, should not be a surprise either to the student or to his or her parents. Teachers should frequently communicate student learning progress so that no one is surprised at the last minute by a low grade that may not have been anticipated.

COMPETENCY 004

The teacher understands learning processes and factors that impact student learning and demonstrates this knowledge by planning effective, engaging instruction and appropriate assessments.

The following are the stated characteristics of a beginning teacher who meets the expectations of this competency.

- Understands the role of learning theory in the instructional process and uses instructional strategies and appropriate technologies to facilitate student learning (connecting new information and ideas to prior knowledge and making learning meaningful and relevant to students).
- Understands that the middle-level years are a transitional stage at which students may exhibit characteristics of both older and younger children and that these are critical years for developing important skills and attitudes (working and getting along with others, appreciating diversity, making a commitment to continued schooling).
- Applies knowledge of the implications for learning and instruction of middle-level students' wide range of thinking abilities.
- Stimulates reflection, critical thinking, and inquiry among middle-level students (engages students in structured, hands-on, problem-solving activities that are challenging; encourages exploration and risk taking; creates a learning community that promotes positive contributions, effective communication, and the respectful exchange of ideas).
- Enhances learning for middle-level students by providing instruction that encourages the use and refinement of higher-order thinking skills (prompting students to explore ideas from diverse perspectives; structuring active learning experiences involving cooperative learning; problem solving, open-ended questioning, and inquiry; promoting students' development of research skills).
- Teaches, models, and monitors organizational and time-management skills at an age-appropriate level (keeping related materials together, using organizational tools).
- Teaches, models, and monitors age-appropriate study skills (using graphic organizers, outlining, note taking, summarizing, test taking) and structures research projects appropriately (teaches students the steps in research, establishes checkpoints during research projects, helps students use time-management tools).
- Recognizes how social and emotional characteristics of middle-level students (interacting with peers, searching for their identities, questioning principles and expectations) impact teaching and learning.
- Analyzes ways in which teacher behaviors (teacher expectations, student grouping practices, teacher-student interactions) affect student learning, and plans instruction and assessment that minimize the effects of negative factors and enhance all students' learning.
- Analyzes ways in which factors in the home and community (parent expectations, availability of community resources, community problems) impact student learning and plans instruction and assessment with awareness of social and cultural factors to enhance all students' learning.

- Understands the importance of self-directed learning and plans instruction and assessment that promote students' motivation and their sense of ownership of and responsibility for their own learning.
- Analyzes ways in which various teacher roles (facilitator, lecturer) and student roles (active learner, observer, group participant) impact student learning.
- Incorporates students' different approaches to learning (auditory, visual, tactile, kinesthetic) into instructional practices.

IN SUMMARY

The competencies in this domain cover a wide range of aspects that have a major impact on the academic and social progress of middle-level learners. The modeling that a teacher does may have a lasting effect (either positively or negatively) on students' academic and social growth. Teachers must demonstrate a love of learning, model how they think and learn, exhibit excitement about the lesson or unit, and model effective skills of organization and self-monitoring.

Students of these ages may not be as organized as teachers would like. With so much of their energy focused on peer influence, study skills, organizational skills, and self-directed learning may require frequent scaffolding by the teacher. Look for ways to model strategies for learning such as brainstorming, K-W-L charts, critical analysis grids, models, and Venn diagrams. As teachers model these strategies, students learn by observation how effective these tools can be. Students may also require considerable guidance in learning how to keep their desks, materials, and supplies (including textbooks) organized and readily accessible.

Frequent opportunities for creative and critical thinking are imperative for these students. As learners move to higher stages of development, they need a chance to express their new feelings, describe their expanded experiences, and ask questions in a risk-free environment. A wise teacher employs an array of strategies to give students venues for sharing, expressing, and being creative. Infusion of the fine and performing arts into the regular curriculum may make learning more inviting and motivating. Physical activities, such as gardening, painting, cooking, drama, and skating, offer opportunities for youth to develop their creative abilities and to be recognized for their successes.

Whenever possible, teachers should take advantage of students' interests. If the teacher has clearly defined learning goals/outcomes, when students indicate interest in a particular area that fits within the planned goals, the teacher should be adept at altering the planned lesson and going with the flow of students' interests, for optimal learning. Which learning activity is chosen is of less importance than the learning goal, so if students express interest in or request a different approach to learning, the teacher should have the flexibility to make this adjustment without any challenge to the learning outcomes.

Students should be engaged in interesting, motivating activities that capitalize on their styles of learning and their interests. Community projects, service learning, and physically engaging activities will encourage motivation and participation.

KNOWLEDGE AND APPLICATION COMPONENTS FOR GRADES 8–12

Secondary teachers in Texas must have extensive knowledge and understanding of the intellectual, social, physical, and emotional developmental characteristics of students in grades 8–12. This includes an understanding of factors that affect growth in the physical, cognitive, social, and emotional domains and how growth in one domain affects growth in one or all of the other domains. Teachers must be knowledgeable about the physical growth and health of secondary students (diet, nutrition, sleep, exercise). They must have a knowledge and understanding of social and emotional development as well, particularly at this level.

Social and Emotional Development

Secondary students often demonstrate an increasing need for affection and attention, primarily from their peers. In some settings, verbal interactions may seem restricted. In other situations, communication is critical to the self-esteem of youth. Changes in family structure may significantly impact the emotional and social status of youth of these ages. Teachers must have a knowledge of the developmental changes in thinking skills and strategies as youth move from concrete thinking to formal reasoning and thinking, as they expand their abilities to think abstractly, analyze logically, understand cause and effect, and see events from varying and diverse perspectives. Teachers must be able to demonstrate knowledge and skills related to how development in one domain can positively or negatively affect development in one or more of the other domains. This is especially true for the social domain at this level. Peer acceptance and influence are significant factors and may positively or negatively influence academic progress. It is imperative that secondary teachers have the knowledge and skills necessary to plan, deliver, and assess lessons that reflect an understanding of students' developmental characteristics and needs.

Developmental Differences

A second knowledge component of Standard I relates to how students' developmental characteristics have implications for planning appropriate instruction. Beginning teachers must recognize the impact that personal and academic experiences in previous grades have had on a youth's individual development. Teachers must know the wide range of individual developmental differences that characterize students in any grade and recognize the impact of the rate of development on all domains. When planning instruction, secondary teachers must know how developmental characteristics affect learning and performance, such as varying skills of processing and differences in physical development. Even at these advanced grade levels, teachers must understand the importance of helping youth apply decision-making skills, hone organizational skills, and refine goal-setting skills. Cognitive, social, emotional, and reasoning stages must be understood as teachers design, develop, and implement developmentally appropriate instruction and assessment. Finally, teachers must know how to use their knowledge of developmental characteristics to plan meaningful and interesting learning experiences that promote development of the whole person.

Effective teachers demonstrate an ability to adapt lessons that address students' varied backgrounds, skills, interests, and learning needs, including the needs of English language learners.

Varied Needs

The third component of this standard is related to the characteristics and instructional needs of students with varied backgrounds, skills, interests, and learning needs. Teachers must be able to use effective approaches that address varied learning needs and preferences. Instructional strategies should include spontaneous activities that promote quality learning as well as capitalize on teachable moments when youth see relevance to their learning.

A fourth area of Standard I is related to different approaches to learning that may be exhibited by secondary learners. Teachers must know what motivates secondary students to be actively engaged in the learning environment. They must be aware of and able to use various motivational strategies appropriate for these ages, including extrinsic as well as intrinsic motivators. Teachers must be able to adapt and adjust to teachable moments when secondary learners exhibit excitement about learning or bring their own personal experiences to the learning setting. Using personal experiences is an appropriate way to make connections and to help youth see relevance to their required learning. Opportunities must be provided that activate prior knowledge and capitalize on prior experience.

Cultural Differences

The final elements of Standard I relate to cultural and socioeconomic differences and their significance when designing and delivering instruction. Teachers must acknowledge and respect the cultural and socioeconomic differences of secondary students when determining appropriate instructional goals, learning activities, learning outcomes, and assessment strategies. They must know appropriate strategies for instructing English language learners of these ages. Although fewer students enter school as second-language learners in these grades, a significant number immigrate to this country in the secondary grades. Teachers must understand the impact of not knowing the target language on the academic, social, and emotional growth of secondary students. As the state of Texas becomes more and more diverse and as more languages are represented in Texas classrooms across the state, it is imperative that all teachers have the knowledge and skills that allow them to address the needs of English language learners rather than leaving this solely to the bilingual or ESL teacher. Although it is logical to expect support from teachers who have specialized in helping learners acquire the English language, these specialists should not be expected to meet all the needs of language learners. All teachers must possess the knowledge and skills required to assist in the learning of students from all cultural, socioeconomic, and language backgrounds.

Readers are encouraged to review the explanatory notes for Domain I competencies presented in the EC–6 and 4–8 sections. Although not all characteristics of learners are the same, many of the elements of the various competencies cross all grade levels, so rather than lengthen this study guide, you are asked to preview the expanded notes in the EC–6 and 4–8 sections of this chapter.

Competencies: Domain I, 8–12

COMPETENCY 001

The teacher understands human developmental processes and applies this knowledge to plan instruction and ongoing assessment that motivate students and are responsive to their developmental characteristics and needs.

The following are the stated characteristics of a beginning teacher who meets the expectations of this competency.

- Recognizes the importance of helping students in grades 8 through 12 learn and apply life skills (self-direction, decision-making skills, goal-setting skills, workplace skills) to promote lifelong learning and active participation in society.
- Knows the typical stages of the cognitive, social, physical, and emotional development of students in grades 8–12.
- Recognizes the wide range of individual developmental differences that characterizes students in grades 8–12 and the implications of this developmental variation for instructional planning.
- Demonstrates an understanding of the physical changes associated with adolescence and ways in which these changes impact development in other domains (cognitive, social, emotional).
- Recognizes typical challenges for students during adolescence and young adulthood (self-esteem, physical appearance, eating disorders, identity formation, educational and career decisions) and effective ways to help them address these challenges.
- Understands ways in which student involvement in risky behaviors (gang membership, drug and alcohol use) impacts development and learning.
- Demonstrates knowledge of the importance of peers, peer acceptance, and conformity to peer group norms and expectations for adolescents, and understands the significance of peer-related issues for teaching and learning.
- Understands that social and emotional factors in the family (parental divorce, homelessness) impact the learning and development of students in grades 8–12 in other domains.
- Uses knowledge of the cognitive changes in students in grades 8–12 (refinement of abstract thinking and reasoning, reflective thinking, focus on the world beyond the school setting) to plan instruction that promotes learning and development.
- Analyzes ways in which the developmental characteristics of students in grades 8–12 impact learning and performance; applies knowledge of students' developmental characteristics and needs to plan effective learning experiences and assessments.
- Understands that development in any one domain (cognitive, social, physical, emotional) impacts development in other domains.

IN SUMMARY

Students in grades 8–12 face many challenges, both in the educational setting and the external environment. Teachers should work diligently to ensure that these high school learners have a strong sense of self-direction and independent approaches to learning. These students need proven decision-making skills to deal with the many exposures they have to factors that might negatively influence their lives. With strength in their ability to establish personal, academic, and career goals, students will have confidence and a strong sense of self-efficacy as they prepare to enter the world beyond school and the workplace. Not only do they need successful records in academic work, but they also need increasingly challenging workplace skills so that they can adjust to changing jobs, respond to leadership opportunities, and retain employment that will provide a comfortable lifestyle. Business and industry leaders today tell us that far too many high school graduates have limited skills in effective communication and mathematical reasoning. Too much focus on the mandated standardized tests may be the culprit in this phenomenon. Teachers must keep clear goals for student learning far beyond those dictated by the knowledge and skills tested by state examinations.

Development

To ensure that high school learners make optimal academic and social progress, teachers must understand the stages of their cognitive, social, physical, and emotional development. See Table 6 for a quick summary of these characteristics. Teachers should also understand how growth in one domain might directly affect growth in the other domains. Of course, the reverse is true as well; if students do not make satisfactory progress in one domain, other domains may be negatively impacted. Teachers are typically faced with a wide range of individual development at these ages and thus must be adept at managing multitasking environments that support a variety of learners.

Self-Esteem

Upper-level learners face issues of self-esteem similar to those encountered by middle-level learners. At these ages, students are very critical of their physical appearances and often follow fads in clothing, dieting, or hair styles. They see themselves through the eyes of others and thus may change their personal habits and patterns to fit in with peers they esteem. Their own sense of self-esteem may be based more on what their peers think of them than on the influence of any other person(s). Eating disorders seem to be on the rise among students in these age groups. Depression is often prominent among high school students, especially if they feel they do not belong to a group or if they are experiencing what is to them devastating family changes, such as parental divorce.

If high school students do not feel an attachment to a peer group that has a positive influence, they may turn to gangs for a sense of belonging. Recent reports indicate that gang activity is on the rise in Texas, especially in large, urban settings. Teachers must be knowledgeable about gang indicators and be able to identify changes in stu-

TABLE 6

Developmental Characteristics of Grades 8–12		
Domain	Ages 14–18	Grades 8–12
Physical	Physically mature; often sexually active; eating disorders; substance abuse; hormonal changes and influences	Physical body is important; need more sleep for developing body; refined motor skills; strength, power, and flexibility well developed
Cognitive	Formal operations; independent learning; abstract thinking; problem solving; critical thinking	Able to deal with abstractions; can form hypotheses; can see different perspectives
Social	Identity versus role confusion; moving into intimacy versus isolation; greater concern for others	Establishing self-identity; peer group influence critical; focusing on career goals
Emotional	Concern for immediate future; depression; role confusion; developing independence	Law-and-order orientation moving into social contract orientation

dent behavior that might indicate involvement in gang activity and/or drug or alcohol use. Sudden changes in behavior, changes in attitude, changes in dress or appearance, and changes in peer group may each or all be indicators of involvement in unhealthy choices. Teachers should watch for physical signs of drug or alcohol use, such as red or unfocused eyes or unusual and noticeable odors indicative of drugs or alcohol. If the secondary teacher has **reasonable suspicion** that a student is engaged in such activities, it is imperative that the counselor, school nurse, and/or campus administrator be notified immediately.

As high school students form and refine their identities, they may have an exceptionally high focus on their physical appearance. If they deem it necessary to fit in by having their body tattooed, they may well choose this route even if their parents are adamantly against it. If they consider their bodies to be overweight, they may develop eating disorders in order to control their weight. Again, teachers must have a knowledge of the characteristics of these disorders. With all the changes in family and social structures occurring in our nation, high school students are engaging in sexual activity and drug use more frequently. A recent report indicates that one out of four high school students will have a sexually transmitted disease. Often, involvement in sexual activity is a result of participation in the use of illegal drugs. Teachers have a responsibility to be on the watch for signs of drug use or inappropriate sexual activity. They might argue that these environmental factors are not their responsibility, but the fact is that far too often teachers see youth more hours per day than do the students' parents or caregivers. Teachers must work closely with counselors, school nurses, and campus administrators to stay on top of issues concerning inappropriate social activities on the part of high school students.

Career Advisor

Another role of the high school teacher is that of career advisor. Although students are likely to discuss career options with the school counselor, a closer relationship is often developed with the classroom teacher. Thus students often turn to the teacher for career advice and emotional support. They may also ask the teacher to provide guidance regarding preparation for college or the workplace.

One of the most important elements of this competency is the teacher's role in ensuring that high school graduates have refined skills in abstract thinking and reasoning, problem solving, reflective thinking, and preparation for life beyond school. Even though high school teachers typically focus more on their subject areas, they have other roles, too. Teachers should focus on the student learner so that all students leave high school fully capable and confident in their abilities to enter the workforce or to continue their education.

COMPETENCY 002

The teacher understands student diversity and knows how to plan learning experiences and design assessments that are responsive to differences among students and that promote all students' learning.

The following are the stated characteristics of a beginning teacher who meets the expectations of this competency.

- Demonstrates knowledge of students with diverse personal and social characteristics (those related to ethnicity, gender, language background, exceptionality) and the significance of student diversity in teaching, learning, and assessment.
- Accepts and respects students with diverse backgrounds and needs.
- Knows how to use diversity in the classroom and the community to enrich all students' learning experiences.
- Knows strategies for enhancing one's own understanding of students' diverse backgrounds and needs.
- Knows how to plan and adapt lessons to address students' varied backgrounds, skills, interests, and learning needs, including the needs of English language learners and students with disabilities.
- Understands cultural and socioeconomic differences (including differential access to technology) and knows how to plan instruction that is responsive to cultural and socioeconomic differences among students.
- Understands the instructional significance of varied student learning needs and preferences.

IN SUMMARY

As Texas becomes more diverse, teachers must know how to work with a classroom of students who represent five to ten nationalities, three or four disabilities, four or five intellectual ability levels, and various cultural and family variances. Issues of ethnicity, gender, language background, and exceptionality challenge teachers beyond the academic aspects of teaching. It is estimated that within the next few years, the state will become a minority-majority state. Since the Texas Higher Education Coordinating Board established a "closing the gaps" strategic plan, high school teachers have been asked to explore more ways to keep students in school until graduation and to encourage all students to go to college for an advanced degree. Unless the gap is closed, the state may face a shortage of well-educated leaders over the next 20–25 years.

Getting Along with Others

Teachers engage learners in activities that will help them get along with workers, family members, or peers who are different than they. Assigning high school students to work in cooperative and collaborative groups helps develop skills of accepting others' points of view, working as a team, fulfilling roles and responsibilities, and completing tasks as a team. To prepare high school graduates for the workplace, teachers should encourage students to consider how other people might react in a given situation, how groups of people can work together effectively even when they differ, how to bring about consensus in a work group, and how to listen effectively to arguments on opposing sides of an issue.

Diverse Backgrounds

Finally, for this competency, teachers must capitalize on the strengths of students from diverse backgrounds. English language learners have much to offer in learning activities that provide cultural, social, geographical, or historical opportunities for sharing. Infusion of the arts into other curriculum areas allows students from all areas to demonstrate how their ancestors contributed to the world's aesthetic enjoyment. Assuming the roles of others in a study of historical events is an effective strategy for taking on the perspective of someone with a possibly conflicting point of view. Keeping a journal (personal, simulated, or learning) is effective for capturing the perspectives, attitudes, and dispositions of secondary-level learners.

COMPETENCY 003

The teacher understands procedures for designing effective and coherent instruction and assessment based on appropriate learning goals and objectives.

The following are the stated characteristics of a beginning teacher who meets the expectations of this competency.

- Understands the significance of the Texas Essential Knowledge and Skills (TEKS) and of prerequisite knowledge and skills in determining instructional goals and objectives.
- Uses appropriate criteria to evaluate the appropriateness of learning goals and objectives (clarity; relevance; significance; age-appropriateness; ability to be assessed; responsiveness to students' current skills and knowledge, backgrounds, needs, and interests; alignment with campus and school district goals).
- Uses assessment to analyze students' strengths and needs, evaluate teacher effectiveness, and guide instructional planning for individuals and groups.

- Understands the connections among various components of the Texas statewide assessment program, the TEKS, and instruction, and analyzes data from state and other assessments using common statistical measures to help identify students' strengths and needs.
- Demonstrates knowledge of various types of materials and resources (including technological resources and resources outside the school) that may be used to enhance student learning and engagement, and evaluates the appropriateness of specific materials and resources for use in particular situations, to address specific purposes, and to meet varied student needs.
- Plans lessons and structures units so that activities progress in a logical sequence and support stated instructional goals.
- Plans learning experiences that provide students with opportunities to explore content from integrated and varied perspectives (by providing intradisciplinary and interdisciplinary instruction, encouraging students' application of knowledge and skills to the world beyond the school, designing instruction that reflects students' increasing abilities to examine complex issues and ideas).
- Allocates time appropriately within the lessons and units, including providing adequate opportunities for students to engage in reflection, self-assessment, and closure.

IN SUMMARY

Learners in grades 8–12 need to see relevance in their learning activities. Although not all components of all lessons have immediate relevance, if teachers can guide secondary learners to see value in learning, students will be much more receptive to the academic tasks. Goals and objectives should be clearly stated. The teacher *and* the students should develop routines and procedures for classroom efficiency so that an environment conducive to optimal learning is in place. Inviting civic, business, or industry leaders to speak to the class is helpful in establishing significance and relevance for a given lesson.

Curriculum Planning

The curriculum must be adequately and effectively planned, delivered, and assessed for secondary students to make satisfactory progress in their academic learning. Lessons and units must be age-appropriate, motivating, connected with prior and future learning, and readily assessable. Lessons should respond to students' current knowledge bases and skill development. Background knowledge and experiences, as well as students' needs and interests, should be considered when designing instructional activities that will meet the preestablished goals and identified learning outcomes. The curriculum must be aligned with campus and district goals. Teachers should work together in both vertical and horizontal teams to ensure that there are no gaps in the curriculum and no boring redundancies.

Resource Use

Interesting and motivating resources should be employed for effective lessons and units. Extensive use of technological resources is vital for students in these grades. As they prepare for a technologically advanced workplace, they must have refined skills across the various technologies available. Integrating word processing, spreadsheets, databases, presentations, and other technologies into the teacher's instructional plans and into the students' assignments will ensure that students leave high school well accomplished in technology.

Making Connections

Finally, the practice of making intradisciplinary connections within lessons and units, as well as interdisciplinary ones, is not always found in secondary schools. Subject-centered teachers often find it challenging to integrate other content areas; however, students make better connections when they see the relevance of refining technical writing skills learned in the English classroom applied to reporting scientific data in the biology classroom. If secondary teachers work together to identify curriculum threads or even curriculum themes in more than one subject area, students will make better connections and be more adept at employing the skills learned. Teachers must also use a wider variety of questioning techniques to help learners in grades 8–12 find meaning in their lessons. Probing questions, cuing questions, guiding questions, and so on provide a means of extending learning and holding the learner responsible for the intended learning outcome.

COMPETENCY 004

The teacher understands learning processes and factors that impact student learning and demonstrates this knowledge by planning effective, engaging instruction and appropriate assessments.

The following are the stated characteristics of a beginning teacher who meets the expectations of this competency.

- Understands the role of learning theory in the instructional process and uses instructional strategies and appropriate technologies to facilitate student learning (connecting new information and ideas to prior knowledge, making learning meaningful and relevant to students).
- Knows the implications for learning and instruction of students' increasing ability to engage in abstract thinking and reasoning.
- Enhances learning for students in grades 8–12 by providing instruction that encourages the use and refinement of higher-order thinking skills (prompting students to explore ideas from diverse perspectives, structuring active learning experiences involving cooperative learning, problem solving, open-ended questioning, and inquiry; building the capacity of students to learn through in-depth study and research).

- Teaches, models, and monitors organizational and time management skills at an age-appropriate level (using effective strategies for locating information, organizing information systematically).
- Recognizes how various characteristics of students in grades 8–12 (interacting with the larger community, building relationships, establishing an identity, questioning values, exploring long-term career and life goals, being aware of the importance of peers) impact teaching and learning.
- Analyzes ways in which teacher behaviors (teacher expectations, student grouping practices, teacher-student interactions) affect student learning, and plans instruction and assessment that minimize the effects of negative factors and enhance all students' learning.
- Analyzes ways in which factors in the home and community (parental expectations, availability of community resources, community problems) impact student learning, and plans instruction and assessment with an awareness of social and cultural factors to enhance all students' learning.
- Understands the importance of self-directed learning and plans instruction and assessment that promote students' motivation and their sense of ownership of and responsibility for their own learning.
- Analyzes ways in which various teacher roles (facilitator, lecturer) and student roles (active learner, observer, group participant) impact student learning.
- Incorporates students' different approaches to learning (auditory, visual, tactile, kinesthetic) into instructional practices.

IN SUMMARY

Howard Gardner's work with multiple intelligences has given teachers a new way to look at how students learn. Secondary students will likely exhibit mastery of most of the ways of learning described by Gardner. The teacher must have the skills, disposition, and knowledge needed to allow learners of all types to capitalize on their strengths and to develop their weaknesses. Whether a student exhibits greater strength in bodily-kinesthetic learning than in spatial learning should be informational to the teacher. In any given classroom, there are likely to be learners in grades 8–12 with strength in logical sequential ways of learning, spatial intelligence, intra- or interpersonal learning strengths, and/or naturalist ways of knowing and learning. Combined with Gardner's intelligences is a needed knowledge of perceptual modality strength potentials. To ensure that all students have optimal learning opportunities, teachers should try to include auditory, visual, tactile, and kinesthetic activities in as many lessons and units as possible. With all the studies on how the brain functions, teachers must stay current on the latest research and theories about learning and apply this knowledge in the classroom.

Upper-level learners have refined skills in abstract thinking, critical thinking, and problem solving. It is the teacher's responsibility to offer frequent learning opportunities where these skills can be used for designing, approaching, and solving problems. The degree to which the teacher models these higher-level thinking skills impacts the desire of students to employ such advanced thinking.

Teachers in secondary schools must also model effective organization and time management. Teacher behaviors clearly have an effect on student behavior. Teachers should be aware of their influence in areas such as keeping the classroom organized; having materials and supplies ready, operable, and available; and modeling continuous self-reflection about how well the learning environment is working. Appropriate and effective modeling by the teacher can help ensure that secondary-level learners become adept at independent and self-directed learning.

Significant in this competency is the connection among the school, the home, and the community. Service learning projects, apprenticeships with adults in the workplace, activities designed to enhance the school campus environment, or any "other-oriented" activities help students learn the importance of giving to others and of becoming a productive member of society. Teachers who know their students well, who become involved in the interests and activities of their students, and who focus on the whole learner rather than only on the subject area will be effective in developing lifelong learning in secondary school graduates.

Standard II: Creating a Positive, Productive Classroom Environment

> **The teacher creates a classroom environment of respect and rapport that fosters a positive climate for learning, equity, and excellence.**

> Note to EC–12 candidates: Read this chapter in its entirety because test items will cover all the competencies for each of the three grade level clusters.

The climate of the learning environment is critical to the learning outcomes of students at any age or grade level. From the era of the effective schools movement, we know that how teachers structure the learning environment directly correlates with how students learn. From the lighting (either natural or artificial) to the temperature (too warm, too cool, or just right) to the air quality (contaminant-laden or clean), the controllable aspects of the classroom are important considerations when planning the academic year.

How tables, chairs, or desks are arranged indicates how much the teacher is interested in a student-centered classroom. If the teacher sets up the furniture so that all learners face the instructional board, projector screen, or teacher's desk, it is clear that he or she has a teacher-centered approach to teaching and learning. On the other hand, if the teacher arranges the furniture so that learners have small working areas, clusters of tables, chairs, or desks for cooperative learning activities, a teacher's desk that is off to the side or in the back of the room, and areas around the room where demonstrations or projections can be shown indicates that a teacher is totally student-centered in his or her approach.

The climate of the classroom has a direct impact on student motivation, active engagement in learning, and success in academic and social growth. The climate also affects issues of student diversity. Teachers must ensure that students with disabilities have an optimal space that is protected and that meets the specific disability needs. Students of other nationalities also have classroom climate needs. Teachers should arrange seating so that it is easy to assign small work groups, provide for literature discussion groups, offer quiet places for studying and reflecting, and move learners about in multitasking activities.

In addition to the physical classroom environment, the affective environment is perhaps just as important. The tone set by the teacher indicates his/her expectations. How the teacher communicates with learners and others depicts the type of environment in which the teacher feels comfortable. The degree to which the classroom walls are covered with various pictures and text documents indicates how the teacher views spatial components. Too much work on the walls could be very distracting to visually challenged or attention-challenged learners. Too little work could result in a boring, non-motivating learning environment. Ultimately, for optimal student learning, the classroom environment should be pleasing, supportive, and engaging.

KNOWLEDGE AND APPLICATION COMPONENTS FOR GRADES EC–6

What factors must teachers know to establish a well-designed classroom for early childhood and elementary level learners? Because young children need lots of space for movement, several stations for active engagement in learning, and frequent opportunities to move about, the classroom should be set up in a manner that responds to these needs. Even older elementary students need space for cooperative learning groups, learning centers/stations, and artistic activities. The teacher's desk should be placed off in a corner or in the rear of the classroom. Primary grade teachers have little or no time to sit at their desks during the instructional part of the day. Several areas should be dedicated to the posting of student work in order to help learners value their work and see the reactions of their peers. A sense of pride is developed when young students view their work displayed, even if the work is not at the level of an optimal grade. Displayed work is motivating for older elementary students as the approval of their peers becomes more important. Clusters of desks or tables should be arranged to provide space for small student work groups, teacher conferencing with students, or learning stations. The arrangement of classroom furniture should form a safe and optimal learning environment.

Competencies: Domain II, EC–6

COMPETENCY 005

The teacher knows how to establish a classroom climate that fosters learning, equity, and excellence and uses this knowledge to create a physical and emotional environment that is safe and productive.

The following are the stated characteristics of a beginning teacher who meets the expectations of this competency.

- Uses knowledge of the unique characteristics and needs of students in grades EC–6 to establish a positive, productive classroom environment (encourages cooperation and sharing, teaches children to use language to express their feelings, provides opportunities to collaborate with peers, promotes students' awareness of how their actions and attitudes affect others, includes kinesthetic experiences and active learning within a planned, structured environment).
- Establishes a classroom climate that emphasizes collaboration and supportive interactions, respect for diversity and individual differences, and active engagement in learning by all students.
- Analyzes ways in which teacher-student interactions and interactions among students impact classroom climate and student learning and development.
- Presents instruction in ways that communicate the teacher's enthusiasm for learning.
- Uses a variety of means to convey high expectations for all students.
- Knows the characteristics of physical spaces that are safe and productive for learning, recognizes the benefits and limitations of various furniture arrangements in the classroom, and applies strategies for organizing the physical environment to ensure physical accessibility and to facilitate learning in various instructional contexts.
- Creates a safe, nurturing, inclusive classroom environment that addresses students' emotional needs and respects students' rights and dignity.

IN SUMMARY

In the primary grades, children need encouragement to develop skills and dispositions that will help them learn to cooperate with their peers. They must have an environment that supports the sharing of supplies, materials, space, ideas, and experiences. A classroom climate that is conducive to learning provides a safe physical space and a place where children feel free to take risks and explore in an inquiring manner. The environment must nurture the natural curiosity of young children and offer opportunities to engage in hands-on learning activities. Children must have easy and ready access to supplies and materials as they make things, perform learning activities, or produce products that demonstrate their knowledge development. The classroom environment should encourage children to use language to express their feelings, such as by providing role-playing centers, problem-solving activities, or simulations of events. Students in the upper-elementary grades need a learning environment that encourages their motivation to learn. Students at these ages want to interact with their peers. The teacher needs to provide appropriate classroom spaces for learning stations, cooperative learning group activities, research activities, and concrete learning activities. In addition, the environment should be conducive to helping all learners develop respect for diversity and individual differences.

Diversity

Today's classrooms represent a wide range of diversity. Teachers must pay careful attention to how students from various backgrounds may contribute to the learning of all students. For example, teachers could hang up posters that display diverse cultures.

They could also add more cooperative learning areas so that students may learn from each other naturally.

Disabilities

When the classroom is arranged to meet the needs of students with disabilities, students begin to view the inclusion of all children as a positive and natural occurrence. All areas of the classroom must be safe, free from clutter, and inviting for students with all abilities or disabilities. For students who move about in wheelchairs or walkers, classroom space must be adequate for maneuvering the equipment. Classroom supplies must be placed at levels all students can easily access, even those in wheelchairs. Access to restroom or water facilities is also important to support the learning of students with physical disabilities.

COMPETENCY 006

The teacher understands strategies for creating an organized and productive learning environment and for managing student behavior.

The following are the stated characteristics of a beginning teacher who meets the expectations of this competency.

- Analyzes the effects of classroom routines and procedures on student learning and knows how to establish and implement routines and procedures to promote an organized and productive learning environment.
- Demonstrates and applies an understanding of how students function in groups; designs group activities that ensure that students work together cooperatively and productively in various settings.
- Recognizes the importance of creating a schedule for young children that balances restful and active movement activities and provides large blocks of time for play, projects, and learning centers.
- Schedules activities and manages time in ways that maximize student learning, including using effective procedures to manage transitions; to manage materials, supplies, and technology; and to coordinate the performance of noninstructional duties (taking attendance) with instructional activities.
- Uses technological tools to perform administrative tasks such as taking attendance, maintaining grade books, and facilitating communication.
- Works with volunteers and paraprofessionals to enhance and enrich instruction and applies procedures for monitoring the performance of volunteers and paraprofessionals in the classroom.
- Applies theories and techniques related to managing and monitoring student behavior.
- Demonstrates awareness of appropriate behavior standards and expectations for students at various developmental levels.
- Applies effective procedures for managing student behavior and for promoting appropriate behavior and ethical work habits (academic integrity) in the classroom (communicating high and realistic behavior expectations, involving stu-

dents in developing rules and procedures, establishing clear consequences for inappropriate behavior, enforcing behavior standards consistently, encouraging students to monitor their own behavior and to use conflict resolution skills, responding appropriately to various types of behavior).

IN SUMMARY

How teachers set up their classrooms for effective and efficient management of time, resources, and student behavior tells a lot about how they view the educational process. Teachers who establish clear classroom rules, based on the greater rules of the campus, help young learners understand the expectations of the entire campus learning community. The routines and procedures established by the teacher with the input of the students clarify for learners what they are expected to do and how they should manage themselves in the learning environment. The manner in which teachers establish and organize group activities models for learners how they can be successful in their group tasks.

Ensuring Balance

Teachers must ensure that early childhood students have a logical balance between restful and active movement activities. Young children have short attention spans and thus need frequent changes in activity. Older students also need motion and variety in their learning activities. A good balance that includes smooth transitions from one activity to another lets students know that their needs are being met in a supportive climate. Older elementary students need routines and procedures as well. Teachers should let students know the rules and the consequences of breaking them so that students more readily abide by those rules. It is better to have only a few firm rules, paired with as many classroom procedure statements as are needed. Older students usually like helping ensure that the classroom runs smoothly. So the teacher should assign students to roles that help maintain a democratic classroom environment.

The teacher should have several strategies that can be employed in making wise use of time during transitions between activities or between classrooms. Hand signals, voice signals, or other cues used consistently help learners know what to expect when it is time to make transitions. Consistent signals should be used for putting away materials, for going to the restroom, for lining up to move to the cafeteria or to another classroom, or for stopping for an announcement or some instruction from the teacher. Some teachers employ hand signals whereby one raised finger indicates get quiet, a second indicates listen carefully, and so on, until the children are all seated and ready to listen. Classroom procedures are needed so that students know in advance how to manage materials and resources transitioning from one activity to another. Written schedules should be clearly displayed help students know the daily schedule.

Managing Resources

Within this competency are ideas about how to manage materials, supplies, and human resources. Most teachers today have a desktop computer either in their classroom or in an adjacent office. They use it to record grades, communicate with parents or peers, develop presentations, prepare word-processing documents, or search the Internet. Effective classroom management involves the teacher's communication skills. Efficient use of technology for managing grades, communicating with parents, or delivering instruction ensures more time for teaching.

Often teachers have the privilege of inviting parent or community volunteers into their classrooms for certain events or for regular assistance with instructional tasks. These teachers must have all the materials organized and ready for the volunteer to use.

In addition to volunteers, many teachers have paraprofessionals who are assigned to assist them with instructional preparation, meeting the needs of special-needs learners, or taking care of routine tasks that otherwise would be time consuming for the teacher. The use of a chart listing times and tasks is helpful for the efficient management of these resources. Teachers also need to prepare materials for a substitute teacher. These materials should outline the classroom routines and procedures, explain where materials and supplies are kept, describe the daily schedule and routine, and suggest ways to encourage individual students.

Managing Behavior

This competency includes concepts about behavior management. Young children often need guidance in developing their own self-management. Older students may be more adept at managing their own behavior. However, they still need teacher guidance in this area. Teachers must prevent off-task behaviors, redirect inappropriate behaviors, and stop risky behaviors before they become dangerous. Something as simple as a student leaning back in a chair could present a legal issue for a teacher if the student fell and was injured. Teachers must have the capacity to see every part of the classroom at all times and to notice when any given student is engaged in off-task or inappropriate behavior. Kounin suggested that teachers must be aware of everything that goes on in the classroom at all times. Teachers who have "withitness" skills are fully on top of things at all times.

Behavior management strategies such as redirection, moving the student to a time-out station within the classroom, signing a behavior contract, or holding a private conference with the student are appropriate measures to take to help learners develop self-management and self-direction. Raising one's voice, yelling at students, placing students out in the hallway, and sending students to the principal's office are not appropriate measures to take in managing student behavior. The teacher is responsible for what goes on in the classroom and thus must take care of behavior issues to the ultimate extent possible. In an emergency behavior management situation, the teacher must never leave the class unattended. Notify a nearby teacher that you have an emergency. Ask that teacher to oversee your classroom by standing in the hallway between the two classrooms until other assistance arrives. Otherwise, the teacher might easily place other students at risk. Many teachers make a prior agreement with the teacher next door or across the hall to step in and monitor students if the teacher needs to escort an out-of-control student to the office.

Competencies: Domain II, 4–8

COMPETENCY 005

The teacher knows how to establish a classroom climate that fosters learning, equity, and excellence and uses this knowledge to create a physical and emotional environment that is safe and productive.

The following are the stated characteristics of a beginning teacher who meets the expectations of this competency.

- Uses knowledge of the unique characteristics and needs of middle-level students to establish a positive, productive classroom environment (provides opportunities to collaborate with peers; promotes students' awareness of how their actions and attitudes affect others; includes kinesthetic experiences and active learning within a planned, structured environment).
- Establishes a classroom climate that emphasizes collaboration and supportive interactions, respect for diversity and individual differences, and active engagement in learning by all students.
- Analyzes ways in which teacher-student interactions and interactions among students impact classroom climate and student learning and development.
- Presents instruction in ways that communicate the teacher's enthusiasm for learning.
- Uses a variety of means to convey high expectations for all students.
- Knows the characteristics of physical spaces that are safe and productive for learning, recognizes the benefits and limitations of various furniture arrangements in the classroom, and applies strategies for organizing the physical environment to ensure physical accessibility and facilitate learning in various instructional contexts.
- Creates a safe, nurturing, inclusive classroom environment that addresses students' emotional needs and respects students' rights and dignity.

IN SUMMARY

Frequent opportunities for working in cooperative and collaborative settings with their peers will help students develop skills necessary for secondary grades and the future workplace. Small groups provide a venue for problem solving, role responsibility, understanding others' points of view, and accountability for the completion of chosen or assigned tasks. Students must have an environment where supplies, materials, space, ideas, and experiences are shared. At these ages students need to demonstrate a disposition of respect for the possessions of others. Keeping personal spaces within the classroom well organized helps avoid problems with missing supplies.

A Nurturing Classroom

A classroom climate that is conducive to learning provides a safe physical and emotional space where students feel free to take risks and explore in an inquiring manner.

The environment must nurture students' natural curiosity and offer opportunities to engage in learning activities involving concrete and higher-level thinking. The classroom environment should encourage children to use language to express their feelings, such as in role-playing historical events, acting out problem-solving activities, or simulating conflict resolution events. If students learn to use words more effectively, they will be able to better control their behaviors in conflict situations.

Classroom Arrangement

The environment should be conducive to helping students develop an attitude of respect for diversity and individual differences. Because students often form groups at these grade levels, opportunities for exchanging ideas and experiences are helpful in promoting the acceptance of others who differ from what students perceive themselves to be. When the classroom is arranged to meet the needs of students with disabilities, this helps students view the inclusion of all children as a positive and natural occurrence. If students who are new to this country are readily invited to participate in active learning experiences, middle-level learners will see the teacher's disposition of inclusion modeled effectively. Because it is natural for students at this age to be competitive, learning how to work cooperatively rather than competitively is necessary for the growth and development of middle-level learners. Activities that help students understand the value of respecting the rights and dignity of others will help them confirm their own rights and develop their sense of dignity, self-efficacy, and self-esteem.

COMPETENCY 006

The teacher understands strategies for creating an organized and productive learning environment and for managing student behavior.

The following are the stated characteristics of a beginning teacher who meets the expectations of this competency.

- Analyzes the effects of classroom routines and procedures on student learning and knows how to establish and implement routines and procedures to promote an organized and productive learning environment.
- Applies procedures for organizing and managing groups to ensure that students work together cooperatively and productively in various settings (problem-solving teams, group projects, research groups, skits, student-created multimedia presentations).
- Schedules activities and manages time in ways that maximize student learning, including using effective procedures to manage transitions; to manage materials, supplies, and technology; and to coordinate the performance of noninstructional duties (taking attendance) with instructional activities.
- Uses technological tools to perform administrative tasks such as taking attendance, maintaining grade books, and facilitating communication.
- Works with volunteers and paraprofessionals to enhance and enrich instruction and applies procedures for monitoring the performance of volunteers and paraprofessionals in the classroom.

- Applies theories and techniques related to managing and monitoring student behavior.
- Demonstrates awareness of appropriate behavior standards and expectations for students at various developmental levels.
- Applies effective procedures for managing student behavior and for promoting appropriate behavior and ethical work habits (academic integrity) in the classroom (communicating high and realistic behavior expectations, involving students in developing rules and procedures, establishing clear consequences for inappropriate behavior, enforcing behavior standards consistently, encouraging students to monitor their own behavior and to use conflict resolution skills, responding appropriately to various types of behavior).

IN SUMMARY

Particularly in the middle grades, teachers should be thoughtful about the message they send regarding how they establish the classroom environment. The way teachers establish their classrooms for the efficient management of time, resources, and student behavior says a lot about the teacher's perspective as either a teacher-centered or a student-centered instructor for middle-grades learners. Teachers who establish clear classroom rules, routines, and procedures (with the participation of the students) set the tone for a well-managed classroom where middle-level learners know what to expect. The manner in which a teacher establishes and organizes group activities informs learners about what the teacher expects and how the groups can function effectively. Students of these ages need frequent opportunities to collaborate with peers in cooperative learning groups, service learning activities, or community action design. Engagement in such learning approaches promotes students' awareness of how their actions and attitudes affect others. They can see that they have an influence on society, have a potential to bring about change, and have the knowledge and skills needed for solving problems in the greater community.

Teacher's Attitude

The teacher's enthusiasm for learning and for teaching is critical to the motivation of middle-level learners. If students perceive that the teacher is bored with the subject, is not interested in the curriculum, is not interested in the students as individuals, or is just burned out as a teacher, many students will misbehave or lack interest. Teachers must ensure that middle-level students have a well-designed, effectively planned, appropriately structured learning environment. A good balance between active and inactive activities helps with motivation for learning while engaging the whole learner in the learning process. Having several strategies for smooth transitions from one activity to another cuts down on the potential for misbehavior and helps to manage time efficiently. Hand signals, voice signals, or other cues used consistently inform students about what to expect when it is time to make transitions. Consistent signals should be used for putting away materials, for going to the restroom, for lining up to move to the cafeteria or to another classroom, or for stopping for an announcement or some instruction from the teacher.

Managing Resources

The management of materials, supplies, and human resources must also be considered in a well-managed classroom. The use of technology has made teachers' work easier and sometimes more efficient. Files can be stored on a computer rather than in a desk drawer or filing cabinet. Most middle-level teachers today have a desktop computer either in their classroom or in an adjacent office. Tasks such as recording grades, communicating with parents or peers, developing presentations, and preparing documents are much more effectively completed with the use of technology. Effective classroom management also involves the skill the teacher has in using tools for communication. Again, a computer can be an efficient means for frequent and effective communication with parents, colleagues, or community partners.

Teachers must have materials organized and ready for volunteer workers or paraprofessionals assigned to assist them with instructional preparation, working with special-needs learners, or taking care of routine time-consuming tasks. The use of a chart that indicates times and tasks is helpful in the efficient management of these resources. The same is true for any potential substitute teachers. To ensure that learning takes place when a substitute is needed rather than using the substitute as a babysitter, the teacher should have all materials and supplies prepared in advance. The teacher should prepare documents that inform the substitute about classroom rules and procedures, where materials are stored, what nearby teachers are available for helping in an emergency, and which students might be called on for information or assistance.

Managing Behavior

Behavior management is often a source of concern for beginning teachers in the middle grades. Students should have developed their own self-management by this age; however, unless the teacher establishes high expectations from the very beginning, he or she is likely to be challenged by youth who need to test their boundaries. Teachers must have skills in preventing off-task behaviors, redirecting inappropriate behaviors, or stopping risky behaviors before they become dangerous. Redirection techniques should be employed. These include moving a student from one mode of thinking to another, using compliance terms like *please* and *thank you*, using body proximity, and using positive voice and body language. Never react to a student's misbehavior in anger. Wait until you both have had time to calm down before addressing the problem. Of course, if the misbehavior is such that other students are at risk, other strategies must be used. Following successful redirection, discuss with the student more appropriate ways to manage his or her actions. Focus on getting the behavior under control and then work on appropriate redirection. Teachers must also have the capacity to oversee all areas of the classroom at all times. Beginning teachers often lack the ability to be completely aware and find that students are off task too often.

The teacher is the primary enforcer of behavior rules, but the goal should be to scaffold learners toward complete self-management and self-direction. Behavior management strategies such as redirection, moving the student to a time-out station in the classroom, signing a behavior contract, or holding a private conference with the student are appropriate measures to take in managing challenging situations. Raising one's voice, placing students in the hallway, or sending them to the principal's office are not appropriate measures to take in managing student behavior. Teachers of youth of these ages sometimes make an agreement with a teacher colleague so that if a major problem occurs and the teacher must leave the classroom for any length of time, the teacher next door or across the hall can step in to monitor students to avoid any disruption in learning or to manage any behavior conflicts that arise. This agreement among teachers can also be used to provide a student with an alternate work environment should the need arise.

Conflict resolution skills are critical for middle-level learners. As students of these ages become more independent and establish their roles and their identities, it is natural that conflicts will arise between individuals and groups. Time should be spent teaching and practicing conflict resolution strategies such as both students or groups of students sitting facing each other and talking through an issue. Guide students toward focusing on the problem or issue, not on the person(s). Model how dealing with the present situation is necessary rather than bringing up past actions or events. Guide students in learning how to come to consensus when a decision has to be made. Teach students how to *save face* and not back themselves into a corner where they might feel defeated or perceive the need to be antagonistic. Facilitate the opportunity for each person (or side) to present his or her case. Help students understand and acquire the skill of seeing things from another's point of view.

Competencies: Domain II, 8–12

COMPETENCY 005

The teacher knows how to establish a classroom climate that fosters learning, equity, and excellence and uses this knowledge to create a physical and emotional environment that is safe and productive.

The following are the stated characteristics of a beginning teacher who meets the expectations of this competency.

- Uses knowledge of the unique characteristics and needs of students in grades 8–12 to establish a positive, productive classroom environment (encourages respect for the community and the people in it, promotes the use of appropriate language and behavior in daily interactions).
- Establishes a classroom climate that emphasizes collaboration and supportive interactions, respect for diversity and individual differences, and active engagement in learning by all students.
- Analyzes ways in which teacher-student interactions and interactions among students impact classroom climate and student learning and development.
- Presents instruction in ways that communicate the teacher's enthusiasm for learning.
- Uses a variety of means to convey high expectations for all students.

- Knows the characteristics of physical spaces that are safe and productive for learning, recognizes the benefits and limitations of various furniture arrangements in the classroom, and applies strategies for organizing the physical environment to ensure physical accessibility and facilitate learning in various instructional contexts.
- Creates a safe, nurturing, inclusive classroom environment that addresses students' emotional needs and respects students' rights and dignity.

IN SUMMARY

Inherent in the stated or the hidden curriculum for grades 8–12 are skills in being respectful, solving problems, accepting others' points of view, and resolving conflicts. Students in these upper grades need encouragement in developing dispositions that will ensure their success in future work and family situations. Learning activities that require working in cooperative groups with their peers are supportive of acquiring or enhancing skills in collaboration, forming a consensus, and problem solving. Having students work in pairs or in small groups provides a venue for improving knowledge and skills for assuming role responsibility, completing chosen or assigned activities on time and with high-quality results, listening to others' perspectives and points of view, and producing quality work as the result of a team effort.

Especially with secondary-level learners, the environment must support the sharing of supplies, materials, space, ideas, and experiences. A classroom climate that is conducive to learning provides an environmentally, emotionally, and physically safe space where students feel free to take risks, ask questions, propose hypotheses, and challenge assumptions. The environment must nurture students' curiosity and offer opportunities to engage in abstract, higher-level thinking activities.

To promote problem-solving skills, the classroom environment should encourage students to express their feelings in activities such as problem solving, simulations, debates, and small-group role playing. The environment should be conducive to developing an attitude of respect for diversity and individual differences. Secondary classrooms that include students with disabilities provide an opportunity for students to view the inclusion of all learners as a positive and natural occurrence. Students in grades 8–12 must explore their own sense of identity, be open to the diverse experiences and views of others, and develop a strong sense of respect for cultural diversity. Classrooms that provide academic and social opportunities for the development of dispositions that result in positive behaviors offer a support system for personal growth and development.

COMPETENCY 006

The teacher understands strategies for creating an organized and productive learning environment and for managing student behavior.

The following are the stated characteristics of a beginning teacher who meets the expectations of this competency.

- Analyzes the effects of classroom routines and procedures on student learning and knows how to establish and implement routines and procedures (by teaching, modeling, and monitoring students' organizational and time management skills) to promote an organized and productive learning environment.

- Organizes and manages individual and group activities that promote students' ability to assume responsible roles and develop collaborative skills and individual accountability applicable in real-world settings.

- Schedules activities and manages time in ways that maximize student learning, including using effective procedures to manage transitions; to manage materials, supplies, and technology; and to coordinate the performance of noninstructional duties (taking attendance) with instructional activities.

- Uses technological tools to perform administrative tasks such as taking attendance, maintaining grade books, and facilitating communication.

- Works with volunteers and paraprofessionals to enhance and enrich instruction and applies procedures for monitoring the performance of volunteers and paraprofessionals in the classroom.

- Applies theories and techniques related to managing and monitoring student behavior.

- Demonstrates awareness of appropriate behavior standards and expectations for students at various developmental levels.

- Applies effective procedures for managing student behavior and for promoting appropriate behavior and ethical work habits (academic integrity) in the classroom (communicating high and realistic behavior expectations, involving students in developing rules and procedures, establishing clear consequences for inappropriate behavior, enforcing behavior standards consistently, encouraging students to monitor their own behavior and to use conflict resolution skills, responding appropriately to various types of behavior).

IN SUMMARY

Students in secondary grades readily pick up on the teacher's attitude toward classroom management. Teachers should be thoughtful about the message they send regarding how they establish their classrooms for efficient management of time, resources, and student behavior. Often secondary teachers are teacher-centered or subject-centered rather than student-centered; therefore, you must think about how you can let students know that you have a passion for your subject area yet have a strong commitment toward their individual and collective learning.

Well-managed Classroom

Teachers who have well-established classroom routines and procedures (developed with the participation of students) set the tone for a well-managed classroom where secondary-level learners feel comfortable, safe, and free to take risks. Students of these ages must know what to expect from the teacher and the school. Clear boundaries must be firmly in place. However, they should be flexible enough so that in a given situation, they can be adjusted to meet the specific needs of a student while remaining equitable.

The manner in which teachers establish and organize group activities informs the learners about what the teacher expects as well as about how the groups can function effectively. Students of these ages need frequent opportunities to collaborate with peers in cooperative learning groups, service learning activities, and community action projects. Engagement in such learning activities promotes students' awareness of how their actions and attitudes affect others. They can see that they have an influence on society, have potential to bring about change, and have the knowledge and skills for solving problems in the greater community.

Enthusiasm for the Subject

The teacher's enthusiasm for the subject, for learning, and for teaching is critical to the motivation of secondary learners. If students perceive that the teacher is bored with the subject, not interested in the curriculum, or just burned out as a teacher, there is a high potential for student misbehavior and a lack of interest in the lessons and units the teacher presents. Dispositions modeled by the teacher have a direct impact on how students respond.

Balance in the Classroom

Teachers must ensure that students have a well-designed, effectively planned, appropriately structured learning environment. A good balance between teacher direction and student choice, between abstract and concrete engagements, and between sedentary and active assignments helps with motivation for learning while engaging the whole person in the learning process. Having several strategies for smooth transitions from one activity to another ensures the best use of time during the school day and may cut down on the potential for misbehavior. Hand signals, voice signals, or other cues used consistently inform students about what to expect when it is time to make transitions or for behavior self-management.

Managing Resources

Effective management of materials, supplies, and human resources is also necessary in a well-managed classroom. The use of technology has made teachers' work easier and sometimes more efficient. Files can be stored on a computer rather than in a desk drawer or filing cabinet. Most secondary teachers today have a desktop computer either in their classroom or in an adjacent office. Tasks such as recording grades, developing presentations, and preparing documents, are much more effectively completed with the use of contemporary technology. Effective classroom management also involves the skill the teacher has in using tools for communication. Again, a computer can be an efficient means for frequent and effective communication with students, parents, colleagues, and community partners. Secondary students often have more knowledge and ability related to the use of technology than their teacher(s). Wise teachers benefit themselves and their students by engaging such advanced learners in activities that benefit the whole group, such as the development of projects or presentations using technology, sending or receiving messages for the whole class, and searching the World Wide Web for learning resources. Teachers must stay abreast of the latest technological tools so they can help secondary students who are preparing to enter the workplace.

Teachers must have materials organized and ready for any volunteer workers or paraprofessionals assigned to assist them with instructional preparation, special-needs learners, or routine time-consuming tasks. The use of a chart listing times and tasks is helpful for efficient management of these resources. The same is true for any potential substitute teacher. Secondary students often challenge a substitute teacher. If the regular teacher provides the substitute with as much information about the classroom as possible, those challenges may be less stressful or may impact student learning at a lower level. The substitute should find clear directions from the teacher regarding where materials and supplies are stored, what the classroom routines and procedures are (such as restroom privileges), what the daily schedule is, and which students might be called on for information or assistance.

Managing Behavior

Behavior management is often a major source of concern for beginning teachers in the secondary grades. Students should have developed substantial self-management skills by this age; however, unless the teacher establishes high expectations from the very beginning, students are likely to challenge the teacher as they test their boundaries and confirm their independence. Teachers must have skills in preventing off-task behaviors, redirecting inappropriate behaviors, or stopping risky behaviors before they become dangerous. Redirection techniques should be employed, such as moving a student from one mode of thinking to another, using compliance terms like *please* and *thank you*, and using positive voice and body language. Never react to a student's misbehavior in anger. Wait until you both have had time to calm down before addressing the problem. Of course, if the misbehavior is such that other students are at risk, other strategies must be used. Focus on getting the behavior under control and then work on appropriate redirection. Following successful redirection, discuss with the student more appropriate ways to manage his or her actions. Teachers must also have the capacity to oversee all areas of the classroom at all times. Beginning teachers often lack a sense of complete awareness and find that students are off task too often. You might try videotaping yourself and your students during an instructional phase to learn about your skills of **withitness** (being aware of and in control of all that occurs in the classroom at all times) and the behavior of your students. Just be very cautious about the tape and erase it as soon as you and your mentor have reviewed it. Students must be protected, so leaving a tape lying around could put them at risk.

The teacher is the primary enforcer of behavior rules, but the goal should be to scaffold learners toward complete self-management and self-direction. Behavior management strategies such as redirection, moving the student to a time-out station, employing a sense of humor, signing a behavior contract, or holding a private conference with the student are appropriate measures to take to manage challenging situations. Raising one's voice, placing students in the hallway, and sending them to the principal's office are not appropriate measures for managing student behavior unless the behavior is completely out of control and students are at risk. Teachers need to make an agreement with a teacher colleague in case of problems. If a major problem occurs and the teacher must leave the classroom for any length of time, the teacher next door or across the hall can step in to monitor students to avoid any disruption in learning or to manage any behavior conflict that arises while the teacher of record is out handling the emergency.

Conflict Resolution

Conflict resolution skills are critical for secondary-level learners. As students of these ages become fully independent and confirm their roles and their identities, it is natural that conflicts will arise between individuals and groups. Time should be spent teaching and practicing conflict resolution strategies. For example, both students or groups of students should sit facing each other and talking through an issue. Guide students toward focusing on the problem or issue, not on the person(s). Model how dealing with the present situation is necessary rather than bringing up past actions or events. Guide students in learning how to come to consensus when a decision has to be made. Teach them how to *save face* and not back themselves into a corner where they might feel defeated or perceive the need to be antagonistic. Facilitate the opportunity for each person (or side) to present his or her case. Help students understand and acquire the skill of seeing things from another's point of view.

Teachers should establish their classroom and behavior management techniques early in the year so that there is no doubt on the part of students as to what is expected. High expectations for academic and social learning should pave the way for positive interactions between the teacher and the students, as well as between or among students.

Standard III:
Implementing Effective,
Responsive Instruction
and Assessment

> The teacher promotes student learning by providing responsive instruction that makes use of effective communication techniques, instructional strategies that actively engage students in the learning process, and timely, high-quality feedback.

> Note to EC–12 candidates: Read this chapter in its entirety because test items will cover all the competencies for each of the three grade level clusters.

If you think that this standard covers everything the teacher does in the context of instruction, you are correct. Think about what happens on a daily basis for teachers at any grade level. First, the teacher must acquire knowledge of the required and extended curriculum for the grade level or subject area teaching assignment. An overall horizontal and vertical curriculum map should be developed to determine a big picture of what is included in the curriculum. A good strategy for the beginning teacher is to work with the assigned mentor to map out the curriculum for the entire year using a big picture approach. From that, teachers can select learning outcomes for developmentally appropriate lessons and units designed and prepared to ensure coverage of the curriculum.

Student Readiness

Teachers must ascertain the readiness of their students as well. Using some form of diagnostic assessment, looking at past academic records, and observing students' learning behaviors tells you whether or not your students already possess the knowledge and skills required by the curriculum. If prior knowledge is firmly in place, a quick review of that part of the curriculum might be in order. If you find that there are gaps in your students' knowledge bases, you should then prepare remediation activities to bring them to grade level expectations. These steps comprise the readiness stage of preparing for effective and developmentally appropriate instruction.

Although the Texas curriculum is carefully paired with state-mandated tests, teaching to the test does little more than prepare students for a one-day look at academic knowledge and test-taking skills. The larger purpose of schools is to prepare well-educated citizens for productive contributions to a democratic society. To do this, teachers must ensure coverage of the required curriculum and then extend the curriculum to develop well-educated students. We must not be satisfied with simply reaching the norm; we must strive to educate our youth to achievement levels beyond this norm.

Analyzing Outcomes

Once the initial readiness steps of instruction are completed, the teacher then turns to an analysis of the learning outcomes. What would be the most effective and efficient means of reaching the instructional goals and ensuring that students acquire and retain the concepts inherent in the learning outcomes? The learning activity is of less importance than the instructional goal. It should matter less what activity is used to learn the concepts than that the concepts are learned. Teachers logically plan learning activities, but if there is good reason to change and take another path to reach the same goal, this should be an option for the teacher. Wise teachers capitalize on students' interests and personal experiences to capture teachable moments and to explore students' motivation for learning.

Teaching the Lesson

Now it is time for teaching the unit or lesson—the knowledge, skills, concepts, and dispositions to be learned and applied. Teachers have numerous options for instructional delivery. From direct instruction to cooperative groups to independent learning, pedagogical knowledge about instruction offers teachers many avenues for capturing students' motivation for learning. Teacher modeling of the concept is always a vital part of instruction. The use of technology for instruction is also primary for today's learners. Whatever instructional modality is chosen, the teacher must be well prepared, capable, and confident in the content knowledge of the lesson. Teachers must monitor student learning to ensure that misconceptions are not occurring and that students are making satisfactory progress toward the stated goals and identified learning outcomes. If the teacher recognizes that any student is not grasping a concept, there should be some type of redirection or reteaching to scaffold the learner's development of the concept. There should be time for guided and independent practice/rehearsal of what is learned. Both mass and distributed practice opportunities are important in confirming concept attainment. Frequent feedback should be provided to learners about the extent to which they are meeting expectations. Students should be encouraged to and have the freedom to ask questions and to clarify their understanding or misconceptions. At or near the end of the lesson, there should be an opportunity for learners to confirm their learning through some type of closure activity. This can be a K-W-L chart, a summary paragraph, a class discussion, or the development of some type of performance or product that demonstrates the learning.

Assessment and Feedback

Now that the lesson has been delivered, the teacher is responsible for affirming that expected learning outcomes have occurred. Some type of assessment is critical to the overall evaluation of both teaching and learning. Among the numerous approaches to assessment are those most often reported in the media—standardized tests. Teachers must be competent in reporting to students and parents the outcomes of standardized tests. That means that teachers must have some knowledge of statistical measures and how to report and explain statistical data. In addition to this type of summative assessment, other end-of-unit or end-of-grading-period assessments can be used. These include, but are not limited to, a unit test, a research report, a unit culminating performance, an oral exam, a portfolio, or any creative means of demonstrating that students have attained the knowledge and skills intended in the lessons that were delivered.

Some forms of formative assessment must occur along the way to complement the summative assessment. Students have the right to know how well they are doing along the way and how close they are to reaching the anticipated learning goals. They need frequent feedback and some form of periodic assessment, rather than having to wait until the end of the instructional period when they receive their final grade. In summary, a variety of assessment tools should be used, both formative and summative, to guide students toward becoming adept at self-monitoring and self-assessment. Peer assessment, student self-assessment, and teacher assessment should be combined for optimal knowledge about the learners' growth and concept attainment.

We can't leave this competency without talking about the cycle that should now occur. This cycle is a continuous progression of planning, delivering, and assessing that leads straight back to planning. The purpose of assessment is to know whether or not the goals and outcomes have been achieved. If the assessment does not indicate achievement, then the teacher is accountable for finding other ways to develop the concepts. Far too often, teaching occurs but learning is not confirmed. This creates gaps in the knowledge base and skill development of students.

KNOWLEDGE AND APPLICATION COMPONENTS FOR GRADES EC–6

EC–6 teachers are vital in the primary periods of a student's life as these are the teachers that help learners establish patterns of learning and habits of mind. Although the strategies used in the early grades may differ from those used in the upper grades, good teaching is always good teaching. Primary grade teachers understand the importance of hands-on learning, engagement of the whole mind, development of an inquisitive attitude, and participation in social interaction. Whatever learning strategy leads to these outcomes is appropriate for the primary grade teacher. The assessment of young children also differs from the assessment of upper-level learners; however, the purpose of assessment is the same. This purpose is to confirm that students have achieved the goals and objectives of each lesson and that there is continuous progress toward academic growth. Included in this domain are the following state-mandated technology applications standards:

1. All teachers use technology-related terms, concepts, data input strategies, and ethical practices to make informed decisions about current technologies and their applications.
2. All teachers identify task requirements, apply search strategies, and use current technology to acquire efficiently, analyze, and evaluate a variety of electronic information.
3. All teachers use task-appropriate tools to synthesize knowledge, create and modify solutions, and evaluate results in a way that supports the work of individuals and groups in problem-solving situations.
4. All teachers communicate information in different formats and for diverse audiences.
5. All teachers know how to plan, organize, deliver, and evaluate instruction for all students that incorporates the effective use of current technology for teaching and integrating the Technology Applications Texas Essential Knowledge and Skills (TEKS) into the curriculum.

Competencies: Domain III, EC–6

COMPETENCY 007

The teacher understands and applies principles and strategies for communicating effectively in varied teaching and learning contexts.

The following are the stated characteristics of a beginning teacher who meets the expectations of this competency.

- Demonstrates clear, accurate communication in the teaching and learning process and uses language that is appropriate to students' ages, interests, and backgrounds.
- Engages in skilled questioning and leads effective student discussions, including using questioning and discussion to engage all students in exploring content; extends students' knowledge; and fosters active student inquiry, higher-order thinking, problem solving, and productive support interactions, including appropriate wait time.
- Communicates directions, explanations, and procedures effectively and uses strategies for adjusting communication to enhance student understanding (by providing examples, simplifying complex ideas, using appropriate communication tools).
- Practices effective communication techniques and interpersonal skills (including both verbal and nonverbal skills and electronic communication) for meeting specified goals in various contexts.

IN SUMMARY

Teachers must be able to communicate effectively with their learners. Knowing that young children often have short attention spans, EC–6 teachers must plan a wide variety of learning activities, be prepared to make smooth and efficient transitions between learning activities, and engage students in various ways of learning. Effective questioning techniques are important at these ages. Learners must understand the value of asking and responding to questions. They must be guided in how to think beyond simple dichotomous responses to questions. Teachers should employ guiding questions, probing questions, cuing questions, and open-ended questions, as appropriate, throughout lessons. For young children especially, proper wait time is vital to the development of thought and the capacity to respond thoughtfully. The first wait time is that between when the teacher asks the question and when learners are permitted to respond to the question. The second wait time is between when the response is given and when the reaction from the teacher is presented. It is at this time that teachers may need to clarify the question, restate the question, probe for more of an explanation, or address misconceptions that are obvious. The use of this wait time allows learners to engage in higher-level thinking.

Teachers of young children must be capable of giving distinct and easily understood directions. EC–6 students may need directions and assignments given in various modalities. Directions and assignments can be written on the board or projected on a screen. They can also be given orally to allow students to write down the teacher's comments. Teachers may need to restate directions or further explain assignments as children of these ages learn to grasp the patterns of taking notes and other study skills. Part of communication is nonverbal. Sometimes students remember nonverbal communication better than verbal communication. Since students come from diverse backgrounds, teachers must be cautious about the nonverbal signals they use. Teachers must be aware of cultural practices and avoid any nonverbal practices that might be offensive to their students. One example is eye contact. Often teachers expect and even require that students look them clearly in the eye in given situations. For some students, their cultural background opposes, believing it to be a sign of disrespect. Although all students should follow the norms of the classroom culture, teachers gain students' respect and develop a stronger rapport with students if they are thoughtful about the impact of nonverbal communication.

COMPETENCY 008

The teacher provides appropriate instruction that actively engages students in the learning process.

The following are the stated characteristics of a beginning teacher who meets the expectations of this competency.

- Employs various instructional techniques (discussion, inquiry) and varies teacher and student roles in the instructional process, and provides instruction that promotes intellectual involvement and active student engagement and learning.

- Applies various strategies to promote student engagement and learning (structuring lessons effectively, using flexible instructional groupings, pacing lessons flexibly in response to student needs, including wait time).
- Presents content to students in ways that are relevant and meaningful and are linked to students' prior knowledge and experiences.
- Applies criteria for evaluating the appropriateness of instructional activities, materials, resources, and technologies for students with varied characteristics and needs.
- Engages in continuous monitoring of instructional effectiveness.
- Applies a knowledge of different types of motivation (internal and external) and factors affecting student motivation.
- Employs effective motivational strategies and encourages students' self-motivation.

IN SUMMARY

Primary grade children are automatically motivated to learn if they are provided an environment conducive to learning. They are naturally inquisitive, interested in almost everything around them, ready to ask lots of questions, and able to use what they already know to make connections with new learning in fun-oriented environments. The problem is that too many schools are not structured for these learners' curiosity or eagerness. Kindergarten classrooms are typically designed to encourage exploration as children play in centers with natural materials. As the grades progress, however, there seems to be less and less focus on the student and more focus on the content to be tested, which is certainly not the ideal. Early childhood teachers do well at integrating the curriculum and building concept clusters around themes that tie together two or more subject areas. Elementary level teachers integrate curriculum and building concepts most of the time. As students get older, teachers have more difficulty integrating the curriculum across content areas. Certain well-known strategies help teachers at all levels present lessons that help learners make appropriate connections among content concepts.

A Discovery Approach

To help young learners make connections, a discovery approach to learning is helpful. If learners can see how a concept learned in science is directly useful in learning mathematics, they will begin to see the relevance of learning. If what is learned in music can be transferred to concepts learned in science, motivation is higher and more connections are made. Teachers must take every opportunity to integrate curricular ideas in ways that mimic how people learn and problem solve in real-life situations.

Because children are rapidly developing language during early elementary years, instructional approaches that encourage an exchange of ideas and experiences are useful. Small groups for learning social skills, responsibility, language development, and cooperation lead to learners scaffolding each other. Active learners are more engaged and less likely to be off task. Capitalizing on prior knowledge allows learners to acquire new knowledge in developmentally appropriate ways. Overall, elementary age learners need a wide variety of experiences, a highly motivating environment, and instruction that is designed to reveal overarching concepts and to make real connections.

Varying Roles

Throughout the teaching and learning process there are many opportunities for teachers to vary their roles and those of their students. Teachers should be capable of moving fluidly from the role of direct instruction to working with small groups of individuals in a particular part of the classroom. Teacher modeling, demonstration, and explanation are usually appropriate for any lesson. Direct instruction is sometimes needed, particularly if all the students in the classroom or group need the same information. Facilitating learning is another teacher role that is frequently appropriate. As teachers move about the classroom while all learners are actively engaged, they are able to effectively facilitate the learning process. Students also have various roles to play, such as listener, responder, creator, author, speaker, facilitator, and role player. If students have many opportunities to vary their role as a learner, they can more readily develop the skills of independence and lifelong learning.

Engaging the Students

Young learners must be kept engaged at all times unless it is time for quiet rest or small breaks from the rigor of learning. Teachers must monitor student learning progress as well as student behavior in the early grades. By using **multitasking** skills, teachers can work with several groups or individuals at one time while monitoring and responding to all the children. Young children are more reliant on the teacher than are upper-level learners, so the teacher of primary grade children is very busy and usually very tired at the end of the day. As elementary students develop more capacity to be self-directed learners, the teacher still must be ready to work in various ways and contexts to support students' personal, social, and academic growth.

The teacher should be adept at monitoring and evaluating the success of the chosen teaching strategy. If the teacher observes that learners are off task, seem to be bored, are inattentive, or simply are not grasping the concepts, there must be a redirection or a change in the planned activities. Teacher reflection is critical in this process, including reflection even when engaged in instruction.

COMPETENCY 009

The teacher incorporates the effective use of technology to plan, organize, deliver, and evaluate instruction for all students.

The following are the stated characteristics of a beginning teacher who meets the expectations of this competency.

- Demonstrates knowledge of basic terms and concepts of current technology (hardware, software applications and functions, input/output devices, networks).
- Understands issues related to the appropriate use of technology in society and follows guidelines for the legal and ethical use of technology and digital information (privacy guidelines, copyright laws, acceptable use policies).
- Applies procedures for acquiring, analyzing, and evaluating electronic information (locating information on networks, accessing and manipulating information

from secondary storage and remote devices, using online help and other documentation, evaluating electronic information for accuracy and validity).

- Knows how to use task-appropriate tools and procedures to synthesize knowledge, create and modify solutions, and evaluate results to support the work of individuals and groups in problem-solving situations and project-based learning activities (planning, creating, and editing word-processing documents, spreadsheet documents, and databases; using graphics tools; participating in electronic communities as a learner, initiator, and contributor; sharing information through online communication).
- Knows how to use productivity tools to communicate information in various formats (slide show, multimedia presentation, newsletter) and applies procedures for publishing information in various ways (printed copy, monitor display, Internet document, video).
- Knows how to incorporate the effective use of current technology; uses technological applications in problem-solving and decision-making situations; implements activities that emphasize collaboration and teamwork; and uses developmentally appropriate instructional practices, activities, and materials to integrate the Technology Applications TEKS into the curriculum.
- Knows how to evaluate students' technologically produced products and projects using established criteria related to design, content delivery, audience, and relevance to the assignment.
- Identifies and addresses equity issues related to the use of technology.

IN SUMMARY

The above-described standards and competencies indicate the extent to which primary grade teachers must infuse, employ, and value technology for teaching, learning, assessment, communication, and product development. Teachers must have competence in developing motivational presentations using tools such as Microsoft Power-Point, projection transparencies, video and audio clips, white boards, smart boards, or any other modern technological tool. Use of the Internet has become commonplace in today's classrooms. Teachers must have the ability to easily navigate the Internet as well as to readily assess the quality of information found at various uniform resource locators (URLs). Students must also develop skill and competence in the use of various technologies, which means that the teacher should provide guidance, leadership, and modeling for technology use. As technology changes rapidly, teachers must keep learning about new technological terms, tools, and strategies in order to prepare all learners for using technology.

COMPETENCY 010

The teacher monitors student performance and achievement; provides students with timely, high-quality feedback; and responds flexibly to promote learning for all students.

The following are the stated characteristics of a beginning teacher who meets the expectations of this competency.

- Demonstrates knowledge of the characteristics, uses, advantages, and limitations of various assessment methods and strategies including technological methods and methods that reflect real-world applications.
- Creates assessments that are congruent with instructional goals and objectives and communicates assessment criteria and standards to students based on high expectations for learning.
- Uses appropriate language and formats to provide students with timely, effective feedback that is accurate, constructive, substantive, and specific.
- Knows how to promote students' ability to use feedback and self-assessment to guide and enhance their own learning.
- Responds flexibly to various situations (lack of student engagement in an activity, occurrence of an unanticipated learning opportunity) and adjusts instructional approaches based on an ongoing assessment of student performance.

IN SUMMARY

As stated previously, assessment is a major component in the instructional process. Teachers must know the language of assessment, be able to communicate assessment information, and demonstrate wisdom in the selection of developmentally appropriate evaluation tools. Providing feedback is critical to young learners, as they are developing their understanding of how to judge their learning and success. Any assessment tool selected should be carefully paired with the instructional goals and intended learning outcomes.

Teachers should be well-versed in the development of teacher-made tests, checklists, rubrics (scoring guides), and portfolio guidelines and assessments. Teachers must also know how to move from using visual symbols (pictures, icons, and so on) for checklists and rubrics to developing detailed descriptors that explain the degrees of success for each criterion on a scoring guide.

Communication of learning expectations and frequent feedback on progress ensure that learners know where they stand in their academic progress. Teachers should be able to explain progress in terms that students can understand. Teachers must also be competent in explaining assessments and grades to parents. This includes knowledge of statistical reports that explain standardized tests such as the TAKS.

KNOWLEDGE AND APPLICATION COMPONENTS FOR GRADES 4–8

Teachers of children in grades 4–8 face basically the same challenges as those teaching the early grades. There are differences, however, related to the selection of assessment, ways to communicate growth, and monitoring of student learning. Middle-level teachers face more demands from standardized tests, and thus must be more adept at administering examinations in the standardized format. Teachers are not allowed to explain test items or answer student questions during a standardized test as they might if the assessment were a teacher-made test. All the guidelines stated in the standards must be carefully followed. Otherwise, the test will no longer be standardized. Teachers must never take any action that would reveal or even suggest to students the correct answer when administering a standardized test.

In addition to standardized assessments, middle-level learners can demonstrate their academic growth through more authentic assessments. These include products, performances, and portfolios. Teachers must guard against subjective assessments for authentic measures. So **rubrics** (scoring guides) are often used. A rubric offers more than a simple checklist that simply says yes or no as to whether learning has occurred. A rubric indicates a scale of learning with clearly defined criteria and levels of potential success.

Communication skills for teachers of middle-level learners can also present more challenges. The tools of technology become more advanced in these grades. Students demand more explanations. Questioning becomes more critical to the development and retention of concepts. Parents may demand more sophisticated explanations about all aspects of their child's academic life. Ultimately, the teacher of middle-level learners must be competent and confident in communicating about instruction, learning, and assessment.

Competencies: Domain III, 4–8

COMPETENCY 007

The teacher understands and applies principles and strategies for communicating effectively in varied teaching and learning contexts.

The following are the stated characteristics of a beginning teacher who meets the expectations of this competency.

- Demonstrates clear, accurate communication in the teaching and learning process and uses language that is appropriate to students' ages, interests, and backgrounds.
- Engages in skilled questioning and leads effective student discussions, including using questioning and discussion to engage all students in exploring content; extends students' knowledge; and fosters active student inquiry, higher-order thinking, problem solving, and productive support interactions including appropriate wait time.
- Communicates directions, explanations, and procedures effectively and uses strategies for adjusting communication to enhance student understanding (by providing examples, simplifying complex ideas, using appropriate communication tools).
- Practices effective communication techniques and interpersonal skills (including both verbal and nonverbal skills and electronic communication) for meeting specified goals in various contexts.

IN SUMMARY

Teachers of students in grades 4–8 need strong skills in communication. These students rely on you for accurate information, wise counsel, and frequent feedback. Because homework typically becomes more demanding at these grade levels, students may need to communicate with you electronically for assistance. Many teachers provide parents with e-mail addresses so that they can be in frequent contact with the teacher. Such use of technology makes contact with parents much more effective as parents can routinely know the status of their child's academic and behavior progress. Most schools now use a campus website where teachers post a variety of information about their classroom. This information includes homework assignments, events on the calendar, classroom norms, and information about the teacher. In addition, schools now use software that allows parents to access the school website for seeing their child's academic progress (grades). This way, parents remain well-informed throughout the grading period about whether or not students are turning in homework, passing exams, and achieving satisfactory course grades.

Communication with colleagues is also important. Providing timely replies to requests, correct information sharing, and privacy regarding data about students within the team is of the utmost importance. Teachers on a team should discuss individual students and their progress; however, they must be very cautious about any behavior that might be deemed as denigratory toward the student. Teachers must maintain students' rights and protections at all times.

Appropriate Teaching Strategies

Using the Socratic method, discovery learning, or inquiry approaches to study are important for learners at these grade levels. To use these strategies, teachers must have skill in the use of questioning techniques. Much research has been conducted regarding the effective use of questions in the educational setting. Most researchers conclude that if the teacher employs questions throughout the development and attainment of concepts, learners will be much more engaged and will retain the knowledge much longer. Middle-level teachers should have skills in planning questions, including guiding questions to open and facilitate a lesson, extending questions to take learners beyond just the basics of the concept, cuing questions when learners seem to be at a loss as to the meaning of the question asked, probing questions when more information is needed, and reflective questions that require thought and time to process. The use of wait time when questioning is also important at these ages. One of the teacher's main goals is to encourage learners to extend their thinking. To do this, the teacher asks the question, waits for all the learners to process the question and formulate a response, and then calls on a student for the answer. Be sure to give all students equitable opportunities to respond. After the question is answered, employ the second wait time between the answer and the teacher's response to the answer. This allows learners to think about whether or not the answer is correct or to consider how they would have answered the question.

An important aspect of communication is how well the teacher gives directions and makes explanations. Middle-level learners may need clarification or repetition of directions, as well as explanations. Try to use more than one strategy for giving directions, such as outlining the directions orally and then having students restate them. When making assignments and explaining related expectations, provide a written version (if feasible for the grade level) and an oral version and have students write the assignment in their homework log.

COMPETENCY 008

The teacher provides appropriate instruction that actively engages students in the learning process.

The following are the stated characteristics of a beginning teacher who meets the expectations of this competency.

- Employs various instructional techniques (discussion, inquiry) and varies teacher and student roles in the instructional process, and provides instruction that promotes intellectual involvement and active student engagement and learning.
- Applies various strategies to promote student engagement and learning (structuring lessons effectively, using flexible instructional groupings, pacing lessons flexibly in response to student needs, including wait time).
- Presents content to students in ways that are relevant and meaningful and that link with students' prior knowledge and experience.
- Applies criteria for evaluating the appropriateness of instructional activities, materials, resources, and technologies for students with varied characteristics and needs.
- Engages in continuous monitoring of instructional effectiveness.
- Applies knowledge of different types of motivation (internal and external) and factors affecting student motivation.
- Employs effective motivational strategies and encourages students' self-motivation.

IN SUMMARY

Students in grades 4–8 learn better when a variety of instructional strategies are employed. From discovery learning in cooperative groups to independent research using technology, students should be provided numerous opportunities to expand their skills in self-directed learning. Teachers must be capable of changing their instructional approaches to meet the needs or interests of their learners. From direct instruction to multitasking facilitation, teachers at these grade levels should constantly guide learners in the development of knowledge, skills, and dispositions. Teacher modeling becomes important as concepts are developed more fully. Demonstrations and explanations help learners acquire concepts better than reading from a text and completing worksheets. Beginning teachers often do not know how to effectively pace during instructional times, and so overplanning may be the key to success in ensuring that middle-level learners remain engaged at all times.

Focus on the Student

A focus on the student is imperative in these grades. As educators recognize the need for a student-centered environment in the middle grades, more attention is given to teaching and learning strategies that place the learner on center stage rather than the teacher. Direct instruction remains a viable strategy; however, inquiry learning and other approaches for developing higher levels of thinking are absolutely necessary as well.

The middle-level teacher is often the facilitator of learning rather than the expositor of knowledge. The learning process is monitored and confirmed as teachers move about the classroom while middle-level learners are on task with the learning assignment. Students have different roles as well, including role player, listener, speaker, writer, creator, team member, and so on. By varying teacher and student roles, learners become more fluent in the skills of independence and lifelong learning.

When you observe the time lost during transition periods, it becomes clear that teachers must carefully monitor and evaluate the success of their students. Students must cover more curriculum and satisfy more demands from standardized testing than ever before. Therefore, time is simply not available for students to be off task or to learn material not directly connected to the stated learning goals. The teacher must monitor progress, provide frequent constructive feedback, and use numerous tools of assessment to ensure that the expected progress is being made.

COMPETENCY 009

The teacher incorporates the effective use of technology to plan, organize, deliver, and evaluate instruction for all students.

The following are the stated characteristics of a beginning teacher who meets the expectations of this competency.

- Demonstrates knowledge of basic terms and concepts of current technology (hardware, software applications and functions, input/output devices, networks).
- Understands issues related to the appropriate use of technology in society and follows guidelines for the legal and ethical use of technology and digital information (privacy guidelines, copyright laws, acceptable-use policies).
- Applies procedures for acquiring, analyzing, and evaluating electronic information (locating information on networks, accessing and manipulating information from secondary storage and remote devices, using online help and other documentation, evaluating electronic information for accuracy and validity).
- Knows how to use task-appropriate tools and procedures to synthesize knowledge, create and modify solutions, and evaluate results to support the work of individuals and groups in problem-solving situations and project-based learning activities (planning, creating, and editing word-processing documents, spreadsheet documents, and databases; using graphics tools; participating in electronic communities as a learner, initiator, and contributor; sharing information through online communication).
- Knows how to use productivity tools to communicate information in various formats (slide show, multimedia presentation, newsletter) and applies procedures for publishing information in various ways (printed copy, monitor display, Internet document, video).
- Knows how to incorporate the effective use of current technology; use technology applications in problem-solving and decision-making situations; implement activities that emphasize collaboration and teamwork; and use developmentally appropriate instructional practices, activities, and materials to integrate the Technology Applications TEKS into the curriculum.

- Knows how to evaluate students' technologically produced products and projects using established criteria related to design, content delivery, audience, and relevance to the assignment.
- Identifies and addresses equity issues related to the use of technology.

IN SUMMARY

How exciting it is to watch middle-level learners refine their skills with technology. With so many electronic games available on today's market, middle graders often come to school with more interest in learning through the manipulation of some type of technology than they are in reading or calculating. The use of calculators is more enticing in learning computations than a textbook and worksheets. Teachers must capitalize on this trend in order to use skills children already have.

Using Computers

The use of computers helps children learn independence, responsibility, and self-direction. Working through simulation software programs helps students conceptualize a historical event better than just reading about it in a textbook. Drill and practice games on a computer can be much more fun than worksheets. Word processing offers the ability to focus on thoughts while writing rather than on handwriting. Revisions are much easier on a computer than on paper.

Examples of the effective and appropriate use of technology in the middle grades could go on and on. Computers or other technologies should never take the place of other more traditional learning approaches (such as reading and writing), but they should be used to increase motivation and to ensure that learners develop or refine technological skills that will be needed in the upper grades. A wise teacher knows how to balance the inclusion of technology with textbooks and other resources. A computer is only a tool. So the focus should remain on what is to be learned, not on the machine.

Caution!

Careful monitoring of computer or other technology use is necessary in the middle grades. As learners gain more skills in the use of the Internet, safeguards must be put in place to ensure that children are protected from inappropriate pop-up ads or branching off to inappropriate websites. Most schools have firewalls in place to prevent unwanted exposure to inappropriate sites.

The Teachers' Roles

As technology becomes more advanced and complex, teachers must keep learning about new technology applications. Many classrooms now have white boards or smart boards for interactive instruction. In some schools, students have individual technological response devices so that learning is instantly confirmed or clarified. Through the use of such devices, teachers readily know which students need further study or reteaching.

COMPETENCY 010

The teacher monitors student performance and achievement; provides students with timely, high-quality feedback; and responds flexibly to promote learning for all students.

The following are the stated characteristics of a beginning teacher who meets the expectations of this competency.

- Demonstrates knowledge of the characteristics, uses, advantages, and limitations of various assessment methods and strategies, including technological methods and methods that reflect real-world applications.
- Creates assessments that are congruent with instructional goals and objectives and communicates assessment criteria and standards to students based on high expectations for learning.
- Uses appropriate language and formats to provide students with timely, effective feedback that is accurate, constructive, substantive, and specific.
- Knows how to promote the ability of students to use feedback and self-assessment to guide and enhance their own learning.
- Responds flexibly to various situations (lack of student engagement in an activity, the occurrence of an unanticipated learning opportunity) and adjusts instructional approaches based on an ongoing assessment of student performance.

IN SUMMARY

Middle-level learners often need teacher monitoring as they work independently or in groups. They need frequent feedback that gives specific guidance as to their academic progress. They need scaffolding to make satisfactory progress toward their educational goals.

Various assessment tools are needed to ensure that adequate evaluation of student progress is made. Teacher modeling of self-assessment strategies helps learners to see the effectiveness of asking themselves questions, monitoring their own learning, and adjusting their thinking strategies. Teachers should model thinking aloud about their learning processes as they guide students to be more self-directed learners who know how to ask themselves questions and monitor their own thinking.

Make Adjustments

Middle-grade teachers should be able to make instant adjustments to the planned instructional and learning strategies and in matching assessments in order to capture teachable moments. Teacher guidance during unanticipated learning opportunities helps learners use their interests and experiences for learning while the teacher ensures that learning activities remain congruent with instructional goals. Learners in grades 4–8 are refining their preferences for how they learn, so taking advantage of their interests and motivation helps ensure successful learning. As students make strong connections, they are able to transfer their learning to other contexts and therefore attain and retain concepts more easily.

Give Feedback

Constructive feedback that gives specific information about academic progress is a primary instructional strategy in the middle grades. For any lesson, teachers should provide frequent feedback as they monitor students' progress. Feedback and assessments (both formative and summative) must be congruent with instructional goals and objectives to ensure that intended learning outcomes are achieved.

KNOWLEDGE AND APPLICATION COMPONENTS FOR GRADES 8–12

Secondary-level teachers face high-stakes demands from standardized tests and thus must be very adept at administering examinations in the standardized format. Teachers must carefully monitor students during the test administration. Teachers are not allowed to explain test items or give any clue as to the correct response to a test item during a standardized test, as they might if the assessment were a teacher-made test. All the guidelines stated in the standards must be carefully followed; otherwise, the test will no longer be standardized.

Other Assessment Methods

In addition to standardized assessments, secondary learners can demonstrate their academic growth through authentic assessments such as projects, products, performances, and portfolios. Teachers must guard against subjective assessments for authentic measures. Providing **rubrics** (scoring guides) either when the assignment is given or later when completing the developmental stage of the project is a safeguard against a teacher's subjective approach to assessment. At this age, students should be included in the development of the rubric. So a good time to establish this assessment framework is in the earliest stage of work on the assignment. A rubric offers more than a simple checklist that simply says yes or no to whether learning occurred. A rubric indicates a scale of learning with clearly defined criteria and levels of potential success.

Communicate with Students

Communication skills for teachers of secondary learners must be highly refined and must provide effective modeling of high standards of communication. Tools of technology become more advanced in these grades. Questioning becomes more critical in the development and retention of concepts. All types of questions should be employed to refine skills in thinking, speaking, and social interaction. Ultimately, secondary learners must be competent and confident in communicating. As teachers provide instruction, monitor learning, and engage in the assessment of student learning, they must apply and model appropriate means of communication.

Competencies: Domain III, 8–12

COMPETENCY 007

The teacher understands and applies principles and strategies for communicating effectively in varied teaching and learning contexts.

The following are the stated characteristics of a beginning teacher who meets the expectations of this competency.

- Demonstrates clear, accurate communication in the teaching and learning processes and uses language that is appropriate to students' ages, interests, and backgrounds.
- Engages in skilled questioning and leads effective student discussions, including using questioning and discussion to engage all students in exploring content; extends students' knowledge; and fosters active student inquiry, higher-order thinking, problem solving, and productive support interactions including appropriate wait time.
- Communicates directions, explanations, and procedures effectively and uses strategies for adjusting communication to enhance student understanding (providing examples, simplifying complex ideas, using appropriate communication tools).
- Practices effective communication techniques and interpersonal skills (including both verbal and nonverbal skills and electronic communication) for meeting specified goals in various contexts.

IN SUMMARY

Secondary teachers must have refined skills in communication. As upper-level learners prepare for entrance into the workplace, they must have high capabilities in writing and speaking, as well as with the technological tools of communication. Teachers therefore must model such skills and be able to provide effective feedback and constructive criticism for students' improvement in communication skills.

Using Technology

Secondary teachers must use technology to communicate with parents and students. Teachers simply do not have time to waste. So any technological tool that helps them stay in touch with parents, students, or the broader community is helpful. Newsletters, information on websites, announcements, and so on, should be frequently provided to all members of the learning community in order to keep everyone fully informed about the academic world of secondary students. Many teachers provide parents with their e-mail address so that parents may be in frequent contact. Such use of technology makes contact with parents much more effective in that they can know on a routine basis the status of their child's academic and behavioral progress.

Most campuses today use the Internet to allow parents access to the teacher's grading system and to the teacher's website. On the website, the teacher provides a variety of tools that help students and parents fulfill school expectations. The teacher typically places: the school or course calendar, the course or grade level learning objectives, the learning resources or materials, and an outline of the curriculum on the school's website.

Communicate with Colleagues

Communication with colleagues is also important. Respect for timely replies to requests, correct information sharing, and privacy regarding data about students on the team is of the utmost importance. Teachers on a team should discuss individual students and their progress. However, teachers must be cautious about any behavior that might be deemed to be denigrating toward the student. Ultimately, teachers must guard students' rights to privacy even though teachers need to discuss students' learning issues at times.

Instructional Methods

Instructional approaches that use the Socratic method, discovery learning, or an inquiry approach to studying are especially beneficial for learners at these upper-grade levels. To use these strategies, teachers must have skill in the use of questioning techniques. Much research has been conducted regarding the effective use of questions in an educational setting. Most researchers conclude that if a teacher employs questions throughout the development and attainment of concepts, learners will be much more engaged and will retain the knowledge much longer.

Teachers of grades 8–12 should plan questions, including guiding questions to open and facilitate a lesson, extending questions to take learners beyond just the basics of the concept, cueing questions when learners seem to be at a loss as to the intent of the asked question, probing questions when more information is needed, and reflective questions that require thought and time to process. It is imperative that teachers employ the use of Benjamin Bloom's taxonomy of cognitive objectives when developing questions, focusing on the higher levels of analyzing, evaluating, and creating. Be sure you know the verbs associated with the objectives at these levels. Those verbs will help you write learning objectives that ensure higher-level learning.

Motivating Students

The use of wait time when questioning is also important as secondary students confirm their independent thought capabilities and learn to continually hold themselves responsible for their own learning. One of the teacher's main goals is to motivate learners to extend their thinking. To do this, the teacher should ask the question, wait for all the students to process the question and formulate a response, and then call on a student for the answer. Be sure to give all the students equitable opportunities to respond. After the question is answered, employ a second wait time between the answer and the teacher's response to the answer. This allows learners to think about whether or not the answer is correct or to consider how they would have answered the question.

Giving Directions

An important aspect of communication is how well the teacher gives directions and provides explanations. Because the curriculum is so extensive in these grades, no time should be wasted in repeating directions or explanations. Try to use more than one strategy for giving directions or explanations, such as speaking the directions and then having students restate them. When making assignments and explaining related expectations, provide a written version and an oral version and have students write the assignment in their planners. Whatever tools of communication secondary teachers use, they must be effective and efficient and meet the goals and objectives of the learning environment.

COMPETENCY 008

The teacher provides appropriate instruction that actively engages students in the learning process.

The following are the stated characteristics of a beginning teacher who meets the expectations of this competency.

- Employs various instructional techniques (discussion, inquiry, problem solving, in-depth study and research) and varies teacher and student roles in the instructional process; and provides instruction that promotes intellectual involvement and active student engagement and learning.
- Applies various strategies to promote student engagement and learning (structuring lessons effectively, using flexible instructional groupings, pacing lessons flexibly in response to student needs, including wait time).
- Presents content to students in ways that are relevant and meaningful and are linked to students' prior knowledge and experiences.
- Applies criteria for evaluating the appropriateness of instructional activities, materials, resources, and technology for students with varied characteristics and needs.
- Engages in continuous monitoring of instructional effectiveness.
- Applies a knowledge of different types of motivation (internal and external) and factors affecting students' motivation.
- Employs effective motivational strategies and encourages students' self-motivation.

IN SUMMARY

Students focused on specific content areas in secondary grades need diversity in how the lessons are designed and delivered. To capitalize on advanced learning abilities, teachers need to ensure that lessons are interesting, are connected, have relevance, and are developmentally appropriate. Using effective grouping strategies works well for learners in grades 8–12 if the task is clearly defined and all members of the group have a specific role. Students at this level still enjoy discovery learning, as it provides a venue for higher-level thinking. Secondary students are often engaged in independent research activities, frequently using technology. They should be provided numerous opportunities to access various primary sources and documents. Secondary-level learners have expanded skills of self-directed learning. Beginning teachers would be wise to make use of this independence.

Be Flexible

Teachers must be capable of changing their instructional approaches to meet the needs or interests of their learners. From direct instruction to multitasking facilitation, teachers should constantly guide learners in the development of knowledge, skills, and dispositions. Teacher modeling becomes important as concepts are developed more fully. Demonstrations and explanations help learners acquire concepts better than reading from a textbook and completing worksheets.

Focus on the Student

Although the focus in secondary schools is often on the content area, a focus on the student also remains important in these grades. To prepare a high school graduate who will be able to effectively join the workforce, teachers must keep the student at the center of the agenda. A student-centered environment where attention is given to teaching and learning strategies that place the learner on center stage is critical. Direct instruction remains a viable strategy. However, inquiry learning, problem solving, and other approaches for developing higher levels of thinking are absolutely necessary.

High school teachers are often facilitators of learning rather than expositors of knowledge. The learning process is monitored and confirmed as teachers move about the classroom while students are on task with the learning assignment. Secondary students have different roles as well, including those of communicator, researcher, team member, and so on. By varying teacher and student roles, learners become more fluent in the skills of independence and lifelong learning.

Evaluate Students

When you observe the time lost during transition periods, it becomes clear that teachers must carefully monitor and evaluate the success of their students. Students must cover more curriculum and satisfy more demands from standardized testing than ever before. Therefore, time simply is not available for students to be off task or to learn material not directly connected to the stated learning goals. The teacher must monitor progress, provide frequent constructive feedback, and use numerous tools of assessment to ensure that the expected progress is being made.

COMPETENCY 009

The teacher incorporates the effective use of technology to plan, organize, deliver, and evaluate instruction for all students.

The following are the stated characteristics of a beginning teacher who meets the expectations of this competency.

- Demonstrates knowledge of the basic terms and concepts of current technology (hardware, software applications and functions, input/output devices, networks).

- Understands issues related to the appropriate use of technology in society and follows guidelines for the legal and ethical use of technology and digital information (privacy guidelines, copyright laws, acceptable-use policies).
- Applies procedures for acquiring, analyzing, and evaluating electronic information (locating information on networks, accessing and manipulating information from secondary storage and remote devices, using online help and other documentation, evaluating electronic information for accuracy and validity).
- Knows how to use task-appropriate tools and procedures to synthesize knowledge, create and modify solutions, and evaluate results to support the work of individuals and groups in problem-solving situations and project-based learning activities (planning, creating, and editing word processing documents, spreadsheet documents, and databases; using graphics tools; participating in electronic communities as a learner, initiator, and contributor; sharing information through online communication).
- Knows how to use productivity tools to communicate information in various formats (slide show, multimedia presentation, newsletter) and applies procedures for publishing information in various ways (printed copy, monitor display, Internet document, video).
- Knows how to incorporate the effective use of current technology; use technological applications in problem-solving and decision-making situations; implement activities that emphasize collaboration and teamwork; and use developmentally appropriate instructional practices, activities, and materials to integrate the Technology Applications TEKS into the curriculum.
- Knows how to evaluate students' technologically produced products and projects using established criteria related to design, content delivery, audience, and relevance to the assignment.
- Identifies and addresses equity issues related to the use of technology.

IN SUMMARY

Secondary students come to school with extensive skills in technology. They have had years of experience with electronic devices and games, multimedia communication, and e-mail. They know how to navigate the Internet to conduct searches when engaged in research. The use of calculators is common for computations and is much more desirable than using a textbook and worksheets. Reading with an electronic reader offers some learners more ready access to text material or narrative readings. Even cell phones have a vast array of applications that students may use for learning activities. Secondary students will likely be very interested in websites such as GoogleEarth as they study the geography of other continents. Teachers must employ instructional strategies that require the use of current technological knowledge as they extend and expand grade 8–12 learners' knowledge of contemporary technology.

Benefits of Computers

The use of computers ensures skills of independence, responsibility, and self-direction. Working through simulation software programs at these ages helps students conceptualize a historical event better than just reading about it in a textbook. When needed, especially for scaffolding students who are not at the expected level of performance, drill and practice games on a computer can be much more fun than using worksheets. Word processing offers the ability to focus on thoughts while writing, rather than on handwriting. Revisions are much easier to make on a computer than on paper. Communicating with students in other countries via Skype or e-mail may motivate secondary students to become actively engaged in the learning goals identified by the teacher (or the state). Many secondary students have personal laptops where they can store their homework files, their research data, or even an electronic form of their textbooks.

Be Balanced

Computers or other technologies should never take the place of other more traditional learning approaches (such as reading and writing), but they should be used to enhance motivation and to ensure that learners develop or refine technological skills that will be needed in life beyond school. Secondary students preparing for immediate entrance into college must be adept at using technology because they will be facing advanced requirements for learning that are benefited by the use of technology. A wise teacher knows how to balance the inclusion of technology with textbooks and other resources. A computer is only a tool. The focus should remain on what is to be learned, not on the machine.

Careful monitoring of cell phones, computer, or other technology use is necessary in all grades but especially at the secondary level. Students in these grades have sophisticated knowledge of and experience with the Internet, and so safeguards must be in place to ensure that they are protected from branching off to inappropriate websites. Most schools have firewalls in place to prevent unwanted exposure to such sites. Teachers often bookmark appropriate websites in advance of the assignment for secondary students to use when conducting Internet research.

COMPETENCY 010

The teacher monitors student performance and achievement; provides students with timely, high-quality feedback; and responds flexibly to promote learning for all students.

The following are the stated characteristics of a beginning teacher who meets the expectations of this competency.

- Demonstrates knowledge of the characteristics, uses, advantages, and limitations of various assessment methods and strategies, including technological methods and methods that reflect real-world applications.
- Creates assessments that are congruent with instructional goals and objectives and communicates assessment criteria and standards to students based on high expectations for learning.
- Uses appropriate language and formats to provide students with timely, effective feedback that is accurate, constructive, substantive, and specific.

- Knows how to promote students' ability to use feedback and self-assessment to guide and enhance their own learning.
- Responds flexibly to various situations (lack of student engagement in an activity, occurrence of an unanticipated learning opportunity) and adjusts instructional approaches based on an ongoing assessment of student performance.

IN SUMMARY

Secondary-level learners need teacher monitoring as they work independently or in groups. Although they are very capable of independent learning, self-direction, and self-monitoring, they still need teacher guidance that provides confidence and that ensures competence as they work. They require frequent feedback that gives specific guidance to their academic progress. They often need scaffolding to make satisfactory progress toward their educational goals. Various tools of assessment are needed to ensure that adequate evaluation is made of student progress. Teacher modeling of self-assessment strategies helps older learners to value the effectiveness of asking themselves questions, monitoring their own learning, and adjusting their thinking strategies. Peer assessment may be appropriate for some instructional goals as secondary students place high value on interaction with peers. Rubrics may be used for peer assessment as well as teacher or self-assessment. At this level, students benefit from performance or product assessment such as science demonstrations, social studies models, and artistic creativity.

Make Adjustments

Secondary teachers should make instant adjustments to planned instructional and learning strategies. They should adjust assessments in order to capture teachable moments. Secondary learners are likely to have their own preferences as to how they learn. Taking advantage of students' interests and motivation helps ensure that they make strong connections, are able to transfer their learning to other contexts, and attain and retain concepts more easily. Such practices assure that secondary students are able to move into college or the workplace as independent learners who have the capacity to self-direct and monitor their own learning.

Give Feedback

Constructive feedback that gives specific information about academic progress is helpful in all situations, but especially in guiding unanticipated learning opportunities. In all lessons, teachers should provide frequent feedback as they monitor students' progress. Feedback and assessments (both formative and summative) must be congruent with instructional goals and objectives to ensure that intended learning outcomes are achieved.

Standard IV: Fulfilling Professional Roles and Responsibilities

> The teacher fulfills professional roles and responsibilities and adheres to the legal and ethical requirements of the profession.

You are strongly advised to read, comprehend, and analyze the Texas Code of Ethics and Standard Practices for Texas Educators in Appendix C of this study guide. This domain/standard is extremely important to teachers at all grade levels. The questions you see on the state test will likely be close to actual cases of how teachers have not followed this code of ethics. Ethical issues involve the use of school equipment, copyright laws, adherence to school policies, respect for the rights of students and parents, respect for colleagues, privacy of information about students, the use of school funds, personal responsibility, and adherence to the provisions of your contract. Be sure you know all the principles included in the code and recognize when and how they should be applied.

Role Models

In addition to ethical behavior, there are many other components of professionalism. Teachers must understand that they serve as role models for their students at any grade level. Let students know that you are continually learning and keeping current with information about your content area and teaching strategies. Report to students the latest research that you have read in professional journals, learned in professional/staff development sessions, or learned in graduate school classes. Apply it to their learning. Demonstrate lifelong learning skills for students and a commitment to high academic standards by letting your students know that you are continually learning.

Cooperation

Working effectively and cooperatively with colleagues/peers is an important part of being a professional. Beginning teachers in Texas are required to have an assigned mentor. Hopefully, this person has volunteered to serve as your mentor and preferably is a teacher with experience who teaches at your grade level or in your content area. Your mentor is the person to whom you turn for instructional guidance, for help with preparing a curriculum map, for advice about classroom and behavior management, for counsel about the culture of the campus, and for information about numerous other areas. Plan to have time each week for a cognitive coaching conference with your mentor. Ask your mentor to observe you as often as possible and then give you feedback about your strengths and about areas where you could improve. If possible, observe your mentor in class to learn about his or her practiced instructional strategies.

In addition to being responsible for what takes place within your assigned classroom(s), as a professional you will be working with teacher partners, on a teaching team, or on committees that make decisions such as textbook selection. Respectful communication is very important in these roles. Contribute to the effectiveness and efficiency of your teaching team. Carry your weight in performing team chores. Attend as many staff development opportunities as you can in order to support your team. Respect the decisions of your team leader and offer to support and assist in any way possible.

Teaching Contract

Your first teaching contract will be one referred to as a **term contract**. This means that you will be employed for a given period of time (usually 9 months or 185 days). At the end of that time period, there is no requirement that your contract be renewed. In most cases, the contract is readily renewed. If not, the district may simply not offer you another one. You should be offered a **continuing tenure contract** after you have effectively served as a teacher for a specified number of years (typically three to five). This means that you will have continual employment unless you are released for just cause or unless the district undergoes a major cutback in the teaching force and claims financial exigency. Such a move is called a *reduction in force*. Just cause is typically a result of your breaching the Code of Ethics.

Teaching Certificate

Another important document is your teaching certificate—your license—which verifies to parents and the district that you are qualified to teach. Texas currently requires a renewal of this certificate every five years. Renewal requires continual professional development throughout that period of time. This can include staff development and/or university course work. Be careful to keep accurate records of your continued professional development, as you will be asked to document what you have done to meet the requirements for certificate renewal. If for some reason you decide to break your contract, you must give the district reasonable and sufficient notice so that a replacement can be found. The district has the right to not accept your resignation if a replacement teacher cannot be found. Typically, with advance notice, districts do release teachers from their contracts. If this does not happen and you leave your position anyway, the state may withdraw your certificate for at least one year. This means you cannot teach in another district in the state. These consequences are understandable because abandoning your students is a grave matter.

State and Federal Regulations

There are many state and federal laws related to education that must be followed (Appendix E). These laws include, but certainly are not limited to, federal regulations that guarantee a **least restrictive environment** for students with disabilities; all the rules in the Individuals with Disabilities Education Act (IDEA), including the right to an individualized education plan (IEP) and an admission, review, and dismissal (ARD) committee; Title IX, which requires that both male and female genders receive equitable opportunities; copyright laws; and court rulings that apply to bilingual education, religion and schools, and so on. In some cases, adherence to federal rules and regulations is tied to the district's right to federal funding, such as in the case of Title I.

In addition to the principles of the Code of Ethics and Standard Practices for Texas Educators, state rules must be followed. These include regulations regarding the administration of the TAKS, adherence to the state-mandated curriculum, knowledge about education for gifted students, inclusion of students with disabilities, and so on. Be sure to read your district's faculty handbook, which will provide most of the vital information you need along these lines.

KNOWLEDGE AND APPLICATION COMPONENTS FOR GRADES EC–6

Embedded in the Texas Educators' Code of Ethics is the overarching theme that teachers must protect their students' privacy, respect their colleagues and interact professionally with them, and abide by all laws and rules related to copyrighted materials. Teachers must know the laws about child abuse. They must know the terms of their contracts and be responsible and accountable for these terms. These ethical procedures apply to teachers at all grade levels; however, there are a few specifics that are pertinent for teachers of young children. These will be discussed below, following each competency in this standard.

Competencies: Domain IV, EC–6

COMPETENCY 011

The teacher understands the importance of family involvement in children's education and knows how to interact and communicate effectively with families.

The following are the stated characteristics of a beginning teacher who meets the expectations of this competency.

- Applies a knowledge of appropriate ways (including electronic communication) to work and communicate effectively with families in various situations.

- Engages families, parents, guardians, and other legal caregivers in various aspects of the educational program.
- Interacts appropriately with all families, including those that have diverse characteristics, backgrounds, and needs.
- Communicates effectively with families on a regular basis (to share information about students' progress) and responds to their concerns.
- Conducts effective conferences with parents, guardians, and other legal caregivers.
- Effectively uses family support resources (community, interagency) to enhance family involvement in student learning.

IN SUMMARY

Parents and caregivers must be involved in their child's academic life. Teachers must be responsible communicators who find ways to invite families into the learning environment. Parents should be made to feel welcome at school and should have no fears about interactions with teachers and administrators.

Parent-Teacher Conferences

Elementary grade teachers typically have success in getting parents to attend conferences. One strategy to support this is to send home frequent messages about the student's progress, both making positive comments and noting areas of concern. If all a parent hears from a teacher is about a child's misbehavior or low grades, why would he or she feel good about coming to the school for a conference? During a parent-teacher conference, appropriate strategies are to arrange the seating area away from the teacher's desk; use a round table if possible rather than a table that might indicate a position of power for the teacher. Use common sense about how to help parents feel that they are part of the team in helping their child make progress in school. Remember the admonition that it takes more than school and more than home to raise a child—it takes us all. Focus on decisions that will foster academic and behavior progress, not on the negatives that have occurred.

Begin the conference by focusing on the student's successes. Then listen to the concerns of the parents. Certainly, the major concern the teacher may have will be the challenges the student may be facing. However, it is important to help parents feel that you, as their child's teacher, cares about the student and wants the best for the student's academic and social success. If the teacher begins the conference by talking about the negative aspects, the parents will likely immediately be defensive rather than willing to partner with the teacher to help the student improve.

Community Resources

Teachers must know about community resources and should have effective means of communicating information about these resources to families. Some schools now have a community center approach at the campus level. Parents may find it more convenient to have their child's health-care needs, afterschool care, and other needs met at or near the school campus. Teachers should provide community resource information to parents, not make appointments for the parents with such agencies. To simplify this process, routinely provide all parents with a list of community resources that they might need.

COMPETENCY 012

The teacher enhances professional knowledge and skills by effectively interacting with other members of the educational community and participating in various types of professional activities.

The following are the stated characteristics of a beginning teacher who meets the expectations of this competency.

- Interacts appropriately with other professionals in the school community (vertical teaming, horizontal teaming, team teaching, mentoring).
- Maintains supportive, cooperative relationships with professional colleagues and collaborates to support students' learning and to achieve campus and district goals.
- Knows the roles and responsibilities of specialists and other professionals at the building and district levels (department chairperson, principal, board of trustees, curriculum coordinator, technology coordinator, special education professional).
- Understands the value of participating in school activities and contributes to the school and the district (by participating in decision making and problem solving, sharing ideas and expertise, serving on committees, volunteering to participate in events and projects).
- Uses resources and support systems effectively (mentors, regional education, service centers, state initiatives, universities) to address professional development needs.
- Recognizes the characteristics, goals, and procedures associated with teacher appraisal and uses appraisal results to improve teaching skills.
- Works productively with supervisors, mentors, and other colleagues to address issues and to enhance professional knowledge and skills.
- Understands and uses professional development resources (mentors and other support systems, conferences, online resources, workshops, journals, professional associations, coursework) to enhance knowledge, pedagogical skills, and technological expertise.
- Engages in reflection and self-assessment to identify strengths, challenges, and potential problems; improve teaching performance; and achieve professional goals.

IN SUMMARY

Elementary-level teachers typically work in horizontal or vertical teams to accomplish effective planning, to determine appropriate instructional practices, to coordinate with specialists, or to make site-based decisions. Beginning teachers should be prepared to serve on campus committees, such as the textbook selection committee. You should also be adept at seeking ways you can make positive contributions for the good of the grade level or campus.

Be a Protégé

One significant role of the beginning teacher is that of protégé. You should be assigned a mentor for your first year, someone who is experienced and teaches in your area. Plan to go to this person for advice, guidance, counsel, and general assistance with what may seem to be overwhelming responsibilities and challenges in your first year. Simple tasks like recording daily student attendance or preparing lunch counts might seem overwhelming the first week of school, but with quick advice from your mentor, you should experience little stress over these tasks.

Periodic Evaluation

Teachers must be evaluated throughout the school year to ascertain whether or not effective teaching practices are being employed. You should be familiar with the Texas Professional Development and Appraisal System (PDAS), which is not state-mandated but is frequently used by districts to respond to the state requirement for a teacher appraisal system. Districts may develop their own appraisal system or use the PDAS. Information about the PDAS can be found on the Texas Education Agency website (www.state.tea.tx.us). Part of the PDAS is a requirement that teachers have an established plan for personal professional growth. You are responsible for documenting your professional activity, and so when you attend workshops, conferences, or external staff development offerings, make sure you keep documentation of that activity.

Professional Resources

There are many resources for professional development. Teachers of young children should consider membership in either the National Association for the Education of Young Children (NAEYC) or the Association of Early Childhood International (ACEI). These professional associations provide journals, newsletters, conferences, and other professional development opportunities. Of course, continued university study at the graduate level is always useful. The district and/or campus provides appropriate staff development sessions on the professional days dedicated for such. Take advantage of all these resources and learn all you can. Read the journals that come with membership in professional associations in order to remain current on the latest research about best educational practices. Propose papers and make presentations at state, regional, national, or international conferences. Attend sessions to learn what others are doing effectively.

COMPETENCY 013

The teacher understands and adheres to legal and ethical requirements for educators and is knowledgeable of the structure of education in Texas.

The following are the stated characteristics of a beginning teacher who meets the expectations of this competency.

- Knows the legal requirements for educators (those related to special education, the rights of students and families, student discipline, equity, child abuse) and adheres to legal guidelines in education-related situations.

- Knows and adheres to the legal and ethical requirements regarding the use of educational resources and technologies (copyright, fair use, data security, privacy, acceptable-use policies).
- Applies a knowledge of ethical guidelines for educators in Texas (those related to confidentiality, interactions with students and others in the school community), including policies and procedures described in the Code of Ethics and Standard Practices for Texas Educators.
- Follows procedures and requirements for maintaining accurate student records.
- Understands the importance of and adheres to required procedures for administering state- and district-mandated assessments.
- Uses a knowledge of the structure of the state education system, including relationships among campus, local, and state components, to seek information and assistance.
- Advocates for students and for the teaching profession in various situations.

IN SUMMARY

All teachers must have full knowledge of the laws, rules, policies, and procedures related to legal and ethical issues. Examine the brief list of legal issues in Appendix E of this study guide. Refer to the ethics principles provided in Appendix C of this study guide, which provide the full language of the Code of Ethics and Standard Practices for Texas Educators.

Teachers are allowed to make a certain number of copies of copyrighted material for educational purposes for one-time use. You must be knowledgeable about the rules and regulations regarding the copying of print or electronic documents, as well as computer software. Go to your local library or ask your campus librarian for a copy of the copyright laws. Even though you may have colleagues who freely duplicate copyrighted materials, it is unlawful to copy large portions of materials for continued use. There are no excuses for such behavior. If you find a need to use copies of copyrighted materials continually, you must obtain permission from the copyright holder. The same is true if you need large portions of print or electronic text.

All students must be protected from invasion of their privacy. The federal Family Rights and Privacy Act provides clear guidelines indicating when parents can view the academic records of their children. Unless there is a restraining order, both custodial and noncustodial parents have the right to examine these records, which are housed in protected files in the main office at your campus. Parents should make an appointment to view these files, just as they should make an appointment for a conference with you, rather than simply stopping by to claim these rights and privileges. If you believe that taking photographs of your students is needed for an educational purpose, be sure that you have written agreements from parents and permission from your team leader or principal for such action. The same is true about videotaping your students. In most cases the campus leader has on file permission from parents who are willing to have their child photographed or videotaped for educational purposes. If these written permissions are not on file, teachers must avoid including non-permit-granted students in any recording that might be viewed by others.

Teachers must be advocates for their students. Never discuss a student with other teachers in a setting other than one appropriate for sharing educational concerns.

Avoid any comment about a student that might be disparaging to the student or harmful to the student's reputation. Although other teachers may vent their frustrations about troublesome students in places such as the teacher workroom, such practices are unethical. Only if the conversation is focused on seeking information about or help for the student should teachers engage in conversation about a student.

Competencies: Domain IV, 4–8

COMPETENCY 011

The teacher understands the importance of family involvement in children's education and knows how to interact and communicate effectively with families.

The following are the stated characteristics of a beginning teacher who meets the expectations of this competency.

- Applies knowledge of appropriate ways (including electronic communication) to work and communicate effectively with families in various situations.
- Engages families, parents, guardians, and other legal caregivers in various aspects of the educational program.
- Interacts appropriately with all families, including those with diverse characteristics, backgrounds, and needs.
- Communicates effectively with families on a regular basis (to share information about students' progress) and responds to their concerns.
- Conducts effective conferences with parents, guardians, and other legal caregivers.
- Effectively uses family support resources (community, interagency) to enhance family involvement in student learning.

IN SUMMARY

Parents of middle-level learners must be involved in their child's academic life to the greatest extent possible. Teachers must be responsible communicators who find ways to invite families into the learning environment. Parents should be made to feel welcome at school and should have no fears about interactions with teachers and administrators. When youth at this age begin to switch from seeking approval from authority figures (parents and teachers) to approval from peers, they express this blossoming sense of independence by moving toward compartmentalization of their lives. They do this by attempting to keep parental interactions for home and peer interactions for school. This may result in youth asking that their parents not be as involved in school as they were in the early grades. They may also fail to communicate invitations in ways that inform parents about opportunities for involvement. Older middle-level learners want their parents fully involved in school and extracurricular activities one day and want them to stay completely out of their school lives the next day.

Parent-Teacher Conferences

Middle-level teachers may face challenges in getting parents to attend conferences. Teachers may need to expend engergy to make a partnership between home and school more inviting. One strategy to support this is to send home frequent messages about the student's progress, including positive comments and noting areas of concern. If all a parent hears from the teacher is about the child's misbehavior or low grades, why would he or she feel good about coming to the school for a conference?

Another effective means of communication is a school website with a link to pages for each teacher. Most parents have some means of accessing the Internet. Providing parents thorough information about school activities (calendar, curriculum, meetings) on the Internet is a wise practice.

During a parent-teacher conference, appropriate strategies are to arrange the seating area away from the teacher's desk and to use a round table if possible rather than a table that might indicate a position of power for the teacher. Use common sense about helping parents to feel that they are part of the team in helping their child make progress in school. Focus on decisions that will foster academic and behavior progress, not on the negatives that have occurred.

Community Resources

Teachers of middle-level learners must know about community resources and should have effective means of communicating information about these resources to families. If your campus has an afterschool program, be sure parents are aware of and have a sense of comfort about this service. Some schools have a community center approach at the campus level, where parents find it convenient to have their child's health-care needs, afterschool care, and other needs met at or near the school campus. Teachers should provide parents with a list of community resources rather than actually putting parents or caregivers in touch with the resources.

COMPETENCY 012

The teacher enhances professional knowledge and skills by effectively interacting with other members of the educational community and participating in various types of professional activities.

The following are the stated characteristics of a beginning teacher who meets the expectations of this competency.

- Interacts appropriately with other professionals in the school community (vertical teaming, horizontal teaming, team teaching, mentoring).
- Maintains supportive, cooperative relationships with professional colleagues and collaborates to support students' learning and to achieve campus and district goals.
- Knows the roles and responsibilities of specialists and other professionals at the building and district levels (department chairperson, principal, board of trustees, curriculum coordinator, technology coordinator, special education professional).
- Understands the value of participating in school activities and contributes to the school and the district (by participating in decision making and problem

solving, sharing ideas and expertise, serving on committees, volunteering to participate in events and projects).

- Uses resources and support systems effectively (mentors, regional education service centers, state initiatives, universities) to address professional development needs.
- Recognizes characteristics, goals, and procedures associated with teacher appraisal and uses appraisal results to improve teaching skills.
- Works productively with supervisors, mentors, and other colleagues to address issues and to enhance professional knowledge and skills.
- Understands and uses professional development resources (mentors and other support systems, conferences, online resources, workshops, journals, professional associations, coursework) to enhance knowledge, pedagogical skills, and technological expertise.
- Engages in reflection and self-assessment to identify strengths, challenges, and potential problems; improve teaching performance; and achieve professional goals.

IN SUMMARY

In the middle grades, teachers typically work in grade level teams to accomplish effective planning, determine appropriate instructional practices, coordinate with specialists, or make site-based decisions. Middle-level teachers often work in clusters. One set of students is served by a group of teachers. This creates a sense of community or family for the students as they learn to transition from the security of lower-elementary grades into the independence of secondary school life. More and more teachers are working together in vertical teams to ensure that there are no gaps or redundancies in how the curriculum is planned or in what materials and resources are used. Beginning teachers should be prepared to serve on campus committees. You should also be adept at seeking ways you can make positive contributions for the good of the team or the campus.

Be a Protégé

One significant role of the beginning teacher is that of a protégé. Beginning teachers are assigned a mentor for their initial teaching year. This is someone who is experienced and teaches in your area. Recognize and benefit from the role of the mentor by going to this person for advice, guidance, counsel, and general assistance with what may seem to be overwhelming responsibilities and challenges during your first year. This is especially true at the middle school level, as teachers are specifically responsible for one or two content areas. You should be assigned content areas where you have documented evidence of knowledge. However, at times you may need mentor assistance for developing strong pedagogical content knowledge.

Periodic Evaluation

Teachers must be evaluated throughout the school year to ascertain whether or not effective teaching practices are being employed. You should be familiar with the Texas

PDAS, which is not state-mandated but is frequently used by districts to respond to the state requirement for a teacher appraisal system. Districts can develop their own appraisal system or use the PDAS. Information about the PDAS may be found on the Texas Education Agency website (www.state.tea.tx.us). Part of the PDAS is a requirement that teachers have an established plan for personal professional growth. You are responsible for documenting your professional activity, and so when you attend workshops, conferences, or external staff development offerings, be sure to keep documentation of that activity.

Professional Resources

There are many resources for professional development. Teachers of middle-grade learners should consider membership in the national curricular association pertinent to the content area assignment. If you are assigned to teach in a self-contained classroom, the ACEI would be a good choice. Consider membership in the National Council for Teachers of English (NCTE), the National Council for the Social Studies (NCSS), the National Council for the Teaching of Mathematics (NCTM), the National Science Teachers' Association (NSTA), or any other specific content-area professional association. The Association for Supervision, Curriculum, and Development (ASCD) would be a good choice for keeping current with educational issues. These and other professional associations publish journals and newsletters, hold conferences, and offer other professional development opportunities. Of course, continued university study at the graduate level is always useful. Consider pursuing a master's degree in curriculum and instruction or in your content-area assignment if you have a semidepartmentalized or departmentalized assignment. The district and/or the campus will provide appropriate staff development sessions on the professional days dedicated to such. Take advantage of all these resources and learn all you can. Read the journals that come with membership in professional associations and stay current with research-based best practices. Propose papers and make presentations at state, regional, national, or international conferences. Attend sessions at the conferences to learn what others are doing.

COMPETENCY 013

The teacher understands and adheres to legal and ethical requirements for educators and is knowledgeable of the structure of education in Texas.

The following are the stated characteristics of a beginning teacher who meets the expectations of this competency.

- Knows the legal requirements for educators (those related to special education, the rights of students and families, student discipline, equity, child abuse) and adheres to legal guidelines in education-related situations.
- Knows and adheres to the legal and ethical requirements regarding the use of educational resources and technologies (copyright, fair use, data security, privacy, acceptable-use policies).

- Applies a knowledge of ethical guidelines for educators in Texas (those related to confidentiality, interactions with students and others in the school community), including policies and procedures described in the Code of Ethics and Standard Practices for Texas Educators.
- Follows procedures and requirements for maintaining accurate student records.
- Understands the importance of and adheres to the required procedures for administering state- and district-mandated assessments.
- Uses a knowledge of the structure of the state education system, including relationships among campus, local, and state components, to seek information and assistance.
- Advocates for students and for the profession in various situations.

IN SUMMARY

Teachers at the middle-grades level must have knowledge about the legal and ethical laws, rules, policies, and procedures related to students and parents at these age levels. Read the brief list of legal issues in Appendix E of this study guide. Refer to the ethics principles provided in Appendix C of this study guide, which provide you the full language of the Code of Ethics and Standard Practices for Texas Educators. Of particular importance for middle-level teachers is the issue of when a teacher or other school personnel has the right to search students or their school property. Keep in mind that desks, lockers, and so on, are school property, not the personal/private property of the student. Probable cause must be present for a search, and reasonable suspicion must be present for reporting suspected child abuse.

Teachers are allowed to make a certain number of copies of copyrighted material for one-time educational purposes. You must be knowledgeable about the rules and regulations regarding the copying of print or electronic documents, as well as computer software. Go to your local library or ask your campus librarian for a copy of the copyright laws. Do not imitate those colleagues who violate copyright laws. If you continually need to copy copyrighted material, you must first obtain permission for such use from the copyright holder.

Youth in grades 4–8 must be protected from invasion of their privacy. The federal Family Rights and Privacy Act provides clear guidelines regarding when parents can view the academic records of their children. Unless there is a restraining order, both custodial and noncustodial parents have the right to view their child's academic records, which are housed in protected files in the main office on your campus. Parents should make an appointment to view these files, just as they should make an appointment for a conference with you rather than dropping in to claim these rights and privileges. If you believe that taking photographs of your students is needed for an educational purpose, be sure that you have a written agreement from parents and permission from your team leader or principal for such action. The same is true about videotaping your students. Any student whose parent has not provided written permission for recording of any type must not be included in a video or audio tape recording or in any photograph that might be viewed by others. All children must be protected to the greatest extent possible.

Competencies: Domain IV, 8–12

COMPETENCY 011

The teacher understands the importance of family involvement in children's education and knows how to interact and communicate effectively with families.

The following are the stated characteristics of a beginning teacher who meets the expectations of this competency.

- Applies a knowledge of appropriate ways (including electronic communication) to work and communicate effectively with families in various situations.
- Engages families, parents, guardians, and other legal caregivers in various aspects of the educational program.
- Interacts appropriately with all families, including those with diverse characteristics, backgrounds, and needs.
- Communicates effectively with families on a regular basis (to share information about students' progress) and responds to their concerns.
- Conducts effective conferences with parents, guardians, and other legal caregivers.
- Effectively uses family support resources (community, interagency) to enhance family involvement in student learning.

IN SUMMARY

Teachers must be responsible communicators who find ways to invite the families of secondary students into the learning environment. Parents should be made to feel welcome at school and should have no fears about interactions with teachers and administrators. As students progress through the grades, there tends to be less involvement on the part of parents. This does not discount the need for effective communication with parents or the need for them to be involved in the education of their children. Neither does this mean that parents are less interested in their child's academic or social success. When youth switch from seeking approval from authority figures (parents and teachers) to approval from peers, they often express this sense of independence by insisting that their lives be compartmentalized. They do this by attempting to keep parental interactions for home and peer interactions for school. This may result in youth asking that their parents not be as involved in school as they were in the early grades. They may also fail to communicate invitations in ways that inform parents about the opportunities for involvement.

An effective means of communicating with parents of secondary students is a campus website that links to teacher pages. The teachers can provide thorough information about the courses the students are assigned. This might include homework assignments, an outline of the curriculum, a calendar of events, and messages about student activities.

Parent-Teacher Conferences

Secondary teachers need to provide well-planned and efficiently run parent-teacher conferences. Communicate the purpose of the conference in advance. Establish conference times that are supportive of the family and work responsibilities of parents. Send home frequent messages about students' progress, noting both positive comments and areas of concern. If all a parent hears from the teacher is about the student's misbehavior or low grades, why would he or she feel good about coming to the school for a conference? During a parent-teacher conference, appropriate strategies are to arrange the seating area away from the teacher's desk and to use a round table if possible rather than a table that might indicate a position of power for the teacher. Use common sense in helping parents feel that they are part of the team in helping their child make progress in school. Focus on decisions that will foster academic and behavior progress, not on the negatives that have occurred. Begin the conference with positive comments. Offer parents an early opportunity to express their concerns or to ask questions.

Community Resources

Teachers must be aware of community resources that are available for families and should have effective means of communicating information about these resources to parents. Parents of secondary students often have concerns about external environmental influences that could negatively impact their child's academic success. Teachers should be able to provide pertinent information about resources to parents. An effective nonthreatening way to provide such information is to provide all parents or caregivers a list of appropriate community resources so that no one specific student is pointed out as needing this information.

Competency 012

The teacher enhances professional knowledge and skills by effectively interacting with other members of the educational community and participating in various types of professional activities.

The following are the stated characteristics of a beginning teacher who meets the expectations of this competency.

- Interacts appropriately with other professionals in the school community (vertical teaming, horizontal teaming, team teaching, mentoring).
- Maintains supportive, cooperative relationships with professional colleagues and collaborates to support students' learning and to achieve campus and district goals.
- Knows the roles and responsibilities of specialists and other professionals at the building and the district levels (department chairperson, principal, board of trustees, curriculum coordinator, technology coordinator, special education professional).
- Understands the value of participating in school activities and contributes to the school and the district (participating in decision making and problem solv-

ing, sharing ideas and expertise, serving on committees, volunteering to participate in events and projects).

- Uses resources and support systems effectively (mentors, regional education service centers, state initiatives, universities) to address professional development needs.
- Recognizes characteristics, goals, and procedures associated with teacher appraisal and uses appraisal results to improve teaching skills.
- Works productively with supervisors, mentors, and other colleagues to address issues and to enhance professional knowledge and skills.
- Understands and uses professional development resources (mentors and other support systems, conferences, online resources, workshops, journals, professional associations, coursework) to enhance knowledge, pedagogical skills, and technological expertise.
- Engages in reflection and self-assessment to identify strengths, challenges, and potential problems; improve teaching performance; and achieve professional goals.

IN SUMMARY

In the secondary grades, teachers typically work in content-area teams to accomplish effective planning, determine appropriate instructional practices, coordinate with specialists, or make site-based decisions. Beginning teachers should be prepared to serve on campus committees. You should also be adept at seeking ways you can make positive contributions for the good of the team or the campus. A department chair will likely guide your team of teachers. However, you must communicate with other grade-level teachers to assure that the curriculum has no gaps from grade level to grade level. The full scope and sequence of a content area is an important knowledge base for a secondary teacher.

Be a Protégé

One significant role of the beginning teacher is that of protégé. Beginning teachers are assigned a mentor for their initial teaching year. At the secondary level, the mentor is someone who is experienced and is an expert in the beginning teacher's content area, or one that is within the discipline. Recognize and benefit from the role of the mentor by going to this person for advice, guidance, counsel, and general assistance with what may seem to be overwhelming responsibilities and challenges during your first year.

Periodic Evaluation

Teachers must be evaluated throughout the school year to ascertain whether or not effective teaching practices are being employed. You should be familiar with the Texas PDAS, which is not state-mandated but is frequently used by districts to respond to the state requirement for a teacher appraisal system. Districts can develop their own appraisal system or use the PDAS. Information about the PDAS can be found at the Texas Education Agency website (www.state.tea.tx.us). Part of the PDAS is a requirement that teachers have an established plan for personal professional growth. You are responsible for documenting your professional activity, and so when you attend workshops, conferences, or external staff development offerings, make sure you keep documentation of that activity.

Professional Resources

There are many resources for professional development. Teachers of secondary learners should consider membership in the national curricular association pertinent to the content-area assignment. Membership in the National Council for Teachers of English (NCTE), the National Council for the Social Studies (NCSS), the National Council for the Teaching of Mathematics (NCTM), the National Science Teachers Association (NSTA), the National Music Teachers Association (NMTA), or any other specific content area professional association would be appropriate. The Association for Supervision, Curriculum, and Development (ASCD) would also be a good choice for keeping current with educational issues. If the national organization has a state level association, it would be helpful to be a member at this level as well. Sometimes it is easier to attend state level conferences than national conventions. These and other professional associations provide journals, newsletters, conferences, and other professional development opportunities. Of course, continued university study at the graduate level is always useful. Consider pursuing a master's degree in the content area of your teaching assignment or in curriculum and instruction. The district and/or campus will provide appropriate staff development on the professional days dedicated for such. Take advantage of all these resources and learn all you can. Read the journals that come with membership in professional associations to stay current with the latest research-based best practices. Propose papers and make presentations at state, regional, national, or international conferences. Attend sessions at meetings to learn what others are doing.

COMPETENCY 013

The teacher understands and adheres to legal and ethical requirements for educators and is knowledgeable of the structure of education in Texas.

The following are the stated characteristics of a beginning teacher who meets the expectations of this competency.

- Knows the legal requirements for educators (those related to special education, the rights of students and families, student discipline, equity, child abuse) and adheres to legal guidelines in education-related situations.
- Knows and adheres to the legal and ethical requirements regarding the use of educational resources and technologies (copyright, Fair Use, data security, privacy, acceptable-use policies).
- Applies knowledge of ethical guidelines for educators in Texas (those related to confidentiality, interactions with students and others in the school community), including policies and procedures described in the Code of Ethics and Standard Practices for Texas Educators.

- Follows procedures and requirements for maintaining accurate student records.
- Understands the importance of and adheres to required procedures for administering state- and district-mandated assessments.
- Uses a knowledge of the structure of the state education system, including relationships among campus, local, and state components, to seek information and assistance.
- Advocates for students and for the teaching profession in various situations.

IN SUMMARY

Teachers at the upper grade levels must have full knowledge of the specific laws, rules, policies, and procedures related to the legal and ethical issues regarding students and families. Refer to the brief list of legal issues in Appendix E of this study guide. Read the ethics principles presented in Appendix C of this study guide, which provide the full language of the Code of Ethics and Standard Practices for Texas Educators. Of particular importance is the issue of when a teacher or other school personnel have a right to search students or their school property. Keep in mind that desks, lockers, and so on are school property, not the personal/private property of the student. Probable cause must be present for a search, and reasonable suspicion must be present for reporting suspecting child abuse.

Teachers have certain copyright exemptions for educational purposes. You must be knowledgeable about the rules and regulations regarding copying print or electronic documents, as well as computer software. Go to your local library or ask your campus librarian for a copy of the copyright laws. Any argument that you did not know the laws regarding copyright use is no excuse for failure to follow the law.

The federal Family Rights and Privacy Act provides clear guidelines for when parents can view the academic records of their children. Unless there is a restraining order, both custodial and noncustodial parents have the right to see their child's academic records. At age 18, the student has the right to view his or her academic records. Any teacher comments are a matter of public record for parents of post-18-year-old students; so be aware that your notes, e-mails, or any other written comments about the student's academic progress or behavior will be placed in the cumulative file. These records are housed in protected files in the main office on your campus. Parents should make an appointment to view these files, just as they should make an appointment for a conference with you.

PART IV

DIAGNOSTIC
AND SAMPLE TESTS

Types of Test Items and How to Analyze Them

Candidates will benefit from answering the items in the test banks in this study guide to diagnose areas of need and to use the items as a means of learning how to approach the thinking required for such items. It is recommended that small study groups be formed to maximize knowledge and share ideas about how to best approach each set of items or individual items. Some items are clustered into decision sets that provide real-world examples of contemporary classrooms. Other items are single items that address a particular term, concept, or construct. At the beginning of each decision set is a description of the classroom scenario that provides information critical to making the appropriate decision about the best answer. In some cases, more than one response might be applicable to the set. However, there is always one response that is more in line with the background information and/or the item stem than are the other responses.

The information provided may be needed for more than one test item. So careful reading of the initial information is important. Readers should use the strategies of chunk reading, setting a purpose for reading, and carefully gauging time when answering these test items in order to simulate the setting of the state examination appropriately.

Remember that each person has a particular style of thinking. Some people should read and analyze the question before considering answer choices. Others should do the opposite. In those cases, read the answer choices first to get a mindset before reading the question and/or background information. You should practice both approaches to determine what works best for you.

Some test takers benefit from placing a mark by the answer they consider to be best while deciding. You might also mark out an answer that you know is not a good choice or make some kind of mark to help you eliminate that choice from consideration. These practices help you narrow down your thinking as you confirm what you believe to be the best of the four possible choices.

Best practice suggests that teachers follow Bloom's taxonomy of cognitive objectives. So you should look for the verb(s) that are placed early in an answer choice. Action verbs are more likely the correct answer than are passive verbs. Higher-level thinking verbs are typically the best answer.

In some items, all possible responses are good choices. However, if the question/item ask you for what should be done *first*, all responses are possibly favorable. However, only one should be the first action a teacher would take.

You should also analyze whether or not the question is asking you to make a judgment about what the teacher should do to help the student or if the question is asking what would be best for the teacher. Your selection will be based on that information.

If the grade level is identified, think about the characteristics of learners at that age. In general, focus on responses that relate to higher levels of thinking. Administration of the state exams will be in a standardized setting, so be sure that you control interruptions and external influences while you are taking these practice tests. (You will find an answer sheet at the end of each test.)

The following set of test items is intended to demonstrate for you how items may be designed on the state test. There may be two test item formats used in the test you take. These include teacher decision sets and single items. Think about how you make decisions as you read and analyze the practice test items and their response options. Think about your mental processes as you work from item to item. Time yourself to see about how much time you will need to answer ten items. Use these sets to become familiar with the format of the test. Then take the following diagnostic and sample tests to help you determine how much more you need to study.

TEACHER DECISION SET ITEMS

The first type of test item format is the teacher decision set. It consists of a scenario where you may or may not be given the grade level. If you are, it is an important element to consider as you need to think about developmental appropriateness. Following the scenario, you will encounter 3–12 multiple-choice questions directly related to the scenario. Multiple competencies are tested in a decision set as you make decisions about best practice in the situation described by the scenario. As you work through the following test items, think about which competency is being tested. Although you will not be given the competency on the formal state tests, it is helpful at this point to think of competencies so that you will be able to translate this thinking into the test setting at the state level.

Teacher Decision Set 1

Stella Mario is a first-year teacher of kindergarten students in an urban setting. Student demographics include 4 ethnic groups, 90 percent of the students receive free or reduced-price lunches, and 5 of the 24 students speak languages other than English as their native language. Ms. Mario is concerned about the background experiences of her young learners and recognizes the necessity for providing as many developmental experiences as possible. As a first-year teacher, she is working with her assigned mentor to plan developmentally appropriate curriculum activities for the year and to achieve maximum integration of the fine arts. Using this background information, answer questions 1–4.

1. Which of the following cognitive characteristics should Ms. Mario expect of these kindergarten students?

   (A) Complex thinking skills that allow students to analyze elements of a concept abstractly in social studies

   (B) Sensory motor responses to environmental stimuli that support learning in a science learning center

   (C) Preoperational thinking skills that allow students to explore and play with manipulatives in a block learning center

   (D) Advanced concrete operation skills that support young learners' abilities to briefly see a model and then develop a schematic drawing of a simple machine

2. At which of the following social development levels might she expect this group of students to be?

   (A) Interest in selecting friends on the basis of loyalty and potential for lasting friendship

   (B) Parallel play where children play alongside each other in a role-play center but do not necessarily play together

   (C) Working through disagreements via conflict reolution strategies

   (D) Reliance on the teacher to dictate play groups during outdoor free play time

3. From the following list of small-group activities, which is most appropriate for developing decision-making skills in these young learners?

   (A) Teacher-assigned homogeneous groups instructed to explore Internet web quests

   (B) Naturally formed groups in a home living center where students explore roles and responsibilities of family members

   (C) Teacher-directed heterogeneous groups assigned to develop prescribed story characters

   (D) Pairing of two children to visit the next door teacher's classroom to conduct an interview about family members

4. How should this beginning teacher initially capitalize on her mentor's years of experience as she designs and develops the curriculum and her instruction for the year?

   (A) Approach the mentor, ask her for last year's curriculum map, and follow it to gain a year of experience.

   (B) Avoid the mentor until she has the current year's curriculum mapped out to avoid undue influence.

   (C) Develop her own curriculum map for the year and then share it with her mentor.

   (D) Arrange an afternoon meeting with her mentor to look at the TEKS and make an initial curriculum map that provides an overview of the year and that can be later used to develop a more detailed map.

Correct Responses

1. **C** is the most developmentally appropriate answer. (A) requires a much higher thinking skill level than that of these young learners. (B) is more appropriate for children younger than these. (D) is far too advanced.

2. **B** is the most developmentally appropriate response. (A) is too advanced for this age group. (C) is also more advanced than is expected for this age. (D) is not an appropriate teacher activity and would certainly not be supportive of social development.

3. **B** is the most developmentally appropriate response. (A) is not at all focused on students' development of decision-making skills. (C) is teacher-centered, which does not promote student decision making. (D) is more teacher-centered and less inclusive of student decision making.

4. **D** is the initial step in working with her mentor to conceptualize the year's curriculum. (A) does not depict a collaborative approach. (B) is certainly not collegial nor does it indicate a sense of partnership. (C) does not capitalize on the mentor's experience and expertise and thus would be more costly in time and energy for the beginning teacher.

Teacher Decision Set 2

It is the beginning of the academic year, and Marlon White is busy preparing for his first year as a fourth-grade social studies and language arts teacher. He has been assigned two groups of students, his own homeroom group and that of his partner teacher, Sharon, who has been assigned to teach mathematics and science to both groups. Marlon and Sharon set a meeting to discuss environmental effects on student learning. They are aware that three of their students live in single-parent homes and that four students live in government-subsidized housing units. They have met all their students and were excited to notice that each student seems highly motivated to learn and seems to have an appropriate level of background experience, even though most of them come from homes at the poverty level. These two beginning teachers are determined to establish a learning community that will ensure optimal learning for their students. Use this background information for questions 1–5.

1. As Marlon and Sharon talk, which legal implication must they keep in mind regarding the potential for child abuse?

   (A) Teachers who have a reasonable suspicion of child abuse must report it to the appropriate authority within 48 hours of the observation.
   (B) Teachers are not subject to being accountable for the reporting of child abuse as long as they have notified the principal of the observation.
   (C) The first action a teacher should take is to get permission from the principal to notify the appropriate legal authority in child abuse cases.
   (D) As long as the teacher makes written documentation of any reasonable suspicion of child abuse, no further action is necessary.

2. As these two colleagues design a classroom environment that focuses on success for all learners, what should be foremost in their planning related to involvement with the parents of their students?

   (A) Notify the parents of all school events through notes, memos, and student-written letters.
   (B) Make the parents aware of school events through a weekly newsletter that students help to write during language arts class.
   (C) Use notices sent home, weekly newsletters, and student writing projects, as well as notices in the neighborhood newspaper, to keep the parents informed of school events.
   (D) Invite the parents to participate by planning and attending school events through notices sent home, weekly newsletters, and student writing projects, as well as notices in the neighborhood newspaper.

3. Which of the following activities would best promote higher-level thinking in the social studies lessons Marlon teaches?

   (A) Teaching concepts through defining, researching, and proposing action on a problem present in the community
   (B) Hands-on social studies activities that allow students to have a concrete experience in each major concept
   (C) Allowing students to role-play to expand their content knowledge of major concepts
   (D) Allowing student groups to select from a file of activities and prepare mini lessons to share with their classmates on selected main concepts

4. How might Marlon and Sharon best capitalize on their team approach to establish a fourth-grade learning community environment to enhance instruction?

   (A) Ensure that each is alert to the times when class changes are scheduled and respect the teaching time allotted for each subject by always having students ready to transition on time.
   (B) Plan together weekly to ensure that the subjects each teaches are coordinated and integrated to ensure that students have opportunities to practice a concept learned in language arts class during science class.
   (C) Plan together to structure the learning environments in the two classrooms to provide consistency in rules, management, routines, and consequences.
   (D) Meet weekly to discuss the progress and challenges each student is encountering in their subjects.

5. To ensure that all students have the maximum opportunity to learn, which grouping approach would be most beneficial for these fourth-grade learners?

(A) Each teacher groups students with similar skill levels and knowledge in a subject so that students experience working daily with a variety of peers.

(B) Marlon and Sharon together form heterogeneous groups that are the same in all subjects for four weeks based on skill level, prior knowledge, and social background.

(C) Allow students to select the groups they will work with until a problem requires teacher intervention.

(D) Marlon and Sharon together form homogeneous groups that are the same in all subjects for four weeks based on skill level and social background.

Correct Responses

1. **A** is required by Texas law. (B) notifying the principal, should also occur, but not instead of response (A). (C) implies that permission is needed and that no report will or should be made without permission, which is untrue. (D) is inaccurate and is in violation of the law as stated in (A).

2. **D** is the only one to *invite* parent participation rather than to use the term *notify* or *make aware* and is therefore the only one that indicates an expectation of active involvement rather than passive awareness.

3. **A** allows for the most problem solving and critical thinking. The other three responses are all useful techniques, but none of these three responses have the application aspect present in recommending a solution to a well-researched, local problem.

4. **C** shows consistency within the learning environment at the fourth grade and will have the greatest impact. (A), (B), and (D) are all ways to have the team effort work smoothly and support the instructional framework, although (B) is too narrow as it focuses on integration of only two of the four classes.

5. **B** considers multiple reasons for placement in a group while maintaining diversity and allows the group to function long enough for members to bond and to learn cooperative patterns of behavior. (A) has too many groups and interactions with too many individuals on a daily basis for this age. (C) depends more on friendships that shift constantly rather than on effective learning, which is the focus of groups. (D) narrows the learning environment by placing students in heterogeneous ability groups and has a potential for a negative impact on self-concept.

SINGLE-ITEM FORMAT

In a single-item test format, you are presented some information in the stem of the item. This information should provide enough of the context of the situation to guide you in deciding among the four possible responses. You have four options from which to select the one response that is correct according to best practice. Keep in mind that one or two of the other responses may be feasible, but that only one is clearly best as paired with the specifics of the information in the stem of the item. Be alert to distracting or unneeded information in the stem.

Single Items 1–5

1. What is the most appropriate activity for a second-grade teacher to use to develop students' skills in setting goals?

    (A) Develop personal time lines and set goals for the next five years.
    (B) Discuss and plan ways that second-grade learners can assist their parents in home responsibilities.
    (C) Tell students that they are responsible for cleaning their desks.
    (D) Have students write a narrative about how they have seen adults set and achieve goals.

2. According to Maslow's hierarchy of human needs, what must students first experience before developing a strong sense of self-worth?

    (A) Students need a sense of belonging.
    (B) Students need to experience self-actualization.
    (C) Students need opportunities to fail and try again.
    (D) Students need repeated experiences with gaining power over others.

3. According to cognitive development, as described by Piaget, at which stage are young children unable to mentally reverse actions?

    (A) Children in the formal operations stage are unable to reverse actions.
    (B) Children in the sensorimotor development stage are unable to reverse actions.
    (C) Children in the preoperational developmental stage are unable to reverse actions.
    (D) Children in the conservation concept developmental stage are unable to reverse actions.

4. Physical development is an important part of school for children of EC–6 ages. What is an appropriate in-class physical activity to use to develop large muscles?

    (A) Playing organized games that require frequent, active use of the arms and legs during free time develops large muscles.
    (B) Using scissors to cut small objects needed for making a collage develops large muscles.
    (C) Sitting in circles at story time develops large muscles.
    (D) Using the body to make letters and numbers during instructional times develops large muscles.

5. Young children who have developed a sense of inferiority may face academic challenges because of their low self-esteem. How can the teacher best support such children and scaffold them to develop a stronger sense of identity?

   (A) Engage these learners in motivational activities designed to guarantee the success of all learners.
   (B) Explain to these children that their sense of self should not impact their academic growth.
   (C) Place these children in heterogeneous groups where there are two strong-willed children who will attempt to control the group.
   (D) Request that parents talk with their children about the need for improving their attitude toward learning.

Correct Responses

1. **B** includes learners in the goal-setting process and is developmentally appropriate. (A) is far too advanced for second-grade students. (C) is totally teacher-centered. (D) does nothing to help students learn to set their own goals.

2. **A** is stated as a prerequisite for developing a sense of self-worth. (B) requires a level beyond the development of self-worth. (C) is not in the set of needs Maslow identified as being critical to development. (D) is not related to developing a sense of self-worth; rather, it is a negatively based response.

3. **C** is the stage Piaget identified as the time when learners are unable to think in reverse. (A) is the stage beyond this development. (B) is the initial stage where sensory and motor activity direct learning. (D) refers to the ability to recognize that properties stay the same despite changes in appearance.

4. **D** is an activity safe for inside the classroom and uses the large muscles of the body. (A) is inappropriate because of the potential for children to be hurt as they move about the classroom. (B) develops small muscles more than large ones. (C) does little to develop muscles.

5. **A** provides a supportive environment for all learners and ensures the success of those who might be less inclined to do their best, because of past failures. (B) will do little to develop a sense of worth in these children. (C) would do more harm than good, as the strong-willed children would likely push around those with lower self-esteem. (D) would not only discourage the children with a low sense of self but may prevent parents from feeling a sense of partnership with the school.

Note: In Chapters 12–15, which provide diagnostic and sample test items, readers should take advantage of all the different tests in order to obtain more practice in selecting the best answer for any test item. Although certain elements of each test are pertinent only to that grade level cluster, many items are generic across the grade level domains. As a result, taking advantage of all the tests offers an opportunity for as much practice as possible while not adding confusion with grade level specifics that are not germane to your area of certification.

Diagnostic and Sample Tests for Grades EC–6

CHAPTER 12

he diagnostic tests in the following chapters include one question per test competency, except for the EC-12 Diagnostic Test, which includes three questions per competency. These questions are similar to those found at the State Board of Educator Certification (SBEC) website (www.sbec.state.tx.us), where the state agency provides a clear example of the PPR certification test. The SBEC practice test should also be used as a diagnostic tool to ascertain both your areas of strength and the needed areas of knowledge and skill improvement that you must have to be successful on the PPR examinations. The diagnostic items in this book are presented without full follow-up explanations of why all responses are correct or incorrect. This follows the pattern used for the test items for the SBEC practice tests. The state competency is listed at the end of each diagnostic test item to help guide your understanding of how you will be tested on each competency.

According to numerous candidates who have taken and passed the state certification test, there is a correlation between SBEC practice tests and the state certification test. You are encouraged to visit www.sbec.state.tx.us for further information about the SBEC study guide. We encourage you to continue to take the diagnostic tests to confirm exactly what competencies are included on the test and to practice deciding why three responses are incorrect or less effective and why one response is clearly the best answer.

Following the sample tests for each of the state certification levels, you will find a self-analysis framework that will guide you in understanding how to improve your study before taking the state tests. In this framework, the authors explain why three answers are incorrect (or are not the *best* response) and one answer is correct (or is the *best* choice). It would be wise to continue to use this analysis strategy as you continue to practice using the tests in this study guide and the SBEC online test. In Chapter 16, suggestions are made that will help you complete an overall analysis of your success and provide you with a strategy for further study.

Answer Sheet
DIAGNOSTIC TEST (GRADES EC-6)

1 Ⓐ Ⓑ Ⓒ Ⓓ

2 Ⓐ Ⓑ Ⓒ Ⓓ

3 Ⓐ Ⓑ Ⓒ Ⓓ

4 Ⓐ Ⓑ Ⓒ Ⓓ

5 Ⓐ Ⓑ Ⓒ Ⓓ

6 Ⓐ Ⓑ Ⓒ Ⓓ

7 Ⓐ Ⓑ Ⓒ Ⓓ

8 Ⓐ Ⓑ Ⓒ Ⓓ

9 Ⓐ Ⓑ Ⓒ Ⓓ

10 Ⓐ Ⓑ Ⓒ Ⓓ

11 Ⓐ Ⓑ Ⓒ Ⓓ

12 Ⓐ Ⓑ Ⓒ Ⓓ

13 Ⓐ Ⓑ Ⓒ Ⓓ

Answer Sheet

SAMPLE TEST (GRADES EC–6)

1 Ⓐ Ⓑ Ⓒ Ⓓ	26 Ⓐ Ⓑ Ⓒ Ⓓ	51 Ⓐ Ⓑ Ⓒ Ⓓ	76 Ⓐ Ⓑ Ⓒ Ⓓ
2 Ⓐ Ⓑ Ⓒ Ⓓ	27 Ⓐ Ⓑ Ⓒ Ⓓ	52 Ⓐ Ⓑ Ⓒ Ⓓ	77 Ⓐ Ⓑ Ⓒ Ⓓ
3 Ⓐ Ⓑ Ⓒ Ⓓ	28 Ⓐ Ⓑ Ⓒ Ⓓ	53 Ⓐ Ⓑ Ⓒ Ⓓ	78 Ⓐ Ⓑ Ⓒ Ⓓ
4 Ⓐ Ⓑ Ⓒ Ⓓ	29 Ⓐ Ⓑ Ⓒ Ⓓ	54 Ⓐ Ⓑ Ⓒ Ⓓ	79 Ⓐ Ⓑ Ⓒ Ⓓ
5 Ⓐ Ⓑ Ⓒ Ⓓ	30 Ⓐ Ⓑ Ⓒ Ⓓ	55 Ⓐ Ⓑ Ⓒ Ⓓ	80 Ⓐ Ⓑ Ⓒ Ⓓ
6 Ⓐ Ⓑ Ⓒ Ⓓ	31 Ⓐ Ⓑ Ⓒ Ⓓ	56 Ⓐ Ⓑ Ⓒ Ⓓ	81 Ⓐ Ⓑ Ⓒ Ⓓ
7 Ⓐ Ⓑ Ⓒ Ⓓ	32 Ⓐ Ⓑ Ⓒ Ⓓ	57 Ⓐ Ⓑ Ⓒ Ⓓ	82 Ⓐ Ⓑ Ⓒ Ⓓ
8 Ⓐ Ⓑ Ⓒ Ⓓ	33 Ⓐ Ⓑ Ⓒ Ⓓ	58 Ⓐ Ⓑ Ⓒ Ⓓ	83 Ⓐ Ⓑ Ⓒ Ⓓ
9 Ⓐ Ⓑ Ⓒ Ⓓ	34 Ⓐ Ⓑ Ⓒ Ⓓ	59 Ⓐ Ⓑ Ⓒ Ⓓ	84 Ⓐ Ⓑ Ⓒ Ⓓ
10 Ⓐ Ⓑ Ⓒ Ⓓ	35 Ⓐ Ⓑ Ⓒ Ⓓ	60 Ⓐ Ⓑ Ⓒ Ⓓ	85 Ⓐ Ⓑ Ⓒ Ⓓ
11 Ⓐ Ⓑ Ⓒ Ⓓ	36 Ⓐ Ⓑ Ⓒ Ⓓ	61 Ⓐ Ⓑ Ⓒ Ⓓ	86 Ⓐ Ⓑ Ⓒ Ⓓ
12 Ⓐ Ⓑ Ⓒ Ⓓ	37 Ⓐ Ⓑ Ⓒ Ⓓ	62 Ⓐ Ⓑ Ⓒ Ⓓ	87 Ⓐ Ⓑ Ⓒ Ⓓ
13 Ⓐ Ⓑ Ⓒ Ⓓ	38 Ⓐ Ⓑ Ⓒ Ⓓ	63 Ⓐ Ⓑ Ⓒ Ⓓ	88 Ⓐ Ⓑ Ⓒ Ⓓ
14 Ⓐ Ⓑ Ⓒ Ⓓ	39 Ⓐ Ⓑ Ⓒ Ⓓ	64 Ⓐ Ⓑ Ⓒ Ⓓ	89 Ⓐ Ⓑ Ⓒ Ⓓ
15 Ⓐ Ⓑ Ⓒ Ⓓ	40 Ⓐ Ⓑ Ⓒ Ⓓ	65 Ⓐ Ⓑ Ⓒ Ⓓ	90 Ⓐ Ⓑ Ⓒ Ⓓ
16 Ⓐ Ⓑ Ⓒ Ⓓ	41 Ⓐ Ⓑ Ⓒ Ⓓ	66 Ⓐ Ⓑ Ⓒ Ⓓ	
17 Ⓐ Ⓑ Ⓒ Ⓓ	42 Ⓐ Ⓑ Ⓒ Ⓓ	67 Ⓐ Ⓑ Ⓒ Ⓓ	
18 Ⓐ Ⓑ Ⓒ Ⓓ	43 Ⓐ Ⓑ Ⓒ Ⓓ	68 Ⓐ Ⓑ Ⓒ Ⓓ	
19 Ⓐ Ⓑ Ⓒ Ⓓ	44 Ⓐ Ⓑ Ⓒ Ⓓ	69 Ⓐ Ⓑ Ⓒ Ⓓ	
20 Ⓐ Ⓑ Ⓒ Ⓓ	45 Ⓐ Ⓑ Ⓒ Ⓓ	70 Ⓐ Ⓑ Ⓒ Ⓓ	
21 Ⓐ Ⓑ Ⓒ Ⓓ	46 Ⓐ Ⓑ Ⓒ Ⓓ	71 Ⓐ Ⓑ Ⓒ Ⓓ	
22 Ⓐ Ⓑ Ⓒ Ⓓ	47 Ⓐ Ⓑ Ⓒ Ⓓ	72 Ⓐ Ⓑ Ⓒ Ⓓ	
23 Ⓐ Ⓑ Ⓒ Ⓓ	48 Ⓐ Ⓑ Ⓒ Ⓓ	73 Ⓐ Ⓑ Ⓒ Ⓓ	
24 Ⓐ Ⓑ Ⓒ Ⓓ	49 Ⓐ Ⓑ Ⓒ Ⓓ	74 Ⓐ Ⓑ Ⓒ Ⓓ	
25 Ⓐ Ⓑ Ⓒ Ⓓ	50 Ⓐ Ⓑ Ⓒ Ⓓ	75 Ⓐ Ⓑ Ⓒ Ⓓ	

Diagnostic Test (Grades EC–6)

Directions: Read each stimulus and answer every question. Mark your answers in the answer spaces on the accompanying grid.

1. Jeanetta is a four-year-old girl who seems to prefer the construction center during free play time in her preschool class. She enjoys working alone to build things, even though there are several other children in the construction center. Based on these observations by the teacher, what is the *best* assessment of Jeanetta's play in the construction center?

   (A) She is limited in her interpersonal development and needs teacher direction regarding how to play with her peers.
   (B) She is in the predictable stage of parallel play with children this age.
   (C) She is demonstrating signs of behavior disorder.
   (D) She is far advanced for her age and should be considered for placement in a kindergarten classroom at this time.

Competency 001: *The teacher understands human developmental processes and applies this knowledge to plan instruction and ongoing assessment that motivate students and are responsive to their developmental characteristics and needs.*

2. Richard was assigned a class of 30 fifth-grade students who speak four different native languages. To ensure that he addresses the diversity in his class appropriately, how should he plan his assessments?

   (A) Use assessments that focus on students' strengths and give them various ways to demonstrate what they have learned.
   (B) Allow students to determine the method of assessment for each assignment.
   (C) Test students several times during the grading period, so he does not have to give a unit test or other cumulative tests.
   (D) Determine end of unit grades by using only student and peer assessment of major assignments.

Competency 002: *The teacher understands student diversity and knows how to plan learning experiences and design assessments that are responsive to differences among students and that promote all students' learning.*

3. Why should Richard design his learning objectives before he plans the instructional activities for his unit?

(A) To allow students the freedom of choosing their activities, with limited focus on the essential knowledge and skills required by the TEKS.

(B) So his formative and summative assessments are focused on the activities he plans in order to have alignment with the activities.

(C) To have confidence in how he has sequenced the content of the TEKS and paired the learning activities with what he is responsible for teaching.

(D) To evaluate the topic of the unit to see if it is appropriate and if it has activities that his students will enjoy.

Competency 003: *The teacher understands procedures for designing effective and coherent instruction and assessment based on appropriate learning goals and objectives.*

4. Sonya immigrated to the United States two years ago. Since that time, she has changed schools twice. Now, in her kindergarten year, she enters Ms. Alvarez's class halfway through the year. Her teacher noted that Sonya is above average in her social skills, but her play successes are not at the point expected for her age. What must Ms. Alvarez keep in mind regarding this variance in levels?

(A) Students in this group may be highly advanced in their play skills, thus a comparison of Sonya to the others would be inequitable.

(B) Teachers should carefully discourage reluctant children who appear to be reverting to levels of performance below where they should be.

(C) Teacher observation is rarely an accurate record of student performance.

(D) It is normal for young children to revert to previous levels of success in a situation where they might feel a lack of security and belongingness.

Competency 004: *The teacher understands learning processes and factors that impact student learning and demonstrates this knowledge by planning effective, engaging instruction and appropriate assessments.*

5. As a new teacher, Margarette wishes to establish high expectations for her students. What should she do to guide her students to achieve their best?

(A) Make sure students focus mainly on their strength areas and avoid any stress related to learning activities that are challenging.

(B) Give students numerous opportunities to work together on assignments so as not to cause any one student to have total responsibility for his/her learning.

(C) Guide all students to set challenging learning goals and scaffold learners at all times as they strive to meet those goals.

(D) Give lots of praise to all students at all times, even if the praise is not contingently earned.

Competency 005: *The teacher knows how to establish a classroom climate that fosters learning, equity, and excellence and uses this knowledge to create a physical and emotional environment that is safe and productive.*

6. Alma noticed two students in seemingly high levels of conflict when on the playground. What conflict resolution technique would be appropriate?

    (A) Guide the students to work together for a mutual agreement to solve their differences.
    (B) Discipline the student who started the conflict and warn the other student.
    (C) Assign another student the responsibility of being in charge of the resolution.
    (D) Send the students inside and direct them in how to solve their problems.

Competency 006: *The teacher understands strategies for creating an organized and productive learning environment and for managing student behavior.*

7. Mary, a first-grade teacher, plans to address the following science objective:

    > **The student knows that plants are made up of parts, and that if one part is damaged, the plant may suffer and possibly die.**

    Which of the following should Mary use as a strategy for introducing this concept effectively and efficiently to her first graders?

    (A) Tell the first graders several times how important each part of the plant is to the successful growth and health of the plant.
    (B) Bring a slightly damaged plant from home or a store to demonstrate the parts of the plant and to show how damage to one part may impact the whole plant.
    (C) Sketch the parts of a plant on a dry erase board and draw lines from each part of the plant to the vocabulary word for the part.
    (D) List the word for each part of a plant on the board and have students define each word in their vocabulary notebooks.

Competency 007: *The teacher understands and applies principles and strategies for communicating effectively in varied teaching and learning contexts.*

8. Mr. Ramey is a fourth-grade teacher who has planned a Texas geography unit. He includes a teacher PowerPoint presentation, a whole-class discussion, a web quest activity, an Internet streaming video, and a series of multitasking activities. What is the most strategic advantage of this instructional plan?

    (A) Such variety helps the teacher pace the lesson, and observe the students as they engage in various activities.
    (B) The teacher can cover more content material in this manner, leaving time for students to engage in free-choice activities.
    (C) It addresses the multiple learning approaches students may have in order to provide an optimal learning opportunity for all students.
    (D) This approach helps a beginning teacher know that the content is well sequenced and will be presented in a logical manner.

Competency 008: *The teacher provides appropriate instruction that actively engages students in the learning process.*

9. David is aware of the state's inclusion of technology competencies at all grade levels. What should be his focus as he guides his second graders' learning of computers?

(A) to apply as much advanced technology knowledge as possible
(B) to explore the ways a computer may be used and the things it can do
(C) to ensure that his students produce attractive computer products
(D) to teach and assess specific computer skills on a regular basis

Competency 009: *The teacher incorporates the effective use of technology to plan, organize, deliver, and evaluate instruction for all students.*

10. What would be an appropriate way for Julie to engage parents/guardians in the assessment of her students in a third-grade class?

(A) Julie should ask parents their opinions about what tests might be appropriate because a parent knows more about a young child's capabilities than the teacher.
(B) Parents typically know little of their children's learning strengths, so they should have a limited voice in the assessment process.
(C) Julie should encourage parents/guardians to provide information about their children's pertinent background knowledge and learning strengths.
(D) Julie should avoid engaging parents in a discussion about assessment.

Competency 010: *The teacher monitors student performance and achievement; provides students with timely, high-quality feedback; and responds flexibly to promote learning for all students.*

11. As a beginning fourth-grade teacher, Carolyn is preparing to meet with Jamie's parents to discuss his performance on the recently administered fourth-grade TAKS. Which of the following should be Carolyn's primary emphasis during the meeting?

(A) To show and discuss the TAKS report with the parents and ask the parents about their analysis of the report, the results for Jamie, and ways to work together.
(B) To help Jamie's parents understand key principles of standardized assessment and how those principles might have impacted Jamie's performance.
(C) To describe Jamie's academic strengths and needs as indicated by the assessment results and to tell the parents how the teacher will address areas that need improvement.
(D) To explain to the parents by using comparison scores of his peers how Jamie compared with other students on his grade level.

Competency 011: *The teacher understands the importance of family involvement in children's education and knows how to interact and communicate effectively with families.*

12. Martin learned the value of reading professional literature in his university teacher education program. He made a commitment to continue reading these materials. What is the *primary* benefit of this practice for Martin?

(A) Martin can identify reading strategies for working with at-risk students in his classroom.

(B) He can continuously be aware of current research and trends.

(C) Reading may serve as a rewarding distraction from planning and grading.

(D) Journal reading is a good support system for a new teacher.

Competency 012: *The teacher enhances professional knowledge and skills by effectively interacting with other members of the educational community and participating in various types of professional activities.*

13. Martin carefully studied the Texas Educator's Code of Ethics in his education foundation class as an undergraduate. He is well aware of the ethical requirements imposed when administering TAKS. Which of the following practices would be considered *unethical?*

(A) giving students a teacher-made practice test two weeks prior to the administration of the TAKS

(B) using body language clues or answering specific student questions about TAKS questions during the actual administration of the test

(C) paraphrasing what the directions for the different sections of the TAKS will be in order to prepare them for the test

(D) planning specific lessons targeting TAKS objectives in order to prepare students for the day of the test

Competency 013: *The teacher understands and adheres to legal and ethical requirements for educators and is knowledgeable of the structure of education in Texas.*

Answer Key

DIAGNOSTIC TEST (GRADES EC–6)

Question Number	Correct Response	Competency
1	B	001
2	A	002
3	C	003
4	D	004
5	C	005
6	A	006
7	B	007
8	C	008
9	B	009
10	C	010
11	A	011
12	B	012
13	B	013

CORRECT ANSWERS

1. **B** Jeanetta is exhibiting age-appropriate parallel play at the construction center. It is a mistake to read into a situation interpretations not supported by evidence, and there is no evidence for the other three possible answers.

2. **A** By varying the types of assessments used, students are given multiple opportunities to exhibit their learning. Assessment of English Language learners should document areas of learning rather than areas where learning is still needed, which also helps encourage continued effort in a challenging situation.

3. **C** Addressing the required TEKS in an appropriate sequence to enhance student learning is at the heart of planning. Other steps and decisions may then come into play as the plan is developed.

4. **D** The stress of a series of moves and the impact and stress of a new environment on a student's behaviors must be considered.

5. **C** Encouraging students to stretch themselves through participation in goal setting and providing the needed support are part of guiding a student to meet high teacher expectations rather than focusing on areas where students can easily succeed without putting forth an appropriate amount of effort.

6. **A** A major tenet of conflict resolution is to have the parties involved reach an acceptable solution. This is better than having a solution imposed by an outsider.

7. **B** A concrete example such as a plant with a damaged part will help trigger any prior knowledge, give visual examples of the parts, and allow students to concretely observe the importance of the damaged part rather than learning abstractly about plants.

8. **C** is the correct answer. By using a variety of instructional strategies and approaches, the teacher assures that all learners have an optimal opportunity to engage in learning in ways that best meet their needs and preferences. Fourth-grade learners need to be exposed to as many approaches to learning as possible in order to address their developing styles and approaches to learning tasks.

9. **B** Concrete exploration is needed to provide motivation and active engagement in learning new skills. By allowing exploration of what the computer can do and be used for, the teacher provides an environment for creative and independent learning while students acquire grade-level appropriate skills.

10. **C** When teachers engage parents/guardians in sharing information about background and learning strengths, this helps ensure that parents consider themselves vital to the educational program of their children. Also, by asking parents to participate by providing this information, the teacher can gather useful information helpful in understanding the learners, especially from the perspective of the parents/guardians.

11. **A** As the teacher explains the information contained in the report of the student's performance, the parents can identify the information provided by such assessments. By examining the assessment results and by sharing ways the parents can work with the school to assist with the student's progress in the educational program, the teacher is engaging the parents in a partnership approach to optimal learning.

12. **B** To be a highly qualified and effective teacher, all teachers must keep as current as possible with the latest trends and issues as identified by recent research. Reading professional journals is one of the most effective and expedient ways to stay abreast of current research and critical issues facing schools.

13. **B** In standardized tests, there are routines and practices that must be explicitly followed during the administration of the test. A teacher who gives body language clues about answers is behaving unethically. This invalidates the standardization and makes the test results invalid.

Sample Test (Grades EC–6)

This sample test has 90 practice questions to help you review as part of your preparation for the EC–6 PPR test. Please carefully read the domains and competencies that will be tested on the EC–6 PPR before beginning this test. As you read the domains and competencies, think about the mind-set and philosophy of teaching they represent. In this sample test, each practice question is introduced by the competency being measured. The questions and competencies are presented in numerical order for the purpose of logical flow as you learn the competencies. When you reach the teacher decision set near the end of the test, the sample questions will no longer address the competencies in numerical order. *Please be aware that competency statements will not appear on the actual test form and that the questions will not be presented in sequential order by competency numbers.*

Use the frame of reference built from your understanding of the domains and competencies as you select the single best answer for each question. It is recommended that you do an in-depth analysis of each possible answer before making your choice. In addition to selecting the best answer, it is recommended that you consider carefully *why* it is the best answer based on the domains and competencies. In addition, it is recommended that you have a clear reason for rejecting each answer that is not chosen rather than just identifying and marking your preferred answer.

Following the sample test and answer key, a section on correct responses and rationales discusses the strengths and challenges of each of the possible answers. Refer back to the domains and competencies as you read the rationale for each possible answer. Carefully examine the rationale for both the right and the wrong answer choices for the relationship to the domains and competencies. A good strategy is to narrow your choices to two and then reread the question with each answer to make sure that your choice answers exactly what the question is asking. Make a clear connection between the choice you believe to be best and the question posed.

Directions: Read each stimulus and answer every question. Mark your answers in the answer spaces on the accompanying grid.

Competency 001: *The teacher understands human developmental processes and applies this knowledge to plan instruction and ongoing assessment that motivate students and are responsive to their developmental characteristics and needs.*

1. Four-year old Lydia is having a tea party with her mother and grandmother. After pouring all the tea from the teapot into three cups, Lydia states that there is now more tea than before. How would her mother, who is a teacher, best interpret this incident?

    (A) Lydia has not yet developed object permanence.
    (B) Lydia is indicating that she is now at the concrete operational stage of development.
    (C) Lydia has not yet developed conservation of liquid volume.
    (D) Lydia has not yet developed one-to-one correspondence.

2. Barbara Schulte has been assigned a classroom of second-grade students for her first-year teaching assignment. She is aware that there are suggested age ranges for Piaget's identified levels of cognitive development and that in any given classroom the cognitive abilities/readiness of students may range over two or three grade levels. What knowledge about Piaget's stages should she apply in designing an activity where she has students working with math manipulatives?

    (A) Second-grade students are most likely to be in preoperational and/or concrete operational stages of development.
    (B) Second-grade students are most likely to be in concrete operational and/or formal operational stages of development.
    (C) Second-grade students are most likely to be in sensorimotor and/or concrete operational stages of development.
    (D) Second-grade students are most likely to be in sensorimotor and/or preoperational stages of development.

3. Richard is talking with his five-year-old nephew Larry about family connections. Uncle Richard is planning to become a preschool teacher. He wants to check what he has learned in his classes on child development against what he observes with his nephew. When asked how many children his parents have, Larry responds, "Two." When asked if he has any brothers, Larry responds, "No." When asked if he has any sisters, Larry responds, "Yes, one—Chrissie." Uncle Richard then asks Larry if Chrissie has any brothers or sisters and Larry responds: "No, I told you there are only two children, me and Chrissie. Weren't you listening?" What is the best interpretation for Larry's response to Uncle Richard's question about Chrissie having any siblings?

(A) Larry's answer indicates he has not yet developed the ability to reverse his thinking.

(B) Larry's answer indicates he has not yet developed one-to-one correspondence.

(C) Larry's answer indicates he has not yet developed object permanence.

(D) Larry's answer indicates he has become a concrete operational learner.

Use the following information to answer questions 4 and 5.

As a fourth-year teacher, Ms. Sashay discovers during the first week of school that 12 of her 20 second-graders have limited English proficiency. There are nine languages other than English spoken in the homes of these students. As Ms. Sashay makes her plans for the new school year, she is very aware that she has a challenging student population and must revise the plans she used successfully last year.

Competency 002: *The teacher understands student diversity and knows how to plan learning experiences and design assessments that are responsive to differences among students and that promote all students' learning.*

4. Ms. Sashay wants to modify her plans, lessons, and assessments for the limited English proficiency students in ways that will address both their language needs and their learning. How can she best meet these goals?

(A) Ms. Sashay should present lessons to these limited English proficiency students that address less demanding content and concept TEKS than the lessons for the other students.

(B) Ms. Sashay should hold these limited English proficiency students to the same TEKS addressed in the lessons for the other students.

(C) Ms. Sashay should present lessons drawn only from TEKS that can be presented with concrete materials to allow these students language development experiences with real objects.

(D) Ms. Sashay should focus on English language acquisition with these limited English proficiency students and worry about their content learning after their English fluency has improved.

5. When assessing the limited English proficiency students, which of the following plans will give Ms. Sashay the most accurate assessment of their learning?

(A) Ms. Sashay should allow the limited English proficiency students to indicate to her how they are progressing in both their English and their learning. This should be done weekly so they are not overwhelmed by the amount of material addressed.

(B) Ms. Sashay should assess the limited English proficiency students more often than the others to ensure that they are keeping up with the rest of the class. She should hold tutoring sessions if they are not.

(C) Ms. Sashay should assign each limited English proficiency student a "study buddy" who will help her assess them by sharing comments and observations about their knowledge and their English.

(D) Ms. Sashay should assess *all* her students using a wide range of assessment styles to allow each student many ways and multiple opportunities to demonstrate their learning and to make the limited English proficiency students feel they are part of the class.

Use the following information to answer questions 6 and 7.

Following the first six weeks of school, Mr. Beaumont decides to read to his third-grade class for 15 minutes every day after lunch. He wants this listening time to provide a calming effect following the stimulation of the lunch break. He also wants to improve the listening skills of his students and to encourage their interest in and enthusiasm for oral language and reading in a listening context.

Competency 003: *The teacher understands procedures for designing effective and coherent instruction and assessment based on appropriate learning goals and objectives.*

6. What criteria are most important in selecting the book he will read to allow Mr. Beaumont to reach all his goals?

(A) Mr. Beaumont should select books that have a direct connection with content classes so that he does not lose 15 minutes of instructional time daily. His students will absorb content knowledge as they listen but will not really be aware that they are learning.

(B) Mr. Beaumont should select books that describe events and settings that are new to his students. This will expand the learning horizon of the students as they encounter new and unexpected events with which they are presently unfamiliar.

(C) Mr. Beaumont should select books that are interesting and familiar to his students. This will hold their interest more effectively and make it easier for them to be attentive.

(D) Mr. Beaumont should select books that are on a topic that is not too exciting. They should also be focused on word play and patterns such as puns, rhyming words, and alliteration.

7. How can Mr. Beaumont best assess the effectiveness of this daily listening time in meeting his stated goals?

   (A) After three weeks, Mr. Beaumont can claim that a scheduling conflict prevents holding the listening time for three days. By observing the students' reactions, he can assess their affective responses to the oral language and reading in the oral context.

   (B) After three weeks, Mr. Beaumont can add a short set of verbal questions to the listening time. By asking about what is recalled or for predictions about future events, he can assess students' listening and thinking skills and attentiveness.

   (C) After three weeks, Mr. Beaumont can ask students if they wish to continue the book currently being read or shift to another one. Based on their responses, he can judge if they are enjoying the book and learning from it.

   (D) After three weeks, Mr. Beaumont can give a short quiz to determine if individuals are attentive and are using effective listening skills. He can also gain information about the affective value of the book.

Use the following information to answer questions 8 and 9.

Following the winter break, Paula transfers from out of state into Mr. Stewart's first-grade class. Paula will be 7 in February. Her parents and her transferred school records indicate that she is developmentally advanced in social skills. During the first week, all of Mr. Stewart's observations of Paula cause him to question the accuracy of the developmentally advanced label for Paula, as her social behaviors and play seem more appropriate for a student just beginning kindergarten. Mr. Stewart is considering contacting the parents to discuss his concern that Paula has been mislabeled as socially advanced.

Competency 004: *The teacher understands learning processes and factors that impact student learning and demonstrates this knowledge by planning effective, engaging instruction and appropriate assessments.*

8. What is Mr. Stewart's best action plan at this time?

   (A) Mr. Stewart should give Paula additional time to adjust to the new school while keeping a close eye on her social skills.

   (B) Because Mr. Stewart knows that states have different educational standards, he should contact her previous school to determine the differences.

   (C) Mr. Stewart should contact Paula's parents and inform them she has been mislabeled because she came from a class of students who were developmentally delayed.

   (D) Mr. Stewart, knowing expectations vary, should accept that Paula is a developmentally delayed student and wait to avoid upsetting her parents.

9. How can Mr. Stewart best establish an accurate assessment of Paula's social developmental level before visiting with her parents to discuss her adjustment to the new school?

(A) Mr. Stewart should talk privately with Paula and let her know that her behaviors are unacceptable and that he knows from her prior school records that she can do much better.

(B) Mr. Stewart should quietly and calmly call Paula's attention to students showing the social behaviors and play habits he expects from her and ask her to emulate them.

(C) Mr. Stewart should not delay in contacting Paula's parents to request additional information about her social development and to ask for their assistance in obtaining a more accurate picture.

(D) Mr. Stewart should assign Paula two students to guide her and orient her to the new school over the next week while observing to see what effect increased comfort and familiarity have on her social skills.

Competency 005: *The teacher knows how to establish a classroom climate that fosters learning, equity, and excellence and uses this knowledge to create a physical and emotional environment that is safe and productive.*

10. A fifth-grade teacher who expects strong active participation in all class activities by her students begins a unit by having the class brainstorm information on a topic into a K-W-L chart on the board. Ideas from the class are added to the chart throughout the introductory discussion. What is the primary reason that this beginning is a good strategy?

(A) The K-W-L chart indicates that no matter how much an individual knows about a topic, there is still information to learn.

(B) The K-W-L chart gives students notice in a nonthreatening manner that everyone is expected to participate.

(C) The K-W-L chart focuses students' prior knowledge of a topic without placing any individual on the spot.

(D) The K-W-L chart sends the message that the teacher thinks that everyone knows something about the topic to contribute.

11. Ms. Gonzales is a second-grade teacher. The school guidance counselor tells her that her class has a high number of students with significant academic needs. In what way can Ms. Gonzales avoid becoming a barrier to success for these students with significant academic needs?

(A) Ms. Gonzales should set high standards, differentiate instruction, and have high expectations for all her students regardless of their levels of academic need.

(B) Ms. Gonzales must collect information such as ethnicity, socioeconomic status, at-risk status, and parental education levels.

(C) Ms. Gonzales should understand the social challenges some students face and take this into account as she plans instruction and expectations for them.

(D) Because all the students are in the same grade and attended this school last year, she should instruct all students in the same way.

Competency 006: *The teacher understands strategies for creating an organized and productive learning environment and for managing student behavior.*

12. As an elementary teacher dealing with student conflicts on a daily basis, what should be your primary student conflict resolution goal for any given situation?

(A) The goal should be to determine which student is at fault and deal with the behavior that caused the conflict.

(B) The goal should be to end the conflict and refocus students on instructional tasks in as short a time as possible.

(C) The goal should be for you to obtain a clear understanding of the problem and issue a settlement fair to all involved.

(D) The goal should be to guide the students involved toward an amicable and agreeable settlement.

Competency 007: *The teacher understands and applies principles and strategies for communicating effectively in varied teaching and learning contexts.*

13. Following a PDAS observation, your evaluator notifies you that your behaviors vary between two groups of students. You provide higher-achieving students significantly longer wait time than you provide lower-achieving students. In addition, with lower-achieving students you restate a question as many as three times in the same amount of wait time you give the higher-achieving students. Both types of students perceive your restated questions as new questions. How is this practice most likely to affect your classroom?

(A) Increased wait time for higher-achieving students signals all students that you expect more from these top students, and this will produce resentment in both groups.

(B) Shorter wait time and restating questions signal all students that you have differentiated expectation levels and will therefore reinforce feelings of inability to achieve success in lower-achieving students.

(C) Shorter wait time allows lower-achieving students less time to feel they are "on the spot," and the restated questions indicate to all students that you are giving lower-achieving students more opportunities to succeed.

(D) A difference in wait time is an effective instructional differentiation method to allow both groups success opportunities by allowing needed think-and-respond time.

14. Ms. Johnson wants to introduce her third-graders to activities requiring them to use problem-solving skills. She knows she must actively teach her students how to succeed with this type of task rather than just assigning it. As the students first engage in a problem-solving activity, what approach will be most effective?

(A) Ms. Johnson should ask questions until she is able to guide her students toward reaching the correct answer.

(B) Ms. Johnson should promise a prize as motivation to the student who finds the correct answer first.

(C) Ms. Johnson should encourage her students to approach the problem in creative ways to find solutions.

(D) Ms. Johnson should use concrete examples from the students' lives to guide them as they find the answer.

Competency 008: *The teacher provides appropriate instruction that actively engages students in the learning process.*

15. Ms. Swirczynski notices that Tad is having trouble understanding the history chapter she has assigned her fifth-graders. She asks Tad to meet with her and to describe to her what has been read in the chapter. What is the main benefit of Ms. Swirczynski's approach to helping Tad?

    (A) Ms. Swirczynski's approach helps Tad develop a sense of ownership toward learning.
    (B) Ms. Swirczynski's approach provides instruction specific to Tad's needs.
    (C) Ms. Swirczynski's approach encourages Tad to focus and pay attention to the task.
    (D) Ms. Swirczynski's approach encourages Tad to apply higher-order thinking skills to the task.

16. Mr. Flavid plans an integrated unit for his sixth-grade class that addresses science, math, social studies, reading, and art. His lessons will be both whole class and small group. He has included a guest speaker, a field trip, a web quest, and a video as part of the unit. What is the most important *instructional* advantage of Mr. Flavid's plan?

    (A) Mr. Flavid's plan allows students multiple and varied opportunities to process, internalize, and reinforce the unit's content.
    (B) Mr. Flavid's plan allows the teacher to address a large amount of content information in a shorter amount of time.
    (C) Mr. Flavid's plan allows him flexibility in pacing the lessons to meet the needs of students with different ability levels.
    (D) Mr. Flavid's plan allows him to individualize instruction to meet the needs of students with different ability levels.

Competency 009: *The teacher incorporates the effective use of technology to plan, organize, deliver, and evaluate instruction for all students.*

17. What is the primary rationale for including computer instruction in a preschool classroom?

    (A) Computer instruction helps young children develop fine motor skills faster as they are very motivated by computers.
    (B) Very young children do not have the fine motor skills for clear letter formation, but computers overcome this.
    (C) Very young children are naturally curious and ready to begin to explore the uses and capabilities of computers.
    (D) Very young children need to lay a foundation for the future computer skill acquisition needed for success in school.

18. Mr. Nagoya schedules his second-grade class for the computer lab three times a week. What is the most important technology principle related to this use of instructional time?

(A) Drill and practice software allow Mr. Nagoya to instruct his students on content while also helping them acquire strong computer skills.

(B) The interests of Mr. Nagoya's students should determine the software he has them use because motivation improves learning.

(C) Mr. Nagoya should give direct instruction in computer skills in a carefully planned sequence of lessons each visit.

(D) Mr. Nagoya should primarily present and have students practice computer skills within the context of other content lessons.

Competency 010: *The teacher monitors student performance and achievement; provides students with timely, high-quality feedback; and responds flexibly to promote learning for all students.*

19. What would be the best strategy to use to evaluate the effectiveness of a student learning center used as an instructional strategy?

(A) Track how many and which students use the center for a week. Also, monitor the number of times each student returns to the center.

(B) Interview students to determine their interest in the center as an instructional strategy and probe for the reasons for their responses.

(C) Ask colleagues to test the center and give you their professional opinion of its effectiveness. Do this before students use it.

(D) Collect observational data on students as they work at the center. Assess their learning of the center's content formally or informally.

20. Susan's mother wants to be very active in her preschooler's education and approaches Susan's teacher, Ms. Biggs, about how to become actively involved. What would be an appropriate role for Susan's mother to fill in Ms. Biggs's classroom?

(A) Ms. Biggs could ask Susan's mother to provide observational information about Susan outside school and help Ms. Biggs interpret both the in-school and out-of-school information about Susan.

(B) Ms. Biggs could ask Susan's mother to attend class and collect observational data about the students and their peer interactions within the classroom setting because two observers see twice as much.

(C) Ms. Biggs could ask Susan's mother to focus on Susan's personal and social growth and to leave Susan's cognitive or academic growth to Ms. Biggs, as she is the expert in these areas because of her certification.

(D) Ms. Biggs should calmly and professionally explain to Susan's mother that parents are not expected to play a role in a child's education, which should be handled by the school because the parent already has a role.

Competency 011: *The teacher understands the importance of family involvement in children's education and knows how to interact and communicate effectively with families.*

21. What is an important educational principle for Mr. Wu to remember as he has his first parent-teacher conference to discuss difficulties a student is having in his classroom?

    (A) Mr. Wu should make it very clear that he cannot solve the problem and that the parents have a responsibility to ensure that their student overcomes the difficulties at school.

    (B) Mr. Wu should downplay the problem situation by indicating areas of student success so that the parents do not overreact and see the difficulty as greater than it is before Mr. Wu can solve it.

    (C) As Mr. Wu clearly explains to the parents the difficulty being experienced by their student, he should take care to present the information so that it is clear that he is not judging the family.

    (D) Mr. Wu should keep the conference focused on the difficulties at school and keep the parents from complicating the situation by adding information about the student's activities outside school.

22. Ms. Ming wants to arrange a progress conference with Ms. Garcia, Carmen's mother. Ms. Garcia has canceled two scheduled appointments and fails to show up for a third one. Because Ms. Ming is very frustrated but still determined to speak with Ms. Garcia about Carmen's progress, what should she do next?

    (A) When she schedules the fourth conference with Ms. Garcia, Ms. Ming should emphasize how very important this meeting is and indicate how disappointed she will be if it does not occur.

    (B) Ms. Ming should accept that for some reason Ms. Garcia is extremely reluctant to attend a conference at the school and arrange a time to discuss Carmen's progress over the phone.

    (C) Ms. Ming should accept that all parents are not interested in their child's educational progress and stop trying to force Ms. Garcia to care and to participate.

    (D) Ms. Ming should ask Carmen to communicate to her mother how important this conference is, share her embarrassment when her mom doesn't attend, and encourage her mother's participation.

Competency 012: *The teacher enhances professional knowledge and skills by effectively interacting with other members of the educational community and participating in various types of professional activities.*

23. When Mr. Grant discovered how limited the resources were at his new school, he decided to establish business and community–school partnerships like the ones in operation at his last school. What should be his first step in establishing this collaborative effort to improve school resources?

   (A) Mr. Grant should first become comfortable with the families of his students and learn about the community.

   (B) Mr. Grant should immediately contact community businesses and ask for resources to meet the school's needs.

   (C) Mr. Grant should make the school administration aware of the problem and of his intention to personally address it.

   (D) Mr. Grant should determine which large companies employ community members and contact them for resources.

24. Part of the first paycheck Matt received as a teacher went to joining a professional teachers' organization. When the first journal arrived, he read it from cover to cover and is now looking forward to the next issue. What will be a primary benefit to Matt and his students if he continues to read professional journals?

   (A) Matt will become increasingly aware of professional networks, resources, and support systems and pass this benefit on to his students.

   (B) Matt will be able to close any gaps in his professional and content knowledge, and his students will benefit from his increased knowledge base.

   (C) Matt will remain aware and up-to-date on current research, trends, and issues in his field and pass this benefit on to his students.

   (D) Matt will find tried and true teaching ideas and strategies in the journal, which will make lesson planning easier and will benefit his students.

Competency 013: *The teacher understands and adheres to legal and ethical require-ments for educators and is knowledgeable of the structure of education in Texas.*

25. Marilyn is concerned about her third-grade student's noticeable bruises and scars. In a casual conversation, she asks the student what happened to cause the injuries. The student drops her head and mumbles that she fell down at home. Marilyn concludes that she has **reasonable suspicion** of child abuse but is not sure what to do first. What are the legal requirements and respon-sibilities of a teacher who becomes reasonably suspicious that a child is being physically abused?

(A) The teacher should confront the parents and demand an explanation for the signs that initiated the suspicion of abuse.

(B) The teacher should immediately call the state 800 number and report the suspected abuse to state authorities.

(C) The teacher should immediately report the suspected abuse to the principal, nurse, or counselor and allow them to take the next step.

(D) The teacher should question the student about being abused or being hurt but must accept the answer or explanation given.

26. Over lunch, Ms. Nagasaki indicates she plans to take a VCR home this weekend to record some videotapes. Mr. Brown immediately states that that is unethical, and he strongly encourages her to change her mind. Or course, everyone else at the table voices their opinion, and the general response is that it is completely permissible to take school equipment home under certain conditions. What is a situation where it is ethical to take school equipment home?

(A) It is ethical to take school equipment home as long as the school knows you have it and its return is clearly scheduled so that others can use it for instructional purposes.

(B) It is ethical to take school equipment home as long as you have permis-sion and are willing to assume financial responsibility if it is lost, damaged, or stolen.

(C) It is ethical to take school equipment home as long as it is removed from the building with permission and gone only when others do not need it, such as over weekends.

(D) It is ethical to take school equipment home as long as you have permis-sion and the equipment is used only for authorized school business during the time it is checked out.

27. A group of teachers are visiting over coffee. Three of the teachers are first-year teachers. The experienced teachers are providing suggestions about preparing students for administration of the TAKS in the spring. Which suggestion is inappropriate?

(A) Give content unit tests written in the style and format of the TAKS throughout the year to help students become familiar with it.

(B) Give teacher-made practice tests a few weeks before the TAKS and debrief how to answer each question after completing the test.

(C) Teach only content units that address specific objectives measured by the TAKS and give unit tests in the TAKS format.

(D) Clarify for a student the definition of a word or help students interpret questions during the TAKS.

DECISION SET BEGINS HERE

Ms. Cardwell's third-grade class is involved in a science unit that focuses on individual and societal responsibilities to the environment. One topic that has already been discussed is recycling. Paul announces at the end of science class, "The information I have learned so far is very interesting, but I'm just a third-grader. I cannot make a difference in the world's environmental problems." Maggie immediately responds, "Maybe you can't, but I sure can! If I just recycle my paper here at school, it will count and a difference will be made." All the students have opinions on this topic that they want to share even though the time allotted to science class has ended.

Once Ms. Cardwell has the class settled again, she comments about the different perspectives and feelings the students have expressed. She asks the class the following questions:

- Can a third-grader make a difference through recycling? You have indicated that some of you think the answer is yes, and others disagree.
- Maggie says she can make a difference through recycling all by herself. What do you think?
- Do you agree or disagree with her? Why?
- What kinds of information would we need to collect to see if Paul or Maggie is correct?
- What kind of difference could be made if everyone in class recycled here at school?

Competency 007: *The teacher understands and applies principles and strategies for communicating effectively in varied teaching and learning contexts.*

28. What purpose is best served by Ms. Cardwell's expansion of Maggie's hypothesis?

(A) Ms. Cardwell expanded on Maggie's hypothesis to guide future discussions in appropriate directions to find the answer.

(B) Ms. Cardwell expanded on Maggie's hypothesis to assist students in focusing as they express ideas about possible solutions.

(C) Ms. Cardwell expanded on Maggie's hypothesis to tap into students' prior knowledge about possible solutions.

(D) Ms. Cardwell expanded on Maggie's hypothesis to cue students to the correct answer about how to make a difference.

Competency 004: *The teacher understands learning processes and factors that impact student learning and demonstrates this knowledge by planning effective, engaging instruction and appropriate assessments.*

29. What was Ms. Cardwell's primary instructional role until this point in the discussion?

(A) Ms. Cardwell's primary instructional role was to encourage the use of students' higher-order thinking skills in a real-world context where problem-solving skills can be applied.

(B) Ms. Cardwell's primary instructional role was to force students to develop questions about problems and issues that directly relate to the content unit being studied in class.

(C) Ms. Cardwell's primary instructional role was to establish a linkage between students' prior knowledge, community or global events, and school instructional topics.

(D) Ms. Cardwell's primary instructional role was to provide students with foundational and factual information so that they can take future instruction to a higher level than in the past.

Competency 005: *The teacher knows how to establish a classroom climate that fosters learning, equity, and excellence and uses this knowledge to create a physical and emotional environment that is safe and productive.*

30. What important instructional event occurred because Ms. Cardwell allowed the discussion initiated by Paul and Maggie's comments to continue?

(A) Ms. Cardwell allowed students to take the recycling unit in a direction she might not have planned because she recognized the students' interest in the discussion.

(B) When Ms. Cardwell allowed the discussion to continue off schedule, she "short-changed" the next subject scheduled and thus reduced the students' learning of it.

(C) When Ms. Cardwell actively joined the discussion to help the students focus on this issue, she gave implied permission to get off task and students will try to do so again.

(D) When Ms. Cardwell allowed the discussion to continue past the time scheduled for science class, she deviated from her plan but can refocus the recycling unit tomorrow.

Competency 004: *The teacher understands learning processes and factors that impact student learning and demonstrates this knowledge by planning effective, engaging instruction and appropriate assessments.*

31. What is the main advantage in having students play such a strong role in planning the type of information they would need to collect to determine if Paul or Maggie is correct about a third-grader being able to make a difference in the environment through recycling?

(A) Allowing students to play a role in designing the type and amount of data to collect relieves the teacher of some of the burden of planning a lesson heading in a direction different from that originally planned for the unit.

(B) Allowing students to play a role in designing the type and amount of data to collect plays to the strengths of individual students and indicates to them areas they need to strengthen as they work on the project.

(C) Allowing students to play a role in designing the type and amount of data to collect increases student ownership of the lesson and increases their interest in the project.

(D) Allowing students to play a role in designing the type and amount of data to collect gives Ms. Cardwell in-depth insights into individual students' background knowledge.

Competency 005: *The teacher knows how to establish a classroom climate that fosters learning, equity, and excellence and uses this knowledge to create a physical and emotional environment that is safe and productive.*

32. Once the class has a plan for determining if Paul or Maggie is correct about a third-grade student being able to affect the environment through recycling at school, Ms. Cardwell asks the class to consider the possible effects the answer could have on the entire student body and on the world environment. What is the most important outcome of this knowledge?

   (A) Knowledge of the potential impact a third-grader can have on a global problem can help the students recognize the value of discussing problems while waiting for guidance from others to solutions.

   (B) Knowledge of the potential impact a third-grader can have on a global problem can help the students develop a sense of purpose and place in addressing global problems one step at a time.

   (C) Knowledge of the potential impact a third-grader can have on a global problem can help the students value the importance of clear research goals when attempting to answer a question.

   (D) Knowledge of the potential impact a third-grader can have on a global problem can help the students determine the importance of designing a clear question to research.

Competency 008: *The teacher provides appropriate instruction that actively engages students in the learning process.*

33. What is the most important goal Ms. Cardwell can help students reach using the data collected and the conclusion reached as a result of the recycling project?

   (A) Through the recycling project, Ms. Cardwell can help students value group work in solving important problems.

   (B) Through the recycling project, Ms. Cardwell can help students understand the importance of listening to everyone's opinion.

   (C) Through the recycling project, Ms. Cardwell can help students learn the importance of careful research into a problem.

   (D) Through the recycling project, Ms. Cardwell can motivate students to attempt to find solutions to future problems by applying the same process.

DECISION SET ENDS HERE

DECISION SET BEGINS HERE

During July, Ms. Reynolds attended some district-sponsored staff development sessions on using technological resources as a teaching strategy. She is excited about adding these to her instruction. As soon as Ms. Reynolds receives her class list of students for the coming school year, she arranges time to visit with their teachers from the previous year. As the fourth-grade teacher, she wants information on the technological skill levels she can expect from her new group of students before she begins to plan for the coming school year.

Competency 008: *The teacher provides appropriate instruction that actively engages students in the learning process.*

34. How can Ms. Reynolds best use this information appropriately as she plans?

(A) Ms. Reynolds can use this information to determine the problems or weaknesses, as well as the strengths, these students have in technology so that she can teach specific lessons on the skills that need improvement.

(B) Ms. Reynolds can use this information to establish instructional groups based on the technological skill levels of the students as indicated by their third-grade teachers so that she can work to strengthen their weak areas.

(C) Ms. Reynolds can use this information to add to her planned content instruction lessons dedicated to areas of weakness in required technological skills and knowledge diagnosed by the past year's teachers.

(D) Ms. Reynolds can use this information to determine which technological skills and knowledge required by the state her students have not yet achieved so that she can start the school year by asking for parental help in these areas.

Early in the school year Ms. Reynolds takes her fourth-graders to the school's media center to teach them about the resources available to them as they do research on animal habitats. She wants all her students to learn to use the media center's computer stations and technology-based resources for their research. To this end, Ms. Reynolds demonstrates to her class how to use the available resources, which include books, journals and magazines, videotapes and CDs, interactive CD-ROMs, and the Internet.

Competency 003: *The teacher understands procedures for designing effective and coherent instruction and assessment based on appropriate learning goals and objectives.*

35. What is the most important benefit of instructing these students in the use of these resources?

   (A) This instruction assists these students in developing higher-level thinking skills.
   (B) This instruction promotes a sense of personal accomplishment in these students.
   (C) This instruction enables Ms. Reynolds to meet the needs of each individual student.
   (D) This instruction allows students to work in groups as they share resources.

Competency 009: *The teacher incorporates the effective use of technology to plan, organize, deliver, and evaluate instruction for all students.*

36. Because the number of computers with Internet access is limited, Ms. Reynolds schedules several days for online research to ensure that all who wish to use this resource have an opportunity to do so. How can Ms. Reynolds best facilitate her students' work during this time?

   (A) Ms. Reynolds can make sure that each student knows how to bookmark useful URLs.
   (B) Ms. Reynolds can make sure that each student takes notes on the useful information they find.
   (C) Ms. Reynolds can make sure that each student prints all the pages from the sites they find useful.
   (D) Ms. Reynolds can make sure that each student designs a web quest to share useful sites with others.

37. While using an Internet search engine to locate information on the prairie dog, Susan discovers there are more than 3,000 entries on this topic. How can Ms. Reynolds best help Susan avoid tying up the computer as she searches through this huge number of entries?

   (A) Ms. Reynolds can instruct Susan to use another search engine to see if it reduces the number of entries.
   (B) Ms. Reynolds can have Susan conduct a second search within the entries located by this search engine.
   (C) Ms. Reynolds can conduct a second search for Susan to show her how to get a reasonable number of responses.
   (D) Ms. Reynolds can instruct Susan on ways to narrow her search terms to get a reasonable number of responses.

As Ms. Reynolds' students begin to plan their reports on animal habitats, three students approach her requesting permission to use technology as a major component of their final products. At this point Ms. Reynolds realizes she has only suggested paper-pencil type products such as reports and posters rather than some additional options such as Microsoft Powerpoint presentations and web quests.

Competency 003: *The teacher understands procedures for designing effective and coherent instruction and assessment based on appropriate learning goals and objectives.*

38. How can Ms. Reynolds best guide her students toward appropriate final projects useful for assessing their growth in obtaining both content knowledge and technological skills?

   (A) Ms. Reynolds can explain to all her students why she is modifying the original instructions she gave about the project to now include a required technological component.

   (B) Ms. Reynolds can indicate that she wants to know if technology was used in the research process and that technology is acceptable as a format for the final product.

   (C) Ms. Reynolds can remind the three students who asked to use technology in preparing their final products that the criteria she expects them to follow have been clearly indicated.

   (D) Ms. Reynolds can agree that technology can make this report more interesting and change the criteria to require all students to produce a technology-based final product.

DECISION SET ENDS HERE

DECISION SET BEGINS HERE

Mr. Parquet's fourth-grade students are a very diverse group. His special-needs student population includes gifted and talented students as well as content mastery students. He also has five limited English proficiency students who each speak a different native language. Mr. Parquet is also aware that in any given classroom, the Piagetian cognitive abilities/readiness of students can range over two or three grade levels.

Competency 001: *The teacher understands human developmental processes and applies this knowledge to plan instruction and ongoing assessment that motivate students and are responsive to their developmental characteristics and needs.*

39. How can Mr. Parquet best meet the needs of the range of cognitive variation found in his students?

    (A) Assign students to groups based on their cognitive development or readiness to make it easier for them to work successfully in small groups.
    (B) Assign student "study buddies" to help lower-level students achieve success by partnering them with higher-level students.
    (C) Target the instructional level toward the normal fourth-grade level of development and work with the students outside this range individually.
    (D) Use high-engagement instructional strategies such as hands-on activities and projects to introduce and provide instruction to all students.

40. Based on the research on Piagetian cognitive levels, which tasks should Mr. Parquet consider most appropriate as instructional strategies for raising the developmental or cognitive levels of his fourth-grade students?

    (A) Mr. Parquet's students should find individual research projects the most appropriate instructional strategy.
    (B) Mr. Parquet's students should find hands-on, concrete activities for small groups the most appropriate strategy.
    (C) Mr. Parquet's fourth-grade students should find individual reading and discussion of the textbook the most appropriate instructional strategy.
    (D) Mr. Parquet's fourth-graders should find teacher lectures and taking class notes the most appropriate instructional strategy.

Competency 002: *The teacher understands student diversity and knows how to plan learning experiences and design assessments that are responsive to differences among students and that promote all students' learning.*

41. What is *most* important as Mr. Parquet considers how to effectively adapt his instructional strategies as he plans for his special-needs students?

    (A) Mr. Parquet's instructional strategies must ensure that no group of students is singled out and made to feel different or isolated from the other students.

    (B) Mr. Parquet's instructional strategies must ensure that each group of students has ample time to interact with other students at a similar cognitive level.

    (C) Mr. Parquet's instructional strategies must ensure that students occasionally work individually but focus more on collaborative efforts to ensure the success of all students.

    (D) Mr. Parquet's instructional strategies must ensure that students are allowed to select instructional activities based on individual interests and strengths.

Competency 003: *The teacher understands procedures for designing effective and coherent instruction and assessment based on appropriate learning goals and objectives.*

42. Mr. Parquet asks for the state's assessment results from last year. He wants this information as he continues to plan for this school year. How can Mr. Parquet best use this information appropriately as he plans?

    (A) Mr. Parquet can use this information to diagnose problems or weaknesses these students have with the style of assessment used so that he can work to improve their testing skills in fourth grade.

    (B) Mr. Parquet can use this information to establish instructional groups based on the skill levels of the students as shown by the state assessment so that he can work to strengthen their weak areas.

    (C) Mr. Parquet can use this information to focus instruction on areas of weakness in skills and knowledge diagnosed by the past year's test while also addressing the required fourth-grade TEKS.

    (D) Mr. Parquet can use this information to determine which skills and knowledge required by the state his students have not yet achieved so that he can ask for parental help in strengthening these areas.

Mr. Parquet wants all his students to learn to design and conduct simple science experiments. Mr. Parquet wants students to improve their skill levels, their confidence, and their attitudes toward science.

Competency 002: *The teacher understands student diversity and knows how to plan learning experiences and design assessments that are responsive to differences among students and that promote all students' learning.*

43. How can Mr. Parquet best achieve his goals, especially with his lower-achieving students?

    (A) Mr. Parquet can require all students to design and conduct an original science experiment, which will be shared with the class. Every science experiment will be critiqued for its effective use of scientific methods.

    (B) Mr. Parquet can break scientific experimental design into short, clear steps that guide students through the process. Every science class will have some time set aside for working on the project and receiving teacher assistance.

    (C) Mr. Parquet can partner higher-achieving students with lower-achieving students to allow both groups of students to grow, especially if he encourages flexibility in student participation and roles.

    (D) Mr. Parquet can require each student to participate in daily lessons focused on teaching the skills needed to design and conduct experiments. Each student must master each skill or repeat the lesson until mastery is reached.

Mr. Parquet intends to use learning journals on a regular basis to allow his students to practice writing skills in context by integrating these skills into other content areas. He selects the following reflection questions for students to address in their learning journals.

- How did the video we saw on Thomas Edison and his persistence as he worked to invent the light bulb help you with this project?
- What are three things you learned by designing and conducting your own experiment?

Competency 004: *The teacher understands learning processes and factors that impact student learning and demonstrates this knowledge by planning effective, engaging instruction and appropriate assessments.*

44. These questions best reflect Mr. Parquet's use of a learning journal to implement which learning principle?

    (A) Knowledge of how a student learns reinforces that student's ability to learn.

    (B) Actively processing relationships between information in context reinforces learning.

    (C) Meaningful learning occurs from the self-motivated acquisition of knowledge and skills.

    (D) Students who formulate generalizations enhance their learning of the content.

Competency 005: *The teacher knows how to establish a classroom climate that fosters learning, equity, and excellence and uses this knowledge to create a physical and emotional environment that is safe and productive.*

45. Mr. Parquet wants to use the students' learning journals to evaluate classroom climate. Which question is most important for Mr. Parquet to consider when reading the learning journals?

    (A) Is there ongoing individual accountability for student learning in my classroom?
    (B) Is my educational philosophy clearly reflected in my daily instructional styles?
    (C) Are my students actively engaged and intellectually stimulated by my lessons?
    (D) Are the learning experiences my students encounter varied to meet the needs of all?

As Mr. Parquet reads his students' journals, he finds a significant variation in the use of capitalization and in punctuation skills. He assumes that this is due to their varied backgrounds and exposure to prior learning opportunities. He also considers that carelessness in applying these skills during journal writing may be a factor. Mr. Parquet knows it is his responsibility to ensure that all his students reach an appropriate level of competency in these common language arts skills.

46. What assessment system will be most effective for Mr. Parquet in creating a positive and supportive environment for all his students as he guides them toward achieving an acceptable level of competency in these and other fourth-grade writing skills?

    (A) Both teacher and peer assessments of performance of the required skills are included in feedback to students.
    (B) Students are assigned appropriate and varied assessment standards for skills based on their ability groups.
    (C) Progress, process, and product are all part of the assessment used to determine a student's skill level.
    (D) Tests include questions at varying levels of difficulty to ensure that all students encounter some success.

DECISION SET ENDS HERE

DECISION SET BEGINS HERE

Ms. Goldman is frustrated by the lack of self-control exhibited by her third-graders during the first three weeks of school. She often uses group activities as one of her instructional strategies and is concerned that several of her students do not fully participate with their groups. Ms. Goldman decides to alter the management system for her class. She clearly displays a card for each student at the front of the room. Every day begins with all the cards on green. She asks individual students to turn their cards from green to yellow to red each time they disrupt class, are off task during group work, or break a class rule. If a student's card is still green at the end of the day, the student receives a reward or a special privilege. If the card is yellow, there is no reward or privilege. A red card results in a message being sent home asking for parental assistance.

Competency 006: *The teacher understands strategies for creating an organized and productive learning environment and for managing student behavior.*

47. Why is this strategy appropriate for use with young students?

(A) The visual of the green/yellow/red cards allows students to see how their day is progressing and encourages behaviors that will result in gaining the desired privilege.

(B) The visual of the green/yellow/red cards allows other students to see how their classmates are behaving so that they can help each other to gain a desired privilege.

(C) The visual of the green/yellow/red cards indicates to students when Ms. Goldman is about to reach the end of her patience with the class and withdraw the privilege.

(D) The visual of the green/yellow/red cards allows students to overcome their resistance to pleasing adult authority figures and work toward gaining the privilege.

48. What additional strategy can Ms. Goldman implement to help encourage students to keep their cards green?

(A) Ms. Goldman can monitor the groups and quietly remind students they need to participate in their groups or risk having a card turned.

(B) Ms. Goldman can place students with low levels of participation together and discuss how the color of their cards will be impacted if they do not work together.

(C) Ms. Goldman can assign clear rotating roles where the success of the task depends on each student meeting the responsibilities of their role.

(D) Ms. Goldman can assign roles based on skills and abilities and use an individual's group participation to determine the color of the student's card.

As Ms. Goldman plans a unit on open and closed systems, she wants to select teaching strategies that will best assist her students in understanding this important basic science concept.

Competency 008: *The teacher provides appropriate instruction that actively engages students in the learning process.*

49. Which teaching strategy would her third-grade students find most helpful in learning this concept?

    (A) She should begin the lesson with a K-W-L chart to explore prior knowledge of the topic and include a reminder to revisit the L-column of the chart.

    (B) She should ensure that time is built into the unit for her to revisit and repeat these concepts and also allow time for student questions to enhance clarity.

    (C) She should begin the lesson with a list of relevant terms students will encounter during the unit and have them define each as they occur.

    (D) She should share concrete examples in the context of her students' life experiences and ask them to contribute additional familiar examples.

Competency 007: *The teacher understands and applies principles and strategies for communicating effectively in varied teaching and learning contexts.*

50. How could Ms. Goldman encourage her students to think more in depth and have more positive feelings about their knowledge of open and closed systems?

    (A) She could assign individual students different systems and have them write a rationale for why the assigned system is open or closed.

    (B) She could assign teams of students three systems and have them discuss why each system is considered open or closed.

    (C) She could have individual students think of three examples of systems and identify and discuss each system as open or closed.

    (D) She could have teams of students think of three examples of systems, identify each as open or closed, and explain their rationale or evidence.

After she discusses what procedures to follow to successfully complete an experiment, Ms. Goldman routinely asks her third-graders to write an explanation of what they think is the objective or point of the experiment they are about to do and in what order they will need to follow the procedures to successfully complete it.

Competency 008: *The teacher provides appropriate instruction that actively engages students in the learning process.*

51. What is the greatest benefit of this advance writing activity for students?

    (A) This writing activity gives all students an equal opportunity for success with the assignment because they now all have the same background.

    (B) This writing activity assists students in developing a conceptual framework for the purpose of the experiment and guides their learning.

    (C) This writing activity increases the chance that all students will follow the directions and the experiments will have the desired outcome.

    (D) This writing activity increases student focus on the lesson and allows them to work quickly and efficiently because confusion is reduced.

Ms. Goldman is working with her students on clarity in writing as they complete their science logs. She has each student complete their log on open and closed systems and give it to a peer for editing. Ms. Goldman looks at all the edited logs before returning them to the writer. In one log, she writes, "I agree with your peer editor that some of your sentences are hard to follow or understand. You are using many pronouns, which is good, but with limited nouns. This might not be appropriate for clarity with your peers. How can you improve your clarity?"

Competency 010: *The teacher monitors student performance and achievement; provides students with timely, high-quality feedback; and responds flexibly to promote learning for all students.*

52. Based on the research on instructional feedback, what will be the most likely response to this note?

    (A) The comment to the author of the science log will probably be ineffective in prompting improvement as the feedback gives a negative response about clear writing and does not give clear suggestions about how to make appropriate changes.

    (B) The comment to the author of the science log will probably be effective in prompting improvement as the feedback gives a positive response about using pronouns, which counterbalances being told that some of the sentences are hard to understand.

    (C) The comment to the author of the science log will probably be effective in prompting improvement as the feedback encourages the writer to find ways to improve, which counterbalances being told that some sentences are hard to understand.

    (D) The comment to the author of the science log will probably be effective in prompting improvement as the feedback gives a negative response about using pronouns and allows freedom in deciding how to make appropriate changes.

53. What is most important for Ms. Goldman to consider if she wants to design an appropriate teacher-made test?

   (A) The test should use both objective and performance assessment questions.
   (B) The test should align with objectives and content learning opportunities.
   (C) The test should contain questions at several levels of difficulty.
   (D) The test should yield a bell curve as the range of student scores.

The final product for Ms. Goldman's unit on open and closed systems will be a multimedia presentation created by groups of students. She has established clear content requirements for the end product so that content will receive a greater emphasis from the students than presentation design.

Competency 009: *The teacher incorporates the effective use of technology to plan, organize, deliver, and evaluate instruction for all students.*

54. How can Ms. Goldman most effectively encourage an appropriate balance between content and presentation design as the final product is developed?

   (A) Ms. Goldman and the students should design a rubric that clearly establishes the content and design expectations and the balance between these two components before groups begin the project.
   (B) Ms. Goldman should share a list of acceptable product design suggestions that groups can select from after the content part of the project is completed to help restrict the multimedia design aspect of the project.
   (C) Groups must submit a draft of the content portion of the project to the teacher for approval before beginning work on the multimedia project design component, which must also be approved by Ms. Goldman.
   (D) Ms. Goldman should provide daily reminders of the required components and the expected balance between content and project design as groups work on completing the required multimedia product.

DECISION SET ENDS HERE

DECISION SET BEGINS HERE

Dr. Barstow, the principal of Jefferson Elementary School, believes school personnel such as administrators, teachers, and paraprofessionals should be partners working together with parents/guardians to ensure the best possible education for all students. He insists on hiring only personnel who share this philosophy.

Competency 011: *The teacher understands the importance of family involvement in children's education and knows how to interact and communicate effectively with families.*

55. What would be the best information for the teachers working with Dr. Barstow to share with their students' families at the beginning of the year to help create this partnership?

(A) Teachers should discuss with the families the expectations for student academic performance and how by working together they can guide students toward success.

(B) Teachers should inform the families about the instructional resources available to students and about the family's role in the major projects that will be required during the coming school year.

(C) Teachers should explain to the family the relationship between the grades on the teacher-made tests the school will use during the year and the scores on state-required tests.

(D) Teachers should inform families about the developmental levels and traits of elementary grade students and how these traits impact the coming learning opportunities.

Ms. Farquhar is a sixth-grade teacher who strongly agrees with Dr. Barstow's educational philosophy. She also believes it is vitally important for students to be able to apply math concepts learned in school to their daily lives. Because of this and her strong belief in the home-school partnership goal of Jefferson Elementary School, she wants to establish family math time at home.

56. What is the best way for Ms. Farquhar to motivate the families of her sixth-graders to help her in establishing and facilitating family math time?

(A) Ms. Farquhar should send home a textbook and a description sheet explaining the importance of family math time and ask that it become a weekly part of family interactions.

(B) Ms. Farquhar should send home notification of a meeting at which the value of family math time, instructional methods used in school, and assessment rubrics will be explained.

(C) Ms. Farquhar should send an invitation to participate in family math time, an explanation of the requirements, and activities for the family to complete together at home with students.

(D) Ms. Farquhar should invite families to evening seminars to introduce family math time, to discuss ways to participate, and to explain how their participation can help their students.

57. After two months of family math time a parent calls and schedules a conference with Ms. Farquhar. What is the best way to ensure a productive conference?

(A) When the parent arrives, Ms. Farquhar should clearly and calmly state her perspective and then listen to the parent's response.

(B) Ms. Farquhar should prepare herself before the parent arrives by determining why this parent wants a conference when the others do not.

(C) Ms. Farquhar should be friendly as she greets the parent and then listen closely to his or her concerns and perspective before responding.

(D) When the parent arrives, Ms. Farquhar should clearly agree that a conference is needed and indicate that she is glad the parent is proactive.

Ms. Farquhar receives a transfer student, Ernest. After two months she decides to see if he qualifies for special education services and refers him for testing.

Competency 013: *The teacher understands and adheres to legal and ethical requirements for educators and is knowledgeable of the structure of education in Texas.*

58. What is Ms. Farquhar's legal responsibility so that Ernest can have this type of evaluation?

(A) She must share her concerns with and obtain written permission from Ernest's parents/guardians for an evaluation.

(B) She must have clear documentation of the reasons for her concerns about Ernest before she can seek an evaluation.

(C) She must visit with Ernest's other teachers and his parents/guardians to share her concerns before proceeding.

(D) She must notify the district special education director and Ernest's parents/guardians before seeking an evaluation.

Patty is a visually impaired student who has been mainstreamed into Ms. Farquhar's class. Ms. Farquhar is beginning a unit on solid geometry, which will be very visual, and so she arranges a meeting with Patty's special education teacher.

Competency 012: *The teacher enhances professional knowledge and skills by effectively interacting with other members of the educational community and participating in various types of professional activities.*

59. What assistance is appropriate for her to ask the special education teacher for as she plans this highly visual unit?

    (A) She asks that Patty be moved from math class to the resource room for individual help with this highly visual unit.
    (B) She asks that Patty be moved from math class to the resource room for individual help with a different unit to replace this highly visual unit.
    (C) She asks the special education teacher to attend math class daily with Patty to assist her with this highly visual unit.
    (D) She asks for help in designing lessons depending on other senses to identify the geometric shapes so that Patty can participate as much as possible.

About two-thirds of the way through the solid geometry unit, Ms. Farquhar observes several students being inattentive and looking puzzled, and so she gives an objective quiz the next day. All the students do poorly on the quiz even though she has addressed all the tested information. She determines that there is not any one question that everyone missed but that all the students missed some questions.

60. What is the most important step for Ms. Farquhar to take now?

    (A) Ms. Farquhar must decide how to refocus her students' attention on the remainder of the unit so that they can pass the unit test.
    (B) Ms. Farquhar must speak with the students about their responsibilities to learn the information she presents in class to earn good grades.
    (C) Ms. Farquhar must determine an effective way to reteach the material already covered before completing the unit and giving the unit test.
    (D) Ms. Farquhar must determine ways to add daily formative assessments so that she can determine if her students will be able to pass the unit test.

DECISION SET ENDS HERE

DECISION SET BEGINS HERE

Ms. Pasternak is in her second year of teaching fifth grade at Bowman Elementary School. She has high student expectations and knows she plays a major role in helping her students meet her expectations. One of Ms. Pasternak's goals for her mathematics class is that "The learner will demonstrate an understanding of the concept of area."

Competency 003: *The teacher understands procedures for designing effective and coherent instruction and assessment based on appropriate learning goals and objectives.*

61. What would be the best way for Ms. Pasternak to assess student understanding of this goal?

    (A) An effective assessment would be to have the students compute the area of 25–35 squares and rectangles.
    (B) An effective assessment would be to have the students determine how much carpet would be needed to carpet an L-shaped hallway.
    (C) An effective assessment would be to have the students define area and answer ten questions about the area of squares and rectangles.
    (D) An effective assessment would be to have the students compute and compare the perimeter and area of five squares and rectangles.

Ms. Pasternak walks around her classroom as her students work on an inquiry math lesson. This allows her to facilitate the activity, maintain class discipline, and guide the students' learning through question-and-answer techniques.

Competency 008: *The teacher provides appropriate instruction that actively engages students in the learning process.*

62. Which one of the following can best be said about Ms. Pasternak?

    (A) Ms. Pasternak employs various instructional techniques throughout her lessons.
    (B) Ms. Pasternak presents content in a meaningful way for effective student learning.
    (C) Ms. Pasternak encourages self-motivation in her students by allowing choices.
    (D) Ms. Pasternak engages in continuous monitoring of her instructional effectiveness.

As part of an integrated unit on Japan, Ms. Pasternak asks students to fold their paper in half as the first stage of an origami activity. She is frustrated to see that some students folded their paper lengthwise and others by width.

Competency 007: *The teacher understands and applies principles and strategies for communicating effectively in varied teaching and learning contexts.*

63. How could Ms. Pasternak have made her directions clearer?

    (A) Ms. Pasternak should have modeled the folding technique for the students.
    (B) Ms. Pasternak should have supplied written directions for folding the paper.
    (C) Ms. Pasternak should have supplied a picture of a correctly folded paper.
    (D) Ms. Pasternak should give each instruction only after the prior step has been done correctly.

Ten-year-old Michael decided to make a Microsoft PowerPoint presentation for his book report for the Japanese unit. Two weeks before the book report due date, he asked to drop the Microsoft PowerPoint project and just write a report. Ms. Pasternak would not allow Michael to change his project but offered guidance toward success with his originally chosen presentation style.

Competency 001: *The teacher understands human developmental processes and applies this knowledge to plan instruction and ongoing assessment that motivate students and are responsive to their developmental characteristics and needs.*

64. Which of the following is illustrated by Ms. Pasternak's decision not to allow the switch?

    (A) The teacher recognizes emotional factors affecting the development of fifth-grade students.
    (B) The teacher recognizes the importance of helping students complete a self-initiated project.
    (C) The teacher recognizes that the sudden physical growth at this age impacts cognitive growth.
    (D) The teacher recognizes the stages of emotional and cognitive development in ten year olds.

Ms. Pasternak plans to have her students work in pairs to produce a final project for the integrated Japan unit using at least three available technologies. Her goal is to have her students experience closure on the unit, demonstrate an improvement in their technological skills, and share major points they have learned during the unit in an interesting format. She speaks with a colleague about what her rubric should be like for this final project.

Competency 009: *The teacher incorporates the effective use of technology to plan, organize, deliver, and evaluate instruction for all students.*

65. Which of the following criteria should be included in an appropriately designed rubric for students' technology-produced products?

(A) An appropriately designed rubric for students' technology-produced products should include criteria on design, difficulty, creativity, and relevance to the assignment.

(B) An appropriately designed rubric for students' technology-produced products should include criteria on design, content delivery, and relevance to the assignment.

(C) An appropriately designed rubric for students' technology-produced products should include criteria on difficulty, grammar, spelling, and design.

(D) An appropriately designed rubric for students' technology-produced products should include criteria on creativity, grammar, spelling, and design.

DECISION SET ENDS HERE

DECISION SET BEGINS HERE

Ms. Davis is an experienced EC teacher who has been asked by her principal to mentor the first-year EC teacher assigned to the classroom across the hall. Ms. Davis explains to her new colleague that she plans her lessons as short vignettes in which she continuously alternates strategies and keeps students actively engaged.

Competency 004: *The teacher understands learning processes and factors that impact student learning and demonstrates this knowledge by planning effective, engaging instruction and appropriate assessments.*

66. What does this demonstrate about Ms. Davis' knowledge of how students this age best learn?

    (A) Ms. Davis recognizes how much more effectively her students will learn if her teaching is as active and engaging as watching TV.

    (B) Ms. Davis recognizes how much more effectively her students will learn if her teaching acknowledges how movement impacts students' learning.

    (C) Ms. Davis recognizes how much more effectively her students will learn if her inquiry teaching stimulates both learning and retention in students.

    (D) Ms. Davis recognizes how much more effectively her students will learn if her teaching keeps the students motivated by refocusing their attention.

Ms. Davis also shares with her new colleague that she has many centers in her EC classroom because she wishes to help her students become independent. Several of her centers allow for side-by-side play.

Competency 006: *The teacher understands strategies for creating an organized and productive learning environment and for managing student behavior.*

67. What can be said about Ms. Davis' understanding of her students?

    (A) Ms. Davis applies theories and techniques to manage student behavior.

    (B) Ms. Davis recognizes how important it is to create blocks of time for play.

    (C) Ms. Davis understands the importance of students monitoring their own behavior.

    (D) Ms. Davis has appropriate expectations of student interactions at the EC level.

Four-year-old Misty prefers playing with blocks by herself. Ms. Johnson, Misty's mother, is concerned because Misty is so unwilling to interact with others or to share. Ms. Davis assures Mrs. Johnson that Misty is fine and will learn to share.

Competency 001: *The teacher understands human developmental processes and applies this knowledge to plan instruction and ongoing assessment that motivate students and are responsive to their developmental characteristics and needs.*

68. What does this response indicate about Ms. Davis' opinion of Misty?

    (A) The response indicates that the teacher recognizes that Misty is presently developmentally delayed.
    (B) The response indicates that the teacher believes it is better to leave Misty alone and thus avoid conflict.
    (C) The response indicates that the teacher knows that Misty is still in the solitary play stage of development.
    (D) The response indicates that the teacher believes Misty has limited verbal skills and so avoids interactions.

Ms. Davis has another parent conference in 20 minutes. She is able to print a complete profile of the student being discussed, as well as copies of e-mails exchanged with the parents.

Competency 009: *The teacher incorporates the effective use of technology to plan, organize, deliver, and evaluate instruction for all students.*

69. What does this ability show about Ms. Davis?

    (A) This shows that Ms. Davis uses technology to perform administrative tasks.
    (B) This shows that Ms. Davis works with a support staff to enhance communication.
    (C) This shows that Ms. Davis applies techniques related to student management.
    (D) This shows that Ms. Davis manages time effectively to maximize student learning.

DECISION SET ENDS HERE

DECISION SET BEGINS HERE

Mr. Stanford and Ms. Shultize are the science team for Blazon Elementary School. Between them, they teach science to all the students. Ms. Shultize has five years of experience, and Mr. Stanford is in his third year. They meet to plan together but do not always agree or reach a consensus and so often go in their own directions.

Competency 003: *The teacher understands procedures for designing effective and coherent instruction and assessment based on appropriate learning goals and objectives.*

70. Mr. Stanford has the following timeline shown in his plan for a sixth-grade lesson:

    8:30–8:35 Introduce cohesion
    8:36–9:16 Directed teaching of cohesion
    9:17–9:27 Guided practice using cohesion activities
    9:28–9:45 Begin independent practice/homework if not completed

    What lack does this timeline indicate in Mr. Stanford's understanding of planning?

    (A) Mr. Stanford does not have an appropriate understanding of the value of allocated time, student reflection, and participation in closure.
    (B) Mr. Stanford does not have an appropriate understanding of the many steps and details needed in an appropriately designed lesson plan.
    (C) Mr. Stanford does not have an understanding of the appropriate time that needs to be allocated for effective introduction of a new topic.
    (D) Mr. Stanford does not have an appropriate understanding of the time needed to complete guided practice/homework.

Every day Mr. Stanford's students come into the room, place their homework in the homework basket, and then complete the brain-twister problem of the day for their grade level. Brain-twister problems for all grade levels are posted on the board daily. If students have time, they can attempt a brain-twister problem for a more advanced grade for extra points.

Competency 006: *The teacher understands strategies for creating an organized and productive learning environment and for managing student behavior.*

71. What does this show about Mr. Stanford?

    (A) Mr. Stanford recognizes the value of repetition in learning.
    (B) Mr. Stanford recognizes the importance of planned movement activities.
    (C) Mr. Stanford recognizes the value of routines in the learning environment.
    (D) Mr. Stanford recognizes the educational value of daily assignments.

Ms. Shultize has her fifth-grade students explore various hands-on activities to observe the Bernoulli principle before she discusses it with them. After debriefing the students, she shows a video of the first attempts at flight. She then has the students work in pairs to write a story giving the inventors of the first unsuccessful flying machines suggestions on how to improve their machines.

Competency 004: *The teacher understands learning processes and factors that impact student learning and demonstrates this knowledge by planning effective, engaging instruction and appropriate assessments.*

72. What is the main point that this demonstrates about how Ms. Shultize plans for her students?

   (A) Ms. Shultize knows she must analyze her success as a teacher based on students' learning of the content.

   (B) Ms. Shultize knows she must incorporate students' different approaches to learning into her instructional practices.

   (C) Ms. Shultize knows that to produce student learning she must plan instruction that promotes student motivation.

   (D) Ms. Shultize knows that for learning to occur she must stimulate reflection on the lesson among students.

Ms. Shultize always asks herself how science lessons she plans to meet the needs of her students might be interpreted by the various cultures represented in her class.

Competency 002: *The teacher understands student diversity and knows how to plan learning experiences and design assessments that are responsive to differences among students and that promote all students' learning.*

73. What is the primary reason that this is such an important consideration for her?

   (A) It represents Ms. Shultize's respect for students with diverse backgrounds and needs who have an innate desire to learn.

   (B) It represents Ms. Shultize's commitment to plan and adapt lessons to address all students' diverse backgrounds and needs.

   (C) It represents Ms. Shultize's understanding of needs caused by the socio-economic differences in her students.

   (D) It represents Ms. Shultize's understanding of student learning needs and her desire to address their preferences.

Mr. Stanford and Ms. Shultize are meeting to plan second-grade science lessons for the next week and are in disagreement again. Ms. Shultize refuses to teach lessons in the style Mr. Stanford has selected. She tells him that research shows that most second-grade students are in either the preoperational or the concrete operational stage of development.

Competency 001: *The teacher understands human developmental processes and applies this knowledge to plan instruction and ongoing assessment that motivate students and are responsive to their developmental characteristics and needs.*

74. Based on this information, which instructional method would be most appropriate for them to use?

    (A) Hands-on, concrete learning activities would be most appropriate for second-graders.
    (B) Lecture and class discussion activities would be most appropriate for second-graders.
    (C) Reading and class discussion activities would be most appropriate for second-graders.
    (D) Teacher demonstrations for instruction would be most appropriate for second-graders.

DECISION SET ENDS HERE

DECISION SET BEGINS HERE

Ms. Donnell considers it important to reflect on her teaching and to look for patterns in order to grow. In an effort to examine her patterns of teacher-student interaction, she videos her class over three days. Ms. Donnell is concerned that the same students consistently respond first to her questions. She also notices that she calls on students with raised hands most often.

Competency 007: *The teacher understands and applies principles and strategies for communicating effectively in varied teaching and learning contexts.*

75. What would be a better questioning technique to engage other students?

   (A) Ms. Donnell should state the student's name and then ask the question.
   (B) Ms. Donnell should state the question first and then say the student's name.
   (C) Ms. Donnell should only call on students who do not have their hands raised.
   (D) Ms. Donnell should use only a think-pair-share strategy for questions.

Competency 003: *The teacher understands procedures for designing effective and coherent instruction and assessment based on appropriate learning goals and objectives.*

76. Ms. Donnell requests and is given the fifth-grade TAKS results for each of her sixth-grade students. What would be the most appropriate use of this information?

   (A) Ms. Donnell could use this information to assign students to the appropriate cooperative groups.
   (B) Ms. Donnell could use this information to divide students into appropriate groups for reading instruction.
   (C) Ms. Donnell could use this information to plan remediation lessons for students needing additional help.
   (D) Ms. Donnell could use this information to recommend the appropriate students for inclusion in the gifted class.

Ms. Donnell assigns her sixth-grade students to cooperative learning groups that will work together over the next month. Each group contains four students, and each group is comprised of one higher-ability student, two average-ability students, and one lower-ability student.

Competency 005: *The teacher knows how to establish a classroom climate that fosters learning, equity, and excellence and uses this knowledge to create a physical and emotional environment that is safe and productive.*

77. What does this grouping pattern illustrate about Ms. Donnell's goals?

    (A) This grouping pattern shows her understanding of the characteristics of her students as they cooperate.
    (B) This grouping pattern is a means of conveying high expectations to all the students in the class.
    (C) This grouping pattern places the emphasis on collaboration and interaction among students of different abilities.
    (D) This grouping pattern shows her respect for the different levels of students' rights and dignity.

After assigning students to the groups, Ms. Donnell assigns each student a role (i.e., scribe, reporter, observer). Each role is necessary because if a student fails to fulfill his or her assigned role, the group's task cannot be successfully completed.

78. Which of Ms. Donnell's beliefs about effective instruction does this best illustrate?

    (A) Assigning roles is a way for Ms. Donnell to convey respect for diversity in her students' abilities.
    (B) Assigning roles is a way for Ms. Donnell to create a safe environment to facilitate student learning.
    (C) Assigning roles is a way for Ms. Donnell to produce active engagement in learning for all students.
    (D) Assigning roles is a way for Ms. Donnell to present instruction that respects each student's dignity.

In addition to cooperative groups, Ms. Donnell also wants to use problem-based learning strategies with her sixth-grade students.

Competency 007: *The teacher understands and applies principles and strategies for communicating effectively in varied teaching and learning contexts.*

79. What is the best way for Ms. Donnell to do this?

    (A) Have students practice solving a small problem before introducing a larger problem.
    (B) Introduce several ways to solve a problem before letting students try each one.
    (C) Allow students to select a problem and attempt to solve it without giving them any help.
    (D) Allow students to create their own problem and solution.

Competency 009: *The teacher incorporates the effective use of technology to plan, organize, deliver, and evaluate instruction for all students.*

80. Ms. Donnell wants to design a web quest as part of her next instructional unit. What are the appropriate parts of a web quest that she must include?

(A) A web quest should have an introduction, research, a web activity, a reading, and a conclusion.

(B) A web quest should have an introduction, a task, a process, an evaluation, and a conclusion.

(C) A web quest should have an introduction, a task, a reading, an evaluation, and a conclusion.

(D) A web quest should have an introduction, a reading, a task, a process, and a conclusion.

Competency 010: *The teacher monitors student performance and achievement; provides students with timely, high-quality feedback; and responds flexibly to promote learning for all students.*

81. When is the best time for Ms. Donnell to provide students with a rubric for their assigned web quest?

(A) Rubrics should be provided when the web quest is assigned so that students will know the expectations from the beginning.

(B) Rubrics should be provided after the students have had time to understand the web quest project, but before it is due.

(C) Rubrics should be discussed from the beginning and provided in writing at least a week before the web quest project is due.

(D) Rubrics should be provided when feedback is given on the web quest unless requested earlier by a student or the student's parents.

DECISION SET ENDS HERE

DECISION SET BEGINS HERE

During Mr. Wong's first year of teaching he felt that he did not keep parents adequately informed about school events and their students' educational progress. He is determined that he will grow as a teacher the second year by meeting this and other challenges. To this end, Mr. Wong arranges an early morning and an evening meeting monthly that families can attend to hear about class events, see examples of students' work, and discuss ways of becoming more involved.

Competency 011: *The teacher understands the importance of family involvement in children's education and knows how to interact and communicate effectively with families.*

82. What does this demonstrate about Mr. Wong?

    (A) Mr. Wong is determined to communicate effectively with families.
    (B) Mr. Wong is determined to conduct effective parent conferences.
    (C) Mr. Wong is determined to recognize the diverse needs of all families.
    (D) Mr. Wong is determined to effectively use family support resources.

Competency 012: *The teacher enhances professional knowledge and skills by effectively interacting with other members of the educational community and participating in various types of professional activities.*

83. Mr. Wong shares with his mentor that he is having a hard time engaging his fourth-grade students in inquiry lessons. What suggestion might his mentor make to best help Mr. Wong?

    (A) Observe inquiry lessons taught by teachers skilled in inquiry instruction.
    (B) Take a methods course at a nearby college or attend a staff development session on inquiry.
    (C) Do not plan to use inquiry lessons until you have gained more teaching experience.
    (D) Keep planning and trying inquiry lessons because practice is needed to gain skills.

Mr. Wong plans to have both his classes read *Charlie and the Chocolate Factory* in literature circles, but the books he has ordered for the class have not arrived yet. Rather than delay the start, Mr. Wong makes two classroom sets of the story.

Competency 013: *The teacher understands and adheres to legal and ethical requirements for educators and is knowledgeable of the structure of education in Texas.*

84. What is the problem with this?

    (A) It violates copyright laws.
    (B) It violates publication laws.
    (C) It violates royalty laws.
    (D) It costs too much.

As he begins his literature circles, Mr. Wong discovers that part of the fourth-graders read *Charlie and the Chocolate Factory* last year, but others did not. This was also a problem last year, and Mr. Wong wants to solve this problem for future years.

Competency 012: *The teacher enhances professional knowledge and skills by effectively interacting with other members of the educational community and participating in various types of professional activities.*

85. What is the best way for Mr. Wong to handle this problem?

    (A) Ask the principal to reprimand the third-grade team for using a fourth-grade resource.
    (B) Complain to the district team leader and ask that the book be restricted to the fourth grade.
    (C) Have a vertical team meeting to share curriculum expectations for each grade level.
    (D) Have a vertical team meeting to complain about the overlap problems that occur.

Mr. Wong monitors his students during the state assessment test (TAKS). He notices Sherry marking an incorrect answer and bumps her desk slightly.

Competency 013: *The teacher understands and adheres to legal and ethical requirements for educators and is knowledgeable of the structure of education in Texas.*

86. What is the problem with this?

    (A) It shows Mr. Wong's inability to apply knowledge of educational guidelines during the state assessment.
    (B) It shows Mr. Wong's inability to adhere to legal requirements for data security during the state assessment.
    (C) It shows Mr. Wong's inability to advocate for all his students' success during the state assessment.
    (D) It shows Mr. Wong's inability to adhere to the required procedures for administering the state assessment.

DECISION SET ENDS HERE

DECISION SET BEGINS HERE

Mr. Bartholomew is an elementary principal. He is interviewing a prospective new teacher. If Mr. Bartholomew likes the answers given by the candidate to the following questions, he will ask his teaching leadership team to conduct another interview and recommend whether he should hire this teacher. Respond to each item as you think the prospective teacher should answer these questions.

Competency 009: *The teacher incorporates the effective use of technology to plan, organize, deliver, and evaluate instruction for all students.*

87. What is the best method for evaluating Internet information for use in class?

   (A) A teacher should rely on evaluations from professionals to choose appropriate sites.
   (B) A teacher should use online resources to help choose student-appropriate sites.
   (C) A teacher should use an approved evaluation tool as a guide to evaluate a site.
   (D) A teacher should use sources given four stars or higher on approved evaluations.

Competency 010: *The teacher monitors student performance and achievement; provides students with timely, high-quality feedback; and responds flexibly to promote learning for all students.*

88. What is the major value of reflective learning for students?

   (A) Reflective learning helps students respond flexibly to various situations.
   (B) Reflective learning helps students demonstrate knowledge of a topic.
   (C) Reflective learning helps students use self-assessment to guide their own learning.
   (D) Reflective learning helps students communicate assessment criteria to themselves.

Competency 011: *The teacher understands the importance of family involvement in children's education and knows how to interact and communicate effectively with families.*

89. Which of the following activities best engages legal caregivers in an aspect of the education program?

    (A) Creating take-home math manipulatives and giving instructions on how to use them.
    (B) Having caregivers help with nightly homework and record the amount of study time.
    (C) Having caregivers sign that they listened to a student read for 30 minutes a day.
    (D) Having caregivers attend math and/or science fairs or competitions at the school.

Competency 013: *The teacher understands and adheres to legal and ethical require-ments for educators and is knowledgeable of the structure of education in Texas.*

90. What does special education law require from regular classroom teachers of included students?

    (A) Regular classroom teachers can follow only the parts of the individual education plan (IEP) that fit the curriculum.
    (B) Regular classroom teachers must follow a child's IEP as written and accepted.
    (C) Regular classroom teachers are not responsible for writing or following IEPs.
    (D) Regular classroom teachers must have aides to help with included students.

DECISION SET ENDS HERE

Answer Key

SAMPLE TEST (GRADES EC-6)

Question Number	Correct Response	Competency	Question Number	Correct Response	Competency
1	C	001	26	D	013
2	A	001	27	D	013
3	A	001	28	B	007
4	B	002	29	A	004
5	D	002	30	A	005
6	C	003	31	C	004
7	B	003	32	B	005
8	A	004	33	D	008
9	D	004	34	C	008
10	C	005	35	C	003
11	A	005	36	A	009
12	D	006	37	D	009
13	B	007	38	B	003
14	C	007	39	D	001
15	B	008	40	B	001
16	A	008	41	A	002
17	C	009	42	C	003
18	D	009	43	B	002
19	D	010	44	B	004
20	A	010	45	C	005
21	C	011	46	C	005
22	B	011	47	A	006
23	A	012	48	C	006
24	C	012	49	D	008
25	B	013	50	D	007

Answer Key

SAMPLE TEST (GRADES EC-6)

Question Number	Correct Response	Competency	Question Number	Correct Response	Competency
51	B	008	71	C	006
52	A	010	72	B	004
53	B	010	73	B	002
54	A	009	74	A	001
55	A	011	75	B	007
56	D	011	76	C	003
57	C	011	77	C	005
58	A	013	78	C	005
59	D	012	79	A	007
60	C	012	80	B	009
61	B	003	81	A	010
62	D	008	82	C	011
63	A	007	83	A	012
64	B	001	84	A	013
65	B	009	85	C	012
66	D	004	86	D	013
67	D	006	87	C	009
68	C	001	88	C	010
69	A	009	89	A	011
70	A	003	90	B	013

CORRECT RESPONSES

1. **C** Lydia has not yet developed the ability to conserve substance and reverse liquid volume. (A) does not fit because the tea exists for Lydia whether it is visible (in the cups) or not (in the teapot), which would not be true if Lydia were at the sensorimotor stage of development. (B) is also an incorrect developmental stage for Lydia as children can reverse and conserve substances when they are at the concrete operational stage. (D) is unacceptable because there is no one-to-one correspondence present although one cup of tea per person could lead you to this answer if you were not clearly knowledgeable about Piagetian stages of development.

2. **A** The two Piagetian levels of development described in response (A) best fit this student range. The sensorimotor stage begins at about 17 months and ends at about age 7 when students transition into the concrete operational stage. The age ranges for each stage are approximate and dependent on multiple factors such as experiences and maturation rates. (B) pairs two stages in the appropriate order but reaches beyond the expected developmental stages for this student range. Students at the concrete operational stage tend to transition to the formal operational stage beginning at age 11 if all required conditions have been met, which is not a given with any set of students. (C) pairs two developmental stages that do not occur together. Students would transition from the sensorimotor into the preoperational rather than into the concrete operational. (D) has the problem of being accurate for a very developmentally delayed group of students as the transition between these two stages can be expected to begin at 17 months.

3. **A** Larry is egocentric and has not yet developed the ability to reverse thinking from his perspective. (C) does not fit because Larry is aware that he has a sister. She exists in his memory when not visible, which would not be true if he were still at the sensorimotor stage of development and had not developed object permanence. (D) is not an accurate developmental stage because children at the concrete operational child stage can reverse. (B) is unacceptable because there is no one-to-one correspondence.

4. **B** Texas requires each teacher to address the grade level TEKS with each student at that grade level. With these limited English proficiency students, this must be done while also addressing their English fluency. (A) demands less of these students. This would result in putting them behind academically as well as linguistically. Expecting less would result in students learning less. They are not less able students but students that need intensive work with English. (C) again eliminates the TEKS dictated by the state. A plan to use TEKS that demand concrete materials first to strengthen English and saves more abstract TEKS for later would be much wiser. (D) also leaves these students behind on the state-required TEKS while developing English skills. Both must be addressed at the same time to keep these students from falling behind. Research tells us that the further behind a student falls, the harder it is for that student to ever catch up.

5. **D** Feeling part of the class is an important step toward student-student inter-actions and important to language acquisition. It also allows students who do not perform well on one style of assessment to shine on another. This gives a more accurate picture of the learning of all the students. The self-assessment addressed in (A) is good, but it should not be restricted to the limited English proficiency students. Also, these students should not be singled out as being different from the rest of the class. The tutoring for any student that falls behind, as suggested in (B), is a good idea in general. Again, it should not be restricted to the limited English proficiency students nor should the assessment schedule label these students as being different from the rest of the class. (C) is an appro-priate way to gather some observational assessment data but should not be the only assessment used. The "study buddy" is also a second-grader and even with some training would not be able to perform the level of assessment needed.

6. **C** None of Mr. Beaumont's goals can be met if students are not attentive during this time, and interest and familiarity are two good motivators for attentiveness. (A) indicates that the development of listening skills is not an appropriate instructional activity, which is not the case. Students are able to absorb content information without being alert to doing so, but counting on this is not a valid instructional strategy. (B) assumes that third-grade students are able to inter-nalize new and unfamiliar information through abstract encounters such as reading and listening when research indicates they need direct experiences instead. The word patterns mentioned in (D) are good for this age group, although fourth grade is when most students fall in love with puns. The calming effect is more a result of the quiet and stillness that comes with effective listening and will not be lost by choosing exciting books that are highly motivating.

7. **B** The response to his verbal questions will allow him to informally assess stu-dents' responses to both the affective and cognitive domains of his goals. Only the affective domain goal is assessed by (A), and even then he may not get accu-rate information. Students may calmly accept three days without listening to him read although they would strongly protest stopping completely. (C) again focuses on the affective domain without addressing the cognitive domain goals. Wanting to switch books does not mean listening skills have not improved. Adding a formal written assessment, as suggested in (D), will give data on each student's cognitive and affective domain growth in terms of his goals but will be counterproductive for future growth as it causes stress in some students about the resulting evaluation.

8. **A** Mr. Stewart knows a stressful situation such as a move can produce a regres-sion to less advanced social skills and levels of play. There is a difference in edu-cational standards across states, but (B) implies there is also a difference in developmental standards across states, which is not accurate. (C) assumes a great deal based on a limited observation time (one week) for one student and is guar-anteed to get Paula's parents, the principal, and Paula's previous teacher and school upset with him. In (D) Mr. Stewart is making a poor judgment call in lowering his expectations after such a short time and in keeping information about Paula from her parents.

9. **D** Although (D) is correct, it would have been better for Paula if the student friends assigned to help her adjust had been implemented on the first day. Mr. Stewart is wise to allow both Paula and himself ample time before making a judgment about the accuracy of her label as socially advanced. It is also important that he not delay a conference about her adjustment or lack of adjustment too long. (A), (B), and (C) are guaranteed to add more stress for Paula and cause her to regress even more. Her parents will probably be at school to visit with him before he is ready to conference with them. (B) also implies Paula is choosing to regress, which is not the case. (C) also indicates that the parents and the prior school were incorrect in their assessment.

10. **C** Having students contribute ideas encourages accessing prior knowledge and participation. Seeing their contributions added to the chart encourages a sense of success and ownership. Doing so in a brainstorming format reduces pressure on individuals. Students will have a stronger motivation for participation in future lessons. These are all good beginnings for a unit. (A) suggests a touch of a putdown toward a knowledgeable student that should not be present. A strong background should be valued and encouraged while expecting it to become even stronger. (B) and (D) assume that each student will contribute something to the chart, but this is not a valid assumption. With the brainstorming format, some students may not add information even though they have prior knowledge of the topic. Although the teacher may think each student knows something about a topic, this is not a valid assumption. Students at any grade level have wide and varied background knowledge. The teacher has not indicated that each student is required to contribute to the chart.

11. **A** Research indicates that high teacher expectations are one of the most important variables for student success, but we also know that all students do not learn in the same way and so differentiated instruction is important. (B) and (C) open Ms. Gonzales to making faulty instructional decisions based on educational myths about an identified group's ability to learn. Although we have data suggesting that some groups face more learning challenges than others, we must be careful not to use this information as a rationale to expect less from students in these groups. Because all students were in the same school last year and are now in the same grade does not mean they all learned at the same rate or will respond to the same instructional strategies this year. If this were so, as (D) implies, there would not be a distinct group of students with significant academic needs in second grade. (B), (C), and (D) are basically the same. If Ms. Gonzales or any teacher expects students to do less for whatever reason, they will. Each of these responses would result in lower teacher expectations of students.

12. **D** Your goal should be to model or guide students toward acceptable ways to reach a mutually agreeable settlement without having to involve an adult each time. (A) and (B) imply that ending discord now will keep it from reappearing the moment the teacher is no longer involved. Settled is very different than ended. Attempting to establish fault causes the settlement to be delayed. It is not necessary for the teacher to clearly understand the problem, as indicated in

(C), as the teacher will not be issuing a settlement. The goal is for involved students to establish a settlement they agree will be fair to all involved.

13. **B** Shorter wait time and restating questions for the lower-achieving students are different behaviors. However, both signal all students that the teacher has lower expectation levels for some students. This reinforces a feeling of inability to achieve in lower-achieving students because it seems that the teacher doesn't expect success. (A) signals different levels of expectation but doesn't really cause resentment in either group unless it is toward the teacher who doesn't expect success from lower-achieving students. Students are aware that they must work to achieve. (C) is inaccurate because the lower-achieving students actually feel that they are more "on the spot" as they fail to respond to a perceived greater number of questions with less success. Altering wait time for different levels of achievement is not an effective manner of instructional differentiation as stated in (D). Both groups need equal wait time, and teachers need to allow effective wait time before restating a question or passing it to another student.

14. **C** Ms. Johnson should encourage her students to be creative and varied in their approaches to the problem. Many effective solutions are the desired outcome. (A), (B), and (D) all imply there is only one correct solution or answer and one best method for reaching it, which is counter to the problem-solving process.

15. **B** Ms. Swirczynski must determine why Tad is having difficulty before she can help. In (A), Tad will not feel ownership while dependent on Ms. Swirczynski. Ownership comes from independent success. (C) assumes a problem of focus or lack of attention with no supporting evidence. (D) sounds good but does not make sense. Reading with comprehension is a higher-order thinking skill. There is no evidence of why Tad is having difficulty.

16. **A** A variety of content topics and instructional methods are planned for the unit, which will allow students multiple learning opportunities. (B) addresses a common misunderstanding about integrated units. Integration allows for greater instructional time per subject, but this does not always mean less class time is required. Instead, integration means that the time is apportioned in different patterns to allow overlap between content areas. There is no information in the question to support the selection of either (C) or (D). The time required for the unit or pacing is not mentioned or indicated. Neither is individualized instruction.

17. **C** Very young children are naturally curious and have been exposed to computers in multiple environments such as homes and businesses. They are ready to begin to explore the uses and capabilities of computers. (A) and (B) focus on the lack of and need to develop fine motor skills in young children. Computers are motivating and can help with the practice needed to gain these skills but cannot and should not replace all the ways children developed fine motor skills before the invention of computers. Word processing with a computer is not an appropriate replacement for learning to write. We see the situation in (D) often as teachers attempt to teach a skill that is not developmentally appropriate

because the students will need it next year. Instead, it should be learned in the future when it is both needed and developmentally appropriate.

18. **D** The best instructional strategy is computer skills learned and practiced within the context of other content lessons such as math and language arts. The drill and practice software in (A) will help with rote memory content such as math facts but is not the best way to acquire computer skills. As (B) states, motivation enhances learning, but student-selected software results in a limited set of computer skills for his students. If all students are allowed freedom of choice, there will be no consistency in the skills set his students acquire. The direct instruction in (C) is important but should not occur in isolation from content knowledge—skill for the sake of a skill. Also, direct instruction should not be the purpose of each visit as learning is strengthened by practice and application.

19. **D** Observational data can tell you if the center runs smoothly and the instruction is clear. Either a formal or an informal assessment can indicate how effectively learning occurred. (A) can tell you how many and how often students visited a center but cannot indicate if the center was used appropriately or if learning occurred. Students may be visiting the center to play with a magnet or for some other invalid reason rather than participating within the instructional context designed into the center. (B) can give a clear picture of the students' response to the affective domain of the center but cannot give cognitive information about learning. (C) can give information about the center's effectiveness with adults and perceived effectiveness with children, but the center's adult designer already knows this.

20. **A** It gives Susan's mother a real task to allow increased involvement, which is what she wants, while providing Ms. Biggs with information she does not have access to as she does not see Susan outside school. Inviting Susan's mother into the classroom, as in (B) is appropriate for some reasons but not as an untrained observer of all the students. This role opens the door to several potential problems. Susan's altered behaviors due to her mom being in the room are just one example. (C) and (D) will offend Susan's mother, as they both clearly indicate that Susan's mom should go home and leave her education to the professionals. This incorrectly indicates that parental assistance and involvement are not needed to effectively educate a child.

21. **C** Parents become defensive if they feel that either their student or their family is being judged. This defensiveness interferes with finding a solution to the difficulties being experienced by the student. (A) shifts all responsibility to the parents, and (B) shifts all responsibility to the teacher, when a solution needs to be a joint effort among teacher, parents, and student. (D) does not acknowledge the greater knowledge a parent has about a student and ignores information that might be vital to understanding the reasons for the difficulties in school.

22. **B** It is apparent that Ms. Garcia can be reached by phone to schedule a conference but does not want to come to school. The teacher should conference by phone. The value lost by not conferencing face to face is outweighed by the

value of having a conference. In (A), Ms. Ming attempts to add guilt to Ms. Garcia as a motivation to attend the conference, yet she probably already feels badly about being asked to do something that is uncomfortable for her. (D) attempts to use Carmen to guilt Ms. Garcia into participating. There are many reasons parents are reluctant to attend school meetings. Clothing, language difficulties, lack of confidence, and intimidation are a few. To set a child against a parent is unprofessional. (C) makes a negative and unwarranted judgment.

23. **A** Mr. Grant needs to allow himself time to become a member of the community rather than an outside crusader who has arrived to solve the problems community members have been unaware of, which is the scenario depicted by (B), (C), and (D).

24. **C** Matt and his students will benefit from his staying up-to-date on research, trends, and issues. (A) and (B) are also true but are not as significant and far-reaching as (C). (D) is also true, and Matt will find it time-saving, but the significance to his students' falls behind that in (A) and (C).

25. **B** As soon as a teacher has reason to suspect abuse, state law requires it be reported to the state authorities. It is not the teacher's job to investigate suspected abuse, and so (A) and (D) are unacceptable because they are both forms of teacher investigation. This does not mean a teacher cannot gently ask about signs that might indicate abuse such as bruising or numerous accidents. People who report suspected abuse in good faith are protected from legal action, but the individual who has the suspicion is required to act rather than pass the problem off to another as (C) suggests.

26. **D** School equipment is purchased with school funds to be used to conduct school business. It does not matter if the school business occurs on or off campus or during school hours or outside school hours. The ethical and legal position is that school equipment should be used only for school business, which eliminates the other three choices.

27. **D** Assisting students with questions during a standardized test is unethical. Teachers may not read the TAKS questions during testing. They may not prompt students on word meanings or how to answer or code an answer. (A) and (B) are appropriate ways to help students learn how to succeed on the TAKS before the exam. State law requires all TEKS to be taught, whether they are tested or not. So (C) is inappropriate. All assessment should not model the TAKS format. However, students should have sufficient practice with the format to be comfortable when taking the standardized test.

28. **B** Ms. Cardwell expanded on Maggie's hypothesis to help students focus on exactly what the problem is so that they will be ready to brainstorm possible solutions. (A) and (D) imply there is a correct answer or solution, which is not the case. Students do need to stay focused on the problem and not become distracted from solutions by parallel or divergent situations. (C) indicates that there is a solution that has been taught at some earlier point and just needs to be recalled by the students.

29. **A** Ms. Cardwell has encouraged her students to tackle the issue of the impact of one or more third-graders on recycling at school. The issue is real, and possible solutions will be varied and require the students to apply problem-solving skills. (B) shifts the discussion from student-initiated to teacher-initiated and implies that the students were not willing participants. (C) will be a result of the discussion and follow-up tasks as the learning from the unit is moved away from the traditional classroom instructional style. The students have some prior knowledge of recycling from earlier parts of the unit and of ways to collect the data they will need. (D) will also be a result of the student-initiated instructional direction the unit is taking.

30. **A** If Ms. Cardwell had been unwilling to allow the discussion to continue past the time set for science class and had not been open to student-initiated instructional directions, she would have lost a teachable moment that could result in a learning experience for her students more powerful than that originally planned. (B) is not a true statement. There are several ways Ms. Cardwell could adjust for the shift in the time allocation. She could "return" time to the next subject tomorrow by using some science time or integrate the two subjects into the direction students have indicated they want the lesson to move. (C) implies the students and Ms. Cardwell have collaborated in distracting or off-task behaviors that block learning, which is not accurate. Ms. Cardwell actually hopes that in the future students will be so interested and excited by a lesson that they will again take an active role in directing the instructional goal. (D) indicates that although Ms. Cardwell allowed and encouraged the discussion today, she has no plans to follow through on shifting the direction of the unit's focus. It indicates that science class will again be teacher-directed tomorrow, which would close the door on a wonderful teachable moment.

31. **C** Decision making increases student ownership and retention. (A) might be a result of student involvement in designing and planning the type and amount of data to collect but should not be the reason for student involvement. (B) and (D) could also be a result of student participation in planning but are more likely to result from successful completion of the recycling project.

32. **B** Although (A), (C), and (D) will all be outcomes of this class project, only (B) is the most important outcome. A sense of ownership and an ability to impact global problems, as indicated in (B), will encourage students to attack a future problem using the skills identified in responses (C) and (D). (A) is only a slight improvement over Paul's original position. Rather than "I can't make a difference," it becomes "I can make a difference if someone guides me through the steps."

33. **D** The knowledge and skills needed to follow the same process in the future are the most important outcome of the recycling project. The other responses are all attitudes and skills students will hopefully gain while working on answering the recycling question, but the motivation to apply these attitudes and skills again will be more important to the students in the future.

34. **C** (C) allows Ms. Reynolds to work during the coming school year to strengthen weak technological skills during content lessons she plans to teach.

This will allow her students to make adequate yearly progress on the state standards (TEKS) without adding new instructional units to an already full curriculum as she works with her students to meet the state's expectations. Adding technology to lessons already in place is a more appropriate way to add instruction in these skills than teaching a specific lesson with no application opportunity as suggested in (A). (B) has students being placed in ability groups, which is not appropriate. It does not permit students with weaker skills access to the assistance their peers could provide as they work on a project together. Instruction does not have to come from a teacher to be successful. Often peer instruction can be more effective for students. (D) seems to shift the remediation role for diagnosed weak areas to parents. Although it is not inappropriate to ask for parental assistance, the school should play the leadership role. It is not appropriate to begin a new year by focusing on problem areas rather than on positive ones. It can set a negative attitude in the teacher, parents, and students that will impact the entire coming year.

35. **C** The most important benefit, meeting the instructional needs of individual students, is given by (C). The wide range of resources allows individual students to select those that are of high interest, which is a motivator and also permits them to work using their preferred learning styles. (A) assumes that a variety of resources will ensure that students are thinking at a higher level, which is not a valid assumption. Many young students simply copy from a source as they begin to learn research skills. There is no indication of how these students are using these resources. They may be operating at a higher level but can just as easily still be functioning at a lower level. Altering the resources does not automatically alter the level of thinking. (B) is correct but is less important and is a by-product of (C). The sense of accomplishment individual students will feel from successfully using these varied resources to complete their research will result from effectively meeting individual student needs. (D) may or may not be true. Some students might work as a group because they are sharing resources, but group work was not indicated and there are so many resources mentioned that students could work individually as they take turns using them.

36. **A** The best way for Ms. Reynolds to facilitate her students' work on these days is (A). Creating bookmarks allows students to move on and off computers without fear of losing information. Having to take notes from each site, as indicated in (B), keeps a computer tied up with one student while another waits. The printing suggested by (C) uses a lot of paper and ink for information students may or may not want later as they locate other helpful sites. (D) does not fit the task Ms. Reynolds has set for the class. She might later want the students to design a web quest as a way of sharing their research, but at this time her goal is to have students learn to use varied resources to conduct research.

37. **D** The best response is (D). It is very similar to (C) but is stronger because it has Ms. Reynolds instructing Susan rather than doing the task for her. It would be faster for Ms. Reynolds to show Susan what to do in this situation, but by showing rather than teaching, she is establishing a pattern where she will have

to show Susan again when this problem next occurs. Fourth-grade students learn better by doing rather than by watching, as they are concrete learners. (A) will not be helpful, as changing search engines without changing search terms is as likely to increase as reduce the number of hits. (B) is also a problem. If Susan conducts a search within a search without narrowing her search terms, she is likely to get the same results.

38. **B** Although Ms. Reynolds did not originally think to suggest or allow a final product based on technology, (B) fits in clearly with her original goals for this learning activity, and so it is an appropriate modification. (B) is better than (D) because students are allowed rather than required to include this alteration. Some students may have already begun or completed their final product before this modification is made, and it would be inappropriate to make them adjust at this time. In (A), the implication is that technology was not originally a component of the project, which does not fit with the number of technology-based resources used in the instruction. Rather technology was not a required part of the final product. (C) is inappropriate because it actually holds back students with advanced technology skills and indicates a lack of flexibility in Ms. Reynolds.

39. **D** (D) is most effective in addressing the range of student cognitive development present in the class. (A), which suggests that students be grouped by cognitive level, is not supported by research on effective teaching and learning. It is better to have students of different abilities work together to enrich the learning of all students. Assigning "study buddies," as suggested in (B), produces highly structured pairs and is not as effective as using small groups of students with mixed abilities. It is also inappropriate to make students at one ability level responsible for the success of those at another although all students should be encouraged to be supportive of the success of other students. (C) assumes there is a normal fourth-grade level of development and that there is ample time to work with a large number of students individually. This strategy is more likely to overlook the needs of all groups when instructional levels don't match and time for individualization runs short.

40. **B** Fourth-graders are 9–10 years old, which places their developmental range at the end of the preoperational stage moving into the concrete operational stage. This transitional group would find it easier to learn from the concrete events and social strategies offered in (B). The other three choices all focus on instructional strategies requiring abstract thinking by individuals. The abstract processing of information needed in these responses is more appropriate for older students at the formal operational level.

41. **A** Instruction must be differentiated in ways that do not apply or reinforce labels that cause students to feel isolated or different while meeting their instructional needs. (B) is a form of ability grouping, which is neither supported by research nor accepted as a valid instructional strategy because it does not allow students at different cognitive levels to interact and learn from each other. (C) shifts responsibility for learning and success away from individuals and onto

groups. Although group work is very important, it is also important that all members of a group have a responsibility not only to the group but also to themselves. (D) is appropriate as it will enhance student motivation, but it is not the most important aspect to consider. (A) is more important to motivation and effective learning.

42. **C** This choice allows Mr. Parquet to work during the coming school year to strengthen weak areas while continuing to make adequate yearly progress with his students, which matches the state's expectations. This is harder and takes more planning than declining any responsibility for teaching knowledge and skills from earlier grade levels that a student might be lacking. In (A), being sure students have the test-taking skills for a particular format is appropriate but is not the best use of the assessment information. (B) has students being placed in ability groups, which is not appropriate. Nor is it appropriate to consider only one criterion when deciding on instructional practices for a school year. (D) seems to shift the remediation role for diagnosed weak areas to parents. Although it is not inappropriate to ask for parental assistance, the school should play the leadership role. It is not appropriate to establish a stronger focus on negative rather than positive areas, as this can set a negative or defeated attitude in the teacher, parents, and students that results in a poor learning environment. It is more positive to focus on what students do know and how to assist them in gaining any missing information.

43. **B** Mr. Parquet allows students opportunities to learn and apply the skills needed for this task in a step-by-step manner under direct teacher supervision. It allows for individual differences and, because of daily monitoring, prevents students from delaying or falling behind. The success this ensures can help with attitudes toward science. (A) depends on each student already having the skills needed to design and conduct the science experiment. It is not reasonable to expect this level of skill in these students. The class critique will actually foster rather than reduce a negative attitude caused by frustration due to lack of skills. (C) can result in a negative attitude toward the project and toward science in general in students at all levels. The flexibility in participation and roles shifts more responsibility to grade-conscious students. Then learning will be unequal. (D) implies that the skills needed to design and conduct all experiments are the same, which is incorrect. It also does not allow for individuals to already have a skill. Boredom due to the repetition of unnecessary instruction can result because no pretest to opt out of instruction was included. Also, students who must endlessly repeat a lesson they feel they cannot master will develop a negative attitude.

44. **B** This choice describes what students are doing as they answer the reflection questions in their learning journals. They are establishing a relationship between Edison's persistence and determination as he designed the light bulb and their need to design, test, and redesign their own experiments. The statements made in (A), (C), and (D) do not fit this situation.

45. **C** This is the best answer as it is the only question Mr. Parquet can clearly answer based on reading the students' learning journals. (A), (B), and (D) are

also good questions for a self-reflective teacher to ask, but to answer them requires other pathways such as a review of past plans.

46. **C** This allows the teacher to use more than one criterion, such as a grade on a practice lesson, to establish a student's skill level. (A) is also a good idea and can help with a positive and supportive learning environment and increased student awareness of the importance of knowing and using these skills. These fourth-graders will be aided in learning the skills as they provide peer feedback. But adding peer feedback to instructor feedback alone is not sufficient. (B) indicates that it is acceptable for some students to be and stay behind when this is not at all acceptable. (D) describes what any good test should do, which is to allow all students some success while distinguishing students who have mastered a concept from those who have not. Any teacher can develop a test that no one can pass or one where everyone can make a perfect score. Neither situation is effective in assessing student learning and indicating the next step for the teacher, which is one of the desired roles of assessment.

47. **A** A privilege is earned in some way. Through clearly stated behavior expectations, students have independence and a visual cue as they work for the privilege. This assumes the privilege is important to and will be sought by the students. (B) focuses on peer encouragement when students at this age are egocentric and therefore more interested in what they can do than in what happens for others. (C) is expressed in a negative manner as students push the limits of teacher tolerance before withdrawing a privilege rather than focusing on earning the privilege. This attitude of an adult against a student's perspective is not typical of this age. Unlike (D), at this age students are interested in pleasing adults and other authority figures, and so pleasing the teacher shares importance with earning a privilege.

48. **C** The roles should not just be titles but important jobs that impact the completion or success of the task. Each student must perform responsibly in each role as it rotates through the group, and so individual and group success depends on each performance. (A) has Ms. Goldman reminding or nagging the students, which is counterproductive to increasing self-control. The cards are where every student can see them. (B) is also counterproductive. Students who are already not giving full participation to their groups are probably not motivated, and so the threat of a color change alone will not have much effect. They need motivation that appeals to them. Placing them all together almost ensures a color change for each member of the group and greater management challenges for Ms. Goldman. Although the color change for individuals in (D) can help with self-control and static job assignments based on ability level allow everyone to have a job they can do successfully, assuming the students in this class have the right balance of skills, no provisions are made for growth in skills as other jobs are learned and performed through job rotation as occurs with (C).

49. **D** This response is the most concrete, has a high level of student participation, and allows a clear signal to the teacher through examples of when understanding has occurred. (A) and (B) are not incorrect strategies but are not as powerful as

strategy (D) for the reasons mentioned. (A) helps a student activate prior knowledge but also assumes some prior knowledge, which may not be accurate. (B) would be better if students were reviewing and repeating the major concepts rather than listening to the teacher do so because of the greater student engagement. (C) is a traditional way to introduce vocabulary in a unit, but introducing and defining a new term within context have been found to be more effective.

50. **D** This choice has students working in teams to determine and label specific examples of systems and support their ideas with evidence, which is student-centered rather than teacher-directed. Why students reach an answer is as important to the learning process as what answer is reached. (A) and (B) are teacher-directed because Ms. Goldman assigns the systems. (A) requires a written product that must be produced without the support of peers. (B) has peer support but does not require a rationale or supporting evidence for identifying a system as open or closed. (C) is more student-centered but is also missing peer support and again does not require a rationale or supporting evidence for identifying a system as open or closed. Because a group of students agree on an answer does not make the answer correct.

51. **B** Understanding why they are doing the experiment and how it is to be done guides students' formation of a conceptual framework. This helps them focus on the relationships required for true, long-term learning rather than on the memorization of information for short-term acquisition. All students have done the same opening activity for the experiment, but this does not give them all the same background on the subject of the experiment as implied in (A). (C) is true but is not as important as the conceptual framework discussed in (B). (D) is inaccurate because doing the preliminary writing actually extends the time needed to do the experiment, although it probably increases accuracy by forcing students to be attentive to the entire experiment rather than approaching it one step at a time, as so often happens when an advance organizer is not used.

52. **A** The student receives negative feedback and no concrete suggestions for improvement. The initial negative comment may be as far as the student reads or they may interpret all other comments as being negative because of the initial negative tone. (B), (C), and (D) assume the initial negative comment about clarity will be outweighed by the comment about the value of using pronouns. No clear suggested changes are given in either (B) or (C), and so the student may have no idea how to improve. This is not a time for student freedom, as suggested in (D), but for clear modeling of a better style.

53. **B** The alignment in (B) is the most important, making it the best response. Testing what and how you have taught is imperative for accurate assessment of learning. (A), (C), and (D) are appropriate for effective teacher-made tests.

54. **A** By establishing the rubric together, clear teacher expectations are given while student input and ownership of the project are established. Both groups know what balance between content and presentation design is expected. (B) gives most of the control of the final product to Ms. Goldman. Completing the content work before considering any presentation components may block students

from producing a creative product appropriate for the content information but not on the suggested product list. (C) also keeps much of the control and creative process away from the students as they seek Ms. Goldman's approval for each component of the final product. The focus on meeting teacher expectations is greater than on the creative use of media to produce an effective final presentation. The daily reminders in (D) will be perceived as nagging in a very short time. A written rubric, as suggested in (A), is much more effective as it can be referred to throughout the project.

55. **A** (B), (C), and (D) all have value but are details that can help support the desired partnership. (A) is also the only response that indicates an interaction between teachers and family, yet this interaction is a required component of a true partnership.

56. **D** This is the only response that allows a discussion between home and school about ways families can participate. It will receive a much more positive reaction from parents/guardians for this reason. (C) also invites participation rather than demanding it, as do (A) and (B), but none of these three responses has room for input into the program from home.

57. **C** This choice is best as it allows the parent to explain why a conference was requested. This permits the parent to express her concerns or ask for clarification. Listening calmly shows respect but not necessarily agreement with the parent's thoughts while allowing time to compose a thoughtful response. (A), (B), and (D) assume Ms. Farquhar knows or can guess the reason the parent wanted a conference. The assumed reason may be accurate but may also be completely off-base and create another area of concern. It is best to let the parent explain what is on her mind so that together you can work in the student's best interest.

58. **A** Ernest's parents/guardians must give written permission before a teacher or school can seek an evaluation for special education services. (B), (C), and (D) all give steps and procedures that also need to be a part of asking for Ernest to be evaluated. The greater the documentation of concerns, the easier it will be for parents to understand the rationale for the requested evaluation and for them to give written permission.

59. **D** This response uses the expertise of both the special education teacher and the math teacher working together to adapt the lessons in the solid geometry unit to senses other than sight where possible. This allows Patty to have a high level of participation while acknowledging her visual challenge. (A) and (B) both remove Patty from participation with the other students in the math classroom during this unit. Patty is not given a chance to succeed within her mainstreamed environment, and (B) alters the content she will study, which is also unacceptable. Solid geometry is easier to learn through concrete experiences and interactions with peers. (C) assumes that the special education teacher has no other responsibilities during math time and can give his or her total attention to one student, which would rarely be an accurate assumption.

60. **C** This is correct as it is the only response that deals with what students do not know but should know and reteaches to allow students to gain this information

before continuing with the unit. It does no good to continue with the unit, as (A) suggests, when the first part has not been learned. The lecture about responsibility in (B) ignores when and how the missed information will be gained while producing a negative learning environment. Formative assessments, as suggested in (D), are a good idea, but the missing material from prior lessons is addressed only in (C).

61. **B** This choice allows Ms. Pasternak's students to demonstrate their understanding of area by applying it in a daily-life setting. (A) sounds more like practice than assessment. A student who can find the area of 3 to 5 geometric shapes such as squares and rectangles can find the area of 300. Also, shapes other than squares and rectangles have an area. (C) is a traditional style assessment without the application needed for true understanding of a concept. (D) brings perimeter into the assessment when it was not part of the goal.

62. **D** By walking around the room, Ms. Pasternak monitors not only activities but also can monitor the effectiveness of her instruction. (A) and (B) are true but are not supported directly by the scenario. (C) is a by-product of this practice.

63. **A** Modeling adds visual data to the auditory directions, leaving no room for mistakes or misunderstanding. (B) and (C) would add to the clarity, but (A) is still the clearest method. (D) is also effective, especially if combined with modeling which is the best.

64. **B** Ms. Pasternak's reason for refusing to allow Michael to change his presentation style is best illustrated in (B). (A) and (D) both include some accurate information that supports the teacher's refusal to allow the change for the reason stated in (B). (C) is based on an inaccurate assumption.

65. **B** The rubric should reflect the assignment. (A), (C), and (D) would be appropriate for other designs.

66. **D** This response best indicates Ms. Davis' knowledge of how students learn. Teachers cannot compete with the entertainment level possible on TV, and so (A) is unrealistic, although teachers can make lessons highly motivating and interesting with just a little effort and creativity. (B) and (C) are true, but there is no mention of student movement or inquiry lessons although both could be part of her teaching strategy; to assume they are is invalid.

67. **D** Children at the age appropriate for Pre-K are still playing side by side more often than with one another. Allowing for side-by-side parallel play at some of the centers shows that Ms. Davis is aware of this. She also allows for a transition to other types of experiences at the centers. (C) is not reflected in the scenario. Though (A) and (B) are probably true, they are not reflected in the scenario.

68. **C** This choice is an indication of Ms. Davis' opinions about Misty and her stage of development. (A) and (D) are incorrect because Misty is exhibiting the expected age response to sharing. There is no indication of verbal problems. (B)

is unacceptable because a professional teacher does not avoid assisting a child's growth to avoid conflict.

69. **A** Technological tasks completed by Ms. Davis are administrative tasks and indicate basic technology knowledge. (B), (C), and (D) do not relate to the passage at all.

70. **A** This choice indicates the area where Mr. Stanford's planning skills are lacking. He does not allow any time for student reflection and participation in closure. He also needs to adjust his time allocation between direct instruction and guided and independent practice. He uses twice as much time providing instruction as is allotted for applying the new information. There could be more detail in his plan as indicated in (B), but many teachers reduce the amount of detail included as they gain experience. (C) is incorrect as his introduction time is appropriate. Making it longer would shift it from an introduction into instruction. (D) is unacceptable because the independent practice is begun at school and continued at home, which is what homework is.

71. **C** Studies have shown that routines add to instructional time by lessening the time it takes to do daily tasks. (B) and (D) are not supported by the information given in the scenario. Repetative instruction, as mentioned in (A), is very different than classroom routine.

72. **B** By having students take part in various hands-on lessons and then connecting this knowledge to both past experiences and new learning, Ms. Shultize shows her knowledge of students' individuality. She debriefs and then moves on to a lesson that is at a high level in Bloom's taxonomy and incorporates critical and creative thinking. The learning of content by students, in (A), is not the sole criterion for analyzing success. Planning instruction that promotes student motivation, as in (C), and stimulating reflections by students, mentioned in (D), are important in the process of learning; however, none of these responses is the key answer to this scenario.

73. **B** Research indicates that all students can learn rather than that all students can learn in the same way. (B) indicates that Ms. Shultize understands this and is willing to adapt lessons to provide effective learning strategies for her students. (A), (C), and (D) all have to be present in a teacher's knowledge base and philosophy before the adjustment required to apply the knowledge to their instructional strategies can be made by a teacher.

74. **A** This choice indicates the most appropriate instructional activities for the developmental stages typically present in the second grade. (B), (C), and (D) would all be more appropriate instructional strategies for formal abstract learners, which is a developmental level that cannot be expected in second-grade students.

75. **B** Stating the question first gets the attention of everyone because no one knows who will be called on. The question is stated, then there is a pause, and then the person's name is stated. If the name is stated first, as in (A), everyone else

stops paying attention because they are then "off the hook." Calling on students who do not have their hands raised, as in (C), destroys a sense of safety in the classroom. This then leads to students shutting down and being nonresponsive. (D) would be good, but (B) is a better solution.

76. **C** This choice would be the most appropriate use of last year's TAKS score for these students. (A), (B), and (D) all give inappropriate suggestions for using TAKS scores.

77. **C** By using true cooperative grouping strategies, Ms. Donnell shows her understanding of how effectively groups of students with different abilities can learn from each other. (A) does not fit as students' traits and skills other than ability levels are not considered as the groups are formed. One group may have all the best organizers or artists if they are at the three ability levels used for assigning membership. Also, there is no indication of how students will cooperate once they are assigned their groups. (B) and (D) are a by-product of cooperative grouping; however, the passage does not directly indicate this.

78. **C** Assigning roles to group members ensures that all students will have both an active role and a responsibility to that role. This in turn ensures engagement in the learning process for all the students. Knowledge of student diversity, as mentioned in (A), might be a factor for Ms. Donnell to consider when assigning the tasks, but it is not the main reason. Respecting each student by dignifying his/her work and thus creating a safe environment for learning, mentioned in (B) and (D), are also by-products of role assignments but not the main reason for assigning roles.

79. **A** Problem-based learning strategy involves beginning with a small problem, and the activity is usually about 5–10 minutes long. The small problem is debriefed, and then the large problem activity is introduced. (B) is one way to help students experience different ways to solve a problem. (C) is closer to being a constructivist strategy, and (D) is a form of student-led inquiry.

80. **B** Research and the web site of the web quest creator support this answer. (A), (C), and (D) are incorrect as they include or omit appropriate parts of an appropriately designed web quest.

81. **A** Rubrics need to be distributed with the assignments. Giving the rubric shortly after the project is assigned, as in (B), is better than the procedures in (C) and (D), which are not acceptable. Students and parents need to know the grading criteria and expectations before getting too far into the project and definitely before completing the assignment. They should not have to ask what the criteria are. A week before the due date is unacceptable as most projects should be nearing completion at that time.

82. **C** Mr. Wong recognizes that the families of the students in his class have unique needs, including the times of day they can attend meetings. Because of this, he has established a meeting format to help him accomplish (A), but he has failed to consider that some families will not feel comfortable or will not feel a need to attend these monthly meetings. The scenario doesn't support (B) and (D).

83. **A** Observing and debriefing an inquiry lesson successfully conducted by a peer would be very helpful for Mr. Wong, and his mentor would know who to send him to. (B) would work but is not always possible to accomplish in a timely manner. (C) is not true because inquiry lessons can be taught at any experiential level of teaching. Student teachers are able to conduct outstanding ones. It is a matter of knowledge rather than years of experience. Finally, (D) is half true because practice does help but not until the required knowledge and skills are in place.

84. **A** Mr. Wong has violated the copyright laws by making more than one classroom set without permission even though the copies are for educational purposes. (B) and (C) are why we have copyright laws. (D) is true. Making two copies is not the best use of copy ink and paper. However, copyright violation is the main problem, not economic considerations.

85. **C** It is obvious that for some students *Charlie and the Chocolate Factory* is being taught earlier than scheduled in the curriculum. Vertical alignment can locate the problem and resolve it. (A), (B), and (D) all deal with complaining to someone, which resolves nothing and may actually exacerbate the problem.

86. **D** Mr. Wong has violated a procedure of the state-mandated test and is cheating by making the student aware of his or her mistake in the answer. (A), (B), and (C) do not fit the scenario. Educational guidelines refer to teaching the TEKS before testing occurs, which is the acceptable way to advocate for student success on the test. Data security during the test says teachers may not read or copy the test.

87. **C** There are many good evaluation tools available. The teacher planning to use the site should conduct the evaluation as only the teacher knows the exact criteria the site needs to meet for the planned use. (A), (B), and (D) are good supplemental sources for evaluation, but (C) remains the best evaluation source.

88. **C** Reflective learning does use self-assessment to guide learning. (A), (B), and (D) can be a small part of reflective learning, but (C) is the best answer.

89. **A** Sending home homemade math manipulatives and activities to be used with the family is the most engaging activity. (B) and (C) are small ways to include caregivers in home activities. (D) has the family involved in a passive rather than an active manner.

90. **B** If any student in the regular classroom has an IEP, the teacher must follow it. Following only the part of the IEP that fits your class or curriculum, as in (A), is not allowed. (C) is simply untrue. (D) is nice and helpful but is not mandated and is costly.

Diagnostic and Sample Tests for Grades 4–8

The diagnostic tests in the following chapters include one question per test competency, except for the EC-12 Diagnostic Test, which includes three questions per competency. These questions are similar to those found at the State Board of Educator Certification (SBEC) website (www.sbec.state.tx.us), where the state agency provides a clear example of the PPR certification test. The SBEC practice test should also be used as a diagnostic tool to ascertain both your areas of strength and the needed areas of knowledge and skill improvement that you must have to be successful on the PPR examinations. The diagnostic items in this book are presented without full follow-up explanations of why all responses are correct or incorrect. This follows the pattern used for the test items for the SBEC practice tests. The state competency is listed at the end of each diagnostic test item to help guide your understanding of how you will be tested on each competency.

According to numerous candidates who have taken and passed the state certification test, there is a correlation between SBEC practice tests and the state certification test. You are encouraged to visit www.sbec.state.tx.us for further information about the SBEC study guide. We encourage you to continue to take the diagnostic tests to confirm exactly what competencies are included on the test and to practice deciding why three responses are incorrect or less effective and why one response is clearly the best answer.

Following the sample tests for each of the state certification levels, you will find a self-analysis framework that will guide you in understanding how to improve your study before taking the state tests. In this framework, the authors explain why three answers are incorrect (or are not the *best* response) and one answer is correct (or is the *best* choice). It would be wise to continue to use this analysis strategy as you continue to practice using the tests in this study guide and the SBEC online test. In Chapter 16, suggestions are made that will help you complete an overall analysis of your success and provide you with a strategy for further study.

Answer Sheet

DIAGNOSTIC TEST (GRADES 4–8)

1 Ⓐ Ⓑ Ⓒ Ⓓ

2 Ⓐ Ⓑ Ⓒ Ⓓ

3 Ⓐ Ⓑ Ⓒ Ⓓ

4 Ⓐ Ⓑ Ⓒ Ⓓ

5 Ⓐ Ⓑ Ⓒ Ⓓ

6 Ⓐ Ⓑ Ⓒ Ⓓ

7 Ⓐ Ⓑ Ⓒ Ⓓ

8 Ⓐ Ⓑ Ⓒ Ⓓ

9 Ⓐ Ⓑ Ⓒ Ⓓ

10 Ⓐ Ⓑ Ⓒ Ⓓ

11 Ⓐ Ⓑ Ⓒ Ⓓ

12 Ⓐ Ⓑ Ⓒ Ⓓ

13 Ⓐ Ⓑ Ⓒ Ⓓ

Grades 4–8 Answer Sheet

Answer Sheet

SAMPLE TEST (GRADES 4–8)

1 Ⓐ Ⓑ Ⓒ Ⓓ   26 Ⓐ Ⓑ Ⓒ Ⓓ   51 Ⓐ Ⓑ Ⓒ Ⓓ   76 Ⓐ Ⓑ Ⓒ Ⓓ
2 Ⓐ Ⓑ Ⓒ Ⓓ   27 Ⓐ Ⓑ Ⓒ Ⓓ   52 Ⓐ Ⓑ Ⓒ Ⓓ   77 Ⓐ Ⓑ Ⓒ Ⓓ
3 Ⓐ Ⓑ Ⓒ Ⓓ   28 Ⓐ Ⓑ Ⓒ Ⓓ   53 Ⓐ Ⓑ Ⓒ Ⓓ   78 Ⓐ Ⓑ Ⓒ Ⓓ
4 Ⓐ Ⓑ Ⓒ Ⓓ   29 Ⓐ Ⓑ Ⓒ Ⓓ   54 Ⓐ Ⓑ Ⓒ Ⓓ   79 Ⓐ Ⓑ Ⓒ Ⓓ
5 Ⓐ Ⓑ Ⓒ Ⓓ   30 Ⓐ Ⓑ Ⓒ Ⓓ   55 Ⓐ Ⓑ Ⓒ Ⓓ   80 Ⓐ Ⓑ Ⓒ Ⓓ
6 Ⓐ Ⓑ Ⓒ Ⓓ   31 Ⓐ Ⓑ Ⓒ Ⓓ   56 Ⓐ Ⓑ Ⓒ Ⓓ   81 Ⓐ Ⓑ Ⓒ Ⓓ
7 Ⓐ Ⓑ Ⓒ Ⓓ   32 Ⓐ Ⓑ Ⓒ Ⓓ   57 Ⓐ Ⓑ Ⓒ Ⓓ   82 Ⓐ Ⓑ Ⓒ Ⓓ
8 Ⓐ Ⓑ Ⓒ Ⓓ   33 Ⓐ Ⓑ Ⓒ Ⓓ   58 Ⓐ Ⓑ Ⓒ Ⓓ   83 Ⓐ Ⓑ Ⓒ Ⓓ
9 Ⓐ Ⓑ Ⓒ Ⓓ   34 Ⓐ Ⓑ Ⓒ Ⓓ   59 Ⓐ Ⓑ Ⓒ Ⓓ   84 Ⓐ Ⓑ Ⓒ Ⓓ
10 Ⓐ Ⓑ Ⓒ Ⓓ   35 Ⓐ Ⓑ Ⓒ Ⓓ   60 Ⓐ Ⓑ Ⓒ Ⓓ   85 Ⓐ Ⓑ Ⓒ Ⓓ
11 Ⓐ Ⓑ Ⓒ Ⓓ   36 Ⓐ Ⓑ Ⓒ Ⓓ   61 Ⓐ Ⓑ Ⓒ Ⓓ   86 Ⓐ Ⓑ Ⓒ Ⓓ
12 Ⓐ Ⓑ Ⓒ Ⓓ   37 Ⓐ Ⓑ Ⓒ Ⓓ   62 Ⓐ Ⓑ Ⓒ Ⓓ   87 Ⓐ Ⓑ Ⓒ Ⓓ
13 Ⓐ Ⓑ Ⓒ Ⓓ   38 Ⓐ Ⓑ Ⓒ Ⓓ   63 Ⓐ Ⓑ Ⓒ Ⓓ   88 Ⓐ Ⓑ Ⓒ Ⓓ
14 Ⓐ Ⓑ Ⓒ Ⓓ   39 Ⓐ Ⓑ Ⓒ Ⓓ   64 Ⓐ Ⓑ Ⓒ Ⓓ   89 Ⓐ Ⓑ Ⓒ Ⓓ
15 Ⓐ Ⓑ Ⓒ Ⓓ   40 Ⓐ Ⓑ Ⓒ Ⓓ   65 Ⓐ Ⓑ Ⓒ Ⓓ   90 Ⓐ Ⓑ Ⓒ Ⓓ
16 Ⓐ Ⓑ Ⓒ Ⓓ   41 Ⓐ Ⓑ Ⓒ Ⓓ   66 Ⓐ Ⓑ Ⓒ Ⓓ
17 Ⓐ Ⓑ Ⓒ Ⓓ   42 Ⓐ Ⓑ Ⓒ Ⓓ   67 Ⓐ Ⓑ Ⓒ Ⓓ
18 Ⓐ Ⓑ Ⓒ Ⓓ   43 Ⓐ Ⓑ Ⓒ Ⓓ   68 Ⓐ Ⓑ Ⓒ Ⓓ
19 Ⓐ Ⓑ Ⓒ Ⓓ   44 Ⓐ Ⓑ Ⓒ Ⓓ   69 Ⓐ Ⓑ Ⓒ Ⓓ
20 Ⓐ Ⓑ Ⓒ Ⓓ   45 Ⓐ Ⓑ Ⓒ Ⓓ   70 Ⓐ Ⓑ Ⓒ Ⓓ
21 Ⓐ Ⓑ Ⓒ Ⓓ   46 Ⓐ Ⓑ Ⓒ Ⓓ   71 Ⓐ Ⓑ Ⓒ Ⓓ
22 Ⓐ Ⓑ Ⓒ Ⓓ   47 Ⓐ Ⓑ Ⓒ Ⓓ   72 Ⓐ Ⓑ Ⓒ Ⓓ
23 Ⓐ Ⓑ Ⓒ Ⓓ   48 Ⓐ Ⓑ Ⓒ Ⓓ   73 Ⓐ Ⓑ Ⓒ Ⓓ
24 Ⓐ Ⓑ Ⓒ Ⓓ   49 Ⓐ Ⓑ Ⓒ Ⓓ   74 Ⓐ Ⓑ Ⓒ Ⓓ
25 Ⓐ Ⓑ Ⓒ Ⓓ   50 Ⓐ Ⓑ Ⓒ Ⓓ   75 Ⓐ Ⓑ Ⓒ Ⓓ

Grades 4–8 Answer Sheet

Diagnostic Test (Grades 4–8)

Directions: Read each stimulus and answer every question. Mark your answers in the answer spaces on the accompanying grid.

1. Martin accepted a seventh-grade position for his first teaching assignment. He learned a lot about cognitive development in his teacher education program and knows that these students likely operate between concrete and formal operational thought. What would be the best instructional approach for him to follow to accommodate learning?

    (A) Use as many manipulatives as possible while focusing on activities that lead learners to more abstract content.
    (B) Always use cooperative grouping to allow learners to share concepts.
    (C) Offer tutoring each morning before school to assist those who are struggling.
    (D) Don't worry about learners at the higher levels; focus on the average learner in order to assure that all students have some opportunity to grow.

Competency 001: *The teacher understands human developmental processes and applies this knowledge to plan instruction and ongoing assessment that motivate students and are responsive to their developmental characteristics and needs.*

2. Several of Martin's students have special needs and sometimes leave his classroom to work in the school's resource room. In consultation with the special education resource teacher, what would be the best instructional plan for Martin as he strives to ensure that he is meeting the need of students with special needs?

    (A) Limit the special needs students to independent work while in his classroom so they do not negatively impact the other students.
    (B) Plan activities that address social skills rather than cognitive development.
    (C) Use a direct teaching approach so all students learn the same material and do not have an opportunity to interfere with any other student's learning.
    (D) Design interactive activities so all learners have an opportunity to work together.

Competency 002: *The teacher understands student diversity and knows how to plan learning experiences and design assessments that are responsive to differences among students and that promote all students' learning.*

Grades 4–8

3. Martin and the seventh-grade team set aside time early in the year to plan new interdisciplinary units for the year. For the most effective use of their time, what would be the most appropriate *initial* step to take as they begin plans for the units?

(A) List their grade level TEKS and focus on those students will find most interesting.

(B) Design a number of interesting activities across the themes and skills likely to be needed for the units.

(C) Design a matrix to identify how many units are needed and when they should be used.

(D) Spend the first few hours brainstorming topics of interest to the teachers so students will be more motivated by the teachers' enthusiasm for the units.

Competency 003: *The teacher understands procedures for designing effective and coherent instruction and assessment based on appropriate learning goals and objectives.*

4. Knowing the value of independent learning for middle level learners, what would be a fifth-grade teacher's best strategy for helping small groups work effectively?

(A) Determine the number of groups needed, then allow students to choose the membership of each group.

(B) Make sure that at least one dominant and one submissive student is in each group in order to balance the give-and-take necessary for group work.

(C) Assign only group grades for the performance of the group, explaining to students how this translates into the work place.

(D) Working with students, develop a rubric to evaluate the work of the group for students to use in a post-project review and discussion of their work.

Competency 004: *The teacher understands learning processes and factors that impact student learning and demonstrates this knowledge by planning effective, engaging instruction and appropriate assessments.*

5. A sixth-grade teacher opens her lesson on United States geography by posting the question, "What do you know about beaches in Florida?" for students to discuss when they enter the classroom. How could this question stimulate student engagement?

   (A) It gives students an opportunity to demonstrate their knowledge about something they all have first-hand experience with.

   (B) This question tells students that the teacher is more interested in topics that represent easy learning than topics that develop their understanding of complex concepts.

   (C) It addresses a concept that many students will have some prior knowledge of, and offers students an environment where no single correct answer is expected.

   (D) The question implies that the teacher believes all students have been to Florida and therefore will be able make a contribution.

Competency 005: *The teacher knows how to establish a classroom climate that fosters learning, equity, and excellence and uses this knowledge to create a physical and emotional environment that is safe and productive.*

6. Jeremy is a sixth-grade school science teacher who has students work in pairs during multitasking. He noticed that two students (one pair) do not participate effectively. Which of the following strategies might Jeremy employ with this pair of students?

   (A) Move the two students to other pairs so they will learn how to work more effectively with others.

   (B) Tell both of these students that, when they prove they can work together, they may then move to other groups with whom they might be more comfortable.

   (C) Conference with the pair to make sure each member has clear directions and that each understands exactly what role he is to take with the multitasking assignments.

   (D) Move the highest achieving student in the class to work with this pair for two weeks in hopes they can learn from someone more successful.

Competency 006: *The teacher understands strategies for creating an organized and productive learning environment and for managing student behavior.*

7. As Jeremy moves the pairs into cooperative groups, he wants to make sure that all students feel safe in taking risks in their learning and use their creativity effectively. Which of the following would be the most effective for Jeremy to say?

(A) "All of you worked well together the last time we had a cooperative group project. Based on that experience, I am sure you will do as well today."

(B) "This is an important assignment for your six weeks' grade so be sure to work together well in order to finish the group project on time."

(C) "Each member of your group is an important contributor. As you complete your project, remember that there is not one exact way to solve the problem."

(D) "Each group needs to select a leader who will guide the group to figure out the right answer to the problem that is the focus of the group work."

Competency 007: *The teacher understands and applies principles and strategies for communicating effectively in varied teaching and learning contexts.*

8. In her teacher education classes, Heather's teacher always returned work the next class day. Heather believes this is critical for student learning and motivation. What is the most important reason for Heather to return her fifth-grade students' work within one or two days?

(A) Fifth graders need constant encouragement, so returning their work will help them keep up with their grades so they can tell their parents how they are doing.

(B) Continuous grading and returning of papers and products will help Heather when she assigns students time to put their portfolios in order.

(C) Immediate feedback encourages students to continually improve their performance.

(D) Fast turnaround of papers will help Heather keep grades current in her grade book.

Competency 008: *The teacher provides appropriate instruction that actively engages students in the learning process.*

9. As a beginning teacher, Heather and her teammates intentionally include a multimedia presentation assignment in their unit plans. The teachers are concerned that fifth-grade students might be more worried about how the technology product looks than about the content included, so they spend a lot of time talking about appropriate assessments for the technology. How could they best address this concern about loss of content knowledge and guide students as they begin their technology work?

(A) Tell students that they will have equal amounts of time for working on the content part and the design part of their presentations.

(B) Have students draw out their plans for the technology presentation and then critique it to be sure there is sufficient content included.

(C) With the students' help, design a rubric that will serve as a guide for the project and that identifies the important content as well as elements of technology design.

(D) Make sure that the test at the end of the unit is focused on content, rather than what students learned as they created their technology products.

Competency 009: *The teacher incorporates the effective use of technology to plan, organize, deliver, and evaluate instruction for all students.*

10. During the first six weeks of school, Heather applies her knowledge of the importance of teacher feedback. She writes the following note on one paper.

> **You have made a lot of progress in your writing skills. You are making fewer errors with those punctuation challenges you had. I've marked your errors in use of nouns and pronouns, and would like for you to work on how to match the pronoun with the antecedent noun. Be sure a reader knows the reference noun for the pronoun.**

Based on what experts say about effective and corrective feedback, which of the following would be the best analysis of Heather's comments?

(A) Her comments will likely be resented by the student, because there is little praise and the feedback includes comments about errors. This will likely cause the student to be reluctant to make self-corrections on future work.

(B) Heather's feedback might be effective because it equally balances comments about improvement and weaknesses; however, it might cause the student to believe she cannot please the teacher.

(C) Such a comment will likely cause the student to be very confused about what the teacher wants, as it includes both positive and negative feedback. The student could think that the comment sends a mixed message.

(D) Such a comment will likely encourage the student to continually pay attention to her work, because it both recognizes good work and informs the student about ways to continuously improve her work.

Competency 010: *The teacher monitors student performance and achievement; provides students with timely, high-quality feedback; and responds flexibly to promote learning for all students.*

11. In order to involve the family in the overall community of learners she hopes to establish in her classroom, Martha, an eighth-grade English teacher, wants to encourage parents/guardians to be partners with her throughout the year. What would be an effective strategy for Martha to use at the beginning of the school year?

   (A) Bring the parents/guardians in the first week of school to review the textbooks and other instructional materials she will use throughout the year.
   (B) Inform parents of her expectations for students' academic success and engagement.
   (C) Send home a letter that describes developmental characteristics of eighth-graders.
   (D) Post a PowerPoint presentation on her web site that tells about her tests and grading policies.

Competency 011: *The teacher understands the importance of family involvement in children's education and knows how to interact and communicate effectively with families.*

12. Martha is concerned about the inclusion students she will have in her classroom during this first year of her teaching. She has designed an exciting role-playing activity as part of a unit on literature genres. One of her inclusion eighth-graders has a significant physical disability that will impair her participation. What would be the best way for Martha to work with the special education inclusion teacher to resolve this concern?

   (A) Ask the inclusion teacher to come to class the day students conduct the role play so he may work one-on-one with the student.
   (B) Have the special education teacher explain to the student that it would be better if she does not try to participate.
   (C) Work out a time that the special education teacher could meet individually with the student to help her complete the role-play assignment.
   (D) Ask the special education teacher to discuss with her the physical limitations this student has, as indicated on her IEP.

Competency 012: *The teacher enhances professional knowledge and skills by effectively interacting with other members of the educational community and participating in various types of professional activities.*

13. After two weeks of observation, Martha wishes to refer a new student for an evaluation to determine whether he could benefit from special education services. What *legal* step must first be taken before this type of evaluation can occur?

    (A) Martha should first observe the new student for a few weeks.
    (B) Martha should contact the district special education coordinator to set up the evaluation schedule and to tell the coordinator about the probable disability.
    (C) Martha should acquire written permission for the evaluation from the student's parents/guardians.
    (D) The district special education coordinator should first conduct an informal assessment to determine an initial diagnosis of the disability.

Competency 013: *The teacher understands and adheres to legal and ethical requirements for educators and is knowledgeable of the structure of education in Texas.*

Answer Key

DIAGNOSTIC TEST (GRADES 4–8)

Question Number	Correct Response	Competency
1	A	001
2	D	002
3	C	003
4	D	004
5	C	005
6	C	006
7	C	007
8	C	008
9	C	009
10	D	010
11	B	011
12	D	012
13	C	013

CORRECT ANSWERS

1. **A** The strategy indicated in (A) will be effective with both concrete and formal operational students; the other three choices do not address developmental stages of students.

2. **D** It is important that special needs students understand that they are not alone; other students also have unique instructional needs. By interacting, everyone sees that each student brings both strengths and weaknesses to the learning environment, and this is part of what makes them unique.

3. **C** This mapping of the units is the step that needs to come first. Without a clear vision of the overall planning goal the team wishes to achieve, it is difficult to know how best to apportion instructional time to TEKS, skills, themes, topics.

4. **D** This response includes student input into the evaluation process and helps them take ownership of learning and their work habits.

5. **C** The question helps some students activate their prior knowledge. No anticipated correct answer is implied by this open question.

6. **C** Clarifying the roles is a clear signal from the teacher that all students are expected to be active and successful participants.

7. **C** This is the only choice that indicates value for individuals' risk-taking and signals an acceptance of more than one possible answer.

8. **C** By receiving rapid feedback, students are able to track their growth as signaled by grades and teacher comments. This helps encourage them to stretch themselves, which would not happen if the feedback was delayed until it was no longer relevant to students.

9. **C** Student input into a rubric created before work on the project begins is an effective manner of insuring that all criteria concerning content focus and presentation style using technology are clear to students.

10. **D** It follows a positive comment with a very specific plan for improvement, which is one criterion for effective feedback.

11. **B** School and family can best collaborate when clear communication of expectations is present to guide the collaboration.

12. **D** The expertise of the special education teacher should be used to clearly understand the student's limitations so that an appropriate adaptation can be made to insure successful participation by this student.

13. **C** Without permission from the parent/guardian, no evaluation can be legally conducted.

Grades 4–8

Sample Test (Grades 4–8)

This sample test has some practice questions to help you review as part of your preparation for the 4–8 PPR test. Please carefully read the domains and competencies that will be tested on the 4–8 PPR test before beginning this sample test. As you read the domains and competencies, think about the mind-set and philosophy of teaching they represent. In this sample test, each practice question is introduced by the competency being measured. The questions and competencies are presented in numerical order for the purpose of logical flow as you learn the competencies. When you reach the teacher decision set near the end of the test, the sample questions will no longer address the competencies in numerical order. *Please be aware that competency statements will not appear on the actual test form and that the questions will not be presented in sequential order by competency numbers.*

Use the frame of reference built from your understanding of the domains and competencies as you select the single best answer for each question. It is recommended that you do an in-depth analysis of each possible answer before selecting your answer. After narrowing your possible choices to two answers, reread the question with each answer. This can help you ensure that your final choice answers what the question is asking. Stay focused on the specific information provided by the question. Avoid reading more into the question or thinking about extenuating circumstances. In addition to selecting your preferred answer, it is recommended that you consider carefully why it is the best answer based on the domains and competencies. You should have a clear reason for rejecting each answer that is not chosen rather than just identifying and marking your preferred answer.

Following this sample test and answer key, a section on correct responses and rationales discusses the strengths and challenges of each of the possible answers. Refer back to the domains and competencies as you read the rationale for each possible answer. Carefully examine the rationale for both right and wrong answer choices for their relationship to the domains and competencies.

Directions: Read each stimulus and answer every question. Mark your answers in the answer spaces on the accompanying grid.

Use the following information to answer questions 1 and 2.

The students in Ms. Bowman's seventh-grade class are a very diverse group. Her class includes both gifted and talented students as well as students who regularly spend time with the school's resource teacher. In addition, Ms. Bowman is aware that in any given classroom, the Piagetian cognitive abilities/readiness of the students may range over two or three grade levels.

Competency 001: *The teacher understands human developmental processes and applies this knowledge to plan instruction and ongoing assessment that motivate students and are responsive to their developmental characteristics and needs.*

1. How can Ms. Bowman best meet the needs of the range of cognitive variation found in her students?

   (A) Assign students to groups based on their cognitive development or readiness level to make it easier for students to work successfully in small groups.
   (B) Assign student "study buddies" to help lower cognitive level students reach success by partnering them with higher cognitive level students.
   (C) Target the instructional level toward the normal seventh-grade level of development and work with the students outside this range individually.
   (D) Use high-engagement instructional strategies such as hands-on activities and projects to introduce and provide instruction on abstract concepts.

2. Based on the research on Piagetian cognitive levels, which tasks would Ms. Bowman consider appropriate instructional strategies for the developmental or cognitive levels of her seventh-grade students?

   (A) Hands-on concrete operational level activities for these seventh-graders would be the most appropriate strategy.
   (B) Ms. Bowman's students should find group projects and experimentation effective instructional strategies for their developmental level.
   (C) These seventh-grade students should find individual reading of the textbook an effective instructional strategy.
   (D) Ms. Bowman's seventh-graders should prefer teacher lectures and taking class notes as effective instructional strategies.

Competency 002: *The teacher understands student diversity and knows how to plan learning experiences and design assessments that are responsive to differences among students and that promote all students' learning.*

3. What is *most* important as Ms. Bowman considers how to adapt her instructional strategies as she plans for her special-needs students?

(A) Her instructional strategies must ensure that no group of students is singled out and made to feel different or isolated from the other students.

(B) Her instructional strategies must ensure that each group of students has ample time to interact with other students at a similar cognitive level.

(C) Her instructional strategies must ensure that individual work occasionally occurs but that collaborative efforts have a stronger focus to ensure the success of all students.

(D) Her instructional strategies must ensure that students are allowed to select instructional activities based on individual interests and strengths.

4. Ms. Wong is the science teacher for a mixed-abilities group of eighth-graders. She wants all her students to learn how to design and conduct simple science research. Ms. Wong sets a goal for all the students to improve their skill level, their confidence, and their attitude toward science. How can Ms. Wong best achieve her goals, especially with her lower-achieving students?

(A) Ms. Wong can require all her students to design and complete a science research project that will be entered in the school science fair. Every science fair entrant will be given a ribbon for participation.

(B) Ms. Wong can break down scientific research into short, clear steps that guide students through the research process. Every class period has some time set aside for working on the project and receiving teacher assistance.

(C) Ms. Wong can partner students with complementary skill levels and interests. Higher-achieving students working with lower-achieving students allows both groups of students to grow, especially if Ms. Wong encourages flexibility in student participation and roles.

(D) Ms. Wong can require each student to participate in active teaching lessons focused on the skills needed to conduct the research. Each student must master the skill lesson or repeat it until mastery is reached.

Competency 003: *The teacher understands procedures for designing effective and coherent instruction and assessment based on appropriate learning goals and objectives.*

5. An elementary school has decided not to shift to a departmental model but rather to form instructional teams. The fifth-grade team is planning to meet during the summer to develop integrated interdisciplinary units for next year. What needs to happen first to facilitate their planning?

   (A) The fifth-grade instructional team needs to compile the teaching strengths and favorite units of each team member to determine appropriate possible themes.

   (B) The team needs to list units and topics from which they expect strong, positive student responses so that they can determine appropriate possible themes.

   (C) The instructional team needs to map the required curriculum and look for overlapping skills and content topics to determine appropriate possible themes.

   (D) The fifth-grade team needs to establish how long they want each unit to last so that they will know how many possible themes they will need.

6. During late July, Ms. Lopez asks for the state's assessment results for last year's fifth-grade class. As the sixth-grade teacher she wants this information before she begins to plan for the coming school year. How can Ms. Lopez best use this information appropriately as she plans?

   (A) Ms. Lopez can use this information to diagnose the problems or weaknesses the students have with the style of assessment used so that she can work to improve their testing skills in sixth grade.

   (B) Ms. Lopez can use this information to establish instructional groups based on the skill level of the students as shown by the state assessment so that she can work to strengthen their weak areas.

   (C) Ms. Lopez can use this information to plan instruction dedicated to areas of weakness in required skills and knowledge diagnosed by the past year's test while also addressing the sixth-grade information required by the state.

   (D) Ms. Lopez can use this information to determine which skills and knowledge required by the state her students have not yet achieved so that she can start the school year by asking for parental help in these areas.

Competency 004: *The teacher understands learning processes and factors that impact student learning and demonstrates this knowledge by planning effective, engaging instruction and appropriate assessments.*

7. Mr. Baron's two children talk about the fun and effectiveness of working in cooperative groups in their classrooms. Mr. Baron teaches at another school and was not happy with the results when he used small groups in the past. Mr. Baron decides he should guide his students toward establishing rules for effective collaboration. What additional strategy should he use to improve the results in his classroom?

   (A) Students should be helped to conduct evaluations at the end of a project to assess group and individual performances on the assignment.
   (B) Mr. Baron should ensure that there is a strong leader for each group and give permission for students to select the role each wishes to perform.
   (C) Mr. Baron should allow students to select the members of their group and allow those who do not wish to be in a group or who are not selected to work alone.
   (D) Mr. Baron should base most of the project grade on how effectively the members of the group have worked collaboratively.

Competency 005: *The teacher knows how to establish a classroom climate that fosters learning, equity, and excellence and uses this knowledge to create a physical and emotional environment that is safe and productive.*

8. A sixth-grade teacher who wants to encourage strong student engagement in the learning process begins her environmental unit with a K-W-L chart on recycling. The teacher completes a class chart on the board after each student has completed an individual chart. Ideas from the class chart that are not on individual charts can be added. What is the primary reason that this beginning was a good selection?

   (A) The individual K-W-L charts give students notice in a nonthreatening manner that everyone is expected to participate.
   (B) The individual K-W-L charts send the message that the teacher thinks that everyone knows something about recycling to contribute.
   (C) The individual K-W-L charts indicate that no matter how much an individual knows about recycling now, there is still information to learn.
   (D) The individual K-W-L charts allow student prior knowledge on a topic to be accessed without placing any individual on the spot.

Use the following information to answer questions 9 and 10.

During the first two weeks of school the students in Ms. Sandal's sixth-grade class do not seem to have as much self-control as she expects. She often uses group activities as part of her instructional strategies and has noticed that several students do not fully participate with their groups. Ms. Sandal decides to implement a new management system for her class. Each time a student disrupts class, is off task during group work, or breaks a class rule, Ms. Sandal turns one of five cards clearly displayed at the front of the room from green to yellow. Each day begins with all the cards on green. If any of the cards are still green at the end of the day, the entire class receives a special privilege. If none of the cards are green, no one receives a privilege.

Competency 006: *The teacher understands strategies for creating an organized and productive learning environment and for managing student behavior.*

9. Why is this strategy appropriate for use with adolescent students?

   (A) The visual of the green/yellow cards allows independence in students as they can clearly see how many more times someone can mess up today without losing the privilege.

   (B) The visual of the green/yellow cards allows students to see how the day is progressing and when they should encourage behaviors in their peers that will result in gaining the desired privilege.

   (C) The visual of the green/yellow cards informs students nonverbally about when Ms. Sandal is about to reach the end of her patience and remove the privilege.

   (D) The visual of the green/yellow cards allows students to show their strong willingness to take risks and support their peers' desire for the privilege.

10. What additional strategy can Ms. Sandal implement to help students keep the cards green?

   (A) Ms. Sandal can monitor the groups and quietly remind students that they need to participate in their groups or risk having a card turned.

   (B) Ms. Sandal can place students with low participation together and discuss how their grades will be impacted with no one to do the work for them.

   (C) Ms. Sandal can assign clear rotating roles where the success of the task depends on each student meeting the responsibilities of their role.

   (D) Ms. Sandal can assign roles based on skills and abilities and use group participation to assign part of the grade.

11. A fifth-grade teacher is working with two students on resolving a conflict that has resulted from ignoring one of her classroom procedures. What should be her primary goal?

(A) A primary goal of conflict resolution should be to guide students toward reaching a mutually agreeable settlement.

(B) A primary goal of conflict resolution should be for the teacher to make the final call with a solution that is fair to both students.

(C) A primary goal of conflict resolution should be to determine which student is the aggressor and which student is the victim.

(D) A primary goal of conflict resolution should be for the teacher to provide noninvolved, sympathetic, third-party arbitration.

Use the following information to answer questions 12 and 13.

A middle school science teacher is planning a unit on energy transformations within ecological systems. She wants to select teaching strategies that will help her students understand this abstract yet important basic science concept.

Competency 007: *The teacher understands and applies principles and strategies for communicating effectively in varied teaching and learning contexts.*

12. Which teaching strategy would her students find most helpful in learning this concept?

(A) She should ensure that time is built into the unit for her to revisit and repeat these abstract concepts and also allow time for student questions to enhance clarity.

(B) She should begin the lesson with a K-W-L chart to explore students' prior knowledge of the topic and include in the unit plan a reminder to revisit the L-column of the chart.

(C) She should share concrete examples from the context of her students' life experiences and ask students to contribute additional examples with which they are familiar.

(D) She should begin the lesson with a list of relevant terms students will encounter during the unit and have students define each as they occur during the unit.

13. How could she encourage students to think more in depth and have positive feelings about their knowledge of energy transformations in ecological systems?

   (A) She could have individual students think of three examples of ecological systems. Students would research and state whether energy transformations occur within each of the named systems.

   (B) She could assign individual students different ecological systems. Students would research their assigned systems and write a report on the system and state if any energy transformations occur within the given system.

   (C) She could have students write a research paper defining energy transformations within a given ecological system and give an example of an energy transformation in the given system.

   (D) She could give teams of students a set of beginning and ending points of energy transformations within specified systems. Students would explain the energy changes that occur and support their explanations with research.

Competency 008: *The teacher provides appropriate instruction that actively engages students in the learning process.*

14. Timeliness and a strong commitment to a job well done are very important to Ms. Koradji, a middle school teacher. From day 1, she has repeatedly stated to her students that she gets her work done in a timely manner and expects the same from them. She models her commitment by returning graded assignments within one to two days of collecting them. What is the greatest benefit of this attitude and practice to Ms. Koradji's students?

   (A) Ms. Koradji is modeling effective work habits that also encourage her students to increase their expectations of themselves and improve their own performance.

   (B) Ms. Koradji is modeling effective work habits that also allow her students and their families to keep track of their performance levels based on returned grades.

   (C) Ms. Koradji is modeling effective work habits while monitoring her students' completion of assignments to ensure that no student falls behind on handing in work.

   (D) Ms. Koradji is modeling effective work habits that also encourage her students to improve their own work habits, which will be very important to their success in high school.

Grades 4–8

Use the following information to answer questions 15 and 16.

The day after 9/11, students arrive in social studies class wanting to discuss the event. The students have strong opinions about the causes of 9/11 and about possible reactions and repercussions. A unit on tolerance toward differences and responses to violence is planned for two months from now.

Competency 008: *The teacher provides appropriate instruction that actively engages students in the learning process.*

15. What decision would be most appropriate for the teacher to make at this time?

   (A) Indicate to the students that home is the most appropriate setting for the discussion they are asking for and continue with the planned lesson.
   (B) Devote the needed class time to allow students to thoroughly discuss the topic and move the unit forward in time because this event has introduced it.
   (C) Remind students how much information is in the curriculum and promise to leave some time for discussion if they stay focused on today's lesson.
   (D) Acknowledge that the topic is highly emotional and encourage students to form support groups for further discussion outside school.

16. Based on comments from the class about an appropriate response by the U.S. government, how can the teacher guide students to apply skills that will assist them in becoming lifelong learners using this high-interest topic?

   (A) Have students examine the available information of the event and sort it as factual or emotional and discuss the potential impact on the response.
   (B) Split students into two teams and have them conduct a mock debate to guide the government in making a decision about how to respond.
   (C) Brainstorm potential responses the government could make and poll the school to see which response is favored and why.
   (D) Encourage students to select the possible response they support and write a clear rationale for their position supported by evidence.

Competency 009: *The teacher incorporates the effective use of technology to plan, organize, deliver, and evaluate instruction for all students.*

17. Teachers on a middle school teaching team have their students working on an integrated unit where the final product will be multimedia presentations from individual students. Each teacher has established clear content requirements to be included in the end product so that content will receive a greater emphasis from the students than presentation design. How can the teachers most effectively encourage the appropriate balance between content and presentation design as the final products are developed?

   (A) The students and teachers should work together to design a rubric that clearly establishes the content and design expectations and the balance between these two components of the final product before the students begin their projects.

   (B) The teachers should share a list of acceptable product design suggestions that students can select from after the content part of the project is done so that the design aspect of the project does not get out of hand.

   (C) Students must submit a draft of the content portion of the project for approval before beginning on the project design component, which must also be approved.

   (D) All teachers should provide daily reminders of the expected balance between content and project design as students work on completing the required individual final products.

Grades 4–8

Competency 010: *The teacher monitors student performance and achievement; provides students with timely, high-quality feedback; and responds flexibly to promote learning for all students.*

18. A middle-school English teacher is working with her students on clarity in writing as they prepare book reports. She has each student complete a book report and give it to a peer for editing. Then she looks at all the edited reports before returning them to the writer. On one report, she writes, "I agree with your peer editor that some of your sentences are hard to follow or understand. You are using very complex, compound sentences, which is a very sophisticated level of writing but might not be appropriate for clarity with your peers. How can you simplify and still write on an advanced and sophisticated level?" Based on the research on instructional feedback, what will be the most likely response to this teacher's note?

(A) The comment to the author of the book report will probably be ineffective in prompting improvement as the feedback gives a negative response followed by a positive response about using a sophisticated writing style and does not give clear suggestions about how to make appropriate changes.

(B) The comment to the author of the book report will probably be effective in prompting improvement as the feedback gives a positive response about using a sophisticated writing style, which counter-balances being told some sentences are hard to understand, and so they will readily make suggested changes.

(C) The comment to the author of the book report will probably be effective in prompting improvement as the feedback gives a positive response about using a sophisticated writing style and motivates to find ways to improve, which counterbalances being told some sentences are hard to understand.

(D) The comment to the author of the book report will probably be effective in prompting improvement as the feedback gives a negative response followed by a positive response about using a sophisticated writing style and allows freedom in deciding how to make appropriate changes.

Use the following information to answer questions 19 and 20.

Mr. Sanchez arranges a conference with Lilly's parents to discuss her continual failure to complete in-class and homework assignments. He explains to the parents his educational rationale for these assignments and discusses with them the need for everyone—teacher, student, and parents—to work together to help Lilly address this problem. Mr. Sanchez asks for their support at home. They readily agree that Lilly needs to establish better study habits as a fifth-grader to aid her successful move into middle school. They agree to help with this at home but state they are not sure how to do this.

Competency 011: *The teacher understands the importance of family involvement in children's education and knows how to interact and communicate effectively with families.*

19. What is the most appropriate action for Mr. Sanchez to suggest to Lilly's parents?

(A) Select a quiet area of the home where Lilly can be comfortable as she studies. Set a daily schedule of appropriate study times and ensure that she works in the selected area and maintains the schedule.

(B) Work with Lilly to designate a comfortable, quiet area in the home appropriate for study. Help Lilly establish a daily study schedule and monitor her use of the study location and schedule.

(C) Sit with Lilly each evening as she works on her homework. Ask in-depth comprehension questions of her in each subject to determine if she understands the work she is doing.

(D) Keep a written record of the amount of time Lilly spends on her schoolwork each evening and the subject she is studying. Compare this study log to the list of assignments Lilly records daily in school.

20. What action is most appropriate for Mr. Sanchez to take to help Lilly's parents monitor Lilly's progress?

(A) Mr. Sanchez should record Lilly's assignments each day and send home the list and the appropriate texts and materials needed to complete them so the parents can work with Lilly. Have them call if they have questions.

(B) Post assignments in a visible location. Ask all the students to record daily assignments in a log. Let Lilly's parents know he will sign the log if there are no assignments due. Send a weekly report of progress.

(C) Provide the parents with a weekly report of Lilly's daily progress toward completing assignments. Her parents must sign and return the weekly report. If Lilly does not bring home or return the report, set another conference.

(D) Remind all the students of any posted assignments that are due the following day and encourage them to record them in their assignment logs. Encourage them to think about what they need to take with them to finish.

Competency 012: *The teacher enhances professional knowledge and skills by effectively interacting with other members of the educational community and participating in various types of professional activities.*

21. As a first-year teacher, Ms. Panoly is aware of the importance of working with her assigned mentor. She is having trouble getting content area concepts across to her students. So Ms. Panoly invites her mentor to observe her science class to give her specific feedback on how she might improve. Her mentor suggests that she use more concrete hands-on learning activities, high-order questioning strategies, and cooperative learning groups. What will be the most likely benefit of implementing these strategies?

    (A) Students will become even more confused because of the immediate change in the teacher's instructional strategies.
    (B) Students will test the teacher's commitment to these new strategies by exhibiting disruptive behaviors.
    (C) Students will be more motivated to engage in these instructional approaches; therefore, they will be more likely to take ownership of their learning.
    (D) Students will be intrigued by the new instructional strategies and will enjoy working in cooperative learning groups and using the manipulatives.

22. Paul is an eighth-grade visually impaired student mainstreamed into a science class. His teacher is beginning a unit on rock identification where a dozen rock samples are identified in class. She arranges a meeting with Paul's special education teacher. What assistance is appropriate for her to ask the special education teacher for as she plans this highly visual unit?

    (A) She asks that Paul be removed from science class to the resource room for individual help with this highly visual unit.
    (B) She asks the special education teacher to acquire books on tape about rocks for Paul to listen to during this highly visual unit.
    (C) She asks that Paul be removed from science class to the resource room for individual help with a different unit to replace this highly visual unit.
    (D) She asks for help in designing lessons that depend on senses other than sight to identify the rocks so Paul can participate as much as possible.

Grades 4–8

Competency 013: *The teacher understands and adheres to the legal and ethical requirements for educators and is knowledgeable of the structure of education in Texas.*

23. During lunch in the teachers' lounge, a discussion about accepting outside consulting jobs occurs. The English department chairperson has been hired to share with a school in a neighboring state the advanced poetry curriculum she wrote last summer, which is used by the department. The ethics of accepting this contract are discussed. What would make this contract unethical?

    (A) The department chairperson was the only author and the curriculum was written during the summer without pay.
    (B) The curriculum was designed specifically for the English department where it is now being used.
    (C) The curriculum was written on a home computer and was based on resource materials from the department.
    (D) The preparation for the presentation was made during the department chairperson's conference period.

24. Ms. Vick is concerned about a student who has just transferred into her class. He often has noticeable bruises and has several visible scars. In a casual conversation, she asks the student what happened to cause these injuries. The student drops his head and mumbles something about dirt bike spills. Ms. Vick feels something is odd about his answer and wonders if she has reasonable suspicion of child abuse. What are the legal requirements and responsibilities if a teacher becomes suspicious that a student is being physically abused?

    (A) Once suspicious, a teacher should immediately report the suspected abuse to the principal, nurse, counselor, or other district representative.
    (B) Once suspicious, a teacher should immediately call the state 800 number and report any suspected abuse to the state authorities.
    (C) Once suspicious, a teacher should question the student in depth about abuse or being hurt but must accept the answer or explanation given.
    (D) Once suspicious, a teacher should confront the parents of the student and demand an explanation for the signs that initiated the suspicion of abuse.

25. At the beginning of the school year, a group of teachers are visiting over coffee and talking about preparing students for administration of the TAKS in the spring. There are three first-year teachers present, and experienced teachers are giving them suggestions. Which suggestion would be unethical?

(A) Giving content unit tests written in the style and format of the TAKS test throughout the year to help students become familiar with them.

(B) Giving teacher-made practice tests a few weeks before the TAKS and debriefing how to answer each question after completing the test.

(C) Selecting only content units that address specific objectives measured by the TAKS test to teach and giving unit tests in the TAKS format.

(D) Answering student questions about what a question is asking or helping students interpret a question during the TAKS exam.

26. Just before the winter break, Mr. Larson discovered that he had been about to break copyright laws. He planned to make copies of entire trade books for his sixth-grade literature circle group rather than request that the school purchase additional copies for his students' use. In fear of losing his teaching license, he goes to his mentor to ask for advice and to request that he be given explicit copyright rule information. Which of the following is the most accurate adherence to copyright laws in such cases?

(A) Educators may make one copy of a limited number of pages from a book for classroom use for a one-time purpose.

(B) Teachers have the right to make copies of trade books for classroom use as long as they do not attempt to sell those copies.

(C) Educators are not held to the same copyright standards as is the general public, so Mr. Larson copying these trade books is not an issue.

(D) As long as the copies remain at the school campus, Mr. Larson may make numerous copies of the full text of a trade book.

DECISION SET BEGINS HERE

A new middle school has been built in a community where new housing has been added as the area's population has increased. Teachers at the new school want to clearly establish a collaboration between the school and the community as the school opens. They decide one way to do this is to get parents/guardians and community businesses actively involved in school projects. This means the faculty must take an active role in recruiting volunteers and communicating information about school events.

Competency 005: *The teacher knows how to establish a classroom climate that fosters learning, equity, and excellence and uses this knowledge to create a physical and emotional environment that is safe and productive.*

27. How will classrooms at the new middle school benefit from having an active cadre of classroom volunteers?

   (A) Classroom volunteers will increase the diversity of the adults that students encounter at school, which will help them be more accepting of differences.
   (B) Classroom volunteers will foster a strong sense of community and provide more support opportunities for students to achieve success.
   (C) Classroom volunteers will relieve teachers of time-consuming routine tasks and allow more attention for instructional tasks.
   (D) Classroom volunteers will encourage improved student behavior as parents visiting the school will see how students behave.

One of the experienced teachers employed at the new school shares her experience in establishing a parent/guardian classroom volunteer cadre at a prior school. She explains that after a short time some of the parent/guardian volunteers stopped participating because they felt they were not truly welcome at the school. They also indicated that they did not feel that the time they spent on school volunteer work was useful, effective, or productive for either the school or themselves.

Grades 4–8

Competency 011: *The teacher understands the importance of family involvement in children's education and knows how to interact and communicate effectively with families.*

28. What plans can the faculty make to ensure that this set of parent/guardian volunteers feel welcome and that they are making valuable contributions to the school?

    (A) Have a specific place at the school for parent/guardian volunteers to gather and work when they are not active in a classroom. Allow these adults to decide what role will most help the school and fulfill their own sense of worth and participation.

    (B) Have a specific place for parent/guardian volunteers to gather and work at the school. Allow teachers, as they need assistance, to draw from the pool of volunteers, which will make a variety of tasks and opportunities available and reduce volunteer boredom.

    (C) Have a specific place for parent/guardian volunteers to gather and work at the school. Have a variety of tasks that need doing either during or out-side school hours that clearly contribute to the smooth functioning of classrooms.

    (D) Have parent/guardian volunteers work only within classrooms where their child is present. This will allow them to see how their work is directly contributing to an improved educational environment for their child.

A teacher with a background in both elementary and middle school teaching mentions that in her experience "it is easy to get elementary volunteers, but middle school is another story. Middle school students don't want their parents at school, and the parents aren't interested in being here."

29. How can the teachers encourage parent/guardian interactions with the school if the attitude expressed by this teacher has some truth to it?

    (A) The school can set up communication pathways such as newsletters, phone trees, or e-mails to notify the community of school events such as sports events and musical programs where parents can interact in a nonthreatening way.

    (B) The school can schedule times to allow teachers to meet with all the parents to introduce them to the new school and ask them to get involved. Notices sent home and posters about the event displayed at local businesses can help spread the word.

    (C) Students can be motivated to help the school get their parents/guardians to visit by planning an open house where students give tours of the new building and earn bonus points if their parents attend.

    (D) Teachers can schedule individual conferences with the parents of each student to discuss the impact the school wants to make in the community and how their student can take an active role in this process and benefit educationally.

A fourth-grade student's mother who has recently stopped working outside the home indicates to her daughter's teacher that she wants to become more active in her child's education now that she has more time. The mother also says she is not really interested in the general types of activities a parent volunteer performs. She is interested in advancing her daughter's learning rather than working with all the students in the class. She asks the teacher for advice on how to appropriately become more directly involved in her child's education as a classroom volunteer.

Competency 010: *The teacher monitors student performance and achievement; provides students with timely, high-quality feedback; and responds flexibly to promote learning for all students.*

30. Which of the following would be an appropriate role for the mother to fill in her daughter's classroom?

(A) The mother could provide observational information about her daughter outside school and assist the teacher with interpreting both the in-school and out-of-school information.

(B) The teacher could ask the mother to attend class and collect observational data about the students and their peer interactions within the classroom because two observers see twice as much.

(C) The teacher could ask the mother to focus on her daughter's personal and social growth while leaving her cognitive or academic growth to the teacher because she is the expert in these areas.

(D) The teacher should calmly and professionally help the mother to understand that because parents already have a clear role they are not expected to play this strong a role in their student's education.

DECISION SET ENDS HERE

DECISION SET BEGINS HERE

In Ms. Stein's fifth-grade science class, students are studying individual and societal responsibilities related to energy conservation. Students are preparing to take a water break when Diana states that they should turn out the lights while they are out of the classroom. Other students think this is not important. The students state they will be gone only five minutes and this is not a big conservation of energy that can really make a difference. They grumble about Diana's bossiness as they walk down the hall. When students return from the break, Ms. Stein asks them to discuss the two perspectives about energy conservation. She asks each student to create a statement that expresses his or her understanding of the two perspectives.

Competency 007: *The teacher understands and applies principles and strategies for communicating effectively in varied teaching and learning contexts.*

31. What is the best reason for Ms. Stein to ask students to create a statement showing they understand the two perspectives?

(A) A clear statement of the two perspectives will tap into students' prior knowledge as they discuss and make decisions about energy conservation.

(B) By creating their own statement of the two perspectives, students will be able to focus on the topic as they debate possible perspectives and responses to similar situations.

(C) Writing a statement of understanding about the two perspectives will help to guide students toward reaching the correct answer about how to best conserve energy in such situations.

(D) A clear statement of understanding by each student will later help the class discuss appropriate actions that people might take to conserve energy.

Competency 004: *The teacher understands learning processes and factors that impact student learning and demonstrates this knowledge by planning effective, engaging instruction and appropriate assessments.*

32. What role has Ms. Stein played by asking students to create their own individual statements regarding their views of energy conservation in such cases?

    (A) Ms. Stein encouraged higher-order critical thinking skills in a real-world context where problem-solving skills can be applied.

    (B) Ms. Stein guided students to write about basic, factual information in order to take the topic to a higher level from a more personal perspective.

    (C) By having students think about problems and issues that directly relate to the energy conservation unit, Ms. Stein has led students to develop their own questions on the topic.

    (D) Ms. Stein has established a link between energy conservation at the global level and students' personal experiences, such as what they encountered in the classroom that day.

Competency 005: *The teacher knows how to establish a classroom climate that fosters learning, equity, and excellence and uses this knowledge to create a physical and emotional environment that is safe and productive.*

33. What was likely the most positive outcome of Ms. Stein directly applying students' immediate conversation to the unit about energy conservation?

    (A) By writing their own personal statement about varying perspectives on the issue, students were encouraged to go beyond the planned unit and engage in learning from their point of interest.

    (B) As students write their statement describing their views of the two perspectives, they are able to take a break from the normal instructional routine.

    (C) Actively encouraging critical thinking about the current issue can later be used to help schedule different elements of the energy conservation unit.

    (D) Ms. Stein has successfully used a teachable moment in a way that saves her time because she may be able to alter what she had planned as a result of students' early writing.

Competency 004: *The teacher understands learning processes and factors that impact student learning and demonstrates this knowledge by planning effective, engaging instruction and appropriate assessments.*

34. What is the main advantage of allowing students to take the topic (energy conservation) in a direction that capitalizes on students' observation of an element of energy conservation within their own classroom?

   (A) Allowing students to be active participants in determining how a unit will flow can alter the direction Ms. Stein planned for the unit but will not take away from any important concepts.

   (B) Asking students to engage immediately in an activity related to the unit, although the topic was not yet in discussion, will help Ms. Stein determine which students need more help during the unit.

   (C) Student interest in a unit increases student ownership of the concepts.

   (D) Having students begin the unit with an activity that resulted from their own conversation gives Ms. Stein insight into their possible interest in the topic of energy conservation.

Competency 005: *The teacher knows how to establish a classroom climate that fosters learning, equity, and excellence and uses this knowledge to create a physical and emotional environment that is safe and productive.*

35. At the end of the day, Ms. Stein asks the class to consider the possible effects that their writing and discussion could have on the entire student body and possibly on the global community. What will be the most important impact of this request?

   (A) By having students consider the impact that they might have on an energy conservation issue, they will have a better understanding of the value of research when they seek to find solutions to global problems.

   (B) A sense of purpose in addressing local or global problems such as energy conservation is developed when students take ownership of their learning by connecting to their interests.

   (C) By having students write their views of energy conservation perspectives early in the unit, they will have a clear topic to research in a logical sequence of steps.

   (D) Writing and discussing the issue related to energy conservation early in the unit will help students find solutions to the questions Ms. Stein has planned for later.

Competency 008: *The teacher provides appropriate instruction that actively engages students in the learning process.*

36. The next day, Ms. Stein directs students to research the two perspectives to determine whether turning off lights for a brief period of time can actually conserve energy. What is the most critical aspect of collecting data and drawing conclusions in such lessons?

   (A) This strategy can guide students to value group work in solving global problems in the future.
   (B) This approach can help students understand the importance of listening to everyone's opinion.
   (C) This lesson can help students understand the importance of carefully researching a global problem before identifying an answer.
   (D) This lesson can guide students to establish thinking skills using the same process to solve future problems.

DECISION SET ENDS HERE

DECISION SET BEGINS HERE

Pam Landers is a first-year home-life skills teacher. A teacher with ten years experience is mentoring her. As she begins to plan for her coed middle school classes, which are electives, she wants to ensure that members of both genders have a positive experience in the class.

Competency 002: *The teacher understands student diversity and knows how to plan learning experiences and design assessments that are responsive to differences among students and that promote all students' learning.*

37. What is most important for Ms. Landers to do to create the gender-equitable learning environment she wants?

    (A) She should have differentiated expectations for students based on gender-related attitudes, interests, and abilities. She must acknowledge that these gender differences exist and accommodate for them.

    (B) She should alternate class activities that appeal to one gender more than another but encourage both genders to participate fully in each. This will allow for high interest when the activity fits the gender and never allow either gender to slide.

    (C) She should have clear rubrics for evaluating each activity from the perspective of the appropriate gender. Having separate rubrics for the genders allows accommodation for gender differences in performance.

    (D) She should select activities where both genders will see that having the knowledge and skills addressed is appropriate and of interest. There should be clear rubrics with no gender accommodation of expectations.

Ms. Landers spends some time visiting with her mentor to discuss how she can allow students to work at the different pacing that will result from the varied backgrounds and skill levels of her students while keeping them engaged in purposeful, on-task behaviors. Because the home skills class is an elective, she is worried that students will goof off rather than work independently as this type of class requires.

Competency 006: *The teacher understands strategies for creating an organized and productive learning environment and for managing student behavior.*

38. What is the best advice Ms. Lander's mentor can share?

    (A) Select several students in the class who exhibit the type of purposeful, on-task behaviors she wants and call the other students' attention to these excellent role models.

    (B) Set clear teacher expectations and have students self-evaluate how effectively they think they are meeting these expectations for a weekly participation grade.

    (C) Establish routines and procedures for students to follow as they arrive in class, indicate attendance, collect the materials they will need for a project, and begin work.

    (D) Involve the students in designing classroom rules of behavior, consequences for not following the rules, and grading scales used to determine student success.

Competency 008: *The teacher provides appropriate instruction that actively engages students in the learning process.*

39. What will be the most likely result of Ms. Landers following her mentor's advice to establish routines and procedures for students to follow as they arrive in class, indicate attendance, collect the materials they will need for a project, and begin work?

    (A) Students will reject any changes she tries to make from what they have come to expect.

    (B) Students will gain the skills needed to work independently and productively.

    (C) Students will learn to use problem-solving skills because Ms. Landers is not available.

    (D) Students will begin to arrive late to class because they are not under teacher supervision.

After a teacher-directed lesson on a new skill, Ms. Landers plans for students to work in pairs and small groups as they practice the new skill. This allows peers to offer timely suggestions to help strengthen new skills without waiting until Ms. Landers has time to visit with each group to monitor their progress.

Competency 010: *The teacher monitors student performance and achievement; provides students with timely, high-quality feedback; and responds flexibly to promote learning for all students.*

40. Which approach is most likely to produce constructive and positive interactions between her middle school students during these peer feedback activities?

   (A) Encouraging the teams to discuss the performance criteria explained during instruction to ensure that they are clear to all before they start.
   (B) Allowing students to determine if they want to work alone or to select students they wish to team with as a reward for cooperative behavior.
   (C) Modeling for students some appropriate and positive ways of suggesting changes as they work within their groups to improve their skills.
   (D) Assigning students with widely ranging skill levels to a group to ensure that each group has a range of strengths and skills to draw on.

DECISION SET ENDS HERE

DECISION SET BEGINS HERE

For her third year of teaching, Ms. Shaw accepts a transfer from fifth to eighth grade. She wants to work with older students whom she feels are more autonomous and will need less "mothering" from her. During the first week of school, Ms. Shaw discovers that 20 of her students have limited English proficiency. There are nine languages other than English spoken in the homes of these students. As Ms. Shaw makes her plans for the new school year, she is very aware that she has a challenging student population and must revise the plans she made following notification of her transfer.

Competency 002: *The teacher understands student diversity and knows how to plan learning experiences and design assessments that are responsive to differences among students and that promote all students' learning.*

41. Ms. Shaw wants to address the language needs and content learning of her limited English proficiency students as she modifies her plans, lessons, and assessments. How can she best meet these goals?

   (A) Ms. Shaw can present lessons to these students that address less-demanding concept TEKS than the lessons she plans for her other students.
   (B) Ms. Shaw can provide language development experiences yet hold these students to the same content TEKS addressed in the lessons for other students.
   (C) Ms. Shaw can present lessons drawn only from TEKS taught with concrete materials to provide language development experiences with real objects.
   (D) Ms. Shaw can focus on language acquisition with these students and worry about their content learning after their English fluency has improved.

42. When planning for students with limited English proficiency, which of the following instructional strategies will give Ms. Shaw's students the greatest opportunity for advancing their learning?

   (A) Ms. Shaw should allow the students to indicate to her their frustrations in learning both English and content.
   (B) Ms. Shaw should assess these students daily to ensure that they are keeping up with the rest of the class.
   (C) Ms. Shaw should use a wide range of assessment styles to ensure a clear picture of her students' individual progress.
   (D) Ms. Shaw should assign each student a higher-level learning partner who will help direct the student's work.

Competency 001: *The teacher understands human developmental processes and applies this knowledge to plan instruction and ongoing assessment that motivate students and are responsive to their developmental characteristics and needs.*

43. After the second week of class, it is also apparent to Ms. Shaw that her eighth-grade students are not all at the same cognitive developmental level. What is the best strategy for adapting instruction that will allow the diverse needs of her students to be met?

    (A) She should use the think-pair-share strategy as her primary instructional adaptation.
    (B) She should blend students from each cognitive level present as she forms groups.
    (C) She should target instruction to the main cognitive development level of her students.
    (D) She should illustrate abstract concepts through hands-on instructional activities.

After the fourth week of school, Ms. Shaw approaches the school guidance counselor and tells her that she needs to speak with him. She explains to Mr. Garcia that she recently transferred to eighth grade and that her prior experience had been in a fifth-grade class. She now finds that her newly assigned class has a high number of students with significant academic needs and she feels unsure and a bit overwhelmed because it is not what she had expected. She indicates her desire to rise to the challenges she is facing.

Competency 005: *The teacher knows how to establish a classroom climate that fosters learning, equity, and excellence and uses this knowledge to create a physical and emotional environment that is safe and productive.*

44. How can Ms. Shaw best avoid becoming a barrier to success for her students with their significant academic needs?

    (A) Ms. Shaw should set high standards, differentiate instruction, and have high expectations for all the students regardless of their level of academic need.
    (B) Because all the students are in the same grade and attended this school last year, Ms. Shaw should have the same expectations of and instruct all the students in the same way.
    (C) Ms. Shaw should understand the social challenges some students face and take this into account as she plans instruction, assessments, and expectations for them.
    (D) Ms. Shaw must collect information such as ethnicity, socioeconomic status, at-risk status, or parental education levels to set reasonable expectations for the students.

Mr. Garcia wishes to aid Ms. Shaw in successfully facing the challenges of her new teaching assignment. He suggests that he observe her interactions with her students and she agrees. During his observation, he notices that Ms. Shaw's behaviors vary between two groups of students. In their follow-up conference he states, "You provide higher-achieving students significantly longer wait time than you provide lower-achieving students. In addition, with lower-achieving students you restate a question as many as three times within the same amount of wait time you allow the higher-achieving students. Both types of students indicate they perceive your restated questions as totally new questions."

Competency 007: *The teacher understands and applies principles and strategies for communicating effectively in varied teaching and learning contexts.*

45. How is this behavior most likely to affect Ms. Shaw's classroom?

   (A) A difference in wait time is an effective instructional differentiation. It allows both groups success opportunities by giving different thinking and response times.

   (B) Longer wait time for higher-achieving students signals all students that more is expected from these top students. This produces resentment in both groups.

   (C) Shorter wait time allows lower-achieving students less time to feel that they are "on the spot." Restated questions indicate that lower-achieving students are given more opportunities to succeed.

   (D) Shorter wait time and restated questions signal differentiated expectation levels to all students. This reinforces feelings of an inability to achieve in lower-achieving students.

After listening to her students talk before class, Ms. Shaw asks Mr. Garcia to visit with Lilly, a student who has indicated to her friends that she plans to become pregnant so she can get out of school. Lilly readily admits that school has no meaning for her and that she sees no reason to continue. She explains she wants a child so that someone will love her.

Competency 001: *The teacher understands human developmental processes and applies this knowledge to plan instruction and ongoing assessment that motivate students and are responsive to their developmental characteristics and needs.*

46. What background information on adolescent students must Mr. Garcia, the middle school counselor, have in order to conduct an effective discussion with Lilly about her decision?

    (A) Many students this age are focused on present needs and desires rather than on long-term consequences.

    (B) Many students this age have not found a place in the school's society and feel they do not fit.

    (C) Many students this age are not able to apply logical reasoning patterns to planning their lives.

    (D) Many students this age do not recognize adults as being able to give valid advice to their age group.

DECISION SET ENDS HERE

DECISION SET BEGINS HERE

At the beginning of the year, Mr. Zastrow, a middle school principal informs his faculty that he expects them to do long-term rather than short-term planning during the coming year. To this end, he expects to see integrated unit plans. To make this easier to accomplish he has scheduled the same conference periods for members of teaching teams. He also indicates that unit plans must be completed and submitted to him at least one week before any instruction on the unit occurs. Teachers must decide how long each unit is to last, but he will not accept a string of week-long units.

Competency 003: *The teacher understands procedures for designing effective and coherent instruction and assessment based on appropriate learning goals and objectives.*

47. What is the primary reason the principal feels so strongly about having the entire unit planned before instruction begins?

    (A) Having the entire unit planned before beginning instruction increases the likelihood that content and learning activities will be sequenced in a logical manner to increase student retention of the material.

    (B) Having the entire unit planned before beginning instruction allows for the selection of age-appropriate presentation formats for the integrated content and topic development needed for a cohesive unit.

    (C) Having the entire unit planned before beginning instruction allows a clear overview of the unit so more interesting approaches can be inserted where instruction style was not stimulating in the original draft.

    (D) Having the entire unit planned before beginning instruction allows for integrated content topics and age-appropriate learning activities to be selected and presented based on indicated student needs.

Mr. Blalock plans and submits to Mr. Zastrow an integrated unit for his sixth-grade class that addresses science, math, social studies, reading, and art. He plans both whole-class and small-group lessons as part of the unit. He has included a guest speaker, a field trip, a web quest, a video, and learning centers as some of the instructional activities for the unit.

Competency 008: *The teacher provides appropriate instruction that actively engages students in the learning process.*

48. What is the most important instructional advantage of Mr. Blalock's integrated unit plan?

(A) Mr. Blalock's integrated unit plan allows him to address a large amount of content information in a shorter period of instructional time.

(B) Mr. Blalock's integrated unit plan allows students multiple and varied opportunities to process, internalize, and reinforce the unit's content.

(C) Mr. Blalock's integrated unit plan allows him to individualize instruction to meet the needs of students with different ability levels.

(D) Mr. Blalock's integrated unit plan allows him flexibility in pacing the lessons to meet the needs of students with different ability levels.

Mr. Blalock has never used learning centers for instruction but has noticed that Ms. Green used them successfully last year. After visiting with her, he is ready to give them a try.

Competency 010: *The teacher monitors student performance and achievement; provides students with timely, high-quality feedback; and responds flexibly to promote learning for all students.*

49. What would be the best strategy for Mr. Blalock to use in determining how well his students are progressing as a result of including literature circles?

(A) Use a checklist to monitor the number of times each student engages in the literature discussion each time that strategy is used.

(B) Interview students to determine their preference for participating in literature circle groups versus working alone at their desk to read the assigned literature.

(C) Ask Ms. Green to visit during a literature circle time and give her professional opinion of the effectiveness of this strategy.

(D) Collect observational data on students' active participation in the literature circle discussions to determine that all students are learning through this strategy.

Mr. Blalock wants his sixth-graders to use problem-solving skills during some of the unit's learning activities. He knows he must do some active teaching to guide his students toward success with this type of task rather than just expecting success when he assigns these tasks.

Competency 007: *The teacher understands and applies principles and strategies for communicating effectively in varied teaching and learning contexts.*

50. As Mr. Blalock's students first engage in a problem-solving activity, which of these approaches would be most effective?

    (A) Mr. Blalock should guide students toward the solution using concrete examples.

    (B) Mr. Blalock should reward the student who finds the correct answer first.

    (C) Mr. Blalock should encourage creative approaches to solving the problem.

    (D) Mr. Blalock should ask questions to guide the students toward the correct answer.

Competency 008: *The teacher provides appropriate instruction that actively engages students in the learning process.*

51. Mr. Blalock notices that Pat is having trouble understanding some of the reading he has assigned during the unit. He asks Pat to meet with him and to explain what has been read. What is the main benefit of Mr. Blalock's approach to helping Pat?

    (A) Mr. Blalock's approach helps Pat succeed and develop a sense of ownership toward learning.

    (B) Mr. Blalock's approach allows him to determine and provide instruction specific to Pat's needs.

    (C) Mr. Blalock's approach encourages Pat to focus and pay attention to the assigned reading.

    (D) Mr. Blalock's approach encourages Pat to use higher-order thinking skills when reading.

Mr. Blalock wants to calm his students and encourage them to be prompt as they enter his class following lunch. He decides to read to them for the first five minutes of class. He wants this calm listening time to also improve the students' listening skills. In addition, he hopes to encourage interest and enthusiasm for oral language and reading in a listening context through the books he selects.

Competency 003: *The teacher understands procedures for designing effective and coherent instruction and assessment based on appropriate learning goals and objectives.*

52. What criteria are most important for selecting the book he will read to allow Mr. Blalock to reach all his goals?

(A) Mr. Blalock should select books that have a direct connection to his class's content so that he does not lose 25 minutes of instructional time per week because students absorb content knowledge as they listen.

(B) Mr. Blalock should select books that describe plots, events, and settings new to his students to expand their learning horizon as they encounter new and unexpected events with which they are presently unfamiliar.

(C) Mr. Blalock should select well-written books on topics that are interesting and familiar to his students, as these traits will help hold their interest more effectively and make it easier for them to be attentive.

(D) Mr. Blalock should select books with topics that are not too exciting but are focused on word play and patterns such as puns, rhyming words, or alliteration so that these topics can be discussed in class later.

53. How could Mr. Blalock best assess the effectiveness of this daily listening time?

(A) After two weeks with listening time, Mr. Blalock can cancel the listening time for three days. He can then observe the students' reaction to assess their response to not having the listening time.

(B) After three weeks with listening time to assess students' listening and thinking skills, Mr. Blalock can add questions to determine whether students remember the concepts about predicting future events.

(C) After ten days with listening time, Mr. Blalock can ask students if they wish to continue the book that he has used or if they prefer that he begin another book.

(D) After the first week with listening time, Mr. Blalock can give a short quiz to determine if students are attentive and are using effective listening skills.

Mr. Blalock is so pleased with the improved listening skills exhibited by his class following lunch that he decides to begin each class the same way. As a learning goal, he states, "Students will increase their appreciation of the aesthetic beauty of the English language in an oral context."

54. What is the most significant problem with this learning goal?

   (A) The desired outcome of this learning goal is hard for eighth-graders to achieve because English is the only language they encounter in school.

   (B) It will be difficult to find or create listening activities that will appeal and motivate eighth-graders to achieve this learning goal.

   (C) This learning goal does not indicate the students' prior level of appreciation, which is their starting point to meet this goal.

   (D) This goal is difficult to measure using objective, meaningful assessments, and so it will be difficult to determine if it has been met.

DECISION SET ENDS HERE

DECISION SET BEGINS HERE

In the spring, Mr. Gonzales receives a transfer student, Paula, from another district. Her parents indicate that she is a gifted student and has been taking pre-advanced placement (pre-AP) classes. During the first week of her attendance, Mr. Gonzales' observations cause him to question the accuracy of this student's placement as she appears to be struggling to do the pre-AP work. Her transferred school records have not yet arrived. Mr. Gonzales is considering contacting the parents and explaining that Paula has been mislabeled as gifted and being ready for advanced classes.

Competency 004: *The teacher understands learning processes and factors that impact student learning and demonstrates this knowledge by planning effective, engaging instruction and appropriate assessments.*

55. What is Mr. Gonzales's best action plan at this time?

    (A) Mr. Gonzales knows that moving isn't easy and that he needs to give her additional time to adjust before expecting her to be able to do the work.
    (B) Because Mr. Gonzales knows that school districts have different standards, he should contact her previous school to discuss the differences.
    (C) Mr. Gonzales should contact her parents and inform them that she has been mislabeled and apparently has come from a less demanding situation.
    (D) Mr. Gonzales should keep a close eye on her work and wait until her prior school records arrive to contact her parents about her placement.

56. How can Mr. Gonzales best establish an accurate assessment of this student's academic developmental level before visiting with her parents to discuss his concerns about her adjustment to the new school and placement in appropriate classes?

    (A) Mr. Gonzales should quietly and calmly call Paula's attention to students showing the appropriate academic performance levels and state that he expects the same level of performance from her.
    (B) Mr. Gonzales should question the student in depth about the content addressed in her pre-AP classes and have her retested for gifted and talented placement to gain a more accurate picture.
    (C) Mr. Gonzales should assign two student "buddies" to guide and orient the new student to the new school while observing to see what effect increased familiarity has on her academic performance.
    (D) Mr. Gonzales should talk privately with the student and let her know her academic performance is unacceptable because he knows from her parents that she is capable of much better.

Mr. Gonzales is holding progress conferences with his students' parents/ guardians during the first nine weeks of school. Raul's mother cancels three scheduled appointments and does not attend a fourth one. Mr. Gonzales is very frustrated but is determined to speak with each student's parents/ guardians.

Competency 011: *The teacher understands the importance of family involvement in children's education and knows how to interact and communicate effectively with families.*

57. What is an appropriate next step for Mr. Gonzales?

(A) When Mr. Gonzales schedules the next conference with Raul's mother, he should emphasize the importance of this meeting and his disappointment about the ones she has missed.

(B) To encourage her participation, Mr. Gonzales should ask Raul to communicate to his mother the importance of this conference and how he feels when she doesn't attend.

(C) Mr. Gonzales should accept that Raul's mother is extremely reluctant to attend a school conference and arrange to discuss Raul's progress over the phone.

(D) Mr. Gonzales should accept that all parents are not interested in their children's educational progress and stop trying to force Raul's mother to care and to participate.

After observing Mr. Gonzales in class, the principal meets with him. She tells Mr. Gonzales that she has observed something that concerns her. She indicates that during this observation, at least one-fourth of his class seemed either unable or unwilling to follow his oral directions correctly.

Competency 007: *The teacher understands and applies principles and strategies for communicating effectively in varied teaching and learning contexts.*

58. What is the best way for Mr. Gonzales to ensure that directions are communicated effectively and understood by all?

(A) Provide oral and written directions with examples and modeling.
(B) Provide written directions with examples and modeling.
(C) Provide oral directions and have students repeat them to check for clarity.
(D) Provide short-step written and oral directions with examples and modeling.

59. When his principal analyzes the effectiveness of an observed class discussion with Mr. Gonzales, which of the following should receive the greatest focus in the meeting?

   (A) Mr. Gonzales repeatedly corrected students who were laughing as they told responding students they were wrong.
   (B) Mr. Gonzales ignored students who repeatedly directed comments to each another rather than to him.
   (C) Mr. Gonzales ignored students who jumped in to add to the discussion without waiting to be recognized.
   (D) Mr. Gonzales repeatedly ignored students who interrupted and did not listen to responses.

Competency 010: *The teacher monitors student performance and achievement; provides students with timely, high-quality feedback; and responds flexibly to promote learning for all students.*

60. What is most important if Mr. Gonzales wants to design an appropriate teacher-made test?

   (A) The test should use both objective and performance assessment questions.
   (B) The test should align with objectives and content learning opportunities.
   (C) The test should yield a bell curve for the range of student scores.
   (D) The test should contain questions at several levels of difficulty.

DECISION SET ENDS HERE

DECISION SET BEGINS HERE

Ms. Dixon, a seventh-grade science teacher, notices that 13-year-old Jason has been less attentive in class today. When Ms. Dixon finishes giving the science assignment, Jason slams his book shut and rests his head on his desk with his eyes closed.

Competency 001: *The teacher understands human developmental processes and applies this knowledge to plan instruction and ongoing assessment that motivate students and are responsive to their developmental characteristics and needs.*

61. What is the best way for Ms. Dixon to respond to Jason's actions?

    (A) Ignore Jason and continue without him, expecting him to work out his problems independently.
    (B) Call Jason to her desk and give him detention, telling him his behaviors must improve immediately.
    (C) Go to Jason and, quietly say, "I notice you seem upset. What is wrong? Can I possibly help you?"
    (D) Ask Jason why he was so rude and how he plans to handle being upset in a different way in the future.

62. Later in the day, Ms. Dixon meets with the counselor to discuss the rather dramatic recent change she has noticed in Jason's behavior. She is concerned that he may be using drugs. What does this show about the teacher's concern for and knowledge of middle grade students?

    (A) She recognizes the academic, family, and social challenges for students Jason's age.
    (B) She recognizes individual developmental differences between Jason and his peers.
    (C) She recognizes that student involvement in risky behaviors impacts development and learning.
    (D) She recognizes the structure of middle schools and the characteristics of middle school children.

Given Jason's recent behaviors, the teacher realizes that he may simply be experiencing a lack of self-confidence and self-efficacy. She believes that the use of a science portfolio might be a way to build Jason's sense of confidence and competence.

Competency 002: _The teacher understands student diversity and knows how to plan learning experiences and design assessments that are responsive to differences among students and that promote all students' learning._

63. What is the best guidance the teacher can give Jason in order to scaffold his development of a quality learning portfolio?

   (A) Provide a list of portfolio divisions and required examples the teacher has chosen.
   (B) Make available a sample portfolio he might use as a model, explaining how he can prepare a similar one.
   (C) Explain the purpose of a portfolio and ask him to create what he thinks is best to meet that purpose.
   (D) Encourage personal ownership of the portfolio by allowing him to choose section labels and work examples unique to each label.

At Jason's school, the teachers recognize that the inner-city school setting does not allow students to experience the grandeur of nature. However, the teachers feel that student appreciation of the aesthetic beauty and grandeur of nature is an important learning goal.

Competency 003: _The teacher understands procedures for designing effective and coherent instruction and assessment based on appropriate learning goals and objectives._

64. What is the most significant problem Jason's science teacher might have with this learning goal?

   (A) This aesthetic learning goal is difficult to address in this environment. Objectively and meaningfully assessing this goal is also difficult.
   (B) The desired outcome indicated by the learning goal is unattainable with these students in this inner-city environment that provides no daily examples.
   (C) Finding or creating instructional activities that will appeal to this student population will be difficult because they have limited or no experience with nature.
   (D) This learning goal does not indicate the prior content knowledge or experiences that inner-city students need to reach this goal.

65. The social studies teachers for grades 5–8 at Jason's school have decided to align their curricula. What should they look for *first* as they map their curricula?

   (A) Gaps in alignment of the school's curriculum with district goals across grades 5–8
   (B) Gaps, overlaps, and redundancies in the instructional plans across grades 5–8
   (C) Differences between social studies lesson plans for grades 5–8
   (D) Outdated objectives and lesson plans across grades 5–8

66. The seventh-grade social studies team at Jason's school wants to plan an integrated curriculum unit on the cultural history of colonial Texas. What should be the *first* step in organizing this thematic unit?

   (A) Decide what assessment(s) will be employed.
   (B) Locate resources on Texas culture, including technology and external sources.
   (C) Decide what topics will be taught in each area of the curriculum.
   (D) Develop a curriculum map and decide which subject areas will logically fit within the unit.

DECISION SET ENDS HERE

DECISION SET BEGINS HERE

Teachers in an urban middle school routinely plan in teams in order to offer their learners the most equitable learning environment. Teachers work in both horizontal and vertical teams on instructional design. Grades 6–9 are in the same building. Even though all the teachers do not have time to meet frequently for planning, they do their best to schedule a major instructional discussion at least twice each semester.

Competency 004: *The teacher understands learning processes and factors that impact student learning and demonstrates this knowledge by planning effective, engaging instruction and appropriate assessments.*

67. Mr. Dixon, an eight-grade mathematics teacher, wishes to use small groups in his classroom but is concerned that one student in a group might do all the work. What is the *most* effective strategy for the teacher to use to avoid this problem?

   (A) Give each member of a group a specific role for which they are responsible.
   (B) Threaten to split the final grade by 4 if only one person does all the work.
   (C) Monitor the groups closely to make sure no one person takes control of a group.
   (D) Give each group member specific questions to answer and share with the group.

One of the eighth-grade science teachers desires to vary his instructional strategies. He plans what he believes will be a motivational inquiry lesson. He prepares two buckets filled with water and places them on a table in the lab area. One bucket of water has a bar of soap at the bottom; the other has what appears to be the same type of soap bar floating on the top. The problem to be solved is, "Why is the soap in one bucket floating while the soap in the other bucket is on the bottom?"

68. What is the primary reason that this is a good inquiry strategy?

   (A) The problem piques curiosity and questioning by the students.
   (B) The problem requires students to read about different kinds of soap.
   (C) The problem causes the students to form a rationale for why the soap is floating.
   (D) The problem causes students to think independently and question their own judgment.

At this middle school, Mr. Huang has a 30-minute time slot for a math lesson in his sixth-grade class. He prefers to conduct a constructivist lesson to engage his students in effective learning.

69. Which statement is correct in regard to Mr. Huang's wish to employ constructivism as an instructional strategy?

   (A) A constructivist lesson is not appropriate in a math class.
   (B) Fourth- through eighth-graders are too old for constructivist lessons.
   (C) A constructivist lesson is likely to require more than 30 minutes.
   (D) A constructivist lesson cannot fill the 30-minute time slot.

Competency 005: *The teacher knows how to establish a classroom climate that fosters learning, equity, and excellence and uses this knowledge to create a physical and emotional environment that is safe and productive.*

70. Barbara Marikow, a first-year seventh-grade teacher at this campus, is committed to a learning environment where students feel free to take risks from the beginning of the year. She believes that the use of effective questioning strategies will support her students' sense of risk taking. One student's response to a question is only partially correct. What response should the teacher give *first* in order to dignify this student's attempt to answer the question?

   (A) Acknowledge the correct part and cue/prompt the student for the other part.
   (B) Acknowledge the correct part and ask someone else to expand on that answer.
   (C) Restate the question, and call on another student to answer.
   (D) Throw out the question and start again, with a clarified question.

71. An eighth-grade social studies teacher at this campus decides to use Hilda Taba's concept development strategy to introduce a unit on the Civil War. What is the primary reason that this method for ensuring that concepts are attained and retained is a good way to begin?

   (A) The concept development method allows all students to safely interact.
   (B) The concept development method gives the teacher an idea of how well the concept is understood by the students.
   (C) The concept development method allows for practice in grouping, naming, and regrouping.
   (D) The concept development method leads to the drawing of key conclusions by students.

Ms. Marikow is now planning a brainstorming activity for her seventh-grade class. She plans to lay down some ground rules before the activity, such as the following.

- Respect each person's responses and do not make fun of each other.
- Piggybacking on the answers of others (e.g., black bird, red bird, yellow bird) is acceptable if you can't think of a response.
- All answers will be accepted as given; answers can be changed only with the permission of the person who gave the answer.

72. What element of the learning environment is promoted by setting these ground rules?

(A) Student understanding of the value of piggybacking on a peer's idea
(B) Student awareness of the value of collaboration with their peers
(C) Student awareness of the impact of their actions and attitudes on others
(D) Student understanding of the brainstorming experience with peers

There are six science labs and seven science teachers on the seventh-grade team. Because of this lack of sufficient lab space, Ms. Carr, one of the science team members, must teach science in a regular classroom. She is concerned about the safety of her students in an environment that is not designed for the use of lab equipment.

Competency 006: *The teacher understands strategies for creating an organized and productive learning environment and for managing student behavior.*

73. How might she organize her classroom to ensure safety during science instruction?

(A) Cluster desks in groups of four, spacing the groups evenly around the room.
(B) Ask for tables, and space them to allow free movement about the room.
(C) Ask for tables, and create a U shape so that all the students face the teacher.
(D) Keep desks separated so that all the students can work individually.

Ms. Carr encourages her seventh-grade students daily by giving them chances to make choices. She provides many and varied ways for them to feel useful, competent, and like they belong. She truly believes that all her students can achieve and does her best to nurture each individual student.

74. What most significantly indicates Ms. Carr's understanding of how to establish a productive learning environment?

   (A) She knows how to use as many ways as possible to build student resiliency.
   (B) She is able to analyze the ways students and teachers interact.
   (C) She understands that the design for an inclusive classroom environment is critical.
   (D) She recognizes that she should establish a classroom climate that emphasizes collaboration.

Competency 007: *The teacher understands and applies principles and strategies for communicating effectively in varied teaching and learning contexts.*

75. Ms. Carr is planning a unit on energy for her science class. She meets with her mentor to design instructional strategies and learning activities. Which strategy would be most useful at the *initial* stage for communicating to students the concept of energy?

   (A) Using a concept attainment lesson in which both exemplars and nonexemplars are given and students then generate more exemplars
   (B) Using an inquiry lesson in which students interact with different forms of energy
   (C) Using a K-W-L chart in which students explore their prior knowledge of energy
   (D) Using a concept mastery lesson in which students read in pairs about energy, discuss what they have read, and give specific examples.

DECISION SET ENDS HERE

Grades 4–8

DECISION SET BEGINS HERE

In a rural setting, students attend a campus comprised of sixth through ninth grades. Teachers do their best to plan together, but most of their shared planning time is after school. Recently, the district provided professional development workshops to help teachers develop improved skills in questioning, inquiry, hands-on learning, and guiding students in independent learning.

Competency 007: *The teacher understands and applies principles and strategies for communicating effectively in varied teaching and learning contexts.*

76. When giving complicated directions to a group of eighth-grade students on this campus, what is the best approach for ensuring that students have a clear understanding of the task and their assignments?

    (A) Talk slowly to allow time for writing clear notes.
    (B) Use a less complicated vocabulary and model examples.
    (C) Provide the directions in writing and ask if everyone understands them.
    (D) Provide a glossary that explains the key terms used in the directions.

Mr. Wateka encourages his eighth-grade science classes on this campus to work in pairs or small groups while doing hands-on scientific investigations. During follow-up questioning, he encourages the students to confer before answering. He feels that this strategy leads to higher levels of thinking and better thought-out responses.

Competency 008: *The teacher provides appropriate instruction that actively engages students in the learning process.*

77. What does this strategy indicate about Mr. Wateka's understanding of learners at this age?

    (A) Students might cheat on their answers, but the answers are really good.
    (B) Students can help each other in times of academic stress.
    (C) Students retain more of what they hear, see, read, discuss, and do in hands-on activities.
    (D) Students learn best by working in pairs to encourage each other.

78. Mr. Wateka has a very diverse fourth-period class. He wants to make a math lesson about calculating the area of a space as relevant as possible for all the students. What is the best way to do this?

(A) Give the class direct instruction on area and then assign 25 problems from the math textbook.

(B) Put the students in groups of four and give them a diagram of a garden. Have them measure the garden using centimeter cubes and flats.

(C) Ask the students to go home and ask their parents what the measurements of their living room are.

(D) Put the students in groups of four and let them measure the lengths of various objects in the room using yarn.

Competency 009: *The teacher incorporates the effective use of technology to plan, organize, deliver, and evaluate instruction for all students.*

79. The librarian at this middle school wants students to have access to the Internet because some do not have access at home. What should the librarian/media specialist do to ensure appropriate student use of the Internet?

(A) Teach a lesson on appropriate use of the Internet followed by students signing an acceptable-use policy.

(B) Have a lesson on web searches followed by a question-and-answer period.

(C) Have all students sign an acceptable-use policy and then allow them to work independently to search any site.

(D) Bookmark appropriate websites and block access to those deemed inappropriate.

80. Ms. Villareal recognizes that her sixth-grade social studies students have had limited travel experience. She designs a lesson to take her classes at this campus on tours around the world. She does this by uploading to her classroom computer movies from her own video camera showing her world travels. What does this indicate about Ms. Villareal's use of video technology as an instructional tool?

(A) She can take good, informative movies of her travels.

(B) She understands how to bring together video and computer technology.

(C) She knows that virtual tours offer learners valuable opportunities.

(D) She can access and manipulate information from a remote device.

81. Based on her commitment to effective inclusion of current technology, what is the best way for Ms. Villareal to incorporate technology into a sixth-grade activity in which student groups design a scavenger hunt using web resources?

    (A) Teach the students how to use Microsoft PowerPoint to show a scavenger hunt.
    (B) Teach the students how to build a scavenger hunt using a web quest.
    (C) Teach the students how to type their scavenger hunt directions in Microsoft Word.
    (D) Teach the students how to download a scavenger hunt from the web.

After having students experience several kinds of inquiry cubes, Mr. Dolezol gives the following directions to his eighth-grade math class at this campus: "In groups of two, design an inquiry cube that will have a minimum of three attributes. Construct the cube and then give the cube and a feedback sheet to at least three other groups for their exploration."

Competency 010: *The teacher monitors student performance and achievement; provides students with timely, high-quality feedback; and responds flexibly to promote learning for all students.*

82. What kind of assessment would be appropriate for this assignment to gain knowledge about students' understanding of and ability to use inquiry cubes?

    (A) A short-answer test about inquiry cubes
    (B) An essay about inquiry cubes and how they work
    (C) A rubric denoting specific criteria for chosen areas to be assessed
    (D) A portfolio section on inquiry into which students insert examples

Ms. Witt has tried for several days to help her lower-level sixth-graders at this campus understand the concept of fractions. She finally decides to introduce the class to fraction squares. Students work with the squares and soon obtain an understanding of fractions.

83. What does this approach demonstrate about Ms. Witt's flexibility in providing supportive instructional strategies?

    (A) She responded to the situation by adjusting her instructional approach to meet the needs of her learners.
    (B) She listened to students' frustration and then demonstrated her knowledge of manipulatives.
    (C) She promoted student self-assessment to guide their learning.
    (D) She provided students with timely feedback on their learning.

Competency 011: *The teacher understands the importance of family involvement in children's education and knows how to interact and communicate effectively with families.*

84. Ms. Villareal has ESL family night once a month. During this time, she not only works with families for which English is a second language but also incorporates useful strategies for working with students at this age. These events form strong parent-child-teacher bonds. What does this illustrate about Ms. Villareal's professional commitment to the family and the community?

(A) She conducts effective conferences and lessons with parents and other caregivers.

(B) She responds to family concerns and tries to help families solve problems.

(C) She understands how to appropriately interact with families of diverse backgrounds.

(D) She understands the various challenging situations that each student faces daily.

Competency 012: *The teacher enhances professional knowledge and skills by effectively interacting with other members of the educational community and participating in various types of professional activities.*

85. Mr. Witt keeps a journal in which he comments on the lessons he has taught each day, his interactions with students, and other important matters regarding his teaching. What is the most important reason why this is a good practice for any teacher?

(A) Journaling allows teachers to record their interactions with both the school and the community.

(B) Journaling allows a teacher to engage in reflection to identify strengths weaknesses and to plan changes.

(C) Journaling allows a teacher to remember which resources and support systems are available.

(D) Journaling allows a teacher to better understand the value of participating in school, district, and community activities.

86. Mr. Renshaw has learned from a social studies colleague at this campus that Ms. Johnson will be teaching about ancient writing forms in her language arts class at the same time Mr. Renshaw is teaching about ancient Egypt. What would be an appropriate way for Mr. Renshaw to act on this information?

   (A) Ask Ms. Johnson to meet with him about possibly team-teaching the unit.
   (B) Ask Ms. Johnson to include ancient Egyptian writings in her unit.
   (C) Change his unit to something else and delay teaching about ancient Egypt.
   (D) Ask Ms. Johnson to change her unit or delay teaching ancient writings.

87. Ms. Baker is quite frustrated with her last-period seventh-grade class in this small-town district. She cannot seem to get her students to pay attention. As a first-year teacher, she is ready to quit. How might her assigned mentor be of help?

   (A) The mentor can give Ms. Baker some suggestions on managment and possible ways to deal with the class's behavior.
   (B) The mentor can have Ms. Baker observe a class where there are no managament or discipline problems.
   (C) The mentor can conduct a workshop for all teachers having management and discipline problems with their classes.
   (D) The mentor can schedule a time to observe Ms. Baker's class and then give feedback on her management and student discipline.

DECISION SET ENDS HERE

DECISION SET BEGINS HERE

Three first-year teachers have been meeting with their mentors in a group setting after their students leave each afternoon. They have talked about the Texas Educators' Code of Ethics and have mentioned several instances involving classroom teachers that have been in the news lately. The beginning teachers are familiar with the Texas Educators' Code of Ethics but are unsure about some practices they have seen their peers engage in recently.

Competency 013: *The teacher understands and adheres to legal and ethical requirements for educators and is knowledgeable of the structure of education in Texas.*

88. Mr. Lee, a veteran mathematics teacher at this campus, recently served on the state's item review committee for preparation of the seventh-grade math TAKS. He has asked to be given library duty during TAKS testing this spring. Why is this the ethical thing for Mr. Lee to do?

   (A) Mr. Lee gets nervous when the class tests and does not want to make students nervous.
   (B) Mr. Lee is afraid he might weaken and give away some answers.
   (C) Mr. Lee signed a legal document stating he would not disclose test information in any way.
   (D) Mr. Lee does not have a class taking the TAKS, so he should volunteer.

89. Ms. Lock, a veteran social studies teacher, was overheard discussing the health issues of her teammate, Ms. Smith. This information had been shared with Ms. Lock in confidence. The beginning teachers ask their mentors what makes Ms. Lock's actions unethical. Which is most likely their reply?

   (A) Ms. Lock was not sure that what Ms. Smith told her was true.
   (B) Ms. Lock said that Ms. Smith willingly told her about her condition.
   (C) There was no lawful reason for Ms. Lock to reveal what Ms. Smith told her.
   (D) Ms. Smith had previously shared confidential information about Ms. Lock.

Grades 4–8

90. Mr. Dotson, a three-year veteran science teacher at this campus recently requested a student's confidential IEP folder so that he could make modifications to the student's science assignments. Mr. Dotson was suddenly called to the office and in his haste left the student's folder open on his desk. The novice teachers wonder if there is any danger in such a happening. Why might this be a problem?

(A) The open file on the desk can be seen by anyone who enters the room.

(B) The window next to the desk is open, and the papers might be blown away.

(C) The file might become buried under other papers and valuable information could be lost.

(D) The student might come in, see his or her folder open, and read private information.

DECISION SET ENDS HERE

Answer Key

SAMPLE TEST (GRADES 4–8)

Question Number	Correct Response	Competency	Question Number	Correct Response	Competency
1	D	001	26	A	013
2	B	001	27	B	005
3	A	002	28	C	011
4	B	002	29	A	011
5	C	003	30	A	010
6	C	003	31	B	007
7	A	004	32	A	004
8	D	005	33	A	005
9	B	006	34	C	004
10	C	006	35	B	005
11	A	006	36	D	008
12	C	007	37	D	002
13	D	007	38	C	006
14	A	008	39	B	008
15	B	008	40	C	010
16	A	008	41	B	002
17	A	009	42	C	002
18	A	010	43	D	001
19	B	011	44	A	005
20	B	011	45	D	007
21	C	012	46	A	001
22	D	012	47	A	003
23	D	013	48	B	008
24	B	013	49	D	010
25	D	013	50	C	007

Answer Key
SAMPLE TEST (GRADES 4–8)

Question Number	Correct Response	Competency	Question Number	Correct Response	Competency
51	B	008	71	B	005
52	C	003	72	C	005
53	B	003	73	B	006
54	D	003	74	A	006
55	D	004	75	A	007
56	C	004	76	B	007
57	C	011	77	C	008
58	D	007	78	B	008
59	D	007	79	A	009
60	B	010	80	D	009
61	C	001	81	B	009
62	C	001	82	C	010
63	D	002	83	A	010
64	A	003	84	C	011
65	B	003	85	B	012
66	D	003	86	A	012
67	A	004	87	D	012
68	A	004	88	C	013
69	C	004	89	C	013
70	A	005	90	A	013

CORRECT RESPONSES

1. **D** This choice allows for the range of student cognitive development present in the class. (A) groups students by their cognitive levels, and this is not supported by research on effective teaching and learning. It is effective to have students of different abilities work together to enrich the learning of all the students, but the highly structured "study buddies" suggested in (B) are not as effective as small groups with mixed abilities. It is not appropriate to make students at one ability level directly responsible for the success of those at another level, which does not mean that each student should not be supportive of the success of another. (C) assumes that there is a "normal" seventh-grade level of development and ample time to work with individuals. This strategy is more likely to overlook the needs of all groups when instructional levels don't match and time runs short for individualization.

2. **B** Seventh-graders are 12–14 years old, which places them at the end of the concrete operational stage and moving into the formal operational stage. This transitional group would find it easier to learn from the social strategies offered in (B). (C) and (D) focus on instructional strategies required of individuals and do not fully engage these learners. (A) assumes no transitional students.

3. **A** Instruction must be differentiated in ways that do not apply or reinforce labels that cause students to feel isolated or different while having their instructional needs meet. (B) is a form of grouping that is neither supported by research nor generally accepted as a valid instructional strategy. (C) shifts the responsibility for learning and success away from individuals and onto groups. Although group work is very important, it is also important that all members of a group have a responsibility not only to the group but also to themselves. (D) is appropriate as it will enhance student motivation, but it is not the *most* important aspect to consider. (A) is more important to motivation and effective learning.

4. **B** Ms. Wong allows students opportunities to learn and apply the skills needed for this task in a step-by-step manner under direct teacher supervision. This allows for individual differences and, because of daily monitoring, prevents students from delaying or falling behind. The success this ensures can help with their attitude toward science. (A) depends on each student already having the skills needed to complete the science fair project. It does not monitor the students' ability to apply their skills in a timely manner. Receiving a ribbon for participation will not help improve a negative attitude caused by frustration due to a lack of information or skills. (C) can result in a negative attitude toward the project and toward science in general in students at all levels. The flexibility in participation and roles shifts more responsibility to the grade-conscious student, and the learning will be unequal. (D) implies that the skills needed for all scientific research are the same, which is untrue. It also allows for no individuals having a skill already, and this can result in boredom caused by repetition. Students who feel they must endlessly repeat a lesson they are not clear on and so cannot master will develop a negative attitude and fall behind on the project.

5. **C** This is the first step the team needs to take. Without knowing what is expected and without some common skills and topics, the task becomes overwhelming. This step also keeps inappropriate material from being added to an overcrowded curriculum and important information from being lost as themes are selected and units planned. (A), (B), and (D) are all appropriate tasks for the team to address but not as a beginning or first step. A clear picture of the required curriculum needs to be the foundation of the planning efforts.

6. **C** This choice allows Ms. Lopez to work during the coming school year to strengthen weak areas while continuing to make adequate yearly progress with her students, which matches the state's expectations. This is harder and takes more planning than declining any responsibility for teaching knowledge and skills from earlier grade levels that students might be lacking. In (A), the idea of being sure that students have the test-taking skills for a particular format is appropriate but is not the best use of the assessment information. In (B), students are being placed in ability groups, which is not appropriate. Nor is it appropriate to consider only one criterion when deciding on instructional practices for a school year. (D) seems to shift the remediation role for diagnosed weak areas to parents. Although it is not inappropriate to ask for parental assistance, the school should play the leadership role. It is also not appropriate to begin a new year by focusing on problem areas rather than on positive ones as this can produce a negative attitude in teacher, parents, and students that will impact the entire coming year.

7. **A** Mr. Baron has helped his students set criteria for collaborative work and now should guide them through self-evaluation and group evaluation based on following these criteria. (B) assigns leadership roles rather than letting unexpected leaders emerge during the process. It also allows students to choose very different levels of participation rather than encouraging them to become a supportive team. (C) permits students to discriminate against each other and can cause hurt feelings. It does not teach teamwork and results in groups based on friendships, which might be fun but not necessarily effective. (D) focuses on learning the skill of collaborating on the lesson being taught during group work. This might be appropriate to do once when actively teaching the skill of grouping. However, doing this repeatedly wastes instructional time by not giving value to the content the grouping activity provided as part of the learning experience. It is more efficient to consider both aspects—group performance and knowledge acquisition.

8. **D** Having individual time allows students to think and access prior knowledge. Being able to add forgotten or new information from the class discussion reduces pressure. Being able to place at least one idea on an individual chart establishes a pattern of success for the unit. Having the idea written on the chart before another student mentions it during the class discussion gives it additional value. Students who are correct have a stronger motivation in terms of future lessons. These are all good beginnings for a unit. (A) assumes that each student will write something on the chart, but this is not a valid assumption. Students sometimes add information only during the class discussion, and some students do not add any information. Although the teacher may think each student

knows something about a topic, as (B) indicates, this too is not a valid assumption. Students at any grade level have wide and varied background knowledge. (C) suggests a touch of a putdown toward knowledgeable students that should not be present. A strong background should be valued and encouraged to become even stronger.

9. **B** A privilege is earned in some way. Through clearly stated behavior expectations, students have independence from adults through the visual cue as they encourage each other to behave for peer approval and to work for the privilege. This assumes the privilege is important to and will be sought by the group. These issues are all important to adolescents. (A) and (C) are expressed in a negative manner as students push the limits of teacher tolerance until the privilege is removed rather than earned. This represents an adult-against-adolescent perspective, and there are no winners in this type of encounter. In (D), it is not clear what risk students are taking. Is it being caught breaking a rule? How does this support their peers' desire for the privilege? This response doesn't address the question.

10. **C** The roles are not titles but important jobs that impact the completion or success of the task. Each student must perform responsibly in each role as it rotates through the group, and so peers depend on each other's performance. In (A), Ms. Sandal is nagging the groups, which is counterproductive to increasing the self-control of the students. The cards are where every student can see them. (B) is also counterproductive. Students who are already not giving full participation to their groups are probably not motivated by grades, and so the threat of a lower grade will not have much effect. Placing them all together guarantees that they will achieve less and fall further and further behind. (D) allows everyone to have a job they can do successfully, assuming the students in the class have the right balance of skills, but does not provide for growth in skills as other jobs are learned and performed. Again, grades are used as motivation when other motivators could be more successful.

11. **A** A teacher's role in conflict resolution is to assist in solving the problem in a manner acceptable to all rather than to solve the problem for the students or allow it to continue or escalate. (B) is counter to the principles of conflict resolution because the teacher rather than the students provides the solution. This can also result in a continuation of the problem if student buy-in is lacking. (C) is also counter to the principles of conflict resolution that avoid assigning blame. (D) describes a role a teacher may play in conflict resolution but is not the primary goal of students solving their own problems in an equitable and acceptable manner.

12. **C** The strategy in (C) is both the most concrete of those offered and has a high level of student participation. It also sends a clear signal to the teacher about when enough examples for understanding have occurred. (A) and (B) are not incorrect strategies but are not as powerful as the strategy in (C) for the reasons mentioned above. (A) would be better if students were reviewing and repeating the major concepts rather than listening to the teacher do so as this would be a

stronger engagement for students. (B) is a good strategy because it helps students activate prior knowledge, but it also assumes prior knowledge, which may not be accurate. (C) is more effective as it points out specific examples of prior knowledge that students might have but may not recognize as such because of the abstract nature of the concept. (D) is a fairly traditional way to introduce vocabulary in a unit of study but is not as effective as introducing and defining a new term within a context as it is needed.

13. **D** Choice D provides teams of students with specific examples within a certain system. Working together, they must track the changes between start and stop points for energy transformations and support their ideas with research. This strategy provides students with teacher support and guidance without signaling that there is one acceptable answer. It allows teamwork and research to assist in locating the needed information. Students should feel confident about their answers when using this approach. (A) requires students to name three ecological systems, which is a knowledge-level response although students providing three examples are required to do more thinking than if they are assigned three systems. Questions about energy transformations require yes/no responses, which are also at the lowest level of thinking. (B) is very similar to (A) but omits student interactions, which are very important to student motivation at this age. Without peer support and accountability, some students will focus on just transcribing the required information from a source into the report. Questions about energy transformations still require a yes/no approach rather than a depth of thinking and learning. (C) is almost the same as (B). It adds the requirement of establishing one example of an energy transformation in the given system. This might result in more thinking, but it may consist only of recording an example from the resource materials.

14. **A** Ms. Koradji not only clearly states her expectations but also models them for her students. Research tells us that high expectations of students translate into higher student performances. This is especially so when the expectation is also modeled and it is a case of "Do as I do" rather than "Do as I say." The effects described in (B), (C), and (D) also occur but are not as important as the effect obtained from (A). She must also monitor the students' success on assignments as well as their completion of assignments, as stated in (C). Falling behind on comprehension is worse than falling behind on completion. We also know that completion of an assignment does not ensure comprehension of an assignment. Although an improved work habit is an excellent goal, students need this improvement for much more than success in high school. They need it in middle school as well as throughout their lives.

15. **B** Postponing a topic students want to discuss to stay within an artificial time frame ignores the strong motivation that occurs when a teacher takes advantage of a teachable moment. This event was too powerful to ignore or postpone. (A) and (C) assume that students can be redirected from a topic that sparks such high interest. Being able to avoid this discussion at school is not a reasonable expectation. If the teacher refuses to allow it as part of the class, it will occur as a subtopic while the planned lesson is ignored and will be continued in the halls and the lunchroom. By allowing this discussion, the teacher can guide a bal-

anced student discussion rather than allowing one perspective to overpower another or permitting the most vocal students to impose their thoughts and opinions on others. (D) should be done in addition to (B). The teacher should also make students aware that individuals have very different reactions to such an emotional issue and encourage them to be respectful of the varied ways others handle their reactions. Some students want to discuss such an event endlessly, whereas others want to learn the factual information and then ignore the event for a period of time. Yet another group wants to hear all the information without discussing anything. There are many reactions, and all are valid and must be respected.

16. **A** This response is the least emotional and has the broadest informational rather than emotional basis. Emotions run high following such events and should be tempered rather than fanned, and (A) helps with this. (B) could strengthen an emotional response if the debate forces a student to take a position counter to his or her own and others forget that this is not their actual opinion. (C) allows students to see where opinions lie, but this might not be a good situation for students holding less popular opinions. They could become frightened of expressing their true opinions. (D) allows individuals to purge only if writing is an outlet for them. Asking for evidence to support an opinion will help keep emotions under control. Students who do not write readily will find this task onerous.

17. **A** By designing the rubric together, student input and ownership of the project are established while teacher expectations are clearly stated. Both groups know what is expected in the balance between content and presentation design. (B) gives much of the control of the final product to the teachers. Completing all the content work without considering any presentation components may block students from producing a creative product suggested by the content information but not on the suggested product list. (C) also keeps much of the control and creative process away from the students as they seek the teachers' approval for each component of the final product. The focus is more on meeting the teachers' expectations than on the creative use of media to produce an effective final presentation. The daily reminders in (D) will be considered nagging in a very short time. A written rubric, as suggested in (A), is much more effective.

18. **A** The student receives negative feedback ahead of positive feedback, and no concrete suggestions for improvement. The initial negative comment may be as far as the student reads, missing the positive comment about sophisticated style or perhaps interpreting this comment as also being negative because of the initial negative tone. (B), (C), and (D) assume the initial negative comment about clarity will be outweighed by the comment about sophisticated writing style. No clear suggested changes are given in either (B) or (C) so the student may have no idea how to improve. This is not a time for student freedom, as suggested in (D), but for clear modeling of a better style.

19. **B** This choice involves both Lilly and her parents in the process of improving her study habits. Also, this response does not expect Lilly to be able to make

the change alone without parental monitoring. Nor does it remove the responsibility for the expected change in behavior away from Lilly and shift it to the parents and teacher as (A), (C), and (D) would do.

20. **B** This response is designed to assist all the fifth-grade students rather than singling out Lilly for different treatment. It also encourages in Lilly a sense of involvement through the responsibility for recording assignments while establishing a predictable pattern for weekly parent-teacher communication. (A) and (C) remove Lilly from participation except as a courier and has Mr. Sanchez and Lilly's parents taking all the responsibility for communicating what needs to be done and what has or has not happened. Neither pattern of behavior will help Lilly establish better study habits, but each gets the parents and teacher into a routine. (D) addresses the situation with all Mr. Sanchez's students but does not set up communication with Lilly's parents, and so they are left out of the process when they have indicated a desire to participate in helping Lilly.

21. **C** This is the strongest benefit that will result from these changes over time. The first response from students will be the confusion indicated in (A). This is not a benefit. However, it is to be expected when such a dramatic change in instructional strategies occurs. The challenges indicated in (B) will follow. These behaviors are also to be expected but are not a benefit. The enjoyment indicated in (D) is a benefit but not as great as the one described in (C).

22. **D** Choice (D) uses the expertise of both the special education teacher and the science teacher working together to adapt the lessons in the rock unit to senses other than sight, where possible. This allows Paul to have a high level of participation while acknowledging his visual challenge. (A) and (B) both remove Paul from participation with the other students in the science classroom during this unit. He can learn the same content but in a very different style and without his peers. Rocks are easier to learn about through concrete experiences with samples. Paul is not given a chance to succeed within his mainstreamed environment. (C) assumes that Paul cannot learn about rocks at all because of his visual impairment and replaces the unit, leaving a gap in the content the state expects students to acquire.

23. **D** The situation in (D) would make performing this consulting job unethical because preparing for it during a school conference period would entail being paid twice for the same time. Nothing in (A), (B), and (C) is unethical. The department chairperson did the planning work during the summer when away from school and on her home computer, so no school time or equipment were involved. She did use school resource materials, but we all make plans based on school resources. She is not selling school materials or committing the school to buying materials for use with the curriculum. She is charging the out-of-state school a consulting fee for her time to share the plans she has made, which she has given to the department.

24. **B** As soon as a teacher has reason to suspect abuse, state law requires that it be reported to the state authorities. Although dirt bike spills are a reasonable explanation for the observable injuries, the response was delivered in such a way that

Ms. Vick was still concerned about accepting it, which constitutes reasonable suspicion that must be reported. It is also the responsibility of the teacher who is suspicious to do the reporting rather than passing the task on to another person, as suggested in (A). If the district policy requires notifying the principal or some other district personnel, this must be done in addition to meeting the state requirement. It is not the teacher's job to investigate suspected abuse, and so (C) and (D) are unacceptable because they are both forms of teacher investigation. This does not mean that a teacher cannot gently ask about signs that might indicate abuse, such as bruising or numerous accidents. People who report suspected abuse in good faith are protected from legal action.

25. **D** Assisting students with questions during the TAKS is unethical. Teachers may not read TAKS questions during testing or prompt students on how to answer or code an answer. (A), (B), and (C) are all appropriate ways to help students learn how to succeed on the TAKS before the exam. All assessments should not model the TAKS format, but there should be sufficient practice with it for students to be comfortable.

26. **A** Educators can make a limited number of pages for one-time use in their own classroom. They are held to the same copyright standards as the general public, so (B), (C), and (D) are incorrect. These three responses all cost authors residuals, which the copyright laws were put in place to protect.

27. **B** Volunteers from the community will foster a sense of belonging to the school community rather than the school being perceived as separate from the community and community members not really being sure what is happening at the school and feeling like outsiders. The presence of classroom volunteers will also make school-community communication two-way. (A) could be true if the school is built in a diverse community rather than a homogeneous one. There is no indication which pattern is present in this setting. If the classroom volunteers are given only time-consuming routine tasks, as suggested in (C), tasks that they perceive as trivial rather than tasks where they can see a direct benefit to the classroom from their effort, boredom and feeling devalued will kill the classroom volunteer program. Although (D) has some truth to it, having some parents present will not automatically improve the behaviors of all students. All you have to do is watch parents and students together in a setting outside school to know this makes more difference for some students than for others.

28. **C** Parent/guardian volunteers need a place at the school where they feel comfortable as they do their work. It does not have to be exclusive to the volunteers but must be a place where they do not feel they are in the way or are intruding. The tasks they do should clearly make a contribution, and it should be possible to do some of them outside school hours so that volunteering is not limited to those who do not work during the school day. Phone calls to arrange a field trip can be made from an office as easily as from the school. Preparing math manipulatives can be done in the evening after work and school. (A) provides the welcoming environment parent/guardian volunteers need but does not give them the guidance they need to be most helpful. A task a volunteer sees as needed may

have a very low priority for the teachers. Teachers may have a greater need but hesitate to ask because they do not want to be seen as bossing the volunteers. (B) sounds like a room of volunteers sitting around, waiting to be given a task, which is not a situation that would encourage volunteers to show up. Tasks need to be clearly thought out and communicated to volunteers. Both teachers and volunteers need to know when volunteers will be available and what they will be doing. Volunteers need to know and feel comfortable with the teachers they will be assisting, which does not mean that they will work with only one person or only in one classroom or only in the classrooms where their children are students, as indicated in (D). Volunteers should always know how the task they are performing will benefit students.

29. **A** It gives all community members, not just parents/guardians, a valid reason to visit the school, which they will be curious about because it is new. It does not focus on which students have participating parent/guardians and which do not. If the community members have a positive experience, they will be much more likely to visit again. It also establishes some communication pathways for the community to watch for future announcements. (B) and (C) are more traditional and will draw more active and confident parents/guardians to the school but not those who are shy or hesitant. A student whose parent/guardian falls into the latter group will not be able to earn bonus points and so will be penalized, which is not appropriate. (D) is the most traditional solution and is the hardest to accomplish successfully. It is extremely time-consuming and should be used when there is a problem that must be addressed. When an individual conference is called, the parents/guardians' schedule must be taken into consideration rather than demanding that the conference occur only during teacher planning times or during the school workday, which might not match the parents/guardians' workday.

30. **A** It gives the mother a real task to allow increased involvement in her daughter's education, which is what she wants, while providing the teacher with useful information she does not have access to now because the teacher does not normally see this student outside school. There might be a time or a reason to invite the mother into the classroom to observe her daughter but not as an untrained observer of all students, as indicated in (B). This could cause several potential problems if the mother discussed her observations and reactions outside school. (C) and (D) will offend the mother as they both clearly indicate that she should go home and leave the education of her child to the professionals or accept the same roles as other classroom volunteers. This incorrectly indicates that parental assistance and involvement are not needed to effectively educate a student.

31. **B** In (B), students focus on the problem, allowing them to write about their understanding of the two perspectives. (A) and (D) are useful outcomes of the focusing activity but are not as important as (B). Writing an individual statement, as suggested in (C), can actually be a problem for some students who might struggle with this if the class discussion did not occur.

32. **A** Encouraging students to apply higher-order thinking is one of the most important responsibilities of a teacher. Ms. Stein has her students considering the impact of actions of one or more fifth graders on a global problem. The issue is real. Possible solutions will be varied and will require students to apply problem-solving skills. (B) focuses on factual information that has not been introduced. Students are dealing with personal perspectives at this time. (C) and (D) can be additional outcomes of the unit, but each is of secondary value to (A).

33. **A** By encouraging students to learn about something that intersts them, they are motivated to learn. A teachable moment can result in a more powerful learning experience. (B) is not a meaningful statement. There are no clear indications of how this is different from the normal routine for this class. (C) implies that elements of the energy conservation unit have not been scheduled in advance instead of implying the flexibility and rescheduling to use this teachable moment. There is also no indication of saved time as indicated by (D).

34. **C** The students show more interest and retain more information because they initiated the topic. (A) indicates student input altering the initial direction can reduce the understanding of major concepts in the unit. (B) and (D) can both occur, but neither has the importance of (C).

35. **B** (A) and (C) will both be outcomes of this instructional unit, but (B) is the most important outcome. A sense of purpose and ownership, as indicated in (B), will encourage students to attack a future problem using the skills identified in (A) and (C). (D) might also occur but is of limited importance at this time in the unit as there is no indication of its relationship to planned questions.

36. **D** The knowledge and skills learned and that can be used in the future is the most important outcome (A) and (B) are attitudes and skills the students will probably gain while collecting data to answer their question. However, the motivation to apply these attitudes and skills will be more important to the students in the future. (C) indicates there is one right answer the students will find by searching, which is an inaccurate response.

37. **D** Most public school and many private school classes are coed. Activities must be selected that appeal to both genders to motive all. (A) encourages and increases gender differences fostered by society and culture at a time when education is trying to decrease differentiated educational opportunities based on gender. (B) is guaranteed to cause management and discipline problems during classes. Planning for part of the student population to have a lower level of participation because of lower interest is poor planning and will produce negative consequences. The different rubrics for each gender, as suggested in (C), is not a good idea as again it sets different expectations for performance based on gender. Performance should be evaluated based on effort and achievement.

38. **C** This is the best advice Ms. Landers can receive and follow. Establishing these routines and procedures early sets clear teacher expectations that students will follow them and be able to work independently. It also sets clear standards of

how this is to occur without the teacher having to remind students of the same information daily. Students will know what is expected of them. This will free Ms. Landers to work with students who need assistance rather than having to constantly address behaviors throughout the entire class. This is the best of some good advice. (A), (B), and (D) each have a value and a flaw. Extreme care must be taken if (A) is used. It is a clear example of a teacher manipulating students and can backfire. Recognizing students who are following the routines is not the problem. Students deserve praise for good behavior. Using the well-behaving students to encourage misbehaving students to improve their behaviors is effective with young students who are strongly interested in gaining the approval of authority figures. This effectiveness declines when working with adolescents who are more interested in gaining the approval of their peers. It is unlikely that adolescents will give an accurate weekly self-assessment as indicated in (B). Self and peer assessments are both valuable, but weekly use can move away from a valuable strategy and into a rubber stamping of actions through overuse. (D) includes some strategies where student input is invaluable to help empower students, but teachers, schools, and school districts set the grading scale. This is different from setting criteria for evaluation in a rubric, which is another area that benefits from student input.

39. **B** As Ms. Landers empowers them, they will respond positively. Knowing what to expect and that the individual teacher assistant will help with this is the opposite of (A). Changes made arbitrarily and regularly will be counterproductive, but adolescents respond to changes in routines made for a valid reason and explained to them. (C) and (D) imply that the students are without teacher supervision or interaction, which is not the case. Instruction does not occur at the same pace for all students daily, which should be a motivator for students of this age who sometimes feel they have no control.

40. **C** If students are unsure what is expected of them, their appropriate responses will be limited. Most students of this age are still at the concrete cognitive level in terms of new material and information. Therefore, seeing appropriate techniques modeled will be much more effective than hearing them explained or reading about them. Actually practicing through role-play would also be effective. (A) would be an appropriate way to reinforce the modeling done in (C). Middle school students are more willing to ask a peer for clarification. (B) is counterproductive to the desire to have students work together and to provide additional supervision to ensure they have a greater chance of learning a skill correctly. (D) will not be as productive as (C), although mixed-ability groups are desirable for the reason given.

41. **B** Texas requires each teacher to address the grade level TEKS with each student at that grade level without regard to the student's native language. With these limited English proficiency students, this must be done while also improving their English fluency. (A) demands less of these students. This would result in putting them behind academically as well as behind in English, which is unacceptable. Students achieve less when less is expected. They are not less able students but students who need intensive work with English. (C) again eliminates

at least some of the TEKS dictated by the state. A plan to use TEKS that demand concrete materials first to strengthen English and save more abstract TEKS for later would be wiser. (D) also leaves these students behind on the state-required TEKS while developing English skills. Both problems must be addressed at the same time to keep these students from falling behind. Research tells us that the further behind a student falls, the harder it is for that student to ever catch up.

42. **C** Tracking individual progress is important in planning and reteaching challenging students. The self-diagnosed frustrations addressed in (A) might be helpful for venting but do not advance student learning. The daily assessment for students as suggested in (B) can quickly become overwhelming for both Ms. Shaw and the students. (D) is an appropriate way to provide some additional support for these students but should not be the only support mechanism used.

43. **D** Hands-on instructional activities allow students at both the concrete operational and formal operational cognitive levels opportunities for success. The think-pair-share instructional strategy in (A) is effective with both cognitive levels of development present in the classroom but should not be the primary instructional strategy. Creating groups of blended cognitive levels of development, as suggested in (B) is good. It is more effective than grouping students who are at the same developmental level but again is not a primary instructional strategy. (C)'s effectiveness depends on which cognitive level, concrete operational or formal operational, is predominant since formal level students can learn from concrete strategies much more easily than concrete students can learn from formal strategies.

44. **A** We know research indicates that high teacher expectations are one of the most important variables for student success, but we also know that all students do not learn the same way, and so differentiated instruction is important. (B), (C), and (D) are basically the same. If Ms. Shaw or any teacher expects students to do less for whatever reason, they will. Each of these responses would result in lower teacher expectations of students. Because all students were in the same school last year and continue in school together does not mean they learned at the same rate or will respond in the same manner to instructional strategies. If this were so, as (B) implies, there would not be a distinct group of students with significant academic needs. (C) and (D) open Ms. Shaw to making faulty instructional decisions based on educational myths about the ability of an identified group to learn. Although we have data showing that some groups face more learning challenges than others, we must be careful not to use this information as a rationale to expect less from students in these groups.

45. **D** Shorter wait time and more restated questions for lower-achieving students signal all students there are lower teacher expectations for these lower-achieving students. This reinforces their feelings of inability and reduces efforts by these students to achieve because it is apparent that the teacher doesn't expect success. The altered wait time for different levels of achievement in (A) is not an effective manner of instructional differentiation. All students need equal wait time and

teachers need to allow appropriate wait time before restating a question or passing it to another student. (B) does signal different levels of expectation but is unlikely to cause resentment in the higher achievers unless it is directed toward the teacher who doesn't expect success from lower-achieving students. (C) is inaccurate. Lower-achieving students actually feel that they are more "on the spot" as they perceive they are asked a greater number of questions they cannot answer.

46. **A** Unless the counselor can help Lilly focus on misconceptions and future consequences, she will not see beyond what is most important to her now, and this seems to be leaving school and being loved by a child. She does not see the demands that a child will place on her in return. (B) has some validity as many students do not feel they belong to a group within the school's society or want to fit into a different group. But the counselor cannot provide this student access into a group. Although this might be part of her problem, it doesn't play much of a role in helping her alter her decision. Many middle school students are already planning for their future so (C) is not valid. Adolescents may not care to acknowledge that adults have gone through many of the same experiences they have, as indicated by (D). Yet they know this is true even when they decide not to accept the advice offered.

47. **A** Seeing the overview of the flow of learning activities helps ensure that they have been appropriately integrated and have been sequenced from concrete to abstract, and that content is sequenced from simple to complex. Having age-appropriate activities and selecting interesting and motivating instructional styles for a unit, as indicated in (B) and (C), are also appropriate but are secondary to and supportive of the logical flow indicated in (A). (D) addresses modifications that might need to be made to the unit during instruction as indicated by student responses or problems rather than as a part of the initial planning.

48. **B** This response states the most important *instructional* advantage. A variety of content topics and instructional methods are planned for the unit, which will allow students multiple learning opportunities. (A) addresses a common misunderstanding about the value of integrated units. Integration allows for greater instructional time per subject, but this does not always mean less class time is required. Instead, integration means the time is apportioned in different patterns to allow an overlap between content areas. There is no information in the question to support the selection of either (C) or (D). The time required for the unit or pacing is not mentioned or indicated—nor is individualized instruction.

49. **D** Observational data will show if the literature circle runs smoothly and instruction is clear. Formal and informal assessment, or both, will indicate how effectively learning occurs. (A) will tell how many and how often students participate during a literature circle but will not indicate if learning occurs. (B) will give a clear picture of the students' response to the affective domain of the center but will not give cognitive information about learning. (C) will give Ms. Green's opinion about the literature circle's effectiveness with the students. Even though

she has had experience with this strategy, data about learning through the strategy is important and is clearly addressed in (D).

50. **C** Mr. Blalock should encourage students to be creative and varied in their approaches to the problem. Multiple effective solutions are the desired outcome of problem solving. (A), (B), and (D) all imply that there is only one correct solution or answer and one best method of reaching it, which is counter to the problem-solving process.

51. **B** Mr. Blalock must determine where Pat is having difficulty before he can help. In (A), Pat will not feel success or ownership if unable to explain the reading to Mr. Blalock. Ownership comes from independent success. (C) assumes a problem of focus or lack of attention with no supporting evidence. (D) sounds good but does not fit the information in the question. Reading with comprehension is a higher order thinking skill. There is no evidence given as to why Pat is having difficulty.

52. **C** None of Mr. Blalock's goals can be met if students are not attentive during this time and interest and familiarity are good motivators. (A) indicates that teaching listening skills is not appropriate instruction, which is not accurate. Counting on students to absorb content information without being alerted to the need to do so during the listening instruction is not a valid instructional strategy. (B) assumes that students are able to internalize new and unfamiliar information through abstract encounters such as reading and listening when research indicates they need direct experiences instead unless they are at the formal abstract development level, which would be unusual for all students in eighth grade. The word patterns in (D) are good for this age group, although fourth grade is when most students fall in love with these types of word play. The calming effect Mr. Blalock wants would be one result of the quiet and stillness needed for effective listening and will not be lost by choosing exciting books that are highly motivating.

53. **B** Adding questions allows the effectiveness to be assessed based on recalled events and appropriate predictions. Responses (A) and (C) both address the affective domain. Even though the affective domain is important, the question asks about the cognitive domain. (D) adds a written test and grading time. These have the potential for reducing the effectiveness of the listening time by reducing student and teacher enthusiasm.

54. **D** This selection presents the most significant challenge to assessing the learning of students, and learning goals are the guide for assessment as well as instruction. It is not impossible to assess but needs some visible, measurable indication of increased appreciation, such as "Students will choose to read to each other orally during their free time" to indicate that the goal has been met by the students. (A) presents a very narrow view of eighth-graders and languages present in schools. (B) is just inaccurate. There are lessons on every conceivable topic available from the wide range of resources that teachers can draw on—plus teachers are creative individuals. (C) is also inaccurate. Prior knowledge needed for success must be considered as learning goals are selected but is not included

in the goal. How the prior knowledge will be assessed to determine if it is present is also part of a teacher's planning but not part of a learning goal.

55. **D** Mr. Gonzales knows a stressful situation such as a move can be challenging. He needs to give the student time to adjust without allowing her to flounder or fall behind. He also needs to compare her records from her prior school to his observations before contacting her parents. (A) has the potential for letting this student fall behind in the name of kindness. A difference in standards across schools can occur, but (B) and (C) assume a great deal based on a week of observation and are guaranteed to irritate this student's parents, her prior school, and the administrators at the current school.

56. **C** The correct response is (C) although it would have been better if the student "buddies" assigned to help with her adjustment had been assigned the first day. Mr. Gonzales is wise to allow adjustment time before making a judgment about the accuracy of her label. It is also important that he not delay a conference with her parents about her lack of adjustment too long. (A), (B), and (D) are guaranteed to add more stress and cause her to struggle even more to adjust and perform at her earlier level. Her parents will probably come to the school to visit with him in response to any of these actions.

57. **C** Because Raul's mother can be reached by phone to schedule a conference but is apparently uncomfortable with visiting the school, he should conference by phone. Having a conference is more important than demanding a face-to-face conference. In (A) and (B), Mr. Gonzales' attempt to use guilt to motivate this mother to attend a conference will not work. She probably already feels badly about being repeatedly asked to do something that is so uncomfortable for her. Setting a child against a parent, as in (B), is unprofessional. (D) makes a negative and unwarranted judgment. There are many reasons parents are reluctant to attend school meetings. Clothing, language difficulties, lack of confidence, or intimidation are just a few reasons for this reluctance.

58. **D** Dividing directions into clear steps for both oral and written formats allows for better comprehension of the directions. Modeling directions and examples also adds to understanding. Although (A) is close, the addition of breaking down the directions into shorter steps is important and its omission makes this response as well as (B) incomplete. (C) might be helpful for some students at this age, but others will tune out this repetition.

59. **D** This choice needs the greatest focus during the meeting. The reason for a class discussion is to determine the thoughts of the group members, and this cannot occur without their listening to each other. (A) stops judgmental put-downs that will kill any willingness to participate in a discussion. After being told they are wrong and laughed at, students will refuse to share their ideas because their ideas are not valued. (B) and (C) are not big problems in an effective class discussion, assuming the comments are on topic and students do not speak over each other. Directing all comments through the teacher can seriously curtail the pace of a class discussion as students wait to be recognized. Also, stu-

dents may not be selected in an appropriate order for the comments they wish to make to occur in a logical sequence.

60. **B** The alignment indicated in (B) is most important, and therefore this is the best response. (A), (C), and (D) are all useful for effective teacher-made tests but are not as important. Testing what and how you have taught is imperative for an accurate assessment of learning.

61. **C** This choice allows Ms. Dixon to respond to Jason in a dignified manner and at the same time allows him to own his behavior. (A) would be a temporary solution as Jason will most likely continue to act out as he obviously needs help. (B) and (D) set the stage for more confrontation, as both set Jason up to be embarrassed and thus react to "save face" in front of his peers.

62. **C** (C) most clearly shows that Ms. Dixon understands the warning signs of drug use and their impact on Jason's behavior. Although Jason does have challenges as noted in (A), this is a broad response. (B) refers to development, and this scenario does not address Jason's development nor does it address middle school structure as denoted in (D).

63. **D** Research has shown that preparing a portfolio can create a sense of competence through development of the division titles, rationales, and artifacts chosen, which are unique to the individual and not driven by assigned labels or artifacts. (A) deprives Jason of a chance to create a personally unique portfolio. (B) can plant the notion that the portfolio must look like the examples. Finally, (C) is just not a feasible choice because even if Jason is given basic directions, he is not given even minimal help.

64. **A** Teachers need objective and meaningful ways to assess student learning. Goals are the guides for assessment and instruction. To assess appreciation, there needs to be a clear indicator to establish that the goal has been meet. (B) presents an inaccurate view of what can be taught. Responses (C) and (D) are also inaccurate. Lessons on every conceivable topic are available from the wide range of resources available. Prior knowledge needed for success must be considered as learning goals are selected but are not included in the goal. How the prior knowledge will be verified is part of a teacher's planning but not part of a learning goal.

65. **B** Though all four responses make sense, (B) is the most thorough and appropriate first step as the teams look over existing maps. Once this is done, alignment with district goals, (A), and differences between plans, (C), can be addressed. (D) is addressed after (B), (A), and (C) are addressed.

66. **D** When planning a thematic unit, once the theme is chosen, the next step is to decide which subject areas will logically fit. Therefore, (D) is the correct response. (C) and (A) will take place once the key players are determined. (B) will fall into place next.

67. **A** By giving each group member a specific job, the chance that one student will take over is lessened considerably. The assessment should then reflect each

role and its specific tasks. (B), (C), and (D) are short-term fixes and really do not hold each group member accountable. Threats solve nothing, (B); Ms. Dixon cannot be everywhere at once, (C); and one person could still conceivably answer all the questions, (D).

68. **A** The science teacher stimulates inquiry and critical thinking through this hands-on science experiment. This challenges the students and encourages risk taking. (B) does nothing but lead to a gain in information. Although (C) and (D) are true, they are part of the process covered in (A).

69. **C** The steps in a constructivist lesson generally take longer than 30 minutes. Constructivist lessons can occur as early as EC and continue through adult courses. They are appropriate for any subject area. Therefore, (A) and (B) are not correct. (D) is incorrect since any lesson can fill 30 minutes.

70. **A** Dignifying a student's response to a question involves finding the positives of the answer and prompting to guide the student in responding to the rest of the question. Therefore, (A) is the correct response. (B) could take place if prompting was not effective. Restating the question, as in (C), would be an appropriate method if the original question was not understood but fails to dignify the correct part of the answer. (D) has nothing to do with dignifying an answer.

71. **B** The Taba method begins by asking students to generate lists of all they know about a given topic. Students then form groups and label their groups based on the lists. This gives the teacher a pretty good idea of what students know. The Taba method allows safe interaction, as in (A), only if the ground rules are given beforehand. Although it does give practice in grouping, as in (C), and can lead to drawing conclusions, as in (D), (B) is still the first step.

72. **C** The ground rules set the stage for respect and acceptance, thus generating student awareness of how actions and attitudes might affect others. Both (A) and (D) are answered during the process. There is no real proof that laying ground rules will lead to student awareness of collaboration with peers, (B).

73. **B** Overcrowding is the major cause of accidents in a science lab. Tables large enough for students to have room to work and space for ease of movement around the room cut down on the chances of accidents occurring. Using individual desks, (D), or grouping individual desks, (A), does not allow for enough flat work surfaces area for the safe use of science equipment. (C) does not lend itself to group work and cuts down on free movement around the room.

74. **A** Studies have shown that building a child's competence, creating opportunities for the child to feel useful, and giving opportunities for the child to feel like he or she belongs are keys to building a resilient child. The other three responses do not fit the scenario.

75. **A** Concept attainment gives a clear understanding of how much the students know. If they are unable to identify positive and negative exemplars, they clearly do not understand the concept. A K-W-L chart, (C), does not give as much

detail of what students know about the concept. Inquiry and concept mastery lessons, (B) and (D), would eventually lead to understanding in some form, but (A) is the best initial method.

76. **B** Less complicated vocabulary and modeling lead to better understanding of otherwise complicated directions. Talking slowly and allowing writing time, as in (A), do not ensure an understanding of complicated vocabulary. (C) would not necessarily simplify the directions as most people will say they understand when asked even if they do not understand. Providing a glossary, as in (D), would be too time-consuming and would take away from understanding the directions when they are given.

77. **C** Response (C) is correct due to the variety of tasks and has been shown by research to be true. Students do tend to give better answers when working in supportive pairs, as in (D), because they have more than one perspective. However, (D) is a narrower answer than (C). (A) and (B) really do not deal with strategies.

78. **B** Having students actively participate in determining the area of a garden, even their own garden, makes the problem relevant to everyday life. Going home and inquiring about the area of the living room, as in (C), requires nothing more than an answer. Measuring only lengths, as in (D), does not calculate area. Finally, solving 25 area problems, as in (A), has no connection to daily life.

79. **A** A lesson on appropriate Internet use both reinforces and further explains the acceptable-use policy that the students sign. Having the students simply sign the acceptable-use policy, (C), does not ensure understanding of the policy. (B) and (D) are acceptable safeguards but do not necessarily ensure appropriate Internet use.

80. **D** Uploading movies from her video camera to her PC and then sharing them using a projector actually demonstrates that Ms. Villareal can access and manipulate information from a remote device. The other three answers are more subjective in nature and without a clear focus on her technology skills.

81. **B** A web quest design includes an introduction, an explanation of the task, and other sections that make it an excellent tool for designing a web scavenger hunt. Downloading a scavenger hunt, (D), does not ask students to design but rather to take part. Both (A) and (C) deal with presentation and not with the design of a web scavenger hunt.

82. **C** A rubric designed to assess criteria given in the assignment is more thorough and appropriate. Objective short-answer tests, (A), or an essay, (B), do not assess the creation of the cube. The portfolio section, (D), would be fine for displaying the cube and assessment results but is not itself an assessment of the assignment.

83. **A** Ms. Witt recognized that her current instructional strategy was not working. So she adjusted her instructional approach. If she had started with the manipulatives in (B), she could have avoided much of her students' frustration.

Grades 4–8

Manipulatives should be a beginning activity rather than an afterthought. (C) and (D) do not fit the scenario as the information does not mention self-assessment or timely feedback.

84. **C** Ms. Villareal has used her knowledge of the families in the community to create an ESL night program. ESL night is an interactive night and not a time for parent/caregiver conferences, as suggested in (A). Responses (B) and D are reflected in her creation of ESL night, thus making (C) the best answer.

85. **B** Studies show that reflective journaling helps a teacher to identify strengths, weaknesses, and other components of effective teaching. (A), (C), and (D) may be relevant to the issues in a journal entry, but they are not the best reason why reflective journaling is a good practice.

86. **A** This is a moment when team teaching would be appropriate and beneficial to the students even if it is not regularly done at this school. Ms. Johnson's job is not to teach about Egyptian writing, as stated in (B). Responses (C) and (D) are unnecessary reactions. No reason is given for either teacher to delay the planned unit.

87. **D** Discipline is required when management is lacking. Although visiting classes where good managment is in place is fine, as stated in (B), it is better if the mentor sees Ms. Baker in action and then suggests a plan for improvement. (A) and (C) will take place after (D).

88. **C** The legal document signed by Mr. Lee prevents him from doing reviews, writing study guides, and being present during the test for the grade level for which he prepared the item review. Although his colleagues may not be aware of Mr. Lee's committee work, the ethical thing for him to do is to remove himself from the testing situation. (A), (B), and (D) are assumptions for which there is no supportive information in the passage, thus making (C) the best answer.

89. **C** Principle II, Standard I, of the Texas Educators' Code of Ethics states that confidential health or personal information concerning colleagues cannot be revealed unless it is for lawful professional purposes or is required by law. Ms. Lock violated this code. (A) cannot be assumed. (B) and (D) are not substantiated in the scenario and therefore cannot be considered.

90. **A** Principle III, Standard I, of the Texas Educators' Code of Ethics states that an educator shall not reveal confidential information about students unless it serves lawful professional purposes or is required by law. Leaving the file out and available for anyone to see violates this code. (B) and (C) really do not address the issue. (D) is not a problem because the open records law allows Jamie and his parents to see the file.

Diagnostic and Sample Tests for Grades 8–12

The diagnostic tests in the following chapters include one question per test competency, except for the EC-12 Diagnostic Test, which includes three questions per competency. These questions are similar to those found at the State Board of Educator Certification (SBEC) website (www.sbec.state.tx.us), where the state agency provides a clear example of the PPR certification test. The SBEC practice test should also be used as a diagnostic tool to ascertain both your areas of strength and the needed areas of knowledge and skill improvement that you must have to be successful on the PPR examinations. The diagnostic items in this book are presented without full follow-up explanations of why all responses are correct or incorrect. This follows the pattern used for the test items for the SBEC practice tests. The state competency is listed at the end of each diagnostic test item to help guide your understanding of how you will be tested on each competency.

According to numerous candidates who have taken and passed the state certification test, there is a correlation between SBEC practice tests and the state certification test. You are encouraged to visit www.sbec.state.tx.us for further information about the SBEC study guide. We encourage you to continue to take the diagnostic tests to confirm exactly what competencies are included on the test and to practice deciding why three responses are incorrect or less effective and why one response is clearly the best answer.

Following the sample tests for each of the state certification levels, you will find a self-analysis framework that will guide you in understanding how to improve your study before taking the state tests. In this framework, the authors explain why three answers are incorrect (or are not the *best* response) and one answer is correct (or is the *best* choice). It would be wise to continue to use this analysis strategy as you continue to practice using the tests in this study guide and the SBEC online test. In Chapter 16, suggestions are made that will help you complete an overall analysis of your success and provide you with a strategy for further study.

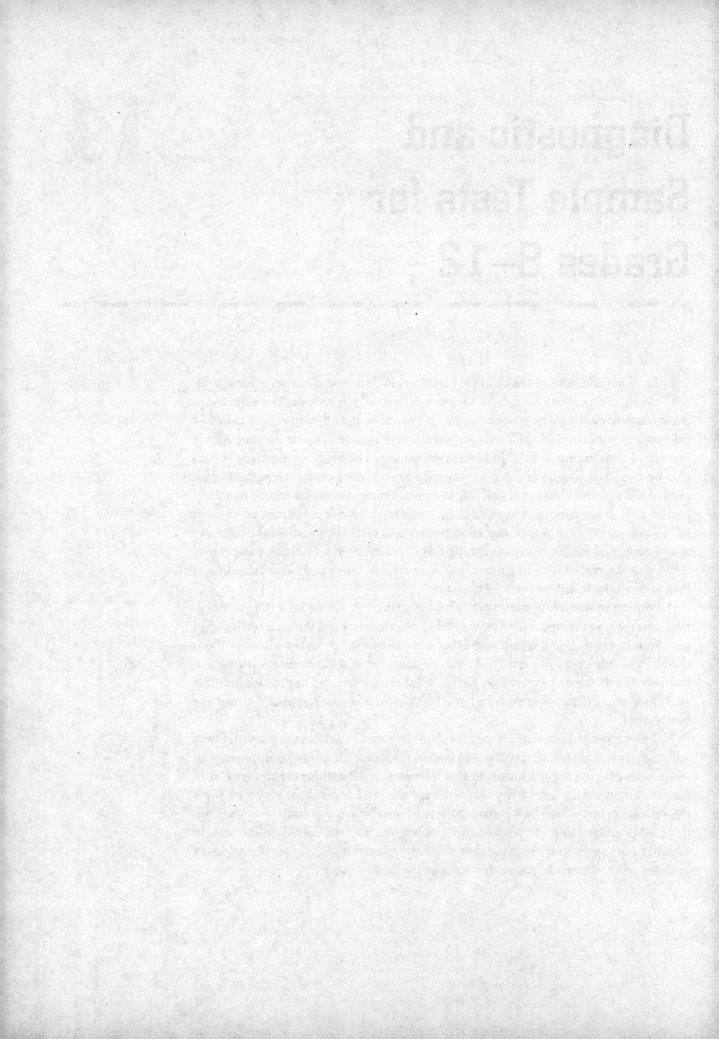

Answer Sheet
DIAGNOSTIC TEST (GRADES 8–12)

1 Ⓐ Ⓑ Ⓒ Ⓓ

2 Ⓐ Ⓑ Ⓒ Ⓓ

3 Ⓐ Ⓑ Ⓒ Ⓓ

4 Ⓐ Ⓑ Ⓒ Ⓓ

5 Ⓐ Ⓑ Ⓒ Ⓓ

6 Ⓐ Ⓑ Ⓒ Ⓓ

7 Ⓐ Ⓑ Ⓒ Ⓓ

8 Ⓐ Ⓑ Ⓒ Ⓓ

9 Ⓐ Ⓑ Ⓒ Ⓓ

10 Ⓐ Ⓑ Ⓒ Ⓓ

11 Ⓐ Ⓑ Ⓒ Ⓓ

12 Ⓐ Ⓑ Ⓒ Ⓓ

13 Ⓐ Ⓑ Ⓒ Ⓓ

Answer Sheet
SAMPLE TEST (GRADES 8–12)

1 Ⓐ Ⓑ Ⓒ Ⓓ	26 Ⓐ Ⓑ Ⓒ Ⓓ	51 Ⓐ Ⓑ Ⓒ Ⓓ	76 Ⓐ Ⓑ Ⓒ Ⓓ
2 Ⓐ Ⓑ Ⓒ Ⓓ	27 Ⓐ Ⓑ Ⓒ Ⓓ	52 Ⓐ Ⓑ Ⓒ Ⓓ	77 Ⓐ Ⓑ Ⓒ Ⓓ
3 Ⓐ Ⓑ Ⓒ Ⓓ	28 Ⓐ Ⓑ Ⓒ Ⓓ	53 Ⓐ Ⓑ Ⓒ Ⓓ	78 Ⓐ Ⓑ Ⓒ Ⓓ
4 Ⓐ Ⓑ Ⓒ Ⓓ	29 Ⓐ Ⓑ Ⓒ Ⓓ	54 Ⓐ Ⓑ Ⓒ Ⓓ	79 Ⓐ Ⓑ Ⓒ Ⓓ
5 Ⓐ Ⓑ Ⓒ Ⓓ	30 Ⓐ Ⓑ Ⓒ Ⓓ	55 Ⓐ Ⓑ Ⓒ Ⓓ	80 Ⓐ Ⓑ Ⓒ Ⓓ
6 Ⓐ Ⓑ Ⓒ Ⓓ	31 Ⓐ Ⓑ Ⓒ Ⓓ	56 Ⓐ Ⓑ Ⓒ Ⓓ	81 Ⓐ Ⓑ Ⓒ Ⓓ
7 Ⓐ Ⓑ Ⓒ Ⓓ	32 Ⓐ Ⓑ Ⓒ Ⓓ	57 Ⓐ Ⓑ Ⓒ Ⓓ	82 Ⓐ Ⓑ Ⓒ Ⓓ
8 Ⓐ Ⓑ Ⓒ Ⓓ	33 Ⓐ Ⓑ Ⓒ Ⓓ	58 Ⓐ Ⓑ Ⓒ Ⓓ	83 Ⓐ Ⓑ Ⓒ Ⓓ
9 Ⓐ Ⓑ Ⓒ Ⓓ	34 Ⓐ Ⓑ Ⓒ Ⓓ	59 Ⓐ Ⓑ Ⓒ Ⓓ	84 Ⓐ Ⓑ Ⓒ Ⓓ
10 Ⓐ Ⓑ Ⓒ Ⓓ	35 Ⓐ Ⓑ Ⓒ Ⓓ	60 Ⓐ Ⓑ Ⓒ Ⓓ	85 Ⓐ Ⓑ Ⓒ Ⓓ
11 Ⓐ Ⓑ Ⓒ Ⓓ	36 Ⓐ Ⓑ Ⓒ Ⓓ	61 Ⓐ Ⓑ Ⓒ Ⓓ	86 Ⓐ Ⓑ Ⓒ Ⓓ
12 Ⓐ Ⓑ Ⓒ Ⓓ	37 Ⓐ Ⓑ Ⓒ Ⓓ	62 Ⓐ Ⓑ Ⓒ Ⓓ	87 Ⓐ Ⓑ Ⓒ Ⓓ
13 Ⓐ Ⓑ Ⓒ Ⓓ	38 Ⓐ Ⓑ Ⓒ Ⓓ	63 Ⓐ Ⓑ Ⓒ Ⓓ	88 Ⓐ Ⓑ Ⓒ Ⓓ
14 Ⓐ Ⓑ Ⓒ Ⓓ	39 Ⓐ Ⓑ Ⓒ Ⓓ	64 Ⓐ Ⓑ Ⓒ Ⓓ	89 Ⓐ Ⓑ Ⓒ Ⓓ
15 Ⓐ Ⓑ Ⓒ Ⓓ	40 Ⓐ Ⓑ Ⓒ Ⓓ	65 Ⓐ Ⓑ Ⓒ Ⓓ	90 Ⓐ Ⓑ Ⓒ Ⓓ
16 Ⓐ Ⓑ Ⓒ Ⓓ	41 Ⓐ Ⓑ Ⓒ Ⓓ	66 Ⓐ Ⓑ Ⓒ Ⓓ	
17 Ⓐ Ⓑ Ⓒ Ⓓ	42 Ⓐ Ⓑ Ⓒ Ⓓ	67 Ⓐ Ⓑ Ⓒ Ⓓ	
18 Ⓐ Ⓑ Ⓒ Ⓓ	43 Ⓐ Ⓑ Ⓒ Ⓓ	68 Ⓐ Ⓑ Ⓒ Ⓓ	
19 Ⓐ Ⓑ Ⓒ Ⓓ	44 Ⓐ Ⓑ Ⓒ Ⓓ	69 Ⓐ Ⓑ Ⓒ Ⓓ	
20 Ⓐ Ⓑ Ⓒ Ⓓ	45 Ⓐ Ⓑ Ⓒ Ⓓ	70 Ⓐ Ⓑ Ⓒ Ⓓ	
21 Ⓐ Ⓑ Ⓒ Ⓓ	46 Ⓐ Ⓑ Ⓒ Ⓓ	71 Ⓐ Ⓑ Ⓒ Ⓓ	
22 Ⓐ Ⓑ Ⓒ Ⓓ	47 Ⓐ Ⓑ Ⓒ Ⓓ	72 Ⓐ Ⓑ Ⓒ Ⓓ	
23 Ⓐ Ⓑ Ⓒ Ⓓ	48 Ⓐ Ⓑ Ⓒ Ⓓ	73 Ⓐ Ⓑ Ⓒ Ⓓ	
24 Ⓐ Ⓑ Ⓒ Ⓓ	49 Ⓐ Ⓑ Ⓒ Ⓓ	74 Ⓐ Ⓑ Ⓒ Ⓓ	
25 Ⓐ Ⓑ Ⓒ Ⓓ	50 Ⓐ Ⓑ Ⓒ Ⓓ	75 Ⓐ Ⓑ Ⓒ Ⓓ	

Grades 8–12 Answer Sheet

Diagnostic Test (Grades 8–12)

Directions: Read each stimulus and answer every question. Mark your answers in the answer spaces on the accompanying grid.

1. Carolyn is concerned about one of her tenth-grade students who misses school more and more frequently. When Carolyn expressed her concern, the student told her that school had no value for her so she was working part time. What human development knowledge does Carolyn need for understanding this student's perspective?

    (A) A person of this age may have more concern with the present than any thought of the future.

    (B) This student may be having financial problems at home, and her single-parent mom may be asking the student to help out.

    (C) This student is likely still operating at the concrete operational stage, and thus has difficulty reasoning through complex problems.

    (D) Students at this age typically place more focus on parents than school, and thus may be following a parent's model of dropping out of school.

Competency 001: *The teacher understands human developmental processes and applies this knowledge to plan instruction and ongoing assessment that motivate students and are responsive to their developmental characteristics and needs.*

2. As a high school teacher in a suburb of a metropolitan area, most of Betty's students are from different cultural backgrounds. How should Betty best respond when she observes tensions caused by several students using demeaning and unacceptable terms when addressing students from both their own culture and other cultures?

    (A) When assigning groups, always place students from the same culture in the same group in an effort to avoid any potential for negative interactions during the time students are in the classroom.

    (B) Each time there is a group activity within a unit, allow students to choose the members of their group in hopes that students who get along well will end up in the same groups.

    (C) Use a shared decision-making process with students to develop clearly defined behavior and language interaction expectations, as well as to determine consequences of not adhering to the guidelines.

    (D) Include participation, attitude, respect, and peer support as elements of the assessment system and explain to students how these elements will carry as much weight as academic performance for determining semester grades.

Competency 002: *The teacher understands student diversity and knows how to plan learning experiences and design assessments that are responsive to differences among students and that promote all students' learning.*

3. Catherine is working with her mentor to design learning objective statements and teaching objectives for an upcoming unit on the integration of aesthetics and history concepts. What challenge will Catherine face with the following objective: "Students will appreciate the role of aesthetics in the study of history"?

(A) This learning objective will be relatively easy to assess because it is easily measurable and is certainly an important concept for this history unit.

(B) There is no clear expectation of learning in this objective so it will be impossible to assess it in any meaningful way.

(C) High school students have no interest in aesthetics, so there is no reason to devote instructional time to this objective.

(D) Objective measurement of "appreciation" is almost impossible, so some other means of assessment must be employed for this objective.

Competency 003: *The teacher understands procedures for designing effective and coherent instruction and assessment based on appropriate learning goals and objectives.*

4. In an eleventh-grade history class, Barbara has students use simulated journal entries for confirming their understanding of historical concepts. The following questions were given to students prior to writing in order to guide their thinking.

> **How do you think the historical figure responded to the event we are studying?**
>
> **If you were the historical figure, do you think you would have reacted in the same way today as the figure did at the time of the historical event? Why or why not?**
>
> **When you discussed the historical figure with your peer partner, how did your conversation help you to understand the importance of the event and the figure?**

What do these questions demonstrate about Barbara's understanding of learning principles?

(A) Students need to be challenged to figure out principles related to any academic concept, especially in the area of social studies.

(B) Students will perform better when they have an opportunity to work with peers to confirm their perceptions about the topic.

(C) It is important to have students regulate their thinking whenever they are challenged to put themselves in the place of another, such as with a simulated journal entry.

(D) When students have an opportunity to actively engage in activities and are challenged to think in reflective ways, learning is reinforced.

Competency 004: *The teacher understands learning processes and factors that impact student learning and demonstrates this knowledge by planning effective, engaging instruction and appropriate assessments.*

Grades 8–12

5. What would be the best strategy for Mary Ellen to use to assess the effectiveness of her classroom learning community design?

    (A) Analyze whether or not her instructions follow her educational philosophy and how her students' responses fit.
    (B) Make a chart of how frequently students are absent and what their excuses are for their absences.
    (C) Evaluate the climate to determine the extent to which lessons engage students' in shared learning, independent thinking, and complex reasoning.
    (D) Determine whether or not students have a clear understanding of the importance of individual responsibility.

Competency 005: *The teacher knows how to establish a classroom climate that fosters learning, equity, and excellence and uses this knowledge to create a physical and emotional environment that is safe and productive.*

6. Daryl works with his mentor to establish routines and procedures that he will put in place early in the first week with his tenth-grade students. What is the most important reason why this approach is a wise strategy for establishing a strong learning climate?

    (A) With routines in place, Daryl will have more time for planning.
    (B) Students will know exactly how each day's instructional activities will occur.
    (C) The teacher will be better able to efficiently and effectively use learning time.
    (D) The teacher will be able to capitalize on students' interest and motivation.

Competency 006: *The teacher understands strategies for creating an organized and productive learning environment and for managing student behavior.*

7. Casey wants to improve the communication skills of her tenth-grade students. From Casey's observations during small group work, which of the following should be of greatest concern for her to address *initially*?

    (A) Often, students do not listen to their classmates and frequently talk over each other.
    (B) In some groups, certain students talk only to one or two others.
    (C) At times, students speak out when others are concentrating on a task.
    (D) In one group, students seem to argue more than target completion of their assignment.

Competency 007: *The teacher understands and applies principles and strategies for communicating effectively in varied teaching and learning contexts.*

8. A first-year ninth-grade teacher is concerned about whether his instruction will result in effective learning. What is the greatest benefit of his requiring students to write in a learning log their understanding/restatement of the lesson objective, what they know about the topic to be studied, and any questions they have about the topic?

(A) This strategy will result in students getting the right answers on quizzes.
(B) Students will be more able to complete their work efficiently.
(C) This approach will facilitate students' development of a conceptual framework for the topic.
(D) This puts all students on an equal status at the beginning of the lesson.

Competency 008: *The teacher provides appropriate instruction that actively engages students in the learning process.*

9. A senior high teacher requires students in his science class to prepare multimedia presentations as a culminating project in their third unit. He is concerned that students may focus more on how the presentation looks than on the content of the concepts to be presented. What procedure should he use to guide students as they begin the work on their presentation?

(A) Ask students to balance their planning time between ideas for presenting the concepts and for designing the presentation.
(B) Require students to draw a concept map after they design the presentation style and set up the slides for the presentation.
(C) In partnership with students, design a rubric that will define the importance of both content and design features.
(D) Explain to students that they must have more focus on the content than on the presentation design.

Competency 009: *The teacher incorporates the effective use of technology to plan, organize, deliver, and evaluate instruction for all students.*

10. What is a major guideline when developing any assessment of learning?

(A) Focus assessment on the defined learning goals and align them with the instructional components previously taught.
(B) Use only multiple-choice questions and ensure that they are written at various levels of cognition to assess all levels of learning.
(C) Always include closed-ended and open-ended items on all assessments so students have an opportunity to use their opinions about what they have learned.
(D) Design assessments that will result in a normal distribution of scores so students can clearly see their position in the group.

Competency 010: *The teacher monitors student performance and achievement; provides students with timely, high-quality feedback; and responds flexibly to promote learning for all students.*

Grades 8–12

11. At the beginning of the second semester, a parent calls Bonita to complain about the amount of homework his senior high student has each night. The parent states that the homework is "excessive and unrelated to what twelfth-grade students need to know." How can Bonita ensure that when she invites the parent in for a conference, the discussion will be productive and will result in a positive outcome for the student?

   (A) Ask the parent what he believes is an appropriate amount of time for a student to do homework each night and how he reached that number.
   (B) Dismiss what the parent says because this student and his parent are the only ones complaining about the amount of homework.
   (C) Carefully listen to the parent, and explain why and how the homework is important to the student's understanding and education.
   (D) Explain to the parent that the homework might be more than what other teachers require because you know students need to be getting ready for college.

Competency 011: *The teacher understands the importance of family involvement in children's education and knows how to interact and communicate effectively with families.*

12. Before the school year begins, Austin meets with his mentor teacher to plan how to integrate library and technology skills throughout the year. He wants his twelfth-grade students to be able to complete their English research papers through the use of library resources and electronic means. After they complete the overarching plans for the research requirements, Austin then asks to meet with the librarian to discuss appropriate tools and processes for research. To have a productive meeting, what information should he be prepared to share?

   (A) The purpose and learning goals for assigning the research project.
   (B) His knowledge of how to use the Internet for searching for resources.
   (C) The likely learning styles of the students he anticipates having this year.
   (D) A list of other resources students may use for the research project.

Competency 012: *The teacher enhances professional knowledge and skills by effectively interacting with other members of the educational community and participating in various types of professional activities.*

13. During the discussion with his mentor about the research assignment, Austin states that he is thinking of taking a school laptop home to do some Internet research on his own. He also plans to use the computer to outline a novel he hopes to publish some day. How does his intent align with aspects of legal/ethical uses of school property?

(A) This is okay as long as he returns the equipment in good condition.
(B) This practice is okay as long as the equipment is not needed at school.
(C) Teachers must use school technology equipment only for authorized school business.
(D) He may keep a laptop for personal use as long as he does not change loaded software.

Competency 013: *The teacher understands and adheres to legal and ethical requirements for educators and is knowledgeable of the structure of education in Texas.*

Answer Key

DIAGNOSTIC TEST (GRADES 8-12)

Question Number	Correct Response	Competency
1	A	001
2	C	002
3	D	003
4	D	004
5	C	005
6	C	006
7	A	007
8	C	008
9	C	009
10	A	010
11	C	011
12	A	012
13	C	013

CORRECT RESPONSES

1. **A** Some high school students can be focused more on themselves, their peers, their environment, and the present than on their futures. It is sometimes difficult for a person of this age to consider long-range consequences of his or her present behaviors and choices. "I will be different" is a common reaction.

2. **C** Working with students to establish clear guidelines for acceptable classroom behaviors and language interactions and the consequences for not following them can reduce or eliminate the inappropriate behaviors and language. Attempting to keep groups of students separate or to ignore the problem will actually increase the negative behaviors and language that are producing the tension.

3. **D** *Appreciation* is a challenging concept for assessment because it would typically result in a subjective rather than objective evaluation. While this area of growth is important, teachers do face challenges when deciding to assess affective domain elements. Catherine would be better served by rewriting her objective statement in a way that can be assessed objectively.

4. **D** Research indicates that active student engagement and reflective thinking as well as reflective writing are all effective ways to help students confirm and clarify their learning and to increase their ownership of the learning process. Barbara's use of these strategies indicates she is knowledgeable about how she can effectively help her students to process new information.

5. **C** As a tool for evaluating classroom climate, Mary Ellen should focus on how engaged students are in the learning process. The main goal of instruction is the development of intellectual growth, so Mary Ellen should focus on how she provides opportunities for students to be involved and actively engaged in higher order thinking during the instructional process.

6. **C** By establishing clear guidelines and classroom routines during the initial week of school, Daryl sets the stage for high standards and high expectations for student learning and efficient use of time. By planning in advance with his mentor, Daryl makes sure he is clear in his own mind and prepared to clearly communicate guidelines and routines to his students to avoid ambiguity and confusion that could allow instructional time to be wasted.

7. **A** When a teacher plans for open discussion among all students in the classroom, typically one of the major goals is for students to develop effective listening skills. The teacher's recognition that some students are not listening while others are talking indicates that she is aware of and can now address one challenge to guiding her students to better communication skills.

8. **C** By having students write briefly about their understanding of the lesson's objective, any prior knowledge they might have, and their questions on the topic, the teacher is focusing on activation of prior knowledge, making connections with prior learning, and identifying any misunderstandings students may have as well as establishing student interest and buy-in.

9. **C** At the high school level, learners will likely be much more motivated to take responsibility for their learning if they have been allowed to participate in the development of how they will be assessed. By using a jointly designed scoring rubric, the teacher has set the stage for student ownership of the multimedia task, and students have a clearly defined set of expectations for the content and presentation requirements of their final product.

10. **A** It is critical that teachers design and develop assessments that are directly paired with learning goals and the concepts developed during instruction. As assessment items are written or alternative assessment methods are selected, these assessment strategies should be at multiple levels of difficulty and in varied formats. Most importantly, the teacher must assure that the items are carefully aligned with the instructional components taught.

11. **C** In a parent-teacher conference, the teacher should always first listen to the parent's concerns. The teacher should explain the purpose and value of the assigned homework so the parent may have a clear understanding of the teacher's instructional goals.

12. **A** Regular classroom teachers frequently partner with specialists. To work most effectively with the librarian, Austin should provide information about the nature, purpose, and learning goals of the research assignment so the librarian can better assist with determining appropriate tools and processes.

13. **C** Any property owned by the school (or district) must be used solely for professional purposes. Teachers must not use school property for their personal reasons, even if they "borrow" the equipment for only a short time.

Sample Test (Grades 8–12)

This sample test has some practice questions to help you review as part of your preparation for the 8–12 PPR test. Please carefully read the domains and competencies that will be tested on the 8–12 PPR test before beginning this test. As you read the domains and competencies, please think about the mind-set and philosophy of teaching they represent. In this sample test, each practice question is introduced by the competency being measured. The questions and competencies are presented in numerical order for the purpose of logical flow as you learn the competencies. When you reach the teacher decision sets near the end of this test, the sample questions will no longer address the competencies in numerical order. *Please be aware that competency statements will not appear on the actual test form and that the questions will not be presented in sequential order by competency numbers.*

Use the frame of reference built from your understanding of the domains and competencies as you select the single best answer for each question. It is recommended that you do an in-depth analysis of each possible answer before making your choice. After narrowing your possible choices to two answers, reread the question with each answer. This can help you ensure that your final choice answers exactly what the question is asking. Stay focused on the specific information provided by the question. Avoid reading more into the question or thinking of extenuating circumstances. In addition to selecting your preferred answer, it is recommended that you consider carefully why it is the best answer based on the domains and competencies. In addition, it is recommended that you have a clear reason for rejecting each answer that is not chosen rather than just identifying and marking your preferred answer.

Following the sample test and answer key, a section on correct responses and rationales discusses the strengths and challenges of each of the possible answers. Refer back to the domains and competencies as you read the rationale for each possible answer. Carefully examine the rationales for both the right and the wrong answer choices for the relationship to the domains and competencies.

Directions: Read each stimulus and answer every question. Mark your answers in the answer spaces on the accompanying grid.

Competency 001: *The teacher understands human developmental processes and applies this knowledge to plan instruction and ongoing assessment that motivate students and are responsive to their developmental characteristics and needs.*

1. A ninth-grade teacher has students in her class at cognitive developmental levels ranging from concrete operational to formal operational. What is the *best* approach for adapting instruction so that all students can achieve?

   (A) The teacher should use cooperative learning groups as the primary instructional method.
   (B) She should create learning teams that include students at each of the cognitive levels.
   (C) She should target her instruction to the middle cognitive level.
   (D) She should model abstract concepts prior to active engagement of students during independent practice.

2. As a first-year teacher, you are concerned about your role in student guidance as well as your role in working cooperatively with the campus counselor. You overhear a junior-level student telling a student in your math class that she plans to drop out of high school because it has no meaning for her. She plans to marry soon and sees no reason to continue with school. Because you do not know the young lady planning to leave school, you ask your student to encourage the junior to discuss the issue with the high school counselor. You then briefly visit with the counselor to inform her that you have recommended help for your student's friend. What must the high school counselor (and you) be aware of about students of this age in order to conduct an effective discussion about not dropping out of school?

   (A) Many students this age are focused on present needs and desires rather than on long-term consequences.
   (B) Many students this age have not found a place in the school's society, and so they feel they do not fit in.
   (C) Many students this age are not able to apply logical reasoning patterns to planning their lives.
   (D) Many students this age do not recognize adults as being able to give valid advice to their age group.

Competency 002: *The teacher understands student diversity and knows how to plan learning experiences and design assessments that are responsive to differences among students and that promote all students' learning.*

3. Since the tragedy of 9/11, a high school teacher has noticed tense relationships among diverse student groups. What would be the best strategy for diffusing this tension?

(A) Reward students who exhibit positive behaviors during the school day.
(B) Use cooperative grouping during instruction to mix diverse students.
(C) Involve students in developing interaction and behavioral guidelines.
(D) Link student attitudes and behaviors exhibited at school to academic grades.

4. A teacher planning to implement a major project with a mixed-ability group also wants to promote resiliency in the students. Which approach will be *most* effective in helping the teacher achieve this goal?

(A) Allow students some choice in topics and in the procedures they will use to complete their research.
(B) Break the project into subtasks and provide students with assistance in planning and accomplishing these subtasks as needed.
(C) Emphasize to students the need to follow processes and procedures as they work on their projects.
(D) Pair lower-achieving with higher-achieving students and allow these partnerships flexibility in determining how the project should be done.

5. A high school teacher is aware that some of her students have had limited exposure to technological tools with which they now need a high level of skill. Which of the following strategies will allow the teacher to best respond to the skills these students lack as they complete a project?

(A) Allow students to have access to the computers and other media equipment available in the library.
(B) Allow students to develop presentations that do not require the use of computer technology.
(C) Provide students with access to written instructions for the use of all the technologies available.
(D) Form heterogeneous groups that have opportunities to explore all the technologies available.

Competency 003: *The teacher understands procedures for designing effective and coherent instruction and assessment based on appropriate learning goals and objectives.*

6. A learning goal for a ninth-grade class states that "students will appreciate the aesthetic beauty of music from a variety of western and eastern cultures." What is the most significant problem with this learning goal?

   (A) The desired outcome indicated by the learning goal is unattainable as ninth-graders are so into their music that they are not open to other types.

   (B) It will be difficult to find or create instructional activities that will appeal and motivate ninth-graders to achieve this learning goal.

   (C) This aesthetic learning goal does not indicate the prior content knowledge the ninth-graders must have to be able to meet it.

   (D) This aesthetic learning goal is difficult to apply objective and meaningful assessment to, and so it will be difficult to determine if it has been met.

7. A middle school principal informs his faculty at the beginning of the year that he will not be collecting and reading lesson plans weekly but that he expects to see unit plans before they are taught. He indicates that unit plans must be completed and submitted to him at least one week before any instruction about the unit occurs. What is the *main* reason the principal feels so strongly about having the entire unit planned before beginning instruction?

   (A) Having the entire unit planned before beginning instruction increases the likelihood that content and learning activities will be sequenced in a logical manner to increase student retention of the material.

   (B) Having the entire unit planned before beginning instruction allows for selection of an age-appropriate presentation format for the content and topic development of the unit.

   (C) Having the entire unit planned before beginning instruction allows a clear overview of the unit so that more interesting approaches can be inserted where instruction style in the original draft was not stimulating.

   (D) Having the entire unit planned before beginning instruction allows for content topics and learning activities to be addressed according to student needs.

Use the following information to answer questions 8 and 9.

Ms. de La Cruz, a high school teacher, has found that including open-ended writing in her physics class has improved student comprehension. So she has students use learning journals on a regular basis in addition to their experimental lab notebooks. Following a recent unit called Physics in Our Daily Life, she selected these reflection questions for students to address in their learning journals.

- What are three things you learned from today's lab on pendulums?
- How is the information in the video we saw on Galileo related to the observations he made in church as he watched the lights swing?
- How was your investigation related to a typical event that occurs in your own life?

Competency 004: *The teacher understands learning processes and factors that impact student learning and demonstrates this knowledge by planning effective, engaging instruction and appropriate assessments.*

8. These reflection questions best demonstrate the teacher's use of a learning journal to implement which learning principle?

   (A) Knowledge of how a student learns reinforces that student's ability to learn.
   (B) Actively processing relationships between content information in context reinforces learning.
   (C) Meaningful learning occurs from self-motivated acquisition of knowledge and skills.
   (D) The formulating of generalizations by students enhances their learning of the content.

Competency 005: *The teacher knows how to establish a classroom climate that fosters learning, equity, and excellence and uses this knowledge to create a physical and emotional environment that is safe and productive.*

9. Ms. de La Cruz wants to use her students' learning journals to help her evaluate classroom climate. Which question is most important for Ms. de La Cruz to consider as she reads her students' learning journals?

   (A) Is there ongoing individual accountability of student learning in my classroom?
   (B) Is my educational philosophy clearly reflected in my daily instructional styles?
   (C) Are my students actively engaged and intellectually stimulated by my lessons?
   (D) Are the learning experiences my students encounter varied to meet the needs of all?

Use the following information to answer questions 10 and 11.

By the second week of school, a first-year high school math teacher has determined that the students in her second-period class differ significantly in their current levels of knowledge and skills. She thinks this is due to their varied prior experiences with mathematical instruction and applications.

10. What assessment system can best create a positive and supportive learning environment for all the students?

   (A) Both teacher and peer assessment of performance are included in feedback to students.
   (B) Students are assigned appropriate and varied assessment standards based on their ability groups.
   (C) Progress, process, and product are all part of the assessment used to determine student grades.
   (D) Tests include questions at varying levels of difficulty to ensure that all students encounter some success.

In a discussion with the school guidance counselor, the math teacher discovers that there is another reason for the differences in her students' levels of knowledge and skills. The counselor tells her that her second-period math class has a high number of students with significant academic needs.

11. In what way can this teacher avoid becoming a barrier to success for the students who have significant academic needs?

   (A) She should set high standards, differentiate instruction, and have high expectations for all students regardless of their level of academic need.
   (B) She must collect information on ethnicity, socioeconomic status, at-risk status, and parental education levels.
   (C) She should understand the social challenges some students face and take this into account as she plans instruction and expectations for them.
   (D) Because all the students are in the same grade and attended this school last year, she should instruct all the students in the same way.

Competency 006: *The teacher understands strategies for creating an organized and productive learning environment and for managing student behavior.*

12. Mr. Argufy is a first-year teacher being mentored by Ms. Cooper, a 12-year veteran from across the hall. Before school begins, Ms. Cooper delivers what she calls her standard "learn to work smart rather than hard" lecture for new teachers. She explains that the school has invested a lot of resources in technology and that teachers do not always use it effectively. She then asks Mr. Argufy to decide which routine task could best be done more efficiently with a spreadsheet program. What should be Mr. Argufy's reponse?

(A) Lesson and unit plan development would be more time-efficient with a spreadsheet program.

(B) Keeping daily attendance and tardiness records would be more time-efficient with a spreadsheet program.

(C) Using a weighted formula to compute student averages would be more time-efficient with a spreadsheet program.

(D) Keeping track of parent-teacher communication, such as signed forms, would be more time-efficient with a spreadsheet program.

Use the following information to answer questions 13 and 14.

During the opening week of school, an eighth-grade teacher spends some of her instructional time daily on emphasizing her expectations that students know and follow her classroom rules, routines, and procedures. She devotes time to this because she feels this is an area where some high school students encounter problems that have a negative impact on their learning.

13. Why is it a major advantage to spend time early in the school year to ensure that students understand and follow classroom routines?

(A) Ensuring that students understand and follow classroom routines promotes the effective use of instructional and learning time.

(B) Ensuring that students understand and follow classroom routines creates a sense of certainty for students and a more positive attitude.

(C) Ensuring that students understand and follow classroom routines reduces management demands and so creates more planning time.

(D) Ensuring that students understand and follow classroom routines reduces confusion and allows for easier student monitoring.

14. This eighth-grade teacher has learned the value of having clear expectations and classroom procedures as well as routines, even at this grade level. She also understands the value of investing time to teach these in depth at the beginning of the school year. She wants to focus on routines and procedures rather than classroom or school rules. She believes that students at this age need more freedom and fewer absolute rules. Which strategy should this teacher use to help her eighth-grade students value and apply classroom rules, routines, and procedures?

   (A) Guiding students to establish and clearly understand classroom rules, routines, and procedures eliminates the need for continual reminders and ensures that students are aware of the expectations for a smoothly running classroom.
   (B) Having students understand the rules, routines, and procedures assures the teacher of having a successful classroom environment for productive student learning.
   (C) Explaining to students how rules, routines, and procedures differ should ensure that the classroom runs smoothly and that students have respect for peers.
   (D) Directing students to record and memorize the rules, procedures, and routines, prior to signing a contract stating that they agree to follow these elements of the classroom, will ensure that the classroom runs smoothly.

Use the following information to answer questions 15–17.

As a beginning 8–12 teacher, you have been assigned an experienced teacher as your mentor. Following a week of daily observation by your mentor, she indicates during your debriefing meeting that your teaching behaviors vary between two groups of students. You provide higher-achieving students significantly longer wait time than you provide lower-achieving students. In addition, with lower-achieving students you restate a question as many as three times during the same amount of wait time you give higher-achieving students. Both types of students perceive your restated questions as new questions.

Competency 007: *The teacher understands and applies principles and strategies for communicating effectively in varied teaching and learning contexts.*

15. Your mentor asks you to respond to the following question: How is continuing this practice of giving variances in wait time, of which you have been unaware, most likely to affect your classroom? What should be your response?

(A) Increased wait time for higher-achieving students signals all students that you expect more from these top students, a practice that is likely to produce resentment in both groups.

(B) Allowing a difference in wait time is an effective instructional differentiation method to permit both groups success opportunities by allowing needed thinking and responding time.

(C) Shorter wait time allows lower-achieving students less time to feel that they are "on the spot," and the restated questions indicate to all students that you are giving lower-achieving students more opportunities to succeed.

(D) Shorter wait time and restating questions send negative signals to students at all differentiated levels and reinforce a feeling of inability to achieve success in lower-achieving students.

16. When considering the effectiveness of a class discussion, which of the following aspects of the discussion should receive the most attention in the meeting with the mentor?

(A) The teacher ignored the fact that students repeatedly told each other that they were wrong.

(B) The teacher ignored the fact that students directed comments to one another rather than to her.

(C) The teacher ignored the fact that students added comments to the discussion without waiting to be called on.

(D) The teacher ignored the fact that students did not listen to their classmates during the discussion.

17. A history teacher concludes a lecture about the War Between the States with the following statements.

> **I hope you are aware that we have spent the past two weeks examining the causes of the War Between the States. We have determined the reasons the North gave for war and the reasons why the South entered the war. Next we will explore the perspective of allies of both the North and South and the reasons they gave for selecting that side to support. Some of the rationales have been alluded to as we have moved through the prior material.**

What is the primary reason for a teacher to conclude a lecture in this way?

(A) A lecture conclusion should be made by the teacher and should be clear, be short, and restate the main points.

(B) A lecture conclusion should guide students toward establishing relationships between main points.

(C) A lecture conclusion should restate the key concepts the teacher expects students to be able to identify on the unit test.

(D) A lecture conclusion should guide students toward recognizing the relevance of the content to their lives.

Use the following information to answer questions 18 and 19.

The day after the events of 9/11, students arrived in social studies class wanting to discuss the event. The class had strong opinions about the cause of 9/11 and the response they felt would be appropriate for the government to take. The class was not scheduled to discuss world violence and tolerance toward differences until a unit scheduled for two months from now.

Competency 008: *The teacher provides appropriate instruction that actively engages students in the learning process.*

18. As a high school teacher, what is an appropriate response for this teacher to make, given that this topic is not part of the planned curriculum?

(A) Explain to students your discomfort in discussing this in class since you do not know how their parents would like such a conversation to be handled.

(B) Give students class time to engage in an open discussion about their concerns, and then find a way to connect this topic with the planned curriculum over the next few days.

(C) Rather than discuss the issue in class, ask students to conduct some Internet research at home and then discuss their concerns with their parents.

(D) Tell students that you empathize with their immediate concerns and their need to talk about this now, yet you must follow the intended curriculum so that they do not fall behind.

19. Based on the comments from the class about an appropriate response by the U.S. government, how can the teacher guide students in applying skills that will assist them in becoming lifelong learners using this high-interest topic?

(A) Have students examine the available information on the event and classify it as factual or emotional and discuss the potential impact on the response.

(B) Split students into two teams and have them conduct a mock debate to guide the government in making a decision about its response.

(C) Brainstorm potential responses the government could make and poll the school to see which response is favored and why.

(D) Encourage students to select the possible response they support and write a clear rationale for their position supported by evidence.

20. A life science teacher routinely asks her students to write an explanation of what they think is the objective or point of the experiment they are about to do and what procedures they will need to follow to successfully achieve this objective. What is the greatest benefit of this advance writing activity to students?

(A) This writing activity gives all students an equal opportunity for success with the assignment because they now all have the same background.

(B) This writing activity increases the chances that all students will follow the directions and the experiments will have the desired outcome.

(C) This writing activity assists students in developing a conceptual framework about the purpose of the experiment and guides their learning.

(D) This writing activity increases student focus on the lesson and allows them to work quickly and efficiently because confusion is reduced.

Competency 009: *The teacher incorporates the effective use of technology to plan, organize, deliver, and evaluate instruction for all students.*

21. A high school teacher has her students working on a unit where the final product will be individual student multimedia presentations. The teacher has established clear content requirements to be included in the end product and has indicated to students that she wants content to receive greater emphasis than presentation design. How can the teacher most effectively encourage the appropriate balance between content and presentation design as the final product is developed?

   (A) Before the project is begun, the students and the teacher should work together to design a rubric that clearly establishes the content and design expectations and the balance between these two components in the final product.

   (B) To ensure that the design aspect of the project does not get out of hand, the teacher should share a list of acceptable product design suggestions that students can select from after the content part of the project is completed.

   (C) Students must submit a draft of the content portion of the project to the teacher for approval before beginning the project design component, which must also be approved.

   (D) The teacher should provide daily reminders of the expected balance between content and project design as students work on completing the required individual final products.

Competency 010: *The teacher monitors student performance and achievement; provides students with timely, high-quality feedback; and responds flexibly to promote learning for all students.*

22. What is most important if you want an appropriately designed teacher-made test?

   (A) The test should yield a bell curve as the range of student scores.
   (B) The test should align with objectives and content learning opportunities.
   (C) The test should contain questions at several levels of difficulty.
   (D) The test should use both objective and performance assessment questions.

Competency 011: *The teacher understands the importance of family involvement in children's education and knows how to interact and communicate effectively with families.*

23. A ninth-grade teacher wants to encourage students to learn to apply math concepts learned in school. Her plan is to accomplish this through family math time at home. What is the best way to motivate families and to facilitate the establishment of family math time?

    (A) The teacher should send home a textbook and assignment sheet explaining the importance of family math time and ask that it become part of each family's interaction during the week.

    (B) The teacher should send home an invitation to participate in family math time with an explanation of the requirements and a description of activities the family can complete together.

    (C) The teacher should conduct seminars in the evenings to help parents understand how their ninth-grade students have changed since middle school and how family math time can help.

    (D) The teacher should send home notification of a meeting in which the value of family math time, instructional methods used in school, and assessment rubrics are explained.

24. A high school principal believes teachers and parents/guardians should be partners working together to ensure the best possible education for students. He shares this philosophy with his teachers as they prepare to begin a new school year. Because his teachers agree, what would be the best information for the teachers to share with their students' families at the beginning of the year to help create this partnership?

    (A) Teachers should discuss with the families the expectations for student academic performance and how by working together they can guide students toward success.

    (B) Teachers should inform the families about the instructional resources available to students and the major projects required during the coming school year.

    (C) Teachers should compare the relationship between scores from teacher-made tests the school will use during the year and those from state-required tests.

    (D) Teachers should inform families about the developmental levels and traits of secondary students and how these produce behaviors different from those of middle school students.

25. A parent has called and scheduled a conference with a teacher to discuss some concerns. What is the best way to ensure a productive conference?

    (A) When the parent arrives, clearly and calmly state your perspective and then listen to the parent's response.

    (B) Prepare yourself before the parent arrives by determining why this parent wants a conference when others do not.

    (C) Be friendly as you greet the parent and then listen closely to the parent's concerns and perspective before responding.

    (D) When the parent arrives, clearly identify why you believe the parent has requested this conference.

Competency 012: *The teacher enhances professional knowledge and skills by effectively interacting with other members of the educational community and participating in various types of professional activities.*

26. Ms. Wolf, an English teacher, asks to meet with the technology coordinator. Ms. Wolf has weak technological skills yet wants her students to use technology as part of an upcoming class project. Her students' technological skills range widely. In order to effectively team with the technology coordinator in planning this student project, what information is most important for the teacher to share?

    (A) Ms. Wolf should make the technology coordinator completely aware of the gaps in her technological skills.

    (B) Ms. Wolf should make the technology coordinator aware of the goals and requirements of the project.

    (C) Ms. Wolf should make the technology coordinator aware of the gaps in her students' technological skills.

    (D) Ms. Wolf should make the technology coordinator aware of how students will be grouped to complete the project.

27. In the coming school year, two teachers plan to share responsibility for the high school drama program. They decide that a drama chairperson is foolish in a department of two and plan to make joint decisions. What is the most important decision they should make before school begins to ensure an effective drama program?

    (A) They should divide the outside school responsibilities necessary for an effective drama program in an equitable manner.

    (B) They should divide the administrative roles and responsibilities of an effective drama program in an equitable manner.

    (C) They should agree on a clear set of goals and expectations for student participation in the drama program.

    (D) They should establish a joint planning time to select learning experiences for their students and discuss problems.

Competency 013: *The teacher understands and adheres to legal and ethical requirements for educators and is knowledgeable about the structure of education in Texas.*

28. Emil is a transfer student who has been in his new school for two months. Emil's transfer records are incomplete, and the school has had no success in getting his previous school to forward the information missing from these records. Emil is struggling with even simple assignments in mathematics, and the math teacher wonders if he had previously been classified as a special education student. Because the new school does not know his classification, the math teacher decides to refer him for testing to see if he qualifies for special education services. Legally, what must occur before Emil can have this type of evaluation?

    (A) Before she can seek an evaluation, the math teacher must document the reasons for her concerns about Emil.

    (B) Before proceeding, the math teacher must visit with Emil's other teachers and parents/guardians to see if they share her concerns.

    (C) Before seeking an evaluation, the math teacher must notify the district special education director of her concerns for Emil.

    (D) Before an evaluation can be requested, the math teacher must first seek written permission from Emil's parents/guardians.

29. Given the high-stakes testing for accountability purposes, two first-year teachers are concerned about the upcoming required state tests that they are to administer. They talk with experienced teachers to make sure that they know exactly the rules and procedures to administer the standardized test. Which of the following suggestions made by one of the experienced teachers is unethical?

    (A) Teachers have the right and responsibility to prepare students for a standardized test by giving unit tests in the same format as the state tests.

    (B) Teachers may write practice tests to be given to students several days prior to state testing and may discuss with students how to answer the questions after giving the practice tests.

    (C) Teachers may test content knowledge and skills that address the objectives measured by the state test, and they may test students using the same format as that of the state tests.

    (D) Teachers may answer students' questions during the test administration if the questions are about a test item.

DECISION SET BEGINS HERE

Consuela Alvarez is a high school science teacher in her first year of teaching. Five weeks into the school year, another science teacher casually remarks to Ms. Alvarez, "I hear you have Liset Jordan in science this year. She was in my class last year and was a real challenge. She is so smart but not at all interested in school, and so she is impossible to motivate."

Ms. Alvarez is careful not to show her surprise because Liset has been a joy to have in class, as she is one of a dozen students in her second-period class who seems especially motivated. She always completes her homework assignments, takes an active role in class discussions, and does well on quizzes. Ms. Alvarez had assumed that Liset and the other students have always enjoyed science and have been motivated to produce high-quality work because they are studying a subject they obviously enjoy. The comment from the other teacher prompts Ms. Alvarez to investigate the prior academic performance of Liset and the others in order to promote continuing high achievement and resiliency. Her first step is to examine their academic records.

Competency 010: *The teacher monitors student performance and achievement; provides students with timely, high-quality feedback; and responds flexibly to promote learning for all students.*

30. Ms. Alvarez determines from school records that Liset's grades have been good, with some slight variations. Liset's greatest variation in grades has been in science. As she interprets the grades in the file, which of the following points should Ms. Alvarez always keep in mind?

    (A) Stress in the classroom is often indicated by minor fluctuations in a student's grades.
    (B) Grades based on student content work completed over a period of time tend to be inflated.
    (C) Science grades for females are expected to fluctuate because of the difficulty of the content.
    (D) Some variation is normal because of differences in teacher-student interactions and expectations.

As a result of talking with some of Liset's other teachers and examining her school records, Ms. Alvarez concludes that Liset's academic performance was significantly weaker last year. She also establishes that Hung and Steve, two other students from second period, are also performing better this year than last year. Ms. Alvarez requests that Liset, Hung, and Steve meet with her following class. The following is a part of their discussion.

> **Ms. Alvarez:** I wanted to speak with you three students because you are doing so well in my science class but your performance in science last year was much weaker. You have all gone from barely passing science last year to earning an A in my class.
>
> *The students glance at each other and the floor but not at Ms. Alvarez. No one speaks.*
>
> **Ms. Alvarez:** Will you please tell me why your performances in science were so weak last year?
>
> **Hung:** I couldn't get my homework done. I always seemed to run out of time.
>
> **Ms. Alvarez:** What makes such a difference in your time from last year to this year?
>
> **Hung:** *Looking at the floor and seeming reluctant to speak, he mumbles.* I don't know.
>
> **Ms. Alvarez:** What was happening with you two? Liset? Steve? *She gets shrugs and they glance at each other again.* Fine. You can all leave now but think about what I have asked. I really want to know. I want to know how to help you continue to do well and avoid sliding back into last year's patterns.

Competency 005: *The teacher knows how to establish a classroom climate that fosters learning, equity, and excellence and uses this knowledge to create a physical and emotional environment that is safe and productive.*

31. What is a likely outcome of Ms. Alvarez's interaction with these three students?

    (A) These students will feel confused about why Ms. Alvarez has asked about what happened before she taught them.
    (B) These students will begin to think more about their academic efforts but be unsure about why they should be concerned.
    (C) These students will generalize about more effort producing better results and apply themselves more.
    (D) These students will acknowledge Ms. Alvarez's caring and begin to understand how to be more resilient.

Competency 013: *The teacher understands and adheres to legal and ethical require-ments for educators and is knowledgeable of the structure of education in Texas.*

32. How was Ms. Alvarez's behavior inappropriate during her meeting with these students?

(A) Ms. Alvarez indicated to these students that she was disappointed by their past performances and that it has impacted her opinion.

(B) Ms. Alvarez formed her opinion of these students based on others' ideas and past information rather than on her own observations.

(C) Ms. Alvarez violated student confidentiality for these three students when she discussed grades in a group setting.

(D) Ms. Alvarez embarrassed these students as she asked them to share a prior experience of which they were probably not proud.

Ms. Alvarez decides to meet with each student individually to see if they will be more forthcoming with her when alone without the others being present. Liset tells Ms. Alvarez she didn't have time to do all her homework last year because she had to work two part-time jobs. When Ms. Alvarez says she is glad Liset was smart enough to cut down on her afterschool work this year, Liset reacts with anger. She says her family needs her to work but that she has a full class load this year. Also, with her father unemployed since the local factory closed, she must have outstanding grades to get a scholarship for col-lege. She feels torn in two directions. Ms. Alvarez sees that Liset is very stressed about her grades.

Competency 004: *The teacher understands learning processes and factors that impact student learning and demonstrates this knowledge by planning effective, engaging instruction and appropriate assessments.*

33. What principle is best illustrated by this situation?

(A) Teachers should get to know their students as individuals and be aware of home and community factors that affect student learning.

(B) Teachers should ask about student family problems so they can be sensitive to the learning challenges they can produce.

(C) Teachers should make more of an effort to establish collaboration between schools and families so the school can help with problems.

(D) Teachers should realize how strong an impact high and low teacher expectations can have on students' academic performances.

Competency 011: *The teacher understands the importance of family involvement in children's education and knows how to interact and communicate effectively with families.*

34. The day following her second visit with Liset, Ms. Alvarez receives a call from Liset's mother. Ms. Jordan says Liset has discussed Ms. Alvarez's concerns with her, and she wants to talk about helping Liset maintain the grades she will need to be eligible for a scholarship while regaining her income from part-time work. What would be Ms. Alvarez's most appropriate response to Ms. Jordan?

   (A) Ms. Alvarez should direct Ms. Jordan to contact local agencies and organizations that assist families in need until one of the parents can find work.
   (B) Ms. Alvarez should arrange for Ms. Jordan and Liset to meet with her to discuss options for helping Liset continue to achieve well.
   (C) Ms. Alvarez should meet with Ms. Jordan to discuss Liset's grades and encourage Ms. Jordan to seek employment.
   (D) Ms. Alvarez should tell Ms. Jordan not to worry as other teachers think highly of Liset and will help ensure that her grades are good.

Competency 010: *The teacher monitors student performance and achievement; provides students with timely, high-quality feedback; and responds flexibly to promote learning for all students.*

35. When Ms. Alvarez meets privately with Hung, he again states that he is unsure why he could not complete his assignments or maintain his grades last year and indicates that he is just glad that the problem has gone away. Ms. Alvarez assures him that the cause has not just disappeared to never return. She convinces him that he must identify the problem to prevent it from occurring again when least expected. Through careful questioning, Ms. Alvarez helps Hung realize he was overextended with extracurricular activities last year. Ms. Alvarez asks Hung to

   • Compare his key goals for last year to this year's goals.
   • List choices he can make to ensure that he is not overextended again.
   • Identify the benefits he sees in continuing to show strong achievement.

   What is a benefit of guiding Hung through this step-by-step analysis process?

   (A) It models for Hung the many applications of problem-solving strategies in his daily life.
   (B) It models an effective problem-solving strategy Hung can use in maintaining his resiliency.
   (C) It models for Hung that classroom lessons might have applications outside the school setting.
   (D) It encourages Hung to be more self-reflective and open to taking risks in a safe environment.

By asking around, Ms. Alvarez discovers that in the past Steve had been a shy loner. During the summer he made friends with a group of academically gifted students, and his grades are reflecting his improved motivation. When Steve and Ms. Alvarez meet privately, Steve is aloof and unresponsive, responding to all her questions with uninformative brush-off statements. This especially concerns Ms. Alvarez because Steve's behaviors in class have altered during the week since the first conference. She has noticed that his participation is down, he seems confused about directions, and seems sleepy during class. She wonders if he may now be using drugs.

Competency 012: *The teacher enhances professional knowledge and skills by effectively interacting with other members of the educational community and participating in various types of professional activities.*

36. Based on her concerns about Steve, what would be the most effective strategy for her to try first?

   (A) Ms. Alvarez should bluntly ask Steve why such a bright young man would waste his life by using drugs to attempt to shock him into realizing he is not fooling anyone and only hurting himself with his recent bad choices.

   (B) Ms. Alvarez should reiterate the expectations she and the school have for appropriate student behaviors and remind Steve of how he is risking a bright future through the poor choices he may now be making.

   (C) Ms. Alvarez should contact Steve's parents to discuss his sudden change in behavior and be sure they clearly understand the potential consequences of continuing in this manner, especially if she is right that drugs are involved.

   (D) Ms. Alvarez should work with Steve and appropriate school personnel to determine what has changed in Steve's life that might be responsible for the changes observed while keeping in mind her concern about drugs.

DECISION SET ENDS HERE

DECISION SET BEGINS HERE

Ms. Bowerman is the new tenth-grade science teacher at the high school and is finding her homeroom class to be an especially diverse group. The class includes both gifted and talented students as well as students who regularly spend time with the school's resource teacher. English is not the first language for six of the students who have been in the United States less than two years. Four languages other than English are spoken in the homes of these students. In addition, Ms. Bowerman is aware that in any given classroom the Piagetian cognitive abilities/readiness of students may range over two to three grade levels.

Competency 001: *The teacher understands human developmental processes and applies this knowledge to plan instruction and ongoing assessment that motivate students and are responsive to their developmental characteristics and needs.*

37. How can Ms. Bowerman best meet the needs of the range of cognitive variations found in her students?

   (A) Assign students to groups based on their cognitive development or readiness level to make it easier for them to work successfully in small groups.
   (B) Assign student "study buddies" to help students at lower cognitive levels reach success by partnering them with students at higher cognitive levels.
   (C) Present instruction at the normal tenth-grade level of development and remind students that they must take some responsibility for their own learning.
   (D) Use high-engagement instructional strategies such as experiments, activities, and projects to introduce and provide instruction on abstract concepts.

38. Given that Piagetian cognitive levels may range across two to three years, even in a high school classroom, what teaching strategies would be most effective for Ms. Bowerman to use to meet the developmental cognitive levels of all students?

   (A) Typically, students at this age level find reading, taking notes, and using worksheets to be the most effective instructional strategies.
   (B) Tenth-grade students should find inquiry projects, cooperative learning, and scientific experimentation effective instructional strategies.
   (C) Students enjoy whole-class reading of a textbook and discussion of the reading as an instructional strategy.
   (D) Students find lectures, PPT presentations, and guided note taking to be effective instructional strategies.

Competency 002: *The teacher understands student diversity and knows how to plan learning experiences and design assessments that are responsive to differences among students and that promote all students' learning.*

39. What is most important as Ms. Bowerman considers how to adapt her instructional strategies as she plans for her special-needs students?

    (A) Her instructional strategies must ensure that no group of students is singled out and made to feel different or isolated from the other students.

    (B) Her instructional strategies must ensure that each group of students has ample time to interact with other students at a similar cognitive level.

    (C) Her instructional strategies must ensure that students occasionally work individually but that collaborative efforts have a stronger focus to ensure the success of all students.

    (D) Her instructional strategies must ensure that students are allowed to select instructional activities based on individual interests and strengths.

40. Ms. Bowerman knows she must modify her plans, lessons, and assessments for her limited English proficiency students in ways that will address both their language needs and their learning of the science content. How can she best meet these goals?

    (A) Ms. Bowerman should present lessons to these limited English proficiency students that address content and concept TEKS that are less demanding than the TEKS addressed in the lessons for the other students.

    (B) Ms. Bowerman should address the same TEKS for all her students while modifying her presentation of the materials in a way appropriate for her limited English proficiency students.

    (C) Ms. Bowerman should present lessons drawn only from TEKS that can be presented with concrete materials to allow these students ample language development experiences in lessons using real objects.

    (D) Ms. Bowerman should focus only on English language acquisition with these limited English proficiency students and worry about their learning after their English fluency has improved.

41. When assessing the limited English proficiency students, which of the following plans will give Ms. Bowerman the most accurate assessment of these students' learning?

    (A) Ms. Bowerman should allow the limited English proficiency students to indicate weekly how they are progressing in both English and content learning. This weekly conference will help her establish their progress.

    (B) Ms. Bowerman should assess the limited English proficiency students more often than the others to ensure that they are achieving at the same pace as rest of the class. She should hold tutoring sessions for those who are not.

    (C) Ms. Bowerman should assign each limited English proficiency student a "study buddy." This person will help her with assessment by sharing comments and observations about content knowledge and English acquisition.

    (D) Ms. Bowerman should assess *all* her students using a wide range of assessment styles. This will allow each of her students many ways and multiple opportunities to demonstrate their levels of achievement.

As one of her educational goals for the year, Ms. Bowerman wants all her students to learn to design and conduct appropriate scientific research. She wants all the students to improve their skill levels, their confidence, and their attitudes toward science.

Competency 003: *The teacher understands procedures for designing effective and coherent instruction and assessment based on appropriate learning goals and objectives.*

42. How can Ms. Bowerman best achieve her goals, especially with her more challenging lower-achieving students?

    (A) Ms. Bowerman can require all her students to design and complete a science research project, which will be entered in the school science fair. Every science fair entrant will receive a ribbon for participation.

    (B) Ms. Bowerman can break down scientific research into short, clear steps that guide students through the research process. Every class period will have some time set aside for working on the project and receiving teacher assistance.

    (C) Ms. Bowerman can partner students with complementary skill levels and interests. Higher-achieving students working with lower-achieving students will allow both groups of students to grow, especially if Ms. Bowerman encourages flexibility in student participation and roles.

    (D) Ms. Bowerman can require each student to participate in active teaching lessons focused on the skills needed to conduct research. Each student must master each skill lesson or repeat it until it is mastered.

During the first six weeks of school, Ms. Bowerman decides to read to her homeroom class for five to ten minutes every day following morning roll call. She thinks this is a better use of students' time as they prepare for the instructional day to begin than visiting with friends. She wants to improve the listening skills of her students. She wants to encourage their interest in famous scientists and their enthusiasm for language within a listening context.

43. For Ms. Bowerman to reach all her goals what criteria are most important in selecting the book she will read?

    (A) Ms. Bowerman should select books about scientists that have a direct connection with content classes. Her students will absorb content knowledge as they listen but will not really be aware that they are learning.

    (B) Ms. Bowerman should select books that describe scientists and discoveries new to the students. This will expand the students' learning as they encounter new and unexpected events with which they are presently unfamiliar.

    (C) Ms. Bowerman should select books about scientists and discoveries that are already very familiar to her students. This will hold their interest more effectively and make it easier for them to be attentive.

    (D) Ms. Bowerman should select books that are on a topic that is not too controversial. They should also be written in simple-to-understand language and sentence patterns to aid student aural comprehension.

44. How can Ms. Bowerman best assess the effectiveness of this daily listening time in meeting her stated goals?

    (A) During the first week, Ms. Bowerman can alternate using or not using the listening time each day. By observing how students respond to the difference, she can determine their interest in the strategy.

    (B) During the first week, Ms. Bowerman can assess students' listening and thinking skills by asking them questions about what they recall. She can also ask them to make predictions about what might occur later.

    (C) After three weeks, Ms. Bowerman can ask students if they wish to continue the listening time. Based on their responses, she will know whether or not students are enjoying the book.

    (D) After three weeks, Ms. Bowerman can give a short quiz to determine if individuals are attentive and if they are using effective listening skills during the daily listening time period.

DECISION SET ENDS HERE

DECISION SET BEGINS HERE

Ms. Angelino is a high school English teacher who wants to encourage strong student engagement in the learning process, and so she begins her grammar unit with a K-W-L chart. Ms. Angelino completes a class chart on the board after each student has completed an individual chart. Ideas on the class chart that are not on individual charts can be added.

Competency 005: *The teacher knows how to establish a classroom climate that fosters learning, equity, and excellence and uses this knowledge to create a physical and emotional environment that is safe and productive.*

45. What is the primary reason this beginning is a good selection?

(A) The individual K-W-L charts give students notice in a nonthreatening manner that everyone is expected to participate.

(B) The individual K-W-L charts send the message that the teacher thinks that everyone has some prior knowledge to contribute.

(C) The individual K-W-L charts indicate that no matter how much an individual knows at the beginning of the unit, there is still information to learn.

(D) The individual K-W-L charts allow students' prior knowledge of a topic to be accessed without placing any individual on the spot.

Ms. Angelino's own children, who are in high school and middle school, talk about the fun and effectiveness of the cooperative group work they do in their classrooms. Ms. Angelino was not happy with the results she obtained using small groups, yet she believes strongly that high school students can learn more effectively during social interactions. Ms. Angelino decides she should guide her students toward establishing rules for effective collaboration.

Competency 004: *The teacher understands learning processes and factors that impact student learning and demonstrates this knowledge by planning effective, engaging instruction and appropriate assessments.*

46. What additional strategy should Ms. Angelino use to improve the results obtained in her classroom?

   (A) Students should be guided as they conduct evaluations at the end of a project to assess group and individual performances on the assignment.

   (B) Ms. Angelino should ensure that there is a strong leader for each group and give permission for students to select the role each wishes to perform.

   (C) Ms. Angelino should allow students to select the members of their groups and permit those who do not wish to be in a group or who are not selected to work alone.

   (D) Ms. Angelino should base most of the project grade on how effectively the members of the group have worked collaboratively.

During late September, Ms. Angelino asks the guidance counselor for the state's assessment results for last year's tenth-grade class. She wants this information as she continues to plan for the coming school year.

Competency 003: *The teacher understands procedures for designing effective and coherent instruction and assessment based on appropriate learning goals and objectives.*

47. How can Ms. Angelino best use this information appropriately as she plans?

   (A) Ms. Angelino can use this information to diagnose the problems or weaknesses last year's students had with the style of assessment used because it is likely that this year's group will have the same problems.

   (B) Ms. Angelino can use this information to plan instruction dedicated to the areas of weakness in required skills and knowledge diagnosed by the past year's test because this year's group of students will likely have the same problems.

   (C) Ms. Angelino can use this information and instructional preassessments based on the skill levels of the students as shown by last year's state assessment to address weak areas so that this year's group will not have the same deficiencies.

   (D) Ms. Angelino can use this information to determine which skills and knowledge required by the state her students are least likely to have achieved so that she can caution them to get additional help, possibly parental, in these areas.

DECISION SET ENDS HERE

DECISION SET BEGINS HERE

Ms. Klondile, a high school science teacher, considers a strong commitment to a job well done in a timely manner to be very important. From the first day of class, she reminds her students that she gets her work done in a timely manner and expects them to do the same. She models her commitment to this principle by returning graded assignments in one or two days.

Competency 008: *The teacher provides appropriate instruction that actively engages students in the learning process.*

48. By using this strategy, how does the teacher encourage students to be more productive learners and responsible citizens?

    (A) The teacher is demonstrating to students the value of having high expectations for themselves in order to achieve at their highest level academically.
    (B) This model will guide students toward tracking their own performance by keeping a record of their graded assignments.
    (C) The teacher's modeling of effective time management will help her as she monitors students' completion of assignments.
    (D) Students will likely copy the modeling of their teacher by turning in their assignments in a timely manner.

Ms. Klondile is planning a major unit on energy transformations within ecological systems. Because she knows students in the past have had trouble with this abstract concept on the TAKS, she plans to spend part of her summer writing a strong unit based on the school's resource materials. Over lunch, Ms. Klondile says she plans to take a laptop computer home over the summer to use as she writes this unit. Mr. Brown immediately states that this would be unethical and strongly encourages her to change her mind. Of course, everyone else at the table voices their opinion, and the general response is that it is completely permissible to take school equipment home under certain conditions.

Competency 013: *The teacher understands and adheres to legal and ethical requirements for educators and is knowledgeable of the structure of education in Texas.*

49. What is a situation where it is ethical to take school equipment home?

    (A) It is ethical to take school equipment home as long as the school knows you have it and its return is clearly scheduled so that others can use it for instructional purposes.
    (B) It is ethical to take school equipment home as long as you have permission and are willing to assume financial responsibility if it is lost, damaged, or stolen.
    (C) It is ethical to take school equipment home as long as it is removed from the building with permission and gone only when others will not need it, such as over weekends.
    (D) It is ethical to take school equipment home as long as it is removed from the building with permission and is used only for authorized school business.

Competency 007: *The teacher understands and applies principles and strategies for communicating effectively in varied teaching and learning contexts.*

50. As Ms. Klondile plans her unit, she wants to select teaching strategies that will help her students truly understand this important basic science concept. Which teaching strategy would Ms. Klondile's students find most helpful in learning this concept?

    (A) She should build into the unit time to revisit and repeat these abstract concepts and for student questions to enhance clarity.
    (B) She should open the lesson with a K-W-L chart to activate prior knowledge and include a reminder to herself to end with the L-column of the chart.
    (C) She should share concrete examples from her life experiences and have students provide additional examples with which they are familiar.
    (D) She should begin with a list of relevant terms from the unit and have students define each term as it occurs during the unit.

51. How could Ms. Klondile best encourage her students to think more in depth and have positive feelings about their knowledge of energy transformations in ecological systems?

(A) She could have individual students give examples of three ecological systems and then do research to determine if any energy transformations occur within each of the systems.

(B) She could assign individual students an ecological system to research and have them write a report on any energy transformations that occur within the assigned system.

(C) She could have students write a paper defining energy transformation within a given ecological system and give an example of at least one energy transformation.

(D) She could have teams of students explain and support with research the energy changes that occur between beginning and ending points within specified systems.

Near the end of a class discussion of energy transformations, Maggie commented, "It seems that all ecological systems have some sort of transformation of energy occurring. Can this be so?" Ms. Klondile asks the class what they think about Maggie's observation, and a huge debate ensues. Although Ms. Klondile had an activity on another topic planned for the remaining class time, she did not stop the discussion and asked several pointed questions to help students focus their thoughts.

Competency 005: *The teacher knows how to establish a classroom climate that fosters learning, equity, and excellence and uses this knowledge to create a physical and emotional environment that is safe and productive.*

52. What important instructional event occurred because Ms. Klondile allowed the discussion initiated by Maggie's comment to continue?

(A) Ms. Klondile allowed students to take the unit in a direction she might not have planned because she recognized the students' interest in the discussion.

(B) When Ms. Klondile allowed the discussion to continue off schedule, she "short-changed" the next topic scheduled and reduced the students' learning of that content.

(C) When Ms. Klondile joined the discussion to help the students focus on this issue, she gave implied permission to go off task and students will try to do so again.

(D) When Ms. Klondile allowed the discussion to continue past the time scheduled for the topic, she deviated from her plan but can refocus on the unit tomorrow.

During lunch in the teachers' lounge, Ms. Klondile indicates she has had a very positive response to the workshop on her new energy transformation unit that she shared at the state science teachers' conference. Another school district has asked her to share the unit with their teachers as a paid consultant. An in-depth discussion about accepting outside consulting jobs ensues. The chairperson of the English department says it is unethical for Ms. Klondile to accept money to share work she designed for her school.

Competency 013: *The teacher understands and adheres to legal and ethical requirements for educators and is knowledgeable of the structure of education in Texas.*

53. The ethics of accepting this contract are discussed. What would make this contract unethical?

    (A) Ms. Klondile was the only author, and the curriculum was written during the summer without pay.
    (B) The curriculum was designed specifically for the science department where it is now being used.
    (C) The curriculum was written on a home computer and was based on resource materials from the department and the Internet.
    (D) The preparation for the consulting job was made during Ms. Klondile's conference period.

DECISION SET ENDS HERE

DECISION SET BEGINS HERE

Ms. Chavez is an English teacher working with her students on clarity in writing as they summarize novels they are reading. She has each student complete a chapter summary and give it to a peer for editing. Before returning them to the writer, she looks at all the edited summaries. On one summary she writes, "I agree with your peer editor that some of your sentences are hard to follow or understand. You are using very complex, compound sentences, which is a very sophisticated level of writing but might not be appropriate for clarity with your peers. How can you simplify and still write on an advanced and sophisticated level?"

Competency 010: *The teacher monitors student performance and achievement; provides students with timely, high-quality feedback; and responds flexibly to promote learning for all students.*

54. Based on the research on instructional feedback, what will be the most likely response to this teacher's note?

   (A) The comment to the author of the chapter summary will probably be ineffective in prompting improvement as the feedback gives a negative response followed by a positive response about using a sophisticated writing style and does not give clear suggestions about how to make appropriate changes.

   (B) The comment to the author of the chapter summary will probably be effective in prompting improvement as the feedback gives a positive response about using a sophisticated writing style, which counterbalances being told some sentences are hard to understand, and so they will readily make suggested changes.

   (C) The comment to the author of the chapter summary will probably be effective in prompting improvement as the feedback gives a positive response about using a sophisticated writing style and encourages the writer to find ways to improve, which counterbalances being told that some sentences are hard to understand.

   (D) The comment to the author of the chapter summary will probably be effective in prompting improvement as the feedback gives a negative response followed by a positive response about using a sophisticated writing style and allows freedom in deciding how to make appropriate changes.

After reading through the edited summaries, Ms. Chavez notices Bernice is having trouble understanding the assigned chapter in the novel. She asks Bernice to meet with her to describe what she has read.

Competency 008: *The teacher provides appropriate instruction that actively engages students in the learning process.*

55. What is the main benefit of Ms. Chavez's approach to helping Bernice?

    (A) Ms. Chavez's approach helps Bernice develop a sense of ownership toward her own learning.
    (B) Ms. Chavez's approach allows her to diagnose Bernice's needs and provide specific instruction.
    (C) Ms. Chavez's approach encourages Bernice to focus and pay attention while reading the chapter.
    (D) Ms. Chavez's approach encourages Bernice to apply higher-order thinking skills while reading.

Ms. Chavez wants to end her unit on novels with an activity that requires students to use problem-solving skills. She has noticed that many of her students are weak in this skill, and so she knows she must actively teach her students how to succeed with this type of task rather than just assigning it.

Competency 007: *The teacher understands and applies principles and strategies for communicating effectively in varied teaching and learning contexts.*

56. As her students first engage in this problem-solving activity, what approach will be most effective?

    (A) Ms. Chavez should ask questions until she is able to guide her students toward reaching the correct answer.
    (B) As motivation Ms. Chavez should promise a prize to the student who finds the correct answer first.
    (C) Ms. Chavez should encourage her students to approach the problem in creative ways to find a solution.
    (D) Ms. Chavez should use concrete examples from the students' lives to guide them as they seek the answer.

Ms. Chavez plans an integrated unit on a novel for the next six weeks that addresses reading, writing, grammar, and spelling. Her lessons will include whole-class, individual, and small-group activities. She plans to include a guest speaker, a field trip, a learning center, a web quest, a Microsoft PowerPoint presentation, and a video as part of this unit.

Competency 008: *The teacher provides appropriate instruction that actively engages students in the learning process.*

57. What is the most important instructional advantage of Ms. Chavez's plan?

    (A) Ms. Chavez's plan allows students multiple and varied opportunities to process, internalize, and reinforce the unit's content.
    (B) Ms. Chavez's plan allows the teacher to address a large amount of content information in a shorter amount of time.
    (C) Ms. Chavez's plan allows flexibility in pacing the lessons to meet the needs of students with different ability levels.
    (D) Ms. Chavez's plan allows her to individualize instruction to meet the needs of students with different ability levels.

Competency 010: *The teacher monitors student performance and achievement; provides students with timely, high-quality feedback; and responds flexibly to promote learning for all students.*

58. Learning centers are a new idea Ms. Chavez learned about during a seminar she took this past summer. What is the best strategy for Ms. Chavez to use to evaluate the effectiveness of a learning center as a new instructional strategy for her students?

    (A) Track how many and which students use the center for a week while also monitoring the number of times any student returns to the center.
    (B) Probe for the rationales for student responses as she interviews students to determine their interest in the center as an instructional strategy.
    (C) Before letting the students use it, ask colleagues to test the center and give her their professional opinions of its effectiveness.
    (D) Collect observational data on students as they work at the center to assess their learning of the center's content formally or informally.

Competency 009: *The teacher incorporates the effective use of technology to plan, organize, deliver, and evaluate instruction for all students.*

59. What is the primary rationale for Ms. Chavez to include computer-based activities in the integrated unit?

    (A) Computer instruction will help Ms. Chavez's students learn the material as they are very motivated by computers.
    (B) Computer instruction will help Ms. Chavez's special-needs students learn the material more effectively.
    (C) Computer instruction will provide instructional variety to better help Ms. Chavez's students learn the material.
    (D) Ms. Chavez's students need a foundation for future computer skills required for success in the job market.

During the integrated novel unit, Bernice continues to have difficulty and fails to complete several of the assignments. After observations and several discussions with Bernice about why she is unable to complete assignments she begins successfully during class, Ms. Chavez decides it is time to meet Bernice's parent.

Competency 011: *The teacher understands the importance of family involvement in children's education and knows how to interact and communicate effectively with families.*

60. What is an important educational principle for Ms. Chavez to remember as she has her first parent-teacher conference with Bernice's parent?

(A) Ms. Chavez should make it very clear that she cannot remedy the situation and that the parent has a responsibility to ensure that Bernice completes her assignments.

(B) Ms. Chavez should downplay the situation by indicating areas where Bernice is successful so that her parent does not overreact before Ms. Chavez can solve the problem.

(C) As Ms. Chavez clearly explains to Bernice's parent the difficulty being experienced, she should present the information so that it is clear she is not judging the family.

(D) Ms. Chavez should keep the conference focused on the incomplete assignments and keep the parent from adding information about Bernice's outside school activities.

DECISION SET ENDS HERE

DECISION SET BEGINS HERE

Ms. Huber is a first-year teacher assigned to teach ninth-grade language arts although this assignment is not her first choice. The guidance counselor tells her that because she is the newest teacher, she has been given the more challenging group of ninth-grade students.

Competency 001: *The teacher understands human developmental processes and applies this knowledge to plan instruction and ongoing assessment that motivate students and are responsive to their developmental characteristics and needs.*

61. What is the most important thing Ms. Huber should know about ninth-grade students?

   (A) They prefer hands-on activities versus reading and answering questions.
   (B) They are most at risk for dropping out of school at this stage.
   (C) They are very emotional and their reactions to simple events can be extreme.
   (D) The girls are both taller and more mature than the boys, which can be challenging.

Ms. Huber shares her plan to present her challenging students with a clear set of classroom rules during the first week of school with the experienced AP-English teacher across the hall. This teacher indicates that her experience leads her to believe Ms. Huber would be more successful with her students if she involved them in forming the rules for the class rather than dictating them.

Competency 006: *The teacher understands strategies for creating an organized and productive learning environment and for managing student behavior.*

62. Why is it important to allow students to play a role in establishing classroom rules?

   (A) Students will remember the rules better when involved in establishing them.
   (B) Students are more willing to follow the rules they make than those made by teachers.
   (C) Students with a role in establishing rules are harder on others who break the rules.
   (D) Students who help establish rules are more likely to use peer pressure to increase buy-in of other students.

Ms. Huber recognizes that she has students in her class with many unique characteristics. She wants to get to know her students as individuals and enjoy their uniqueness. She feels this will help her establish a positive and productive classroom environment. One of her major goals is to base her instruction on the needs of her students.

Competency 005: *The teacher knows how to establish a classroom climate that fosters learning, equity, and excellence and uses this knowledge to create a physical and emotional environment that is safe and productive.*

63. What is the best way for Ms. Huber to begin this process?

   (A) She should determine each student's grade point average from the previous year.
   (B) She should use a pretest to determine each student's prior knowledge.
   (C) She should use a posttest to determine what each student has learned.
   (D) She should ask each student to write a paragraph about a given topic.

Competency 007: *The teacher understands and applies principles and strategies for communicating effectively in varied teaching and learning contexts.*

64. Ms. Huber notices a pattern when she reflects on her lessons for the past week. It appears that at least one-third of the class is unable to follow her oral directions correctly. What is the best way for Ms. Huber to ensure that directions are communicated effectively and understood by all?

   (A) Provide directions in oral and written format with examples and modeling.
   (B) Provide directions in written format with examples and modeling.
   (C) Provide oral directions and have students repeat them to her to check for clarity.
   (D) Provide short-step directions in written and oral format with examples and modeling.

Competency 009: *The teacher incorporates the effective use of technology to plan, organize, deliver, and evaluate instruction for all students.*

65. Ms. Huber has assigned a multimedia project to her classes. The requirements for their web quest include creative design, appropriate vocabulary for the stated audience, inclusion of the assigned content, and appropriate grammar and spelling. What is the most effective method for her to assess their web quest?

(A) She should assess with a checklist of the appropriate criteria.
(B) She should assess with an evaluation downloaded from an assessment web page.
(C) She should assess with a subjective evaluation in paragraph form.
(D) She should assess with a rubric designed for the specific criteria in the assignment.

The parents of a student contact the school guidance counselor to request a conference with Ms. Huber and Ms. Bowman, the geography teacher. The entire team that teaches the student, plus the counselor, decides to meet with the parents.

Competency 011: *The teacher understands the importance of family involvement in children's education and knows how to interact and communicate effectively with families.*

66. What makes this a good idea?

(A) There is safety in numbers where irate parents are concerned. It also allows everyone to share comments, both positive and negative, with the parents and present a united front about any observed patterns of behavior that parents may not want to admit.
(B) It allows parents to hear comments, both positive and negative, from all the teachers to provide a clear picture of events at school. It also allows everyone to determine if there is a pattern of behavior that may otherwise have been missed.
(C) It allows all teachers to exchange information about the student in many different settings. It also allows everyone to determine if there is a pattern of negative student behavior that may otherwise have been missed by some of the teachers.
(D) It allows the parents hear comments, both positive and negative, from other teachers without having to schedule another meeting. It also allows them to determine if there are negative teacher behaviors that have been overlooked.

DECISION SET ENDS HERE

DECISION SET BEGINS HERE

Mr. Isaacson is a high school principal at a new school on the north side of town. He is having difficulty getting parents to attend PTO meetings at the school, yet he believes students of any age learn best when their parents are actively involved in their children's education. He asks the students, faculty, and staff for suggestions on how to get parents involved.

67. Which of the following suggestions would work the best?

    (A) The school should have PTO breakfast meetings once a month at the school.
    (B) The school should have brown bag lunch PTO meetings once a month at the school.
    (C) The school should have monthly PTO meetings at various community locations.
    (D) The school should have two open-house meetings and stop forcing the PTO issue.

Mr. Isaacson hires a new teacher for the school. During his interview with her, he indicates that in order to maintain her employment, she must earn a minimum of 250 professional development hours over a five-year period, which is higher than the state's requirement. Only hours that meet the state's criteria for professional development will be accepted by the district.

Competency 012: *The teacher enhances professional knowledge and skills by effectively interacting with other members of the educational community and participating in various types of professional activities.*

68. Which of the following methods would meet the criteria for state-recognized professional development hours?

    (A) Attending conferences, approved workshops, and/or graduate credit hours would count toward the required professional development hours.
    (B) Writing a curriculum unit for the school or an article for a professional journal would count toward the required professional development hours.
    (C) Publishing a book on an educational topic relevant to her teaching would count toward the required professional development hours.
    (D) Writing a grant proposal, receiving funding, and implementing the grant would count toward the required professional development hours.

Because he knows the emphasis Mr. Isaacson places on teachers' structuring their lessons to ensure student success, Mr. Robertson works hard at making sure he himself clearly understands all the directions he is going to give to his students.

Competency 007: *The teacher understands and applies principles and strategies for communicating effectively in varied teaching and learning contexts.*

69. What does Mr. Robertson's taking the time to go this extra step ensure?

(A) That he can clearly communicate what he is asking students to do
(B) That the vocabulary he uses is appropriate for higher-achieving students
(C) That the vocabulary he uses is appropriate for lower-achieving students
(D) That he will have a better chance of communicating his high expectations

Competency 011: *The teacher understands the importance of family involvement in children's education and knows how to interact and communicate effectively with families.*

70. Ms. Jones agrees with Mr. Isaacson's philosophy about parental involvement and wants to share classroom success stories and school news with the community. What is the best way for her to do this?

(A) Ms. Jones should create a monthly newsletter to be mailed to community members.
(B) Ms. Jones should post school and class information on the school district's web page.
(C) Ms. Jones should create a "what's new" bulletin board in the hall outside her office.
(D) Ms. Jones should send home a letter with school and class news with her report cards.

Competency 013: *The teacher understands and adheres to legal and ethical requirements for educators and is knowledgeable of the structure of education in Texas.*

71.   Mr. Isaacson reported Mr. Snowden to the state for an unethical TAKS situation, and Mr. Snowden has been suspended from teaching. Which of the following situations would be an unethical practice Mr. Isaacson might have reported?

(A) Mr. Snowden gave all his content tests formatted exactly like the TAKS.
(B) Mr. Snowden gave practice tests with content similar to that on the TAKS.
(C) Mr. Snowden kicked students' desks when they recorded a wrong answer.
(D) Mr. Snowden held required TAKS review workshops prior to the TAKS.

DECISION SET ENDS HERE

DECISION SET BEGINS HERE

Ravenswood High School is located in an area rich with community members of unique and diverse backgrounds. Mr. Woods teaches American history and world history at Ravenswood High. At least once a month Mr. Woods invites a member of the community to be a guest speaker in each of his classes.

Competency 002: *The teacher understands student diversity and knows how to plan learning experiences and design assessments that are responsive to differences among students and that promote all students' learning.*

72. What does this practice show about Mr. Woods?

   (A) Mr. Woods respects students with diverse backgrounds and includes this diversity in his instruction.
   (B) Mr. Woods uses strategies that enhance his own understanding of students' diversity through his instruction.
   (C) Mr. Woods plans and adapts lessons to meet students' needs by acknowledging their diversity.
   (D) Mr. Woods uses the rich diversity in the community to enrich all his students' learning experiences.

Mr. Woods has the following two objectives for his American history class: (a) The learner will understand the Civil War and (b) the learner will understand the causes of the battles.

Competency 003: *The teacher understands procedures for designing effective and coherent instruction and assessment based on appropriate learning goals and objectives.*

73. What is the most significant problem with these objectives?

   (A) The objectives are broad and ask for too much information.
   (B) The objectives are too broad and are not easily measured.
   (C) The objectives are too detailed and address too much information.
   (D) The objectives should be broken down into smaller objectives.

Mr. Woods has noticed during the past two years that his sophomores have little or no prior knowledge of maps and globe skills. According to state TEKS, these skills are taught in sixth-grade social studies and revisited in eighth-grade social studies, yet his students come to him in their second year at Ravenswood High without sufficient skills.

Competency 012: *The teacher enhances professional knowledge and skills by effectively interacting with other members of the educational community and participating in various types of professional activities.*

74. What is the best way for Mr. Woods to address this problem?

   (A) Mr. Woods must reteach the missing skills before moving into the required grade level curriculum.
   (B) Mr. Woods should contact the district social studies coordinator and outline the issue of poor instruction.
   (C) Mr. Woods should meet with the middle school social studies teachers to establish vertical alignment.
   (D) Mr. Woods should create a curriculum map for the social studies teachers for grades 6–12.

Mr. Woods constantly attempts to create unusual learning experiences for his classes. He strives to enhance student learning by using techniques that encourage and refine higher-order thinking skills. One such assignment asks students to approach a familiar topic from a different perspective.

Competency 004: *The teacher understands learning processes and factors that impact student learning and demonstrates this knowledge by planning effective, engaging instruction and appropriate assessments.*

75. What is the best suggestion to students for approaching a topic from a different perspective?

   (A) As a Native American living on the East Coast when the first settlers arrived, write a journal entry.
   (B) List the hardships and changes in circumstances faced by the settlers at Jamestown during the first year.
   (C) Answer the following question: What do you think was the worst hardship on the Oregon Trail?
   (D) Write a narrative for or against the following statement: Miles Standish was a true colonial hero.

Mr. Woods wants his world history students to have access to poetry and early journal entries from other countries. He owns some rare books that contain sixteenth-century Russian poetry. He does not want the books handled extensively as they are old and quite delicate. He decides to make photocopies of the poems he wants to share with his students.

Competency 013: *The teacher understands and adheres to legal and ethical requirements for educators and is knowledgeable of the structure of education in Texas.*

76. What must Mr. Woods know about copyright laws before making these copies?

 (A) It is illegal to make photocopies of rare books even for instructional purposes.
 (B) He must receive permission from the authors or the publishers to make photocopies.
 (C) He can make a one-time-use classroom set of the book of poems without getting permission to copy them.
 (D) Students can make written copies for instructional purposes only with permission.

Mr. Woods has noticed that one of his classes is beginning to divide into cliques. These include a sports clique, a drill team clique, a band clique, and a technology clique. Some of the clique members taunt the members of other cliques. Mr. Woods decides to use a cooperative grouping strategy called jigsaw with this class.

Competency 001: *The teacher understands human developmental processes and applies this knowledge to plan instruction and ongoing assessment that motivate students and are responsive to their developmental characteristics and needs.*

77. What purpose would be served by Mr. Woods using this grouping strategy with this class?

 (A) It would break up the developing cliques before they become engrained.
 (B) It would allow the cliques to concentrate on competing for grades.
 (C) It would allow interaction among students from different cliques.
 (D) It would allow the different cliques to compete academically.

Mr. Woods is becoming discouraged because his third-period students no longer heed his warnings about continued tardiness. He has tried everything from being understanding to withdrawing student privileges. He has tried many different forms of punishment or consequences. His rule for attending class on time is still being broken daily.

Competency 006: *The teacher understands strategies for creating an organized and productive learning environment and for managing student behavior.*

78. What can Mr. Woods do to ensure that his rules are followed?

(A) Mr. Woods should be consistent about enforcing all rules and consequences.

(B) Mr. Woods should make the rules, and consequences for breaking them, more severe.

(C) Mr. Woods should change the rules and consequences because they are not working.

(D) Mr. Woods should let the students establish rules and consequences that they will follow.

Ms. Blankenship also teaches at Ravenswood High. She is having difficulty relating to two Arab-American students in her speech class. She has never perceived herself as having ill feelings toward any group or person. She speaks with Mr. Woods about this new and concerning experience with bias.

Competency 002: *The teacher understands student diversity and knows how to plan learning experiences and design assessments that are responsive to differences among students and that promote all students' learning.*

79. What is the first thing Mr. Woods might suggest to Ms. Blankenship to begin accepting and respecting these two students?

(A) Ms. Blankenship has already taken the first step by admitting that she is biased toward these two students.

(B) Ms. Blankenship must first learn more about Arab-Americans before she will be able to overcome her bias.

(C) Ms. Blankenship must first tell her principal about the problem before she will be able to overcome her bias.

(D) Ms. Blankenship must first transfer the students out of her class so that her bias will not impact them.

DECISION SET ENDS HERE

DECISION SET BEGINS HERE

Mabry High School is staffed by a group of dedicated teachers and administrators truly respected by the community for their commitment to students. Ms. Johnson is a science teacher there. She begins her integrated physics and chemistry lesson by having the students each construct a whirlybird. A piece of 2" × 9" paper is used for the construction. Ms. Johnson models exactly how to make the whirlybird step by step. The students are instructed to observe carefully as they drop their whirlybirds three times and then sit down. Some of the whirlybirds spin clockwise as they drop, whereas others spin counterclockwise. The students are asked to investigate in pairs why there are two directions of spin rather than one although they all followed the same directions.

Competency 005: *The teacher knows how to establish a classroom climate that fosters learning, equity, and excellence and uses this knowledge to create a physical and emotional environment that is safe and productive.*

80. This activity best exemplifies which of the following statements?

(A) Ms. Johnson uses a variety of means to convey high expectations and successful interactions for students.

(B) Ms. Johnson creates a nurturing and supportive environment for high student achievement and learning.

(C) Ms. Johnson establishes a climate that emphasizes collaboration and supportive student interactions.

(D) Ms. Johnson presents instruction in ways that communicate her enthusiasm for student learning.

Competency 004: *The teacher understands learning processes and factors that impact student learning and demonstrates this knowledge by planning effective, engaging instruction and appropriate assessments.*

81. What is the best method of assessing the lesson on determining the reason for two directions of spin?

(A) Have individual students record their reasons for the two directions of spin and provide supporting evidence for their answers.

(B) Have pairs of students record their reasons for the two directions of spin and provide supporting evidence for their answers.

(C) Have pairs of students determine their reasons for the two directions of spin and be able to produce both directions of spin.

(D) Have pairs of students determine and report to the class their reasons for the two directions of spin and their supporting evidence.

A tornado wiped out a neighboring town during April 2003. With tornado season arriving again, Ms. Johnson wants her students to truly understand the destructive nature of a tornado.

Competency 008: *The teacher provides appropriate instruction that actively engages students in the learning process.*

82. What is an effective way for Ms. Johnson to reach this goal?

    (A) Have students do an online search for stories by storm chasers and tornado survivors.

    (B) Have students interview tornado survivors and weather experts from the neighboring town.

    (C) Have students watch the movies "Tornado" and "Storm Stories" and respond to focus questions.

    (D) Have students recreate a tornado in class and compare their model to a video of a tornado.

Competency 009: *The teacher incorporates the effective use of technology to plan, organize, deliver, and evaluate instruction for all students.*

83. Ms. Johnson wants to create a web quest for her students on tornados. What program would be the easiest for her to use yet still have the technology needed for the project?

    (A) Microsoft Excel would be the easiest and most effective software for her to use.

    (B) Microsoft Word would be the easiest and most effective software for her to use.

    (C) Paint/Draw (in Microsoft Word) would be the easiest and most effective software for her to use.

    (D) Microsoft Outlook would be the easiest and most effective software for her to use.

Ms. Johnson shares with her friend Ms. Beaumont how successful and enthusiastic her students were in working through the tornado web quest Ms. Johnson designed. Ms. Beaumont, a fifth-grade teacher, wants her students to have more online experiences but does not know how to design a web quest. Mrs. Johnson volunteers to have her students create a web quest for Ms. Beaumont's fifth-grade science classes.

84. What is the best way for Ms. Johnson to help her class design an effective experience for Ms. Beaumont's fifth-graders?

    (A) Ms. Johnson should give the class a lesson plan with the appropriate steps for designing a web quest.

    (B) Ms. Johnson should have the class do a web search for at least five web quest examples.

    (C) Ms. Johnson should have the class experience another web quest before designing its own web quest.

    (D) Ms. Johnson should have the class interview other students who have designed web quests.

Ms. Nelson and Ms. Johnson attend a conference workshop that stresses the value to students and teachers of collaboration across subjects. On the drive home they discuss how to effectively include this idea in their instruction. Ms. Nelson decides to have her AP English class do a research report using all the appropriate steps of scientific research. Most of her students also have Ms. Johnson for science.

Competency 004: *The teacher understands learning processes and factors that impact student learning and demonstrates this knowledge by planning effective, engaging instruction and appropriate assessments.*

85. What is the first step Ms. Nelson will need to take with her students?

    (A) Ms. Nelson should review the steps of scientific research methods with her students.
    (B) Ms. Nelson should determine the library and technologies information available.
    (C) Ms. Nelson should have students conduct a literature review on the chosen topics.
    (D) Ms. Nelson should determine all the possible types of research to be conducted.

In the past, students in Ms. Nelson's class have complained that they have had no say in or control of any aspect of their learning. Ms. Nelson wants to design a rubric for the research report. She has decided to plan the research rubric with her AP class.

86. Why is including the students in the design process a good strategy?

    (A) Including the students in the design process incorporates different approaches to learning.
    (B) Including the students in the design process allows for self-directed learning to take place.
    (C) Including the students in the design process enhances students' learning by giving them control.
    (D) Including the students in the design process creates a sense of owner-ship and responsibility.

DECISION SET ENDS HERE

DECISION SET BEGINS HERE

Several students in Ms. Henry's history class have brothers and sisters being deployed to Afghanistan or already stationed there. Ms. Henry notices that her students are dividing into two distinct camps over the question of the U.S. government's policy toward Afghanistan. Some of the students feel the United States should leave Afghanistan immediately, whereas others feel the United States should stay until the country becomes more in control and more self-governing. Students favoring either perspective seem unable to clearly express the reasons for the position they have taken.

Competency 008: *The teacher provides appropriate instruction that actively engages students in the learning process.*

87. What is an appropriate first step in helping the class become better informed about the issues of the war in Afghanistan?

   (A) Have the students generate some questions they want answered and brainstorm possible resources to be used in answering these questions.
   (B) Generate some questions appropriate for the students to answer and provide the appropriate resources for use in answering these questions.
   (C) Have student teams research life in Afghanistan before the war and compare and contrast it to life in the United States or another democracy.
   (D) Have a guest speaker from Afghanistan talk to the class about life in Afghanistan before the war compared and contrasted to life in the United States.

88. At the conclusion of her unit called Cities and Their Cultures, Ms. Henry asks her students to generate the big idea or generalize the main points. How does this exercise benefit the students?

   (A) It allows students to break generalizations into specific pieces of information.
   (B) It allows students to combine information and to form generalizations.
   (C) It allows students to brainstorm, group, label, and synthesize information.
   (D) It allows students to recall, review, and connect key points from the unit.

Ms. Henry is becoming frustrated with her assessments. More than half of the class failed the last test. This has become a pattern lately, although this is the largest group to fail. She wants all the students in her class to be successful.

Competency 010: *The teacher monitors student performance and achievement; provides students with timely, high-quality feedback; and responds flexibly to promote learning for all students.*

89. With this in mind, what should be Ms. Henry's next step?

   (A) Review the tested material and give a second test on this information.
   (B) Reteach the same information using different methods of instruction.
   (C) Record the test scores but give students an opportunity to add bonus points.
   (D) Have students correct wrong answers for half-value of the missed points.

Mr. Richards teaches across the hall from Ms. Henry. They share several students, as Mr. Richards teaches math to all English as a second language students. He wants to be sure his ESL math class is able to use a checkbook.

90. What is an ideal way for Mr. Richards to assess the ESL students' understanding of this skill?

   (A) Have students take turns selling and making change for assigned purchases at a model store.
   (B) Have students use grocery ads to design a grocery list, make purchases, and make change.
   (C) Have students shop at a model store using checks and a check register to keep track of their budgets.
   (D) Have students complete worksheets that have students write checks and use a check register.

DECISION SET ENDS HERE

Answer Key
SAMPLE TEST (GRADES 8–12)

Question Number	Correct Response	Competency	Question Number	Correct Response	Competency
1	D	001	26	B	012
2	A	001	27	C	012
3	C	002	28	D	013
4	B	002	29	D	013
5	D	002	30	D	010
6	D	003	31	A	005
7	A	003	32	C	013
8	B	004	33	A	004
9	C	005	34	B	011
10	C	005	35	B	010
11	A	005	36	D	012
12	C	006	37	D	001
13	A	006	38	B	001
14	A	006	39	A	002
15	D	007	40	B	002
16	D	007	41	D	002
17	B	007	42	B	003
18	B	008	43	B	003
19	A	008	44	B	003
20	C	008	45	D	005
21	A	009	46	A	004
22	B	010	47	C	003
23	B	011	48	A	008
24	A	011	49	D	013
25	C	011	50	C	007

Answer Key
SAMPLE TEST (GRADES 8-12)

Question Number	Correct Response	Competency	Question Number	Correct Response	Competency
51	D	007	71	C	013
52	A	005	72	D	002
53	D	013	73	B	003
54	A	010	74	C	012
55	B	008	75	A	004
56	C	007	76	B	013
57	A	008	77	C	001
58	D	010	78	A	006
59	C	009	79	A	002
60	C	011	80	C	005
61	B	001	81	C	004
62	D	006	82	B	008
63	B	005	83	B	009
64	D	007	84	C	009
65	D	009	85	A	004
66	B	011	86	D	004
67	C	011	87	A	008
68	A	012	88	B	008
69	A	007	89	B	010
70	A	011	90	C	010

CORRECT RESPONSES

1. **D** Modeling abstract concepts before engaging students in independent activities allow students at both concrete operational and formal operational cognitive levels opportunities for success. (A) is effective with both levels of cognitive development present in the ninth-grade classroom. However, it should not be the primary instructional strategy used. Creating groups of students with blended levels of cognitive development, as suggested by (B), is good. It is more effective than grouping students at the same developmental level. Again, it is not a primary instructional strategy. (C) requires instructing only the middle range. Students with either higher or lower cognitive levels will miss out on instruction. Delivering daily instructions for students at the two cognitive levels is not time effective and divides the student population rather than pulling them together.

2. **A** Unless the counselor can help this student focus on future consequences, she will not see beyond what is most important to her now, which seems to be leaving school and getting married. (B) has some validity because many students do not feel they belong due to the group within the school's society. The counselor cannot provide this student a group. Although this might be part of the student's problem, it does not play much of a role in helping her make a decision to stay in school. Many high school and even middle school students are already planning for their futures, and so (C) is not valid. Students of this age may not want to acknowledge that adults have gone through many of the same experiences they have encountered, as indicated by (D), yet know that it is true even when they decide not to accept the advice offered.

3. **C** This is the best response because it encourages student participation in addressing the situation, which also increases student ownership of the solution. (A) would be more effective with much younger students who are still focused on pleasing an authority figure. It also attempts to deal with the tensions from an external rather than an internal focus when an internal reason is more powerful for students this age. (B) will help defuse tension as students work together successfully, but it is not as effective a strategy as that suggested by (C). (D) is not effective, ethical, or legal. Student grades should only indicate progress toward learning. If this strategy is used, it will have a potential for actually increasing tensions.

4. **B** It allows the teacher to guide students of all levels through achievable steps toward a successful completion. Each student is able to receive the assistance needed rather than having the teacher provide the same assistance to all students, which does not acknowledge individual differences in backgrounds and skills. (A) and (D) are valid strategies, but neither is as effective as (B) for guiding all students toward successful completion of the project. Some students will find that (A) allows too many choices or more freedom than they are comfortable with and will have the same difficulty with (D). Partnering higher and lower achievers must be done with clear expectations that both members of the part-

nership bring strengths to the task and that each must play a clear role so that the higher-achieving student does not carry the lower-achieving student. (C) is also a valid strategy, but again (B) is stronger. (C) is a way to provide the guidance some students need.

5. **D** This is the best response because it allows for peer instruction in the different technologies available and students in this age group are willing to explore and learn from peers more readily than with formal instruction as suggested in (C). (A) allows access but without the peer support, and so it is not as effective. (B) allows students to continue to avoid or miss gaining technological skills rather than providing a supportive pathway to acquiring these needed skills. (C) is not the strongest answer, as reading the instructions would appeal to adults more than to high school students who readily check with peers before reading. Many adults read the directions only when all else fails. Yet having access to instructions is useful when peers don't know and when trying what seems logical doesn't produce the desired results.

6. **D** Teachers need a way to assess the learning of students and because learning goals are the guide for assessment as well as instruction. It is not impossible to assess but needs some visible indication of appreciation such as "Students will choose to listen to music from other cultures during their free time" to indicate the goal has been met by students. (A) presents a very narrow view of ninth-graders. Music does tend to be important to a large number of students this age, but the types of music they value are very wide-ranging. Openness to new ideas presented in a nonthreatening manner is also a trait of this age. Being told they are being "introduced to good music rather than that trash you have been listening to" will not get far with these students but "See if you also like this music" will be more effective. (B) is just inaccurate. There are lessons on every conceivable topic available from the wide range of resources teachers can draw on—plus teachers are creative individuals. (C) is also inaccurate. Prior knowledge needed for success must be considered as learning goals are selected but should not be included in the goal. How the prior knowledge will be assessed to determine that it is present is also part of a teacher's planning but not part of a learning goal.

7. **A** Seeing the overview of the flow of learning activities helps ensure that they have been sequenced from concrete to abstract and that the content is sequenced from simple to complex. Having age-appropriate activities and selecting interesting and motivating instructional styles for a unit, as indicated in (B) and (C), are also appropriate but are secondary to and supportive of the logical flow indicated in (A). (D) addresses modifications that might need to be made to the unit during instruction. These are indicated by student responses or problems rather than part of the initial planning.

8. **B** Response (B) is what students are doing as they answer the three reflection questions in their learning journals. They are establishing the relationship between the pendulum activity done in class, a video about Galileo's initial

study of pendulums, and where pendulum motion occurs in their own lives. The statements made in (A), (C), and (D) do not fit this situation.

9. **C** This is the only question she can clearly answer based on reading her students' learning journals. (A), (B), and (D) are also good questions for a self-reflective teacher to ask. To be answered, pathways other than the learning journals would be required, such as a review of past plans.

10. **C** This allows the teacher to use more than the number of correct answers to establish progress. (A) is a good idea and will help with a positive and supportive learning environment, but peer feedback is not the same as assessing and assigning grades. (B) indicates that it is acceptable for some students to be and to stay behind when this is not acceptable. (D) describes what any good test should do, which is to allow all students some success while distinguishing students who have mastered a concept from those who have not. Any teacher can develop a test that no one can pass or one where everyone can make a perfect score. Neither situation is effective in assessing student learning or for indicating the next step for the teacher, which is the desired role of assessment.

11. **A** We know research indicates that high teacher expectations are one of the most important variables for student success, but we also know that all students do not learn in the same way and so differentiated instruction is important. Responses (B) and (C) open the teacher to making faulty instructional decisions based on educational myths about an identified group's ability to learn. Although we have data suggesting that some groups face more learning challenges than others, we must be careful not to use this information as a rationale to expect less from students in these groups. Because all students were in the same school last year and are now in the same grade does not mean that they learned at the same rate or will respond to the same instructional strategies this year. If this were so, as (D) implies, there would not now be a distinct group of students with significant academic needs. Responses (B), (C), and (D) are basically the same. Each of these responses indicates lower teacher expectations of students. If any teacher expects a student to do less, for whatever reason, the student will lower to the expectation.

12. **C** The most time-efficient task of using a spreadsheet program is given in (C), using a weighted formula to compute students' grades. It draws on the strength of spreadsheets to speed up a task. The task suggested in (A) would be better done using a word-processing program than a spreadsheet. The daily attendance records from (B) can be easily prepared on a spreadsheet, but limited computing is done on these records. The same is true of the parent/teacher communications paperwork in (D). A spreadsheet does not improve the efficiency of these two tasks in the same way it does in calculating student averages using weighted grades.

13. **A** When students understand and follow classroom routines, the teacher has to spend less instructional time on getting the classroom to operate smoothly, as that is what the routines achieve. (B) can also be a result of students under-

standing and following routines, but the increase in instructional and learning time has a greater payoff. Although a sense of certainty results, a positive attitude might not if a student strongly disagrees with a routine. (C) is true in that should management demands such as discipline decrease, this would increase a teacher's instructional time rather than a teacher's planning time. (D) is accurate in that confusion would be reduced for both the teacher and the students. This may or may not allow for greater ease in student monitoring, but the increase in instructional and learning time in (A) has a greater value.

14. **A** A teacher allowing student input into clasroom rules, routines, and procedures increases student ownership and agreement to following them. Although students tend to follow the rules, routines, and procedures better, this is not assured, as indicated in (B). Explaining the differences between rules, routines, and procedures as in (C) will do nothing to increase the number of students responding cooperatively to the desired smooth operation of the classroom. (D) ensures that every student knows the rules, routines, and procedures. However, it has no impact on whether or not the students follow them. The contract is neither valid nor valuable to them.

15. **D** Shorter wait time and restating questions for lower-achieving students are different behaviors. They signal all students that some students are expected to do less. This reinforces a feeling of inability to achieve in lower-achieving students because it seems that the teacher doesn't expect success. (A) does signal different levels of expectation but doesn't really cause resentment in either group unless it is directed toward the teacher who doesn't expect success from lower-achieving students. Students are aware that they must work to achieve success. Altering wait time for students with different levels of achievement is not an effective manner of instructional differentiation as stated in (B). Both groups need equal wait time, and teachers need to allow effective wait time, before restating a question or passing it to another student. (C) is inaccurate because lower-achieving students actually feel that they are "on the spot" more as they have a shorter response time and therefore fail to respond to a perceived greater number of questions with less success.

16. **D** (D) needs to receive the greatest focus during the meeting with the mentor. The main reason for a class discussion is to determine the thoughts of the members of a group on a topic, and this cannot occur without their listening to each other. (A) ignores the fact that the listening that is vital to an effective discussion must be nonjudgmental. After being told they are wrong, which is another way of saying that their ideas are not valued, many students refuse to share their ideas. The effectiveness of class discussions is seriously curtailed. (B) is not a problem in an effective class discussion, assuming the comments are on topic and students are not speaking over each other, yet many teachers object to this response. Directing all comments through the teacher can seriously limit a class discussion. Comments do not occur logically, as they would in a conversation, because the students have to wait to be called on by the teacher. This is the problem with (C). The teacher needs skill to ensure that students are listening.

17. **B** Research on how students learn explains that they do not comprehend information until they can establish relationships. So (B) is best because it is the only one that helps students focus on relationships. Being able to repeat the information is not the same as understanding and being able to use information during thinking or problem solving. (A), (C), and (D) do not guide students toward looking for or establishing relationships because (A) and (C) focus instead on renaming or repeating concepts without connecting them. (D) does a better job of asking students to connect types of information or establish relationships between them but does not fit this lecture conclusion.

18. **B** Postponing the discussion of a high-interest topic that students want to discuss ignores the strong motivation that occurs when a teacher takes advantage of a teachable moment. (A), (C), and (D) assume that students can be redirected from such a high-interest topic. Avoiding this discussion at school is not a reasonable expectation. If the teacher refuses to allow it during class, it will occur as a subtopic while the students ignore the lesson the teacher attempts. The students will continue the discussion in the halls and the lunchroom. By allowing the topic to be discussed, the teacher can guide a balanced student discussion. One perspective or opinion will then not overpower the perspectives and opinions of other students. The teacher should also remind students that individuals respond differently to such an emotional issue and encourage them to be respectful of the varied ways others handle their responses. Many responses are valid and must be respected.

19. **A** (A) is the least emotional and has the broadest informational rather than emotional basis. Emotions run high following such an event and should be tempered rather than fanned. (B) could strengthen an emotional response when the debate forces a student to take a position counter to his or her own and others forget that this is not their actual opinion. (C) allows students to see where opinions lie, but this might not be a good situation for students holding less popular opinions. They could become afraid to express their true opinions. (D) allows individuals to purge only if writing is an outlet for them. Students who do not readily write will find this task onerous. Asking for evidence to support the opinions will help keep emotions under control.

20. **C** Understanding why they are doing the experiment and how it is to be done guides students in forming a conceptual framework that helps them focus on the relationships required by true, long-term learning rather than memorization of information only for short-term acquisition. All students have completed the same opening activity for the experiment, but this does not give them all the same background on the subject of the experiment as implied by (A). (B) is true but is not as important as the conceptual framework discussed in (C). (D) is inaccurate as doing the preliminary writing actually extends the time needed to do the experiment, although it probably increases accuracy by forcing students to be attentive to the entire experiment rather than approaching it one step at a time, as so often happens when an advance organizer is not used.

21. **A** By creating the rubric together, student input and ownership of the project are established while at the same time clear teacher expectations are presented. Both groups know what balance between content and presentation design is expected. (B) gives most of the control of the final product to the teacher. Completing all the content work without considering any presentation components may block students from producing as creative a product as prompted by the content information if an idea is not on the suggested product list. (C) also keeps much of the control and creative process away from the students, as they must seek the teacher's approval for each component of the final product. The focus is more on meeting the teacher's expectations than on the creative use of media to produce an effective final presentation. The daily reminders in (D) will be tuned out and considered nagging in a very short time. A written rubric, as suggested in (A), with reminders to apply the rubric, is much more effective.

22. **B** Although (A), (C), and (D) are appropriate for effective teacher-made tests, the alignment in (B) is the most important. Therefore it is the best response. Testing what and how you have taught is imperative for accurate assessment of learning.

23. **B** This is the only response that invites families to participate rather than demanding that they do so. It will receive a much more positive reaction from parents/guardians for this reason. Because (A) is so demanding, it probably will not occur. However, the ideas expressed in (C) and (D) are appropriate to increase parent/guardian understanding of an idea the teacher feels is important for enhanced student learning. These ideas will also encourage greater family participation if issued as an invitation.

24. **A** Responses (B), (C), and (D) all have value but are details that can help support the desired partnership. (A) is also the only response that indicates an interaction between teachers and family, yet this interaction is a required component of a partnership.

25. **C** To ensure a productive conference, (C) is the best response. It allows the parent to share why a conference was requested. This response allows the parent to express his or her concerns or ask for clarification. Listening calmly and respectfully shows respect, but perhaps not agreement, with the parent's thoughts. It also allows time for the teacher to compose a thoughtful response. In (A), (B), and (D), the teacher assumes he or she knows or can guess the reason the parent wanted a conference. The assumed reason may be accurate or it may also be completely off base and needlessly open another area of concern. Find out what is on the parent's mind so that you can work together in the student's best interest.

26. **B** Response (B) has the information most needed by the technology coordinator as he assists Ms. Wolf in planning a project that makes effective use of her students' present technological skills and also allows for improvement in their skill level. (A), (C), and (D) all contain suggestions for sharing information that might be interesting to the technology director but are not imperative to allow him to assist Ms. Wolf in planning an effective project. If all her students had strong

technological skills, this information would be important to ensure that the planned project required an appropriate level of skills, but we know that the range is broad and so the project must also require a broad range of skills. Ms. Wolf's gaps in knowledge may be addressed as she improves while helping her students with the project, but this is not a significant goal. Very likely, students with strong skills will help those who need assistance, and the technology director will be asked for help in meeting major technological challenges that arise as the project progresses. The grouping of students is a minor consideration based on available technology and should be a joint decision.

27. **C** This response contains the primary step to ensure an effective drama program, or any other type of program, whether the responsibility falls to a team or to an individual. Without a clear direction and vision, no program can succeed. Therefore, this response is most important. (D) is also important, so consider it a close second. Open and planned communication about a program is also necessary for success. (A) and (B) assume that these responsibilities should be divided rather than shared, which would be more appropriate to a philosophy of team responsibility for the program.

28. **D** Emil's parents/guardians must give written permission before a teacher or school can seek an evaluation for special education services. (A), (B), and (C) all give steps and procedures in asking for Emil to be evaluated. However, no action can be taken prior to obtaining written parental permission. The more documentation of concerns, the easier it will be for the parents to understand the rationale for the evaluation and give written permission.

29. **D** Teachers may not answer any student question during administration of the test. (A), (B), and (C) are all appropriate teacher behaviors as they prepare students for testing on high-stakes standardized tests.

30. **D** Students can interact very differently with individual teachers because of many factors such as respect, classroom control, and an endless variety of other reasons such as students feeling confident or defeated. Also, individual teachers have differing expectations and set different standards for grades. (A) may also be true, but there are other reasons for minor fluctuations as discussed in (D). Rather than being inflated as indicated in (B), grades collected over an extended period of time can be very stable. Note that individual assignment grades could fluctuate widely based on outside events impacting a student's efforts and participation. The more assignments used to assign a grade, the less impact a few wide variations have. (C) states the myth that males and females vary in their ability to learn science. The variation sometimes seen is more dependent on interest, effort, and societal expectations than on gender.

31. **A** Response (A) is the most likely reaction from this interaction. She questioned the students in a group with limited explanation for why she was doing so. They are doing well now and wonder about her interest in their past. They were embarrassed in front of their peers. If the students do give philosophical thought to their academic efforts, as in (B), they will know exactly who planted the idea

because Ms. Alvarez asked them to continue to think about this issue. Ms. Alvarez was trying to produce the results in (C) and (D) but was not successful.

32. **C** The behavior in (C) is unethical as very specific criteria are in place regarding respect for student confidentiality. (A), (B), and (D) also occurred during this conference. These results were unwise and unnecessary but not unexpected in view of the way this meeting was structured. Breaking student confidentiality is the biggest problem although there might be negative repercussions from these students because of her thoughtlessness.

33. **A** Although Ms. Alvarez may not live in the school's neighborhood, a factory closing will have a financial impact on many local families, and this will be seen at school. This information should be obtained from the news and from an awareness of the community in which you teach rather than from questioning students as suggested in (B), which would be perceived as nosiness and intrusiveness. (C) is good, but families face many problems with which the school cannot help. Liset can be guided toward effective ways to locate possible scholarships and how to apply for them, but the school has no money to assist any of the families facing financial problems. (D) is true but is not directly related to the second meeting with Liset.

34. **B** (B) includes both Liset and her mother in the planning discussion. In contrast, (C), which leaves Liset, who is most affected, out of the process. Suggesting that Ms. Jordan seek employment is also out of line because there are many reasons why this may not be desirable or possible for her. The suggestion in (A) must be handled very tactfully so that pride is not injured or offense taken. At this point, Ms. Alvarez's record for tactfulness is not strong. (D) offers either a platitude or a gift of grades, which are inappropriate and possibly undeliverable, rather than constructive assistance to Liset.

35. **B** (B) is the strongest benefit for Hung. (A) indicates that this encounter has given Hung multiple problem-solving skills rather than just one. Yet using one successfully does much for Hung's resiliency. Hopefully this is not the first connection Hung has seen between information learned in school and daily life as indicated in (C). The self-reflection in (D) is accurate, but the risk taking is not. The first time Hung met with Ms. Alvarez, it didn't appear to be a safe environment.

36. **D** The first strategy Ms. Alvarez should try is working with Steve and other school personnel to diagnose and solve whatever problem is causing the new behaviors as suggested in (D). This needs to occur before she involves Steve's parents as in (C). Telling Steve's family that he is using drugs with no supporting documentation is sure to destroy any trust in or respect for her that either Steve or his family has ever had. He may have been spending time with a hospitalized relative after school, which would also account for her observations. The accusation in (A) might shock Steve, but shock is not an especially helpful approach to problem solving. The hectoring and judgmental tone of (B) is also sure to

irritate Steve rather than to invite his confiding in her. Again, she is not using good judgment in her student interactions.

37. **D** (D) provides instruction appropriate for the range of student cognitive development present in the class. (A) groups students by their cognitive levels and this is not supported by research on effective teaching and learning. It is effective to have students of different abilities work together to enrich the learning of all students, but the use of a highly structured "study buddies," as suggested in (B), is not as effective as using small groups of students with mixed abilities. It is not appropriate to make students at one ability level directly responsible for the success of another, which does not mean that one student should not be supportive of the success of another. (C) assumes there is a normal tenth-grade level of development and that a simple reminder that students have some responsibility toward their learning will be effective. This is an attitude that is acquired over an extended period of time through thoughtfully guided experiences.

38. **B** Tenth graders are 15–17 years old, which places those developing at a typical rate in the transition stage between the concrete operational level and the formal operational level. This transitional group would find it easier to learn from the concrete and social strategies offered in (B). There is also sufficient variation possible when using these teaching strategies to allow for the differentiated instruction needed by gifted, remedial, and ESL students. (A), (C), and (D) all focus on instructional strategies that require individual and abstract processing of information and would be more effective if all students were at the transition or formal operational level, which is not the case in this class.

39. **A** Instruction must be differentiated in ways that both meet the teacher's instructional needs but do not apply or reinforce labels that cause students to feel isolated or different. (B) is a form of ability grouping, which is neither supported by research nor accepted as a valid instructional strategy. (C) shifts responsibility for learning and success away from individuals and onto groups. Although group work is very important, all members of a group must have some responsibility, not only to the group but also to themselves. (D) is appropriate as it will enhance student motivation, but it is not the most important aspect to consider. (A) is more important for motivation and effective learning.

40. **B** Texas requires each teacher to address the grade level TEKS with each student at that grade level. With these limited English proficiency students, this must be done to allow content acquisition while also addressing English fluency. (A) would demand less of these students, which would result in putting them behind academically as well as in English fluency. Expecting less will result in students learning less. These are not less able students but students that need intensive work with English. They often know the content from their prior educational experiences but are unable to communicate this knowledge effectively in English. (C) again eliminates the TEKS dictated by the state, which is unacceptable. A plan to use TEKS that demands concrete materials first to strengthen English and saves more abstract TEKS for later would be much wiser. (D) also leaves these students behind on the state-required TEKS while developing their

English skills. Both issues must be addressed at the same time to keep these students from falling behind. Research tells us that the further behind a student falls, the harder it is for that student to ever catch up.

41. **D** (D) allows students who do not score well on one style of assessment a chance to shine on another. This gives a more accurate picture of the learning of all the students and allows for the differentiated instruction needed for this group. It also helps the limited English students to feel they are part of the class, which is an important step toward student-student interactions and in language acquisition. The self-assessment addressed in (A) can be effective but should not be restricted to limited English proficiency students. The tutoring for any student that falls behind, as suggested in (B), is a good idea in general. Again, it should not be restricted to limited English proficiency students nor should the assessment schedule focus attention on ways these students are different from the rest of the class. (C) is an appropriate way to gather some observational assessment data but should never be the only assessment used. A "study buddy," even one with some training, would not be able to provide the level of assessment needed.

42. **B** Ms. Bowerman allows students opportunities to learn and apply the skills needed for this task in a step-by-step manner under direct teacher supervision. It allows for individual differences and, because of the daily monitoring, prevents students from delaying or falling behind. The success this ensures can help with improved attitudes toward science. (A) depends on each student already having the skills needed to do the required science fair project. It does not monitor the students' ability to apply these skills in a timely manner. Receiving a ribbon for participation does not help a negative attitude caused by frustration due to lack of interest, information, or skills. (C) can result in a negative attitude toward the project and toward science in general in students at all levels. The flexibility in participation and roles shifts more responsibility to grade-conscious students, and the learning will be unequal. (D) implies that the skills needed for all scientific research are the same, which is untrue. It also allows for no individuals already having mastery of a skill, and this can result in boredom. Also, students who feel they must endlessly repeat a lesson they cannot or have not yet mastered will develop a negative attitude and fall behind in their work on the project.

43. **B** The scientists and discoveries should also be of high student interest related to their daily lives, such as Velcro and microwaves. None of Ms. Bowerman's goals can be met if students are not attentive during this time, and interest, unexpectedness, and obvious applications are good motivators for attentiveness. (A) indicates that students are able to absorb content information without being alert to doing so, but counting on this is not a valid instructional strategy. It also does not consider how students not in her homeroom will gain the same information. (C) assumes that students will be less attentive to their peers and social needs and more attentive to information they already have because it is presented by the teacher, which is not a valid assumption. The language patterns

in (D) do make oral language easier for some listeners. Controversial topics could add great interest and discussion opportunities, yet they are avoided.

44. **B** The responses to her verbal questions will allow the teacher to assess informally students' responses to both the affective and cognitive domains of her goals. Only the affective domain goals are assessed by (A). Even then, the teacher may not obtain accurate information. Students may calmly accept her not reading on alternative days but strongly protest stopping this activity completely. (C) again focuses on the affective domain goals without addressing the cognitive domain goals. Wanting to continue the activity does not mean listening skills have not improved. Adding a formal, written assessment, as suggested in (D), will give data on each student's growth in terms of the teacher's goals. However, the task will be counterproductive for future growth as it could make some students feel stressed about the anticipated evaluations.

45. **D** Having individual time allows students to think and access prior knowledge. Being able to add forgotten or new information from the class discussion reduces pressure. Being able to place at least one idea on an individual chart establishes a pattern of success for the unit. Having the idea written on the chart before another student says it during the discussion gives additional value to the idea. Students who are correct will have a stronger motivation in future lessons. These are all good beginnings for a unit. (A) assumes that each student will write something on the chart, but this is not a valid assumption. Students sometimes add information only during class discussion. And some students do not add it at all. Although the teacher may think each student knows something about a topic, as (B) indicates, this is not a valid assumption. Students at any grade level have wide and varied background knowledge. (C) suggests a touch of a putdown directed toward knowledgeable students that should not be present. A strong background should be valued while encouraging it to become even stronger.

46. **A** Ms. Angelino has helped her students set criteria for collaborative work and now should guide them through self-evaluations and group evaluations based on these criteria. (B) assigns leadership roles rather than letting unexpected leaders emerge during the process. It also permits students to choose very different levels of participation rather than encouraging them to become a supportive team. (C) allows students to discriminate against each other and can cause hurt feelings. It does not teach teamwork and results in groups based on friendships, which might be fun but not necessarily effective. (D) focuses on learning the skill of collaborating while learning the lesson being taught during group work. It might be appropriate to do this once when teaching the skill of grouping. However, it wastes instructional time by not giving value to the content the grouping activity produced as part of the learning experience. It is more efficient to consider both aspects—group performance and knowledge acquisition.

47. **C** Response (C) allows Ms. Angelino to work during the coming school year to strengthen possible weak areas. This is based on the experience of prior students who have attended the same schools, after confirming the level of student

achievement in these areas. The idea in (A) of being sure students have the test-taking skills for a particular format may be appropriate but is not the best use of the assessment information. Students of this age have experienced these types of tests multiple times in their school careers. It is important that she establish that this group has the same educational gaps before teaching knowledge and skills from earlier grade levels that she just assumes a group of students are lacking as in (B). Nor is it appropriate to consider only one criterion when deciding on instructional practices for a school year. (D) shifts the remediation role for diagnosed weak areas to students or to parents. Although it is not inappropriate to ask for parental assistance, the school should take the leadership role.

48. **A** The teacher is modeling the value of high expectations to reach the highest levels of academic performance, so (A) is the best response. Tracking their performance, as in (B), is helpful to some students. However, some students are not motivated by grades. So this may not have the desired impact. The teacher tracking completed assignments as in (C), removes responsibility from students. The result is reduced value for that strategy. (D) is the least likely to occur. Modeling by the teacher has little likelihood for increasing homework by students who have not been completing homework in the past.

49. **D** School equipment is purchased with school funds and is intended to be used to conduct school business. It does not matter if the school business occurs on or off campus or during school hours or outside school hours. The ethical and legal position is that school equipment should be used only for school business, which eliminates (A), (B), and (C).

50. **C** Response (C) gives the most helpful strategy as it is both the most concrete of those offered and has a high level of student participation. It establishes specific examples of the concept that students might not initially recognize because of the abstract nature of the concept. It also allows the teacher to use these examples to determine when understanding has occurred. (A) and (B) are not incorrect strategies but are not as powerful for the reasons mentioned. (A) would be more effective if the students rather than the teacher were reviewing and repeating the major concepts. (B) is a good strategy because it helps students activate prior knowledge, but it assumes prior knowledge, which may not be accurate. (D) is a traditional way to introduce vocabulary but is not as effective as introducing and defining a new term as needed within a context.

51. **D** Response (D) provides teams of students with specific examples within a specified system. By working together, they must track the changes between start and stop points for energy transformations, which requires higher-order thinking as they support their ideas with research. This strategy also provides students with teacher support and guidance without signaling that there is only one acceptable answer. It allows teamwork and discussions of the needed information. (A) requires students to name three ecological systems, which is asking for a knowledge-level response, although providing three examples requires more thinking than being assigned three systems. Questions on energy transformations require a yes/no response, which represents the lowest level of thinking. (B) removes stu-

dent interactions from the assignment. The question about energy transformations still requires a yes/no approach rather than a depth of thinking and learning. (C) adds the requirement of establishing one example of an energy transformation in the given system. This might result in more thinking, but it may only involve recording an example from the resource materials.

52. **A** If Ms. Klondile had been unwilling to allow the discussion to continue past the time set and was not open to student-initiated instructional pathways, she would have lost a teachable moment that could result in a more powerful learning experience for her students than originally planned. (B) is not a true statement. There are several ways Ms. Klondile could adjust for the shift in the time allocation. She could "return" time to the next topic tomorrow or integrate the two topics in the direction that students have indicated they want the lesson to move. (C) implies that the students and Ms. Klondile have collaborated in distracting or off-task behaviors that block learning, which is not accurate. Ms. Klondile actually hopes that in the future students will be so interested and excited by a lesson that they will again take an active role in directing the instructional goal. (D) indicates that although Ms. Klondile allowed and encouraged the discussion today, she has no plans to follow through on shifting the direction of the unit's focus. It indicates that the class will again be teacher-directed tomorrow, which will close the door on a wonderful teachable moment.

53. **D** This consulting job would be unethical because preparing for it during a school conference period entails being paid twice for the same time. Her preparation should occur outside of school hours. Nothing in (A), (B), and (C) is unethical. Ms. Klondile did the planning work away from school during the summer on her personal home computer. She did not use school resource materials. However, basing plans on school resources is the expected norm and none of these resources were unique to her school. She is not selling school materials or committing the school to buying materials to be able to use the curriculum. She is charging the other school a consulting fee for the time spent sharing the plans she made and has already given to the department.

54. **A** The student received negative feedback ahead of positive feedback and no concrete suggestions for improvement. The initial negative comment may be as far as the student reads, and so the student could miss the positive comment about sophisticated writing style or may even interpret this comment as being a negative because of the initial negative tone. Responses (B), (C), and (D) assume the initial negative comment about clarity will be outweighed by the comment about sophisticated writing style. No clear suggested changes are given in either (B) or (C), and so the student may have no idea how to improve. This is not a time for student freedom as suggested in (D) but for clear modeling of a better style.

55. **B** Ms. Chavez must determine why Bernice is having difficulty before she can help. In (A), Bernice will not feel ownership while dependent on Ms. Chavez for help. Ownership comes from independent success. (C) assumes Bernice has

a problem with focus or lack of attentiveness with no supporting evidence. (D) sounds good but reading with comprehension is a higher-order thinking skill. There is no evidence of why Bernice is having difficulty.

56. **C** Ms. Chavez should encourage her students to be creative and varied in their approaches to the problem. Many effective solutions are the desired outcome. Responses (A), (B), and (D) all imply that there is only one correct solution or answer and one best method for reaching it, which is counter to the problem-solving process.

57. **A** A variety of content topics and instructional methods are planned for the unit, which allows students multiple styles of learning opportunities. (B) addresses a common misunderstanding about integrated units. Integration allows for greater instructional time per subject, but this does not always mean that less class time is required. Instead, integration means the time is apportioned in different patterns to allow overlap between content areas. There is no information in the question to support the selection of either response (C) or (D). Neither the pacing of lessons nor individualized instruction is mentioned or indicated.

58. **D** Observational data can tell Ms. Chavez if the center runs smoothly and the instruction is clear. Either formal or informal assessment can reveal how effectively learning occurs. (A) tells her how many and how often students visited a center but does not indicate if the center was used appropriately or if learning occurred. Students may be visiting the center to play with included materials or for some other invalid reason rather than participating as instructed by the center. (B) gives a clear picture of the students' responses to the affective domain of the center but does not give information about their cognitive learning. (C) gives information about the center's effectiveness with adults and perceived effectiveness with students but not about its actual effectiveness for student learning.

59. **C** Computers are one of many instructional styles planned into the unit and variety helps maintain interest, motivation, and learning. High school students have already had extensive exposure to computers in multiple environments, such as home and businesses. So they would not find including computer activity a major motivation as in (A). (B) seems to indicate that an activity involving computers is the best way to help special-needs students learn, which is inaccurate. (D) is true but not as important a reason for including this type of activity as is varying instructional strategies. High school students without computer skills are most unusual.

60. **C** Bernice's parent will become defensive if he or she feels that either his or her student or family is being judged. This defensiveness will interfere with a solution to the difficulty being experienced. (A) shifts all responsibility to the parent, and (B) shifts all responsibility to the teacher when finding a solution needs to be a joint effort among teacher, parent, and student. (D) does not acknowledge the greater knowledge a parent has about a student and ignores information

that might be vital to understanding the reasons for the difficulty in completing the assignments.

61. **B** Research has shown that most ninth-grade students do not see graduation as an attainable goal. Faced with a myriad of social, emotional, and academic roadblocks, most ninth-graders are at risk. Assigning a novice teacher to this grade serves to exacerbate the problem, making knowledge of the traits of ninth-grade students of utmost importance. (A), (C), and (D) can all be true of a ninth-grader but are not as important to know as (B).

62. **D** Simply put, students are more likely to adhere to rules that they have had a part in creating. Studies have shown that students responsible for establishing their own rules and the consequences for breaking these rules feel they have taken part in the democratic process. This in turn gives them a sense of control and more ownership or buy-in. (A), (B), and (C) might be true but are subjective statements.

63. **B** Giving a pretest is an effective method to determine what students know and allows for more effective planning of what still needs to be learned. Grade point averages, as in (A), are not indicators of prior knowledge but merely a method of reporting last year's grades. (C) measures what has been learned after the lesson has been conducted. (D) is not as precise or effective a method for determining prior knowledge. Will the paragraph be written in a setting that restricts research on the topic?

64. **D** Breaking directions into clear steps for both oral and written formats allows for better comprehension of the directions. Modeling directions and examples further add to understanding. Although (A) is close, the addition of breaking down the directions into shorter steps is important and its omission makes this response as well as (B) incomplete. (C) might be helpful for some students at this age, but others will tune out this repetition.

65. **D** The rubric is the most thorough method of assessing their web quest. (A) and (B) can be used to assist in designing the rubric. (C) is not an appropriate way to assess this activity.

66. **B** Having all the teachers present provides a more complete picture of what is happening with the student. Any negative comments are balanced by positive ones. While meeting together, the teachers can determine if the student is achieving and behaving the same way in all classes or if differences occur in one or more. (A) has teachers ganging up on parents, which is unacceptable as parents and teachers must both focus on what is best for students. The exchange of ideas by teachers in (C) should occur before the conference with the parents. (D) adds convenience for the parents but again involves conflict between parents and teachers that should not be present in an effective conference.

67. **C** For a variety of reasons, some people do not feel comfortable coming to the school. Taking meetings to the people ensures a better turnout. (A), (B), and (D) are good ideas. However, meetings will still be at the school. Many parents/guardians might choose not to attend or may be unable to attend.

68. **A** Approved workshops, conferences, and graduate school hours all count toward the hours of professional development required by the state for renewing a teaching license. All the professionally enriching activities indicated in (B), (C), and (D) are not usually accepted for this credit. If a district indicates that it will use only credits the state accepts, it must ask for and receive state credit before accepting these types of activities even though they value this type of development and require more hours than the state.

69. **A** The first rule of giving clear directions is making sure you understand them yourself. If you clearly understand the directions, you will be able to clearly explain them to your students. (B) and (C) specify appropriate vocabularies for higher- and lower-achieving students. This should also be a consideration when planning directions. (D) is an important consideration based on Mr. Robertson's philosophy but is not related to instructional directions.

70. **A** Creating a monthly newsletter that is mailed to the community is a great way to share class and school information. (B) is a good idea but would reach only those with Internet access. Only community members who come to the school could see the bulletin board in (C). Finally, (D) does not ensure that all community members will get the letter or even that the letter will make it home.

71. **C** Response (C) is the practice reported to the state. Mr. Snowden guided his students toward selecting correct answers, which is cheating, plain and simple. (A), (B), and (D) are actually good strategies to prepare students for the test and are neither unethical nor illegal. In (B), Mr. Snowden would only know what content to address because the TAKS is based on the state's TEKS and teachers are not allowed to view copies of the test.

72. **D** By inviting community members to come in and speak to the students, Mr. Woods is not only exposing his students to the diversity of the speakers but is also making his instruction relevant by having as speakers people the students come in contact with on a daily basis. Having these speakers also supports (A), (B), and (C), but as a secondary effect, which could be the underlying reason for selecting (D).

73. **B** Objectives must be specific and measurable. The word *understand* is broad and not easily measurable. How the learner is to demonstrate that the information has been understood is not specified. (A) and (D) are true, but the inability to clearly measure success is a greater problem. (C) is an incorrect statement for these two objectives.

74. **C** Having a vertical team for curriculum alignment allows problems to be detected and solved. Simple communication among the grade levels does not only solve the problems detected but also helps key players see what occurs before and after their respective grade levels. (A) and (B) do not solve the problem and are short-term responses. (D) will occur during the process of (C).

75. **A** Most American history courses teach about the first settlers in the United States and their hardships. This scenario asks students to approach the familiar

from an unfamiliar perspective—the Native American view of life when the settlers arrived. This also requires the higher-level thinking skills of synthesis and evaluation. (B) is a typical listing activity. (B), (C), and (D) do not require higher-order thinking skills. (B) and (D) ask for knowledge level information in the form of recall. (C) calls for a comprehension level in the form of an opinion based on knowledge.

76. **B** Mr. Woods must get permission before making copies of the books even though he owns the books. (A), (C), and (D) are not true.

77. **C** One of the goals of cooperative grouping is interaction among students with mixed abilities and interests. Research has shown that students not only interact with each other but also tend to learn more about others. Some even form friendships that might not have occurred had they not worked together. Although winning a competition for grades, as in (B), is a goal of jigsaw, it is not the reason Mr. Woods selected the instructional model. (A) and (D) are not supported by the information given and are not goals of jigsaw.

78. **A** Consistency is the key to ensuring that students follow rules. Once students see that the consequences of breaking a rule are not consistently enforced, the rule loses meaning. The teacher needs to reevaluate the rules and determine why he is unable to be consistent in enforcing them. Once this occurs, then (C) might be needed. (B) and (D) would not solve the problem and could create greater problems.

79. **A** First and foremost, Ms. Blankenship has to admit to herself that she is prejudiced toward these two students and possibly toward Arab-Americans as a group. She then has to seek assistance while deciding her own limits and how this will affect the students. Learning more about the students' backgrounds and their nationalities might help as in (B). Should Ms. Blankenship not be able to get beyond her prejudice, (C) would be the next step and might lead to (D), which is a last resort but not always a viable option.

80. **C** Ms. Johnson provides both teacher-student and student-student interactions in the classroom. Peer collaboration creates a support system that allows safe interaction and often leads to responses at higher levels of thinking. The conclusions drawn are generally far more comprehensive. Although (A), (B), and (D) can also be true, (C) is the more likely result of the described learning activity.

81. **C** Because they are able to produce spin in each direction, each pair of students can clearly understand the cause. (A) and (B) have students writing and supporting their thoughts, which require a lower level of thinking. (D) has one group report while others listen. Many groups can report, but the response from the first group will influence the responses of all the following groups.

82. **B** First-hand information is the most reliable and dramatic source of information. Talking to survivors allows students to see personal and emotional aspects of tornado damage that cannot be accurately portrayed by pictures of the destruction. Personal interviews bring many perspectives and consequences to the attention of the students, such as emotional costs, the monetary costs of

starting over, and the physical responses of the survivors. (A), (C), and (D) can be used to supplement and support information learned from the interviews.

83. **B** Microsoft Word is a program that allows the addition of hyperlinks and the inclusion of interactive art. It is user-friendly and readily available. Microsoft Excel, as in (A), is a spreadsheet program. Paint/Draw, as in (C), is a program incorporated into Microsoft Word. Microsoft Outlook, as in (D), is an e-mail program.

84. **C** Experiencing another web quest will give students a clear, first-hand understanding of the design components. (A) can occur after (C). (B) would be part of the design process as well. (D) might be helpful but is not necessary.

85. **A** Before the students can be asked to carry out research using the steps involved in scientific research, Ms. Nelson must be sure that they know and understand the requirements of each step. (B) would be helpful, but it could be the second step. (C) and (D) are also additional steps.

86. **D** The students have input into the criteria chosen for the rubric as well as the assigned point values and critical exemplars. This in turn gives students ownership of the project and garners student responsibility for their own learning. (A) and (B) might occur as a result of this process, but not necessarily. Although student learning can be enhanced as stated in (C), they are not given control.

87. **A** Because the students have some preconceived ideas about Afghanistan and the war, they would be better served if they generated their own questions. The generation of possible resources should be student-led as well. (B) is teacher-led and takes away the buy-in of the students. (C) and (D) can result from the initial research.

88. **B** Generating big ideas requires taking two or more key concepts and forming a generalization. (A) suggests the opposite and therefore is not the correct response. (C) is the Hilda Taba method of concept development. (D) is a component of the generalization process in (B).

89. **B** Obviously, the class did not understand the material as it was originally taught. Reteaching the information using a different instructional method to help students learn the concept is the next step. (A) is what normally occurs; however, if comprehension of the material does not occur, no purpose is served. (C) and (D) also do not correct the problem of students failing to understand the material.

90. **C** For ESL students, beginning with a hands-on activity results in better comprehension of the lesson. The activity also gives the teacher a better idea of whether or not the students can write checks and balance a checkbook. Because they have limited English proficiency does not mean they do not have a skill or knowledge in their original language. (A) and (B) are good activities for lessons on making change but not for a lesson on check writing. (D) is a good reinforcement activity but not an appropriate introductory activity.

Diagnostic and Sample Tests for Grades EC–12

The diagnostic tests in the following chapters include one question per test competency, except for the EC-12 Diagnostic Test, which includes three questions per competency. These questions are similar to those found at the State Board of Educator Certification (SBEC) website (www.sbec.state.tx.us), where the state agency provides a clear example of the PPR certification test. The SBEC practice test should also be used as a diagnostic tool to ascertain both your areas of strength and the needed areas of knowledge and skill improvement that you must have to be successful on the PPR examinations. The diagnostic items in this book are presented without full follow-up explanations of why all responses are correct or incorrect. This follows the pattern used for the test items for the SBEC practice tests. The state competency is listed at the end of each diagnostic test item to help guide your understanding of how you will be tested on each competency.

According to numerous candidates who have taken and passed the state certification test, there is a correlation between SBEC practice tests and the state certification test. You are encouraged to visit www.sbec.state.tx.us for further information about the SBEC study guide. We encourage you to continue to take the diagnostic tests to confirm exactly what competencies are included on the test and to practice deciding why three responses are incorrect or less effective and why one response is clearly the best answer.

Following the sample tests for each of the state certification levels, you will find a self-analysis framework that will guide you in understanding how to improve your study before taking the state tests. In this framework, the authors explain why three answers are incorrect (or are not the *best* response) and one answer is correct (or is the *best* choice). It would be wise to continue to use this analysis strategy as you continue to practice using the tests in this study guide and the SBEC online test. In Chapter 16, suggestions are made that will help you complete an overall analysis of your success and provide you with a strategy for further study.

Answer Sheet
DIAGNOSTIC TEST (GRADES EC–12)

1 Ⓐ Ⓑ Ⓒ Ⓓ

2 Ⓐ Ⓑ Ⓒ Ⓓ

3 Ⓐ Ⓑ Ⓒ Ⓓ

4 Ⓐ Ⓑ Ⓒ Ⓓ

5 Ⓐ Ⓑ Ⓒ Ⓓ

6 Ⓐ Ⓑ Ⓒ Ⓓ

7 Ⓐ Ⓑ Ⓒ Ⓓ

8 Ⓐ Ⓑ Ⓒ Ⓓ

9 Ⓐ Ⓑ Ⓒ Ⓓ

10 Ⓐ Ⓑ Ⓒ Ⓓ

11 Ⓐ Ⓑ Ⓒ Ⓓ

12 Ⓐ Ⓑ Ⓒ Ⓓ

13 Ⓐ Ⓑ Ⓒ Ⓓ

14 Ⓐ Ⓑ Ⓒ Ⓓ

15 Ⓐ Ⓑ Ⓒ Ⓓ

16 Ⓐ Ⓑ Ⓒ Ⓓ

17 Ⓐ Ⓑ Ⓒ Ⓓ

18 Ⓐ Ⓑ Ⓒ Ⓓ

19 Ⓐ Ⓑ Ⓒ Ⓓ

20 Ⓐ Ⓑ Ⓒ Ⓓ

21 Ⓐ Ⓑ Ⓒ Ⓓ

22 Ⓐ Ⓑ Ⓒ Ⓓ

23 Ⓐ Ⓑ Ⓒ Ⓓ

24 Ⓐ Ⓑ Ⓒ Ⓓ

25 Ⓐ Ⓑ Ⓒ Ⓓ

26 Ⓐ Ⓑ Ⓒ Ⓓ

27 Ⓐ Ⓑ Ⓒ Ⓓ

28 Ⓐ Ⓑ Ⓒ Ⓓ

29 Ⓐ Ⓑ Ⓒ Ⓓ

30 Ⓐ Ⓑ Ⓒ Ⓓ

31 Ⓐ Ⓑ Ⓒ Ⓓ

32 Ⓐ Ⓑ Ⓒ Ⓓ

33 Ⓐ Ⓑ Ⓒ Ⓓ

34 Ⓐ Ⓑ Ⓒ Ⓓ

35 Ⓐ Ⓑ Ⓒ Ⓓ

36 Ⓐ Ⓑ Ⓒ Ⓓ

37 Ⓐ Ⓑ Ⓒ Ⓓ

38 Ⓐ Ⓑ Ⓒ Ⓓ

39 Ⓐ Ⓑ Ⓒ Ⓓ

Answer Sheet
SAMPLE TEST (GRADES EC–12)

1	Ⓐ Ⓑ Ⓒ Ⓓ	26	Ⓐ Ⓑ Ⓒ Ⓓ	51	Ⓐ Ⓑ Ⓒ Ⓓ	76	Ⓐ Ⓑ Ⓒ Ⓓ
2	Ⓐ Ⓑ Ⓒ Ⓓ	27	Ⓐ Ⓑ Ⓒ Ⓓ	52	Ⓐ Ⓑ Ⓒ Ⓓ	77	Ⓐ Ⓑ Ⓒ Ⓓ
3	Ⓐ Ⓑ Ⓒ Ⓓ	28	Ⓐ Ⓑ Ⓒ Ⓓ	53	Ⓐ Ⓑ Ⓒ Ⓓ	78	Ⓐ Ⓑ Ⓒ Ⓓ
4	Ⓐ Ⓑ Ⓒ Ⓓ	29	Ⓐ Ⓑ Ⓒ Ⓓ	54	Ⓐ Ⓑ Ⓒ Ⓓ	79	Ⓐ Ⓑ Ⓒ Ⓓ
5	Ⓐ Ⓑ Ⓒ Ⓓ	30	Ⓐ Ⓑ Ⓒ Ⓓ	55	Ⓐ Ⓑ Ⓒ Ⓓ	80	Ⓐ Ⓑ Ⓒ Ⓓ
6	Ⓐ Ⓑ Ⓒ Ⓓ	31	Ⓐ Ⓑ Ⓒ Ⓓ	56	Ⓐ Ⓑ Ⓒ Ⓓ	81	Ⓐ Ⓑ Ⓒ Ⓓ
7	Ⓐ Ⓑ Ⓒ Ⓓ	32	Ⓐ Ⓑ Ⓒ Ⓓ	57	Ⓐ Ⓑ Ⓒ Ⓓ	82	Ⓐ Ⓑ Ⓒ Ⓓ
8	Ⓐ Ⓑ Ⓒ Ⓓ	33	Ⓐ Ⓑ Ⓒ Ⓓ	58	Ⓐ Ⓑ Ⓒ Ⓓ	83	Ⓐ Ⓑ Ⓒ Ⓓ
9	Ⓐ Ⓑ Ⓒ Ⓓ	34	Ⓐ Ⓑ Ⓒ Ⓓ	59	Ⓐ Ⓑ Ⓒ Ⓓ	84	Ⓐ Ⓑ Ⓒ Ⓓ
10	Ⓐ Ⓑ Ⓒ Ⓓ	35	Ⓐ Ⓑ Ⓒ Ⓓ	60	Ⓐ Ⓑ Ⓒ Ⓓ	85	Ⓐ Ⓑ Ⓒ Ⓓ
11	Ⓐ Ⓑ Ⓒ Ⓓ	36	Ⓐ Ⓑ Ⓒ Ⓓ	61	Ⓐ Ⓑ Ⓒ Ⓓ	86	Ⓐ Ⓑ Ⓒ Ⓓ
12	Ⓐ Ⓑ Ⓒ Ⓓ	37	Ⓐ Ⓑ Ⓒ Ⓓ	62	Ⓐ Ⓑ Ⓒ Ⓓ	87	Ⓐ Ⓑ Ⓒ Ⓓ
13	Ⓐ Ⓑ Ⓒ Ⓓ	38	Ⓐ Ⓑ Ⓒ Ⓓ	63	Ⓐ Ⓑ Ⓒ Ⓓ	88	Ⓐ Ⓑ Ⓒ Ⓓ
14	Ⓐ Ⓑ Ⓒ Ⓓ	39	Ⓐ Ⓑ Ⓒ Ⓓ	64	Ⓐ Ⓑ Ⓒ Ⓓ	89	Ⓐ Ⓑ Ⓒ Ⓓ
15	Ⓐ Ⓑ Ⓒ Ⓓ	40	Ⓐ Ⓑ Ⓒ Ⓓ	65	Ⓐ Ⓑ Ⓒ Ⓓ	90	Ⓐ Ⓑ Ⓒ Ⓓ
16	Ⓐ Ⓑ Ⓒ Ⓓ	41	Ⓐ Ⓑ Ⓒ Ⓓ	66	Ⓐ Ⓑ Ⓒ Ⓓ		
17	Ⓐ Ⓑ Ⓒ Ⓓ	42	Ⓐ Ⓑ Ⓒ Ⓓ	67	Ⓐ Ⓑ Ⓒ Ⓓ		
18	Ⓐ Ⓑ Ⓒ Ⓓ	43	Ⓐ Ⓑ Ⓒ Ⓓ	68	Ⓐ Ⓑ Ⓒ Ⓓ		
19	Ⓐ Ⓑ Ⓒ Ⓓ	44	Ⓐ Ⓑ Ⓒ Ⓓ	69	Ⓐ Ⓑ Ⓒ Ⓓ		
20	Ⓐ Ⓑ Ⓒ Ⓓ	45	Ⓐ Ⓑ Ⓒ Ⓓ	70	Ⓐ Ⓑ Ⓒ Ⓓ		
21	Ⓐ Ⓑ Ⓒ Ⓓ	46	Ⓐ Ⓑ Ⓒ Ⓓ	71	Ⓐ Ⓑ Ⓒ Ⓓ		
22	Ⓐ Ⓑ Ⓒ Ⓓ	47	Ⓐ Ⓑ Ⓒ Ⓓ	72	Ⓐ Ⓑ Ⓒ Ⓓ		
23	Ⓐ Ⓑ Ⓒ Ⓓ	48	Ⓐ Ⓑ Ⓒ Ⓓ	73	Ⓐ Ⓑ Ⓒ Ⓓ		
24	Ⓐ Ⓑ Ⓒ Ⓓ	49	Ⓐ Ⓑ Ⓒ Ⓓ	74	Ⓐ Ⓑ Ⓒ Ⓓ		
25	Ⓐ Ⓑ Ⓒ Ⓓ	50	Ⓐ Ⓑ Ⓒ Ⓓ	75	Ⓐ Ⓑ Ⓒ Ⓓ		

Diagnostic Test (Grades EC–12)

Directions: Read each stimulus and answer every question. Mark your answers in the answer spaces on the accompanying grid.

1. Jeanetta is a four-year old girl who seems to prefer the construction center during free play time in her preschool class. She enjoys working alone to build things, even though there are several other children in the construction center. Based on these observations by the teacher, what is the *best* assessment of Jeanetta's play in the construction center?

   (A) She is limited in her interpersonal development and needs teacher direction regarding how to play with her peers.
   (B) She is in the predictable stage of parallel play.
   (C) She is demonstrating signs of behavior disorder.
   (D) She is far advanced for her age and should be considered for placement in a kindergarten classroom at this time.

2. Martin accepted a seventh-grade position for his first teaching assignment. He learned a lot about cognitive development in his teacher education program and knows that these students likely operate between concrete and formal operational thought. What would be the best instructional approach for him to follow to accommodate learning?

   (A) Use as many manipulatives as possible while focusing on activities that lead learners to more abstract content.
   (B) Always use cooperative grouping to allow learners to share concepts.
   (C) Offer tutoring each morning before school to assist those who are struggling.
   (D) Don't worry about learners at the higher levels; focus on the average learner in order to assure that all students have some opportunity to grow.

3. Carolyn is concerned about one of her tenth-grade students who missed school more and more frequently. When Carolyn expressed her concern, the student told her that school had no value for her so she was working part time. What development knowledge does Carolyn need for understanding this student's perspective?

   (A) A person of this age may have more concern with the present than any thought of the future.
   (B) This student may be having financial problems at home, and the single mom may be asking the student to help out.
   (C) This student is likely still operating at the concrete operational stage, and thus has difficulty reasoning through complex problems.
   (D) Students at this age typically place more focus on parents than school, and thus may be following a parent's model of dropping out of school.

Competency 001: *The teacher understands human developmental processes and applies this knowledge to plan instruction and ongoing assessment that motivate students and are responsive to their developmental characteristics and needs.*

4. Several of Martin's students have special needs and sometimes leave his classroom to work in the school's resource room. In consultation with the special education resource teacher, what would be the best instructional plan for Martin as he strives to ensure that he is meeting the need of students with special needs?

(A) Limit the special needs students to independent work while in his classroom so they do not negatively impact the other students. ✗

(B) Plan activities that address social skills rather than cognitive development.

(C) Use a direct teaching approach so all students learn the same material and do not have an opportunity to interfere with any other student's learning.

(D) Design interactive activities so all learners have an opportunity to work together.

5. As a high school teacher in a suburb of a metropolitan area, most of Betty's students are from different cultural backgrounds. How should Betty best respond when she observes tensions caused by several students' use of demeaning and unacceptable terms when addressing students from both their own culture and other cultures?

(A) When assigning groups, always place students from the same culture in the same group in an effort to avoid any potential for interaction during the time students are in the classroom. ✗

(B) Each time there is a group activity within a unit, allow students to choose the members of their group in hopes that students who get along well will end up in the same groups. ✗

(C) Use a shared decision-making process with students to develop clearly defined behavior and language interaction expectations, as well as to determine consequences of not adhering to the guidelines.

(D) Include participation, attitude, respect, and peer support as elements of the assessment system and explain to students how these elements will carry as much weight as academic performance for determining semester grades.

6. Richard was assigned a class of 30 fourth-grade students who represent four different native languages. To ensure that he addresses this diversity appropriately, how should he plan his assessments?

(A) Use assessments that focus on students' strengths and give them various ways to demonstrate what they have learned.

(B) Allow students to determine the method of assessment for each assignment. ✗

(C) Test students several times during the grading period, so he does not have to give a unit test or other cumulative tests. ✗

(D) Determine end of unit grades by using only student and peer assessment of major assignments. ✗

Competency 002: *The teacher understands student diversity and knows how to plan learning experiences and design assessments that are responsive to differences among students and that promote all students' learning.*

7. Martin and the seventh-grade team set aside time early in the year to plan new interdisciplinary units for the year. For the most effective use of their time, what would be the most appropriate *initial* step to take as they begin plans for the units?

    (A) List all the TAKS for their grade level and focus on those most interesting. X

    (B) Design a number of interesting activities across the themes and skills likely to be needed for the units.

    (C) Design a matrix to identify how many units are needed and when they should be used.

    (D) Spend the first few hours brainstorming topics of interest to the teachers so students will be more motivated by the teachers' enthusiasm for the units. X

8. Why should Richard design his learning outcomes before he plans the instructional activities for his unit?

    (A) To allow students the freedom of choosing their activities, with limited focus on the essential knowledge and skills required by the TEKS. X

    (B) So his formative and summative assessments are focused on the activities he plans in order to have alignment with the activities.

    (C) To have confidence in how he has sequenced the content of the TEKS and paired the learning activities with what he is responsible for teaching.

    (D) To evaluate the topic of the unit to see if it is appropriate and if it has activities that his students will enjoy.

9. Catherine is working with her mentor to design learning outcome statements and teaching objectives for an upcoming unit on the integration of aesthetics and history concepts. What challenge will Catherine face with the following outcome statement: "Students will appreciate the role of aesthetics in the study of history"?

    (A) This learning outcome will be relatively easy to assess because it is easily measurable and is certainly an important concept for this history unit.

    (B) There is no clear expectation of learning in this outcome so it will be impossible to assess it in any meaningful way.

    (C) High school students have no interest in aesthetics, so it will be impossible for the majority of these students to meet this objective.

    (D) Objective measurement of "appreciation" is almost impossible, so some other means of assessment must be employed for this objective.

Competency 003: *The teacher understands procedures for designing effective and coherent instruction and assessment based on appropriate learning goals and objectives.*

10. In an eleventh-grade history class, Barbara has students use simulated journal entries for confirming their understanding of historical concepts. The following questions were given to students prior to writing in order to guide their thinking.

> **How do you think the historical figure responded to the event we are studying?**
>
> **If you were the historical figure, do you think you would have reacted in the same way today as the figure did at the time of the historical event? Why or why not?**
>
> **When you discussed the historical figure with your peer partner, how did your conversation help you to understand the importance of the event and the figure?**

What do these questions demonstrate about Barbara's understanding of learning principles?

(A) Students need to be challenged to figure out principles related to any academic concept, especially in the area of social studies.

(B) Students will perform better when they have an opportunity to work with peers to confirm their perceptions about the topic.

(C) It is important to have students regulate their thinking whenever they are challenged to put themselves in the place of another, such as with a simulated journal entry.

(D) When students have an opportunity to actively engage in activities and are challenged to think in reflective ways, learning is reinforced.

11. Knowing the value of independent learning for middle level learners, what would be a fifth-grade teacher's best strategy for helping small groups work effectively?

(A) Determine the number of groups needed, then allow students to choose the membership of each group.

(B) Make sure that at least one dominant and one submissive student is in each group in order to balance the give-and-take necessary for group work.

(C) Assign only group grades for the performance of the group, explaining to students how this translates into the work place.

(D) Working with students, develop a rubric to evaluate the work of the group for students to use in a post-project review and discussion of their work.

12. Sonya immigrated to the United States two years ago. Since that time, she has moved twice. Now, in her kindergarten year, she enters Ms. Alvarez's class halfway through the year. Her teacher noted that Sonya is above average in her social skills, but her play successes are not at the point expected for her age. What must Ms. Alvarez keep in mind regarding this variance in levels?

(A) Students in this group may be highly advanced in their play skills, thus a comparison of Sonya to the others would be inequitable.

(B) Teachers should carefully discourage reluctant children who appear to be reverting to levels of performance below where they should be.

(C) Teacher observation is rarely an accurate record of student performance.

(D) It is normal for young children to revert to previous levels of success in a situation where they might feel a lack of security and belongingness.

Competency 004: *The teacher understands learning processes and factors that impact student learning and demonstrates this knowledge by planning effective, engaging instruction and appropriate assessments.*

13. As a new teacher, Margarette wishes to employ high expectations of her students. What should she do to guide her students to achieve their best?

(A) Make sure students focus mainly on their strength areas and avoid any stress related to learning activities that are challenging.

(B) Give students numerous opportunities to work together on assignments so as not to cause any one student to have total responsibility for his/her learning.

(C) Guide all students to set challenging learning goals and scaffold learners at all times as they strive to meet those goals.

(D) Give lots of praise to all students at all times, even if the praise is not contingently earned.

14. A sixth-grade teacher opens her lesson on United States geography by posting the question, "What do you know about beaches in Florida?" for students to discuss when they enter the classroom. How could this question stimulate student engagement?

(A) It gives students an opportunity to demonstrate their knowledge about something they all have first-hand experience with.

(B) This question tells students that the teacher is more interested in topics that represent easy learning than topics that develop their understanding of complex concepts.

(C) It addresses a concept that many students will have some prior knowledge of, and offers students an environment where no single correct answer is expected.

(D) The question implies that the teacher believes all students have been to Florida and therefore will be able make a contribution.

15. What would be the best strategy for Mary Ellen to use to assess the effectiveness of her classroom learning community design?

    (A) Analyze whether or not her instruction follows her educational philosophy.

    (B) Make a chart of how frequently students are absent and what their excuses are for their absences.

    (C) Evaluate the climate to determine the extent to which lessons engage students' in shared learning, independent thinking, and complex reasoning.

    (D) Determine whether or not students have a clear understanding of the importance of individual responsibility.

Competency 005: *The teacher knows how to establish a classroom climate that fosters learning, equity, and excellence and uses this knowledge to create a physical and emotional environment that is safe and productive.*

16. Jeremy is a sixth-grade school science teacher who has students work in pairs during multitasking. He noticed that two students (one pair) do not participate effectively. Which of the following strategies might Jeremy employ with this pair of students?

    (A) Move the two students to other pairs so they will learn how to work more effectively with others.

    (B) Tell both of these students that when they prove they can work together they may then move to other groups with whom they might be more comfortable.

    (C) Conference with the pair to make sure each member has clear directions and that each understands exactly what role he is to take with the multitasking assignments.

    (D) Move the highest achieving student in the class to work with this pair for two weeks in hopes they can learn from someone more successful.

17. Daryl works with his mentor to establish routines and procedures that he will put in place early in the first week with his tenth-grade students. What is the most important reason why this approach is a wise strategy for establishing a strong learning climate?

    (A) With routines in place, Daryl will have more time for planning and organizing materials.

    (B) Students will know exactly how each day's instructional activities will occur and in what manner the teacher will always present lessons.

    (C) The teacher will be better able to use instructional time efficiently and effectively.

    (D) The teacher will be able to capitalize on students' interest and motivation.

18. Alma noticed two students in seemingly high levels of conflict when on the playground. What conflict resolution technique would be appropriate?

    (A) Guide the students to work together for a mutual agreement to solve their differences.
    (B) Determine which student started the conflict and discipline that student.
    (C) Assign another student the responsibility of being in charge of the resolution through serving as a mediator.
    (D) Send the students inside and direct them in how to solve their problems.

Competency 006: *The teacher understands strategies for creating an organized and productive learning environment and for managing student behavior.*

19. As Jeremy moves pairs of students into cooperative groups, he wants to make sure that all students feel safe in taking risks in their learning and use their creativity effectively. Which of the following would be the most effective for Jeremy to say?

    (A) "All of you worked well together the last time we had a cooperative group project. Based on that experience, I am sure you will do as well today."
    (B) "This is an important assignment for your six weeks' grade so be sure to work together well in order to finish the group project on time."
    (C) "Each member of your group is an important contributor. As you complete your project, remember that there is not one exact way to solve the problem."
    (D) "Each group needs to select a leader who will guide the group to figure out the right answer to the problem that is the focus of the group work."

20. Casey wants to improve the communication skills of her tenth-grade students. Which of the following observations during small group work should be of greatest concern for Casey to address *initially*?

    (A) Often, students do not listen to their classmates and frequently talk over each other.
    (B) In some groups, certain students talk only to one or two others.
    (C) At times, students speak out when others are concentrating on a task.
    (D) In one group, students seem to argue more than target completion of their assignment.

21. Mary, a first-grade teacher, plans to address the following science objective:

> **The student knows that plants are made up of parts and that if one part is damaged, the plant may suffer and possibly die.**

Which of the following should Mary use as a strategy for introducing this concept effectively and efficiently to her first graders?

(A) Tell the first graders several times how important each part of the plant is to the successful growth and health of the plant. ✗

(B) Bring a slightly damaged plant from home (or a store) to demonstrate the parts of the plant and to show how damage to one part may impact the whole plant.

(C) Sketch the parts of a plant on a dry erase board and draw lines from each part of the plant to the proper word for the part.

(D) List the word for each part of a plant on the board and have students define each word in their vocabulary notebooks. ✗

Competency 007: *The teacher understands and applies principles and strategies for communicating effectively in varied teaching and learning contexts.*

22. Mr. Ramez is a fourth-grade teacher who has planned a Texas geography unit. He includes a teacher PowerPoint presentation, a whole-class discussion, a web quest activity, an Internet streaming video, and a series of multitasking activities. What is the most strategic advantage of this instructional plan?

(A) Such variety helps the teacher pace the lesson, as students are engaged in the variety of activities.

(B) The teacher can cover more content material in this manner, leaving time for students to engage in free-choice activities.

(C) It addresses the multiple learning approaches students may have in order to provide an optimal learning opportunity for all students.

(D) This approach helps a beginning teacher know that the content is well sequenced and will be presented in a logical manner.

23. A first-year ninth-grade teacher is concerned about whether his instruction will result in effective learning. What is the greatest benefit of his requiring students to write in a learning log their understanding/restatement of the lesson objective, what they know about the topic to be studied, and any questions they have about the topic?

(A) This approach will ensure that the planned follow-up learning activities will result in students getting the right answers on quizzes.

(B) Students will be more able to complete their work efficiently.

(C) It will facilitate students' development of a conceptual framework for the topic.

(D) This puts all students on an equal status at the beginning of the lesson.

29. What is a major guideline when developing any assessment of learning?

   (A) The assessment should focus on the defined learning goals and be carefully aligned with the instructional components previously taught.

   (B) Use only multiple-choice questions and ensure that they are written at various levels of cognition to assess all levels of learning.

   (C) Always include closed-ended and open-ended items on all assessments so students have an opportunity to use their opinions about what they have learned.

   (D) Design assessments that will result in a normal distribution of scores to determine each student's ranking in the class.

30. During the first six weeks of school, Heather applies her knowledge of the importance of teacher feedback. She writes the following note on one paper.

   > You have made a lot of progress in your writing skills. You are making fewer errors with those punctuation challenges you had. I've marked your errors in use of nouns and pronouns and would like for you to work on how to match the pronoun with the antecedent noun. Be sure a reader knows the reference noun for the pronoun.

   Based on what experts say about effective and corrective feedback, which of the following would be the best analysis of Heather's comments?

   (A) Her comments will likely be resented by the student, because there is little praise and the comment includes comments about errors. This will likely cause the student to be reluctant to make self-corrections on future work.

   (B) Heather's feedback might be effective because it equally balances comments about improvement and weaknesses; however, it might cause the student to believe she cannot please the teacher.

   (C) Such a comment will likely cause the student to be very confused about what the teacher wants, as it includes both positive and negative feedback. The student could think that the comment sends a mixed message.

   (D) Such a comment will likely encourage the student to continually pay attention to her work, because it both recognizes good work and informs the student about ways to continuously improve her work.

Competency 010: *The teacher monitors student performance and achievement; provides students with timely, high-quality feedback; and responds flexibly to promote learning for all students.*

31. At the beginning of the second semester, a parent calls Bonita to complain about the amount of homework his senior high student has. The parent states that the homework is "excessive and unrelated to what twelfth-grade students need to know." How can Bonita ensure that when she invites the parent in for a conference, the discussion will be productive and will result in a positive outcome for the student?

    (A) Ask the parent how much time he thinks the student should spend doing homework.
    (B) Dismiss what the parent says because this student and his parent are the only ones complaining about the homework.
    (C) Carefully listen to the parent and explain why and how the homework is important.
    (D) Explain to the parent that the homework is more than what other teachers require because students need to be getting ready for college work.

32. In order to involve the family in the overall community of learners she hopes to establish in her classroom, Martha, an eighth-grade English teacher, wants to encourage parents/guardians to be partners with her throughout the year. What would be an effective strategy for Martha to use at the beginning of the school year?

    (A) Bring the parents/guardians in the first week of school to review the textbooks and other instructional materials she will use throughout the year.
    (B) Inform parents of her expectations for students' academic success and engagement.
    (C) Send home a letter that describes developmental characteristics of eighth-graders.
    (D) Post a PowerPoint presentation on her web site that tells about her tests and grading policies.

33. As a beginning fourth-grade teacher, Carolyn is preparing to meet with Jamie's parents to discuss her performance on the recently administered fourth-grade TAKS. Which of the following should be Carolyn's primary emphasis during the meeting?

    (A) To show and discuss the TAKS report with the parents and ask the parents about their analysis of the report, the results for Jamie, and ways to work together.
    (B) To help Jamie's parents understand key principles of standardized assessment and how those principles might have impacted Jamie's performance.
    (C) To describe Jamie's academic strengths and needs as indicated by the assessment results and tell the parents how the teacher will address areas that need improvement.
    (D) To explain to the parents how Jamie compared with her grade-level peers by comparing scores with three of her peers.

Competency 011: *The teacher understands the importance of family involvement in children's education and knows how to interact and communicate effectively with families.*

34. Manuela learned the value of reading professional literature in her university teacher education program. She made a commitment to continue reading these materials. What is the *primary* benefit of this practice for Manuela?

    (A) Manuela can identify reading strategies for working with at-risk students in her classroom.
    (B) She can continuously be aware of current research and trends.
    (C) Reading may serve as a rewarding distraction from planning and grading.
    (D) Journal reading is a good support system for a new teacher.

35. Martha is concerned about the inclusion students she will have in her classroom this first year of her teaching. She has designed an exciting role-playing activity as part of a unit on literature genres. One of her inclusion eighth-graders has a significant physical disability that will impair her participation. What would be the best way for Martha to work with the special education inclusion teacher to resolve this concern?

    (A) Ask the inclusion teacher to come to class the day students role play so the teacher can work one-on-one with the student.
    (B) Have the special education teacher explain to the student that it would be better if she does not try to participate.
    (C) Work out a time that the special education teacher could meet individually with the student to help her complete the role-play assignment.
    (D) Ask the special education teacher to discuss the physical limitations this student has, as indicated on her IEP.

36. Before the school year begins, Austin meets with his mentor teacher to plan how to integrate library and technology skills throughout the year. He wants his twelfth-grade students to be able to complete their English research papers through the use of the library resources and electronic means. After they complete the overarching plans for the research requirements, Austin then asks to meet with the librarian to discuss appropriate tools and processes for research. To have a productive meeting, what information should he be prepared to share?

    (A) The purpose and learning goals for assigning the research project.
    (B) His knowledge of how to use the Internet for searching for resources.
    (C) The likely learning styles of the students he anticipates having this year.
    (D) A list of other resources students may use for the research project.

Competency 012: *The teacher enhances professional knowledge and skills by effectively interacting with other members of the educational community and participating in various types of professional activities.*

37. Martin carefully studied the Texas Educator's Code of Ethics in his education foundation class as an undergraduate. He is well aware of the ethical requirements imposed when administering the Texas Assessment of Knowledge and Skills (TAKS). Which of the following practices would be considered *unethical?*

   (A) Giving students a teacher-made practice test two weeks prior to the administration of the TAKS

   (B) Reading specific student questions on the TAKS test while students are answering the questions.

   (C) Explaining to the class what the directions for the different sections of the TAKS will be in order to prepare them for the actual test

   (D) Planning specific lessons targeting TAKS objectives in order to prepare students for the day of the test

38. During the discussion with his mentor about a research assignment, Austin states that he is thinking of taking a school laptop home to do some Internet research on his own. He plans to use the computer to write a novel he dreams of publishing some day. How does his intent align with aspects of legal/ethical uses of school property?

   (A) This is okay as long as he returns the equipment in good condition.

   (B) He will be okay as long as the equipment is not needed at school.

   (C) He can use school equipment only for authorized school business.

   (D) He may keep an unneeded school laptop for personal use as long as he does not change loaded software.

39. After two weeks of observation, Martha wishes to refer a new student for an evaluation to determine whether he could benefit from special education services. What *legal* step must first be taken before this type of evaluation can occur?

   (A) Martha should first observe the new student for a few more weeks.

   (B) Martha should contact the district special education coordinator to set up the evaluation schedule and to tell the coordinator what is the likely disability.

   (C) Martha should acquire written permission for the evaluation from the student's parents/guardians.

   (D) The district special education coordinator should first conduct an informal assessment to determine an initial diagnosis of the disability.

Competency 013: *The teacher understands and adheres to legal and ethical requirements for educators and is knowledgeable of the structure of education in Texas.*

Diagnostic and Sample Tests for Grades EC–12 **405**

Grades EC–12

Answer Key
DIAGNOSTIC TEST (GRADES EC–12)

Question Number	Correct Response	Competency	Question Number	Correct Response	Competency
1	B	001	21	B	007
2	A	001	22	C	008
3	A	001	23	C	008
4	D	002	24	C	008
5	C	002	25	C	009
6	A	002	26	C	009
7	C	003	27	B	009
8	C	003	28	C	010
9	D	003	29	A	010
10	D	004	30	D	010
11	D	004	31	C	011
12	D	004	32	B	011
13	C	005	33	A	011
14	C	005	34	B	012
15	C	005	35	D	012
16	C	006	36	A	012
17	C	006	37	B	013
18	A	006	38	C	013
19	C	007	39	C	013
20	A	007			

CORRECT RESPONSES

1. **B** She is exhibiting age-appropriate parallel play at the construction center. It is a mistake to read into a situation interpretations not supported by evidence, and there is no evidence for the other three possible answers.

2. **A** The strategy indicated in (A) will be effective with both concrete and formal operational students; the other three choices do not address developmental stages of students.

3. **A** Some high school students can be focused more on themselves, their peers, their environment, and the present than on their futures. It is sometimes difficult for a person of this age to consider long-range consequences of his or her present behaviors and choices. "I will be different" is a common reaction.

4. **D** It is important that special needs students understand that they are not alone; other students also have unique instructional needs. By interacting, everyone sees that each student brings both strengths and weaknesses to the learning environment. This is part of what makes them unique.

5. **C** Working with students to establish clear guidelines for acceptable classroom behaviors and language interactions and the consequences for not following them can reduce or eliminate the inappropriate behaviors and language. Attempting to keep groups of students separate or to ignore the problem will actually increase the negative behaviors and language that are producing the tension.

6. **A** By varying the types of assessments used, students are given multiple opportunities to exhibit their learning. Assessment of English Language learners should document areas of learning rather than areas where learning is still needed, which also helps encourage continued effort in a challenging situation.

7. **C** This is the step that needs to come first. Without a clear vision of the overall planning goal the team wishes to achieve, it is difficult to know how best to apportion instructional time to TEKS, skills, themes, topics.

8. **C** Addressing the required TEKS in an appropriate sequence to enhance student learning is at the heart of planning. Other steps and decisions may then come into play as the plan is developed.

9. **D** *Appreciation* is a challenging concept for assessment because it would typically result in a subjective rather than objective evaluation. While this area of growth is important, teachers do face challenges when deciding to assess affective domain elements. Catherine would be better served by rewriting her objective statement in a way that can be assessed objectively.

10. **D** Research indicates that active student engagement and reflective thinking as well as reflective writing are all effective ways to help students confirm and clarify their learning and to increase their ownership of the learning process. Barbara's use of these strategies indicates she is knowledgeable about how she can effectively help her students to process new information.

11. **D** This response includes student input into the evaluation process and helps them take ownership of learning and their work habits.

12. **D** The impact of the stress of a series of moves and of a new school environment on a student's behaviors must be considered.

13. **C** Encouraging students to stretch themselves through participation in goal setting and providing the needed support are part of guiding a student to meet high teacher expectations rather than focusing on areas where students can easily succeed without putting forth an appropriate amount of effort.

14. **C** The question posed helps some students activate their prior knowledge. No anticipated correct answer is implied by this open question.

15. **C** As a tool for evaluating classroom climate, Mary Ellen should focus on how engaged students are in the learning process. The main goal of instruction is the development of intellectual growth, so Mary Ellen should focus on how she provides opportunities for students to be involved and actively engaged in higher order thinking during the instructional process.

16. **C** Clarifying the roles is a clear signal from the teacher that all students are expected to be active and successful participants.

17. **C** By establishing clear guidelines and classroom routines during the initial week of school, Daryl sets the stage for high standards and high expectations for student learning and efficient use of time. By planning in advance with his mentor, Daryl makes sure he is clear in his own mind and prepared to clearly communicate guidelines and routines to his students to avoid ambiguity and confusion that could allow instructional time to be wasted.

18. **A** A major tenet of conflict resolution is to have the parties involved reach an acceptable solution. This is better than having a solution imposed by an outsider.

19. **C** This is the only choice that indicates value for individuals' risk-taking and signals an acceptance of more than one possible answer.

20. **A** When a teacher plans for open discussion among all students in the classroom, typically one of the major goals is for students to develop effective listening skills. The teacher's recognition that some students are not listening while others are talking indicates that she is aware of and can now address one challenge to guiding her students to better communication skills.

21. **B** A concrete example such as a plant with a damaged part will help trigger any prior knowledge and allow students to concretely observe the importance of the damaged part rather than learning abstractly about it.

22. **C** By using a variety of instructional strategies and approaches, the teacher assures that all learners have an optimal opportunity to engage in learning in ways that best meet their needs and preferences. Fourth-grade learners need to be exposed to as many approaches to learning as possible in order to address their developing styles and approaches to learning tasks.

23. **C** By having students write briefly about their understanding of the lesson's objective, any prior knowledge they might have, and their questions on the topic, the teacher is focusing on activation of prior knowledge, making connections with prior learning, and identifying any misunderstandings students may have as well as establishing student interest and buy-in.

24. **C** By receiving rapid feedback, students are able to track their growth as signaled by grades and teacher comments. This helps encourage them to stretch themselves, which would not happen if the feedback was delayed until it was no longer relevant to students.

25. **C** Student input into a rubric created before work on the project begins is an effective manner of insuring that all criteria concerning content focus and presentation style using technology are clear to students.

26. **C** At the high school level, most learners will be much more motivated to take responsibility for their learning if they are interested. Students enjoy using computers because they provide varied instruction.

27. **B** Concrete exploration is needed to provide motivation and active engagement in learning new skills. By allowing exploration of what the computer can do and be used for, the teacher provides an environment for creative and independent learning while students acquire grade-level appropriate skills.

28. **C** When teachers engage parents/guardians in sharing information about background and learning strengths, this helps ensure that parents consider themselves vital to the educational program of their children. Also, by asking parents to participate by providing this information, the teacher can gather useful information helpful in understanding the learners, especially from the perspective of the parents/guardians.

29. **A** It is critical that teachers design and develop assessments that are directly paired with learning goals and the concepts developed during instruction. As assessment items are written or alternative assessment methods are selected, these assessment strategies should be at multiple levels of difficulty and in varied formats. Most importantly, the teacher must assure that the items are carefully aligned with the instructional components taught.

30. **D** It follows a positive comment with a very specific plan for improving, which is one criterion for effective feedback.

31. **C** In a parent-teacher conference, the teacher should always first listen to the parent's concerns. The teacher should explain the purpose and value of the assigned homework so the parent may have a clear understanding of the teacher's instructional goals.

32. **B** School and family can best collaborate when clear communication of expectations is present to guide the collaboration.

33. **A** As the teacher explains the information contained in the report of the student's performance, the parents can identify the information provided by such assess-

ments. By examining the assessment results and by sharing ways the parents can work with the school to assist with the student's progress in the educational program, the teacher is engaging the parents in a partnership approach to optimal learning.

34. **B** To be a highly qualified and effective teacher, teachers must keep as current as possible with the latest trends and issues as identified by recent research. Reading professional journals is one of the most effective and expedient ways to stay abreast of current research and critical issues facing schools.

35. **D** The expertise of the special education teacher should be used to clearly understand the student's limitations so that an appropriate adaptation can be made to insure successful participation by this student.

36. **A** Regular classroom teachers frequently partner with specialists. To work most effectively with the librarian, Austin should provide information about the nature, purpose, and learning goals of the research assignment.

37. **B** The TAKS is a standardized test. So routines and practices must be explicitly followed during the administration. A teacher who responds to students' questions about a TAKS item, gives body language clues about how to answer a TAKS item, or even reads a question on a student's test booklet invalidates the standardization rules of the test. That teacher thus breaks the rules set out by the state for giving the test.

38. **C** Any property owned by the school (or district) must be used solely for professional purposes. Teachers must not use school property for their personal reasons, even if they "borrow" the equipment for only a short time or use it on school property.

39. **C** Without permission from the parent/guardian, no evaluation can be legally made.

Sample Test (Grades EC–12)

This sample test consists of practice questions to help you review as part of your preparation for the EC–12 PPR test. Please carefully read all the domains and competencies that will be tested on the EC–12 PPR test before beginning this test. Keep in mind that the competencies cover the range of EC–12 and thus include all competencies across the other three tests (EC–6, 4–8, and 8–12). As you read the domains and competencies, please think about the mind-set and philosophy of teaching they represent. In this sample test, each practice question is introduced by the competency being measured. The questions and competencies are presented in numerical order for the purpose of logical flow as you learn the competencies. When you reach the teacher decision sets near the end of this test, the sample questions will no longer address the competencies in numerical order. *Please be aware that competency statements will not appear on the actual test form and that the questions will not be presented in sequential order by competency numbers.*

Use the frame of reference built from your understanding of the domains and competencies as you select the single best answer for each question. It is recommended that you do an in-depth analysis of each possible answer before making your choice. After narrowing your possible choices to two answers, reread the question with each answer. This can help you ensure that your final choice answers exactly what the question is asking and is aligned with any information provided as background. Stay focused on the specific information provided by the question. Avoid reading more into the question or thinking of extenuating circumstances. In addition to selecting your preferred answer, it is recommended that you consider carefully why it is the best answer based on the domains and competencies. You should have a clear reason for rejecting each answer that is not chosen rather than just identifying and marking your preferred answer.

Following this sample test and answer key, a section on correct responses and rationales discusses the strengths and challenges of each of the possible answers. Refer back to the domains and competencies as you read the rationale for each possible response. Carefully examine the rationales for both the right and the wrong answer choices for the relationship to the domains and competencies.

Directions: Read each stimulus and answer every question. Mark your answers in the answer spaces on the accompanying grid.

Competency 001: *The teacher understands human developmental processes and applies this knowledge to plan instruction and ongoing assessment that motivate students and are responsive to their developmental characteristics and needs.*

1. Four-year old Lydia is having a tea party with her mother and grandmother. After pouring all the tea from the teapot into three cups, Lydia states that there is now more tea than before. How would her mother, who is a teacher, best interpret this incident?

   (A) Lydia has not yet developed object permanence.
   (B) Lydia is in the concrete operational stage of development.
   (C) Lydia has not yet developed conservation of liquid volume.
   (D) Lydia has not yet developed one-to-one correspondence.

2. Barbara Schulte has been assigned a classroom of second-grade students for her first year's teaching assignment. She is aware that Piaget suggested age ranges for his identified levels of cognitive development and that in any given classroom students' cognitive abilities/readiness may range over two or three grade levels. She has the students working with math manipulatives to learn addition and subtraction. Which of Piaget's stages has she recognized as typical of her second-grade students?

   (A) Second-grade students are most likely to be at the preoperational and/or concrete operational stages of development.
   (B) Second-grade students are most likely to be at the concrete operational and/or formal operational stages of development.
   (C) Second-grade students are most likely to be at the sensorimotor and/or concrete operational stages of development.
   (D) Second-grade students are most likely to be at the sensorimotor and/or preoperational stages of development.

3. The students in Ms. Bowman's seventh-grade class are a very diverse group. Her class includes both gifted and talented students as well as students who regularly spend time with the school's resource teacher. In addition, Ms. Bowman is aware that in any given classroom, the Piagetian cognitive abilities/readiness of students can range over two or three grade levels. How can Ms. Bowman best meet the needs of the range of cognitive variation found in her students?

(A) Assign students to groups based on their cognitive development or readiness level to make it easier for them to work successfully in small groups.

(B) Assign students "study buddies" to help students at lower cognitive levels achieve success by partnering them with students at higher cognitive levels.

(C) Target the instructional level toward the normal seventh-grade level of development and work with the students outside this range individually.

(D) Use high-engagement instructional strategies such as hands-on activities and projects to introduce and provide instruction on abstract concepts.

4. You overhear a high school junior telling a student in your math class that she plans to drop out of high school because it has no meaning for her. She plans to marry soon and sees no reason to continue with her education. Because you do not know the student planning to leave school, you ask your student to encourage her to discuss this with the high school counselor. What must the teacher and high school counselor be aware of about students at this age?

(A) Many students at this age are focused on present needs and desires rather than on long-term consequences.

(B) Many students at this age have not found a place in the school's society, and so they feel they do not fit in.

(C) Many students at this age are not able to apply logical reasoning patterns to planning their lives.

(D) Many students at this age do not recognize adults as being able to give valid advice to their age group.

Use the following information to answer questions 5 and 6.

As a fourth-year teacher, Ms. Sashay discovers during the first week of school that 12 of her 20 second-graders have limited English proficiency. There are nine languages other than English spoken in the homes of these students. As Ms. Sashay makes her plans for the new school year, she is very aware that she has a challenging student population and must revise the plans she used successfully last year.

Competency 002: *The teacher understands student diversity and knows how to plan learning experiences and design assessments that are responsive to differences among students and that promote all students' learning.*

5. Ms. Sashay wants to modify her plans, lessons, and assessments for her limited English proficiency students in ways that will address both their language needs and their learning. How can she best meet these goals?

   (A) Ms. Sashay should present lessons to these limited English proficiency students that address less demanding content and concept TEKS than the lessons for the other students.

   (B) Ms. Sashay should hold these limited English proficiency students to the same TEKS addressed in the lessons for the other students.

   (C) Ms. Sashay should present lessons drawn only from TEKS that can be presented with concrete materials to provide these students language development experiences with real objects.

   (D) Ms. Sashay should focus on English language acquisition with these limited English proficiency students and worry about their learning after their English fluency has improved.

6. When assessing the limited English proficiency students, which of the following plans will give Ms. Sashay the most accurate assessment of their learning?

   (A) Ms. Sashay should allow the limited English proficiency students to indicate to her how they are progressing in both their English and their learning. This should be done weekly so that they are not overwhelmed by the amount of material addressed.

   (B) Ms. Sashay should assess the limited English proficiency students more often than the others to ensure that they are keeping up with the rest of the class. She should hold tutoring sessions if they are not.

   (C) Ms. Sashay should assign each limited English proficiency student a "study buddy" who will help her assess them by sharing comments and observations about their knowledge and their English fluency.

   (D) Ms. Sashay should assess *all* her students using a wide range of assessment styles to allow each student many ways and multiple opportunities to demonstrate their learning and to make the limited English proficiency students feel part of the class.

7. What is most important as Ms. Bowman considers how to adapt her instructional strategies as she plans for her special-needs students?

   (A) Her instructional strategies must ensure that no group of students is singled out and made to feel different or isolated from the other students.

   (B) Her instructional strategies must ensure that each group of students has ample time to interact with other students at a similar cognitive level.

   (C) Her instructional strategies must ensure that students occasionally work individually but that collaborative efforts have a stronger focus to ensure the success of all students.

   (D) Her instructional strategies must ensure that students are allowed to select instructional activities based on individual interests and strengths.

8. Ms. Wong is the science teacher for a mixed-ability group of eighth-graders. She wants all her students to learn how to design and conduct simple science research. Ms. Wong wants all the students to improve their skill levels, their confidence, and their attitudes toward science. How can Ms. Wong best achieve her goals, especially with her lower-achieving students?

   (A) Ms. Wong can require all her students to design and complete a science research project that will be entered in the school science fair. Every science fair entrant will be given a ribbon for participation.

   (B) Ms. Wong can break scientific research into short, clear steps that guide students through the research process. Every class period will have some time set aside for working on the project and receiving teacher assistance.

   (C) Ms. Wong can partner students with complementary skill levels and interests. Higher achieving students working with lower-achieving students allows both types of students to grow, especially if Ms. Wong encourages flexibility in student participation and roles.

   (D) Ms. Wong can require each student to participate in active teaching lessons focused on the skills needed to conduct research. Each student must master each skill or repeat the lesson until mastery is achieved.

9. Since 9/11, a high school teacher has noticed tense relationships among diverse student groups. What would be the best strategy for reducing it?

   (A) Rewarding students who exhibit positive behaviors during the school day.

   (B) Using cooperative grouping during instruction to mix diverse students.

   (C) Involving students in developing interaction and behavioral guidelines.

   (D) Linking student attitudes and behaviors exhibited at school to grades.

10. A teacher planning to implement a major project with a mixed-ability group also wants to promote resiliency among the students. Which approach will be most effective in helping the teacher achieve this goal?

    (A) Give students a choice in topics and procedures used to do the research.
    (B) Break the project into subtasks and provide students with assistance as needed in planning and accomplishing these tasks.
    (C) Emphasize to students the need for following processes and procedures as they work on their projects.
    (D) Pair lower-achieving with higher-achieving students and allow these partnerships flexibility in how the project should be completed.

11. A high school teacher is aware that some of her students have had limited exposure to technological tools for which they now need a high level of skill. Which of the following strategies will allow the teacher to best respond to the missing skills of these students as they complete a project?

    (A) The teacher should allow students access to the computers and other media equipment available in the library.
    (B) The teacher should allow students to develop presentations that do not require the use of computer technology.
    (C) The teacher should provide students with access to written instructions for the use of all technologies available.
    (D) The teacher should form heterogeneous groups that have opportunities to explore all technologies available.

Use the following information to answer questions 12 and 13.

Following the first six weeks of school, Mr. Beaumont decides to read to his third-grade class for 15 minutes every day following lunch. He wants this listening time to provide a calming effect following the stimulation of the lunch break. He also wants to improve the listening skills of his students and to encourage their interest in and enthusiasm for oral language and reading in a listening context.

Competency 003: *The teacher understands procedures for designing effective and coherent instruction and assessment based on appropriate learning goals and objectives.*

12. What criteria are most important for selecting the books he will read to allow Mr. Beaumont to reach all his goals?

(A) Mr. Beaumont should select books that have a direct connection with content classes so that he does not lose 15 minutes of instructional time daily. His students will absorb content knowledge as they listen but will not really be aware they are learning.

(B) Mr. Beaumont should select books that describe events and settings that are new to his students. This will expand the learning horizons of the students as they encounter new and unexpected events with which they are presently unfamiliar.

(C) Mr. Beaumont should select books that are interesting and familiar to his students. This will hold their interest more effectively and make it easier for them to be attentive.

(D) Mr. Beaumont should select books that are on a topic that is not too exciting. They should also be focused on word play and patterns such as puns, rhyming words, and alliteration.

13. How can Mr. Beaumont best assess the effectiveness of this daily listening time in meeting his stated goals?

(A) After three weeks, Mr. Beaumont can claim that a scheduling conflict prevents having the listening time for three days. By observing the students' reactions, he can assess their affective response to oral language and reading in the oral context.

(B) After three weeks, Mr. Beaumont can add a short set of verbal questions to the listening time. By asking about what is recalled or for predictions about future events, he can assess students' listening and thinking skills and attentiveness.

(C) After three weeks, Mr. Beaumont can ask students if they wish to continue with the book currently being read or shift to another one. Based on their responses, he can judge if they are enjoying the book and learning from it.

(D) After three weeks, Mr. Beaumont can give a short quiz to determine if individuals are attentive and using effective listening skills. He can also gain information about the affective value of the book.

14. An elementary school has decided not to shift to a departmental model but rather to form instructional teams. The fifth-grade team is planning to meet during the summer to develop integrated interdisciplinary units for next year. What needs to happen first to facilitate their planning?

(A) The fifth-grade instructional team needs to compile the teaching strengths and favorite units of each team member to determine appropriate themes.

(B) The fifth-grade instructional team needs to list units and topics from which they expect positive student responses so that they can determine themes.

(C) The fifth-grade instructional team needs to map out the required curriculum and look for overlapping skills and content topics to determine appropriate possible themes.

(D) The fifth-grade instructional team needs to establish how long they want each unit to last so that they will know how many themes will be needed.

15. In July, Ms. Lopez asks for the state's assessment results for last year's fifth-grade class. As the sixth-grade teacher, she wants this information before she begins to plan the coming year. How can Ms. Lopez best use this information?

(A) Ms. Lopez can use this information to diagnose problems or weaknesses these students have with the style of assessment used so that she can work to improve their testing skills in sixth grade.

(B) Ms. Lopez can use this information to establish instructional groups based on the skill levels of the students as shown by the state assessment so that she can work to strengthen their weak areas.

(C) Ms. Lopez can use this information to plan instruction dedicated to areas of weakness in required skills and knowledge diagnosed by the past year's test while also addressing the sixth-grade information required by the state.

(D) Ms. Lopez can use this information to determine which skills and knowledge required by the state her students have not yet achieved so that she can start the school year by asking for parental help in these areas.

16. A learning goal for a ninth-grade class states, "Students will appreciate the aesthetic beauty of music from a variety of western and eastern cultures." What is the most significant problem with this learning goal?

    (A) The desired outcome indicated by the learning goal is unattainable as ninth-graders are so into their music that they are not open to other types.

    (B) It will be difficult to find or create instructional activities that will appeal to and motivate ninth-graders to achieve this learning goal.

    (C) This learning goal does not indicate the prior content knowledge the ninth-graders must have to be able to meet this aesthetic learning goal.

    (D) This aesthetic learning goal is difficult to apply objective and meaningful assessment to, and so it will be difficult to determine if it has been met.

17. A middle school principal creates a team of teachers to help him plan campus wide staff development for the second semester. He explains to the team that his goal is to provide teachers efficient professional learning opportunities rather than requiring that they attend sessions/workshops that may have little immediate impact on their students' achievement. What is this principal's main reason for taking this approach to staff development?

    (A) The approach allows the team to suggest professional learning opportunities that will be most effective for meeting campus teachers' specific and immediate needs.

    (B) Including teachers as part of the planning team assures that all teachers will commit to whatever is planned.

    (C) By focusing on professional learning workshops that directly apply to teachers' immediate needs, the principal uses school resources efficiently and effectively.

    (D) Because the team of teachers know what their colleagues need, the planning team will definitely plan appropriate staff development.

Use the following information to answer questions 18 and 19.

Following the winter break, Paula transfers from out of state into Mr. Stewart's first-grade class. Paula will be 7 in February, and both her parents and her transferred school records indicate that she is developmentally advanced in social skills. During the first week, all of Mr. Stewart's observations of Paula cause him to question the accuracy of the developmentally advanced label for Paula as her social behaviors and play seem more appropriate for a student beginning kindergarten. Mr. Stewart is considering contacting the parents and explaining that Paula has been mislabeled as socially advanced.

Competency 004: *The teacher understands learning processes and factors that impact student learning and demonstrates this knowledge by planning effective, engaging instruction and appropriate assessments.*

18. What is Mr. Stewart's best action plan at this time?

(A) Mr. Stewart should give Paula additional time to adjust to the new school while keeping a close eye on her social skills.

(B) Because Mr. Stewart knows that states have different educational standards, he should contact her previous school to determine the differences.

(C) Mr. Stewart should contact Paula's parents and inform them she has been mislabeled because she came from a developmentally delayed class.

(D) Mr. Stewart, knowing expectations vary, should accept that Paula is a developmentally delayed student and say nothing to avoid upsetting her parents.

19. How can Mr. Stewart best establish an accurate assessment of Paula's social developmental level before visiting with her parents to discuss her adjustment to the new school?

(A) Mr. Stewart should talk privately with Paula and let her know that her behaviors are unacceptable and that he knows from her prior school records that she can do much better.

(B) Mr. Stewart should quietly and calmly call Paula's attention to students showing the social behaviors and play habits he expects from her and ask her to emulate them.

(C) Mr. Stewart should not delay in contacting Paula's parents to request additional information about her social development and to ask for their assistance in forming a more accurate picture.

(D) Mr. Stewart should assign Paula two students to guide her and orient her to the new school over the next week while observing to see what effect increased comfort and familiarity have on her social skills.

20. After two years of teaching, Mr. Rivera wishes to improve his use of cooperative learning groups in his fourth-grade classroom. He has attended a district workshop on effective planning and implementation of groups. He has planned to use groups at the beginning of the next school year. What will be the most effective way for him to implement the jigsaw cooperative learning strategy for a unit focused on Texas history?

(A) Place students in groups at the beginning of the unit on Texas history. After forming home groups to study specific regions of Texas, have students then form expert groups to research certain topics. These topics can include landforms, Native-American tribes, natural resources, and so on.

(B) Ask students to form their own groups. Explain to them that within each group will be subgroups. Each subgroup will need to identify a particular area of study and report back to the original group as experts.

(C) Assign students according to ability level to study elements of the Texas history unit. Explain that each group will receive a group grade and an individual grade, based on the participation and behavior management of the group.

(D) Ask students to identify what parts of Texas history they wish to study. Then form groups according to student interest. After groups are formed, give students general guidelines for what product they are to produce that will depict their learning about Texas history.

Competency 005: *The teacher knows how to establish a classroom climate that fosters learning, equity, and excellence and uses this knowledge to create a physical and emotional environment that is safe and productive.*

21. Ms. Gonzales is a second-grade teacher. The school guidance counselor tells her that her class has a high number of students with significant academic needs. How can Ms. Gonzales avoid becoming a barrier to success for these students with significant academic needs?

(A) Ms. Gonzales should set high standards, differentiate instruction, and have high expectations for all students regardless of their levels of academic need.

(B) Ms. Gonzales must collect information on ethnicity, socioeconomic status, at-risk status, or parental education levels.

(C) Ms. Gonzales should understand that some students face social challenges and take this into account as she plans instruction and expectations for them.

(D) Because all the students are in the same grade and attended this school last year, she should instruct them all in the same way.

22. At the end of the first three weeks of school, a high school math teacher has determined that the students in her second-period class differ significantly in their current levels of knowledge and skill because of their varied prior experiences with mathematics instruction and use. What assessment system can best create a positive and supportive learning environment for all her students?

    (A) Including both teacher and peer assessments of performance in feedback to the students.

    (B) Assigning students appropriate and varied assessment standards based on their ability groups.

    (C) Making progress, process, and product all part of the assessment used to determine student grades.

    (D) Including test questions at varying levels of difficulty to ensure that all students achieve some success.

23. By the end of her first year of teaching, a seventh-grade teacher has serious concerns about the classroom climate. She reflects on the times that some students expressed bias toward others, that some students chose acting-out behaviors to get attention, and that some students spoke caustic "put-down" remarks to their peers. While she recognizes that these may be somewhat expected behaviors for students at this age, she has a strong desire to create a safer and more productive emotional climate for next year. What is a primary strategy that she might consider to reach her goal?

    (A) Allow students to rearrange their groups for their second and third unit of study, if they wish, so that they can work more closely with those with whom they feel comfortable.

    (B) Place students in specific groups according to gender, ethnicity, and ability to ensure that similar students are together in hopes of making them feel safer and to encourage them to treat each other with respect.

    (C) Randomly assign students to groups. Explain to the groups that they must not act with bias.

    (D) In the second and third units of study for next year, change the mixture of cooperative learning groups so that all students have opportunity to get to know a cross section of their peers rather than forming cliques or working only in the same clique.

24. Ms. de la Cruz wants to use her students' learning journals to help her evaluate the classroom climate. Which question is most important for Ms. de la Cruz to consider as she reads her students' learning journals?

   (A) Is there ongoing whole class accountability of student learning in my classroom?

   (B) Is my educational philosophy clearly reflected in my daily instructional styles?

   (C) Are my students actively engaged and intellectually stimulated by my lessons?

   (D) Are the learning experiences my students encounter varied to meet the needs of all?

Competency 006: *The teacher understands strategies for creating an organized and productive learning environment and for managing student behavior.*

25. As an elementary teacher dealing with student conflicts on a daily basis, what should be your primary student conflict resolution goal?

   (A) The goal should be to determine which student is at fault and deal with the behavior that caused the conflict.

   (B) The goal should be to end the conflict and refocus students on instructional tasks in as short a time as possible.

   (C) The goal should be for you to have a clear understanding of the problem and issue a settlement fair to all involved.

   (D) The goal should be to guide the students involved toward an amicable and agreeable settlement.

Use the following information to answer questions 26 and 27.

As a first-year teacher, Ms. Sanderson is concerned that her sixth-grade students are not using good self-management skills. She asks her mentor to suggest other strategies to help students improve their self-control. The mentor suggests that Ms. Sanderson implement additional management strategies. For example, when students are off task or disrupting other students' learning, she can use proximity as a behavior management strategy. Each time a student chooses an inappropriate behavior, Ms. Sanderson should move near the student and continue the lesson she is teaching.

26. Why is this strategy appropriate for use with adolescent students?

   (A) Proximity control leads students to understand that the teacher is in charge of what happens in the classroom.

   (B) The use of proximity control helps increase students' awareness of the teacher's interest in and monitoring of their behavior.

   (C) Students become uncomfortable when the teacher is near, so they naturally improve their behavior.

   (D) Students like the teacher to stand near their desks so they can get immediate help or have increased attention.

27. What additional strategy can Ms. Sanderson implement to help students be more successful with their self-control and behavior management?

   (A) She can orally remind students they need to make good choices or lose privileges.
   (B) She can place students who continually choose inappropriate behaviors with other students who need her immediate attention.
   (C) She can assign clear roles and responsibilities for tasks where success depends on each student meeting the role responsibilities.
   (D) She can assign roles and responsibilities based on skills and abilities and can focus on individual behavior as the major part of the grade.

28. Mr. Argufy is a first-year teacher being mentored by Ms. Cooper, a 12-year veteran from across the hall. Before school begins, Ms. Cooper delivers what she calls her standard "learn to work smart rather than hard" lecture for new teachers. She explains that the school has invested a lot of resources in technology and that teachers do not always use it effectively. Which routine task would Mr. Argufy select that could be done more efficiently with a spreadsheet program?

   (A) Lesson and unit plan development would be more time-efficient with a spreadsheet program.
   (B) Keeping daily attendance and tardiness records would be more time-efficient with a spreadsheet program.
   (C) Using a weighted formula to compute student averages would be more time-efficient with a spreadsheet program.
   (D) Keeping track of parent-teacher communication such as signed forms would be more time-efficient with a spreadsheet program.

Use the following information to answer questions 29 and 30.

During the opening week of school, an eighth-grade teacher spends some of her daily instructional time on emphasizing her expectations that students know and follow her classroom rules, routines, and procedures. She devotes time to this because she feels that this is an area where middle school students encounter problems that have a negative impact on their learning.

29. Why is it a major advantage to spend time early in the school year to ensure that students understand and follow classroom routines?

   (A) Ensuring that students understand and follow classroom routines promotes the effective use of instructional and learning time.
   (B) Ensuring that students understand and follow classroom routines creates a sense of certainty for students and a more positive attitude.
   (C) Ensuring that students understand and follow classroom routines reduces management demands and so creates more planning time.
   (D) Ensuring that students understand and follow classroom routines reduces confusion and allows for easier student monitoring.

30. When this teacher is working with two students on resolving a conflict that resulted from ignoring one of the classroom procedures, what should be her primary goal?

(A) A primary goal of conflict resolution should be to guide students toward reaching a mutually agreeable settlement.

(B) A primary goal of conflict resolution should be for the teacher to make the final call, providing a solution that is fair to both students.

(C) A primary goal of conflict resolution should be to determine which student is the initiator and which student is the victim.

(D) A primary goal of conflict resolution should be for the teacher to provide noninvolved, sympathetic third-party arbitration.

Competency 007: *The teacher understands and applies principles and strategies for communicating effectively in varied teaching and learning contexts.*

31. Following a PDAS observation, your evaluator notifies you that your behaviors vary between two groups of students. You provide higher-achieving students significantly longer wait time than you provide lower-achieving students. In addition, with lower-achieving students you restate a question as many as three times during the same amount of wait time you give higher-achieving students. Both types of students perceive your restated questions as new questions. How is this practice most likely to affect your classroom?

(A) Increased wait time for higher-achieving students indicates to all students that you expect more from these top students, and this will produce resentment in both groups.

(B) Shorter wait time and restating questions send signals to all students about differentiated expectation levels and will reinforce a feeling of inability to achieve success in lower-achieving students.

(C) Shorter wait time allows lower-achieving students less time to feel that they are "on the spot," and the restated questions indicate to all students that you are giving lower-achieving students more opportunities to succeed.

(D) A difference in wait time is an effective instructional differentiation method to allow both groups success opportunities by providing needed think and respond time.

32. Ms. Johnson wants to introduce her third-graders to activities requiring them to use problem-solving skills. She knows she must actively teach her students how to succeed with this type of task rather than just assigning it. As her students first engage in a problem-solving activity, what approach will be most effective?

    (A) Ms. Johnson should ask questions until she is able to guide her students toward finding the correct answer.

    (B) As motivation, Ms. Johnson should promise a prize to the student who finds the correct answer first.

    (C) Ms. Johnson should encourage her students to approach the problem in varied ways to find a solution.

    (D) Ms. Johnson should use concrete examples from the students' lives to guide them as they find the answer.

Use the following information to answer questions 33 and 34.

After observing your class every day for a week, your mentor indicates that she has noted the amount of instructional time your students spend writing in their journals or learning logs. She asks you to explain your rationale for this large instructional time investment in the logs. You agree that students are making a large investment by writing much more than their answers. For each new topic, you require students to paraphrase the stated objective, identify their prior knowledge of the topic, and list any questions they have about the topic.

33. When you repond to your mentor, what is the greatest benefit you share for having students write this information in their log?

    (A) The information required in the logs helps student access their prior knowledge of a topic and start from a more uniform perspective.

    (B) The information required in the logs helps focus students on the lesson content so they can score higher on unit quizzes.

    (C) The information required in the logs focuses students on the lesson, which allows more students to complete the lesson in the set time.

    (D) The information required in the logs help students develop a conceptual framework for the topic.

34. When discussing with your mentor the effectiveness of a class discussion, which of the following aspects of the discussion should receive the greatest focus during the meeting?

(A) The teacher ignored the fact that students repeatedly told each other that they were wrong.

(B) The teacher ignored the fact that students directed comments to one another rather than to her.

(C) The teacher ignored the fact that students added to the discussion without waiting to be called on.

(D) The teacher ignored the fact that students did not listen to their classmates during the discussion.

A history teacher concludes a lecture about the War Between the States in the following manner.

> **"I hope you are aware that we have spent the past two weeks examining the causes of the War Between the States. We have determined the reasons the North gave for the war and the reasons the South entered the war. Next we will explore the perspective of allies of both the North and South and the reasons they gave for selecting a side to support. Some of the rationales have been alluded to as we have moved through the prior material."**

35. What is the primary reason a teacher would conclude a lecture in this way?

(A) A lecture conclusion made by a teacher should be clear and short and restate the main points.

(B) A lecture conclusion should guide students toward establishing relationships between main points.

(C) A lecture conclusion should restate the key concepts the teacher expects students to be able to identify.

(D) A lecture conclusion should guide students toward recognizing the relevance of the content within their lives.

36. A middle school science teacher is planning a unit on energy transformations within ecological systems. She wants to select teaching strategies that will help her students understand this abstract yet important basic science concept. Which teaching strategy would her students find most helpful in learning this concept?

    (A) She should ensure that time is built into the unit for her to revisit and repeat these abstract concepts and also allow time for student questions to enhance clarity.

    (B) She should begin the lesson with a K-W-L chart to explore student prior knowledge of the topic and include in the unit plan a reminder to revisit the L-column of the chart.

    (C) She should share concrete examples from the context of her students' life experiences and ask them to contribute additional examples with which they are familiar.

    (D) She should begin the lesson with a list of relevant terms students will encounter during the unit and have them define each as it occurs during the unit.

Competency 008: *The teacher provides appropriate instruction that actively engages students in the learning process.*

37. Ms. Swirczynski notices that Pat is having trouble understanding the history chapter she has assigned her third-graders. She asks Pat to meet with her and describe what he has read. What is the main benefit of Ms. Swirczynski's approach to helping Pat?

    (A) Ms. Swirczynski's approach helps Pat develop a sense of ownership toward learning.

    (B) Ms. Swirczynski's approach allows her to provide instruction specific to Pat's needs.

    (C) Ms. Swirczynski's approach encourages Pat to focus on the task.

    (D) Ms. Swirczynski's approach encourages Pat to apply higher-order thinking skills to the task.

38. Mr. Flavid plans an integrated unit for his second-grade class that addresses science, math, social studies, reading, and art. His lessons will be both whole class and small group. He has included a guest speaker, a field trip, a web quest, and a video as part of the unit. What is the most important instructional advantage of Mr. Flavid's plan?

    (A) Mr. Flavid's plan allows students multiple and varied opportunities to process, internalize, and reinforce the unit's content.

    (B) Mr. Flavid's plan allows the teacher to address a large amount of content information in a shorter amount of time.

    (C) Mr. Flavid's plan allows him flexibility in pacing the lessons to meet the needs of students with different ability levels.

    (D) Mr. Flavid's plan allows him to individualize instruction to meet the needs of students with different ability levels.

39. Timeliness and a strong commitment to a job well done are very important to Ms. Koradji, a middle school teacher. From day one, she has repeatedly stated to her students that she gets her work done in a timely manner and expects the same from them. She models her commitment by returning graded assignments within one or two days of collecting them. What is the greatest benefit of this attitude and practice to Ms. Koradji's students?

   (A) Ms. Koradji is modeling effective work habits that also encourage her students to increase their expectations of themselves and improve their own performances.

   (B) Ms. Koradji is modeling effective work habits that also allow her students and their families to keep track of their performance levels through the returned grades.

   (C) Ms. Koradji is modeling effective work habits while monitoring her students' completion of assignments to ensure that no student falls behind on handing in work.

   (D) Ms. Koradji is modeling effective work habits that also encourage her students to improve their own work habits, which will be very important to their success in high school.

Use the following information to answer questions 40 and 41.

The day after 9/11 students arrive in social studies class wanting to discuss the event. The class has strong opinions about the cause of 9/11 and what response they feel would be appropriate for the government to take. The class is not scheduled to discuss world violence and tolerance toward differences until a unit scheduled for two months from now.

40. In a social studies class, a lot of curriculum must be covered. However, the students are very interested in a current event. They want to discuss it instead of the planned topic. What action should this social studies teacher take?

   (A) Explain to students that although this topic is directly related to the social studies curriculum, the best place for them to express their emotional concerns and to ask their questions is at home.

   (B) Find a way to connect this event to one of the social studies units. Move that unit forward in order to allow students to devote as much time as needed to explore all aspects of this current event.

   (C) Remind students that the social studies curriculum is already packed with content that must be covered, but promise to allow a limited time for discussion if students stay focused on the planned lesson.

   (D) Suggest that students talk with each other after class or discuss this issue with their parents since not enough time is left to have a serious discussion about the topic.

41. Based on the comments from the class about an appropriate response by the U.S. government, how can the teacher guide students toward applying skills that will assist them in becoming lifelong learners using this high-interest topic?

    (A) Have students examine the available information on the event and classify it as factual or emotional and discuss the potential impact on the government's response.
    (B) Split students into two teams and have them conduct a mock debate to guide the government in making a decision about its response.
    (C) Brainstorm potential responses the government could make and poll the school to see which response is favored and why.
    (D) Encourage students to select the possible response they support and write a clear rationale for their position supported by evidence.

42. A life science teacher routinely asks her students to write an explanation of what they think is the objective or point of the experiment they are about to do and what procedures they will need to follow to successfully achieve this objective. What is the greatest benefit of this advance writing activity to students?

    (A) This writing activity gives all students an equal opportunity for success with the assignment because they all now have the same background.
    (B) This writing activity increases the chances that all students will follow the directions and the experiments will have the desired outcome.
    (C) This writing activity assists students in developing a conceptual framework about the purpose of the experiment and guides their learning.
    (D) This writing activity increases student focus on the lesson and allows them to work quickly and efficiently because confusion is reduced.

Competency 009: *The teacher incorporates the effective use of technology to plan, organize, deliver, and evaluate instruction for all students.*

43. What is the primary rationale for including computer instruction in a preschool classroom?

    (A) Computer instruction helps young children develop fine motor skills faster as they are very motivated by computers.
    (B) Very young children do not have the fine motor skills for clear letter formation but computers overcome this.
    (C) Very young children are naturally curious and ready to begin to explore the uses and capabilities of computers.
    (D) Very young children need to lay a foundation for the future acquisition of computer skills needed for success in school.

44. Mr. Nagoya schedules his second-grade class into the computer lab three times a week. What is the most important technology principle related to this use of instructional time?

   (A) Drill and practice software allow Mr. Nagoya to instruct his students on content while also helping them acquire strong computer skills.

   (B) The interests of Mr. Nagoya's students should determine the software he has them use because motivation improves learning.

   (C) Mr. Nagoya should give direct instruction on computer skills in a carefully planned sequence of lessons during each visit.

   (D) Mr. Nagoya should primarily present and have students practice computer skills within the context of other content lessons.

45. A middle school teaching team has students working on an integrated unit where the final product will be a multimedia presentation by individual students. Each teacher has established clear content requirements to be included in the end product as they want content to receive a greater emphasis than presentation design. How can the teachers most effectively encourage the appropriate balance between content and presentation design?

   (A) Students and teachers should work together to design a rubric that establishes the content and design expectations and the balance between these two components in the final product before the project begins.

   (B) The teachers should share a list of acceptable product design suggestions that students can select from after the content part of the project is completed so that the design aspect of the project does not get out of hand.

   (C) Students must submit a draft of the content portion of the project to the teacher for approval before beginning the project design component, which must also be approved.

   (D) All teachers should provide daily reminders of the expected balance between content and project design as students work on completing the required individual final product.

46. A high school teacher has her students preparing presentations about important natural disasters that occurred during the eighteenth century. At least one visual is required as part of the presentation. Several students ask the librarian to assist them in downloading color pictures, and she reminds them to cite their sources. What is the main reason for citing a source?

    (A) Scholastic and creative efforts must always be attributed to their originators.
    (B) Without a citation, it is difficult for the student or the teacher to locate the information for later use.
    (C) If the validity of the picture needs to be verified, the citation will be needed.
    (D) The citation allows the class to build a catalog of valuable resources for later use.

Competency 010: *The teacher monitors student performance and achievement; provides students with timely, high-quality feedback; and responds flexibly to promote learning for all students.*

47. What would be the best way to assess the benefits of placing students in groups for an inquiry project?

    (A) Monitor and record how often each member of the group makes contributions to the project.
    (B) Survey students to determine their preferences for working in groups in order to complete the inquiry project.
    (C) Ask a colleague to give you her opinion of how well groups work for inquiry projects.
    (D) Observe students as they work on the project to evaluate the benefits of the group work.

48. Susan's mother wants to be active in her preschooler's education and approaches her teacher, Ms. Biggs, about how to become involved. What would be an appropriate role for Susan's mother to fill in the classroom?

    (A) Ms. Biggs could ask Susan's mother to provide observational information about Susan's activities outside school. Ms. Biggs could help with materials, supplies, and phone calls during or after class.
    (B) Ms. Biggs could ask Susan's mother to attend class and collect observational data about the students and their peer interactions within the classroom setting because two observers see twice as much.
    (C) Ms. Biggs could ask Susan's mother to focus on Susan's personal and social growth and leave Susan's cognitive or academic growth to Ms. Biggs as she is the expert in these areas because of her certification.
    (D) Ms. Biggs should calmly and professionally explain to Susan's mother that parents are not expected to play a role in a child's education, which should be handled by the school because the parent already has a role.

49. What is most important if you want an appropriately designed test?

    (A) The test should yield a bell curve for the range of student scores.
    (B) The test should align with objectives and content-learning opportunities.
    (C) The test should include questions at several levels of difficulty.
    (D) The test should use both objective and performance assessment questions.

50. A middle school English teacher is working with her students on clarity in writing as they prepare book reports. She has each student complete a book report and give it to a peer for editing. Then she looks at all the edited reports before returning them to the writers. On one report, she writes, "I agree with your peer editor that some of your sentences are hard to follow or understand. You are using very complex, compound sentences, which is a very sophisticated level of writing but might not be appropriate for clarity with your peers. How can you simplify and still write on an advanced and sophisticated level?" Based on the research on instructional feedback, what will be the *most* likely response to this teacher's note?

    (A) The comment to the author of the book report will probably be ineffective in prompting improvement as the feedback gives a negative response followed by a positive response about using sophisticated writing and does not give clear suggestions about how to make appropriate changes.
    (B) The comment to the author of the book report will probably be effective in prompting improvement as the feedback gives a positive response about using a sophisticated writing style, which counterbalances being told that some sentences are hard to understand, and so they will readily make suggested changes.
    (C) The comment to the author of the book report will probably be effective in prompting improvement as the feedback gives a positive response about using a sophisticated writing style and encourages the writer to find ways to improve, which counterbalances being told that some sentences are hard to understand.
    (D) The comment to the author of the book report will probably be effective in prompting improvement as the feedback gives a negative response followed by a positive response about using a sophisticated writing style and allows freedom in deciding how to make appropriate changes.

Competency 011: *The teacher understands the importance of family involvement in children's education and knows how to interact and communicate effectively with families.*

51. A ninth-grade teacher wants to encourage students to learn to apply in their daily life math concepts that they learn in school. Her plan is to do this through family math time at home. What is the best way to motivate families and facilitate the establishment of family math time?

(A) The teacher should send home a textbook and an assignment sheet explaining the importance of family math time and ask that it become part of their family interaction during the week.

(B) The teacher should send home an invitation to participate in family math time with an explanation of the requirements and activities for the family to complete together.

(C) The teacher should conduct seminars in the evenings to help parents understand how their ninth-grade students have changed since middle school and how family math time can help.

(D) The teacher should send home notification of a meeting at which the value of family math time, instructional methods used in school, and assessment rubrics are explained.

52. A parent has called and scheduled a conference with you to discuss some concerns. What is the best way to ensure a productive conference?

(A) When the parent arrives, clearly and calmly state your perspective and then listen to the parent's response.

(B) Prepare yourself before the parent arrives by determining why this parent wants a conference when others do not.

(C) Be friendly as you greet the parent and then listen closely to the parent's concerns and perspective before responding.

(D) When the parent arrives, clearly identify why you agree with the parent that this conference is necessary.

53. What is an important educational principle for Mr. Wu to remember as he has his first parent-teacher conference to discuss a student's difficulties?

(A) Mr. Wu should make it very clear that he cannot solve the problem and that the parents have a responsibility to ensure that their student overcomes difficulties at school.

(B) Mr. Wu should downplay the problem situation by indicating areas of student success so that the parents do not overreact and see the difficulty as more than it is before Mr. Wu can solve it.

(C) As Mr. Wu clearly explains to the parents the difficulty being experienced by the student, he should take care to present the information so that it is clear that he is not judging the family.

(D) Mr. Wu should keep the conference focused on the difficulties at school and keep the parents from complicating the situation by adding information about the student's activities outside school.

54. A high school principal believes teachers and parents/guardians should be partners working together to ensure the best possible education for students. He shares this philosophy with his teachers as they prepare to begin a new school year. Because his teachers agree, what is the best information for them to share with their students' families at the beginning of the year?

    (A) Teachers should discuss with the families the expectations for student academic performance and how they can guide students together.

    (B) Teachers should inform the families about the instructional resources available to students and the major projects that will be required during the coming school year.

    (C) Teachers should compare the relationship between scores from the teacher-made tests the school will use during the year and scores from state-required tests.

    (D) Teachers should inform families of the developmental levels and traits of secondary students and how they produce behaviors different from those of middle school students.

55. Ms. Ming wants to arrange a progress conference with Ms. Garcia, Carmen's mother. Ms. Garcia cancels two scheduled appointments and fails to show for a third one. Because Ms. Ming is very frustrated but still determined to speak with Ms. Garcia about Carmen's progress, what should she do next?

    (A) When she schedules the fourth conference with Ms. Garcia, Ms. Ming should emphasize how very important this meeting is and indicate how disappointed she will be if it does not occur.

    (B) Ms. Ming should accept that for some reason Ms. Garcia is extremely reluctant to attend a conference at the school and arrange a time to discuss Carmen's progress over the phone.

    (C) Ms. Ming should accept that all parents are not interested in their child's educational progress and stop trying to force Ms. Garcia to care and to participate.

    (D) Ms. Ming should ask Carmen to communicate to her mother how important this conference is, share her embarrassment when her mom doesn't attend, and encourage her mother's participation.

Use the following information to answer questions 56 and 57.

Mr. Blackwell agrees to a conference requested by one of his fifth-grade students. Molly's parents wish to discuss her continual tardiness to class and the resulting detentions. He explains to the parents the importance of Molly arriving at class on time each day in order to participate in all class activities and not miss any explanations or assignments. Mr. Blackwell asks for the parents' support. They state that they understand. They agree that Molly needs to handle her time better so she will have fewer detentions and not miss important school information. They discuss possible reasons why Molly is not getting to class on time even though she rides the bus to school each day.

56. What is the most important suggestion Mr. Blackwell can make to Molly's parents to help them guide Molly toward more appropriate behavior?

(A) Suggest that the parents surpervise Molly getting her materials together each night in order to be prepared for the next day.

(B) Work with Molly to design a checklist of items she will need for her first-period class so that she has all materials in her backpack or knows what to pull from her locker.

(C) Suggest to the parents they they stress to Molly her responsibility for getting herself to class on time each day and ask her if she understands why they are upset with her.

(D) Keep a written record of the number of times Molly is tardy to her first-period class. Compare this log to the arrival times of other students who ride the bus.

57. What action should Mr. Blackwell take to help Molly's parents monitor her progress?

(A) Post an arrival time checklist in a visible location in the classroom so that Molly can see the status of her progress.

(B) Have Molly record on a chart her arrival time at class each day. Send this information home each Friday so her parents can keep a close check on Molly's progress.

(C) Have Molly take home for her parents a weekly report of her daily progress. The parents must sign and return the weekly report.

(D) Remind all the students of the necessity of being in class on time. Encourage them to think about why they need to be responsible for their arrival time.

Competency 012: *The teacher enhances professional knowledge and skills by effectively interacting with other members of the educational community and participating in various types of professional activities.*

58. Ms. Wolf, an English teacher, asks to meet with the technology coordinator. Ms. Wolf has weak technological skills yet wants her students to use technology as part of an upcoming class project. Her students' technological skills range widely. In order to team with the technology coordinator in planning this student project, what information is most important for her to share?

(A) Ms. Wolf should make the technology coordinator completely aware of the gaps in her technological skills.

(B) Ms. Wolf should make the technology coordinator aware of the goals and requirements of the project.

(C) Ms. Wolf should make the technology coordinator aware of the gaps in her students' technological skills.

(D) Ms. Wolf should make the technology coordinator aware of how students will be grouped to complete the project.

59. When Mr. Grant discovered how limited resources are at his new school, he decided to establish business community–school partnerships like the ones at his last school. What should be his first step in establishing this collaborative effort to improve school resources?

(A) Mr. Grant should first become comfortable with the families of his students and learn about the community.

(B) Mr. Grant should immediately contact community businesses and ask for resources to meet the school's needs.

(C) Mr. Grant should make the school administration aware of the problem and of his intention to personally address it.

(D) Mr. Grant should determine which large companies employ community members and contact them for resources.

60. Part of the first paycheck Matt received as a teacher was used to join a professional teachers' organization. When the first journal arrived, he read it from cover to cover and is now looking forward to the next issue. What will be a primary benefit to Matt and his students if he continues to read professional journals?

    (A) Matt will become increasingly aware of professional networks, resources, and support systems and pass this benefit on to his students.
    (B) Matt will be able to close any gaps in his professional and content knowledge, and his students will benefit from his increased knowledge base.
    (C) Matt will remain aware of and up-to-date on current research, trends, and issues in his field and pass this benefit on to his students.
    (D) Matt will find tried and true teaching ideas and strategies in the journal, which will make lesson planning easier and will benefit his students.

61. Mr. Jeremy is a first-year tenth-grade biology teacher. Toward the end of the second semester, he recognizes that he has not achieved all of the required learning outcomes that his students must meet in order to move forward to the next level in the science curriculum. Although he has experienced reasonably good classroom management for his first year, he knows that his students are at risk academically. He requests an appointment with his mentor to discuss what he might do to remedy this situation, given the limited amount of time left in the academic year. The two meet for two hours one afternoon to discuss immediate strategies that Mr. Jeremy might use with his students. What might the mentor suggest to meet the academic needs of the students in the time remaining?

    (A) The mentor might suggest that Mr. Jeremy combine as many of the remaining biology lessons as possible to ensure that he covers the required curriculum.
    (B) Mr. Jeremy might be invited by his mentor to team teach the remainder of the semester so that the mentor can make sure that all content concepts are covered.
    (C) The mentor might suggest that Mr. Jeremy be as focused as possible on the remaining required standards to ensure that required concepts are introduced in the time remaining.
    (D) Students might be totally engaged in group work to help Mr. Jeremy better manage his time so that he can work with groups arranged according to ability level.

62. Miranda is a ninth-grade student who has a physical disability that requires that she move about school in a wheelchair. She has been assigned to Mr. Jason's full-inclusion mathematics class. The physical space in this classroom is very limited. Yet Mr. Jason knows the importance of Miranda being placed in a location in the classroom that is least restrictive for her physical needs. In frustration, Mr. Jason requests a meeting with the special education team leader to discuss how this situation might be resolved. What is the most appropriate request for Mr. Jason to make of the special education team leader?

(A) Mr. Jason should ask the team leader to suggest ways that he could modify his mathematics lessons so that Miranda is not at any disadvantage.

(B) Mr. Jason should ask the team leader to sit in on his classes to provide suggestions about how he might rearrange his classroom to meet Miranda's space needs.

(C) The team leader should be asked to team teach the mathematics lessons so that Miranda gets the full advantage of learning.

(D) Mr. Jason should ask the team leader to help him configure the classroom space so that where Miranda sits best fits the guidelines outlined in her IEP.

Competency 013: *The teacher understands and adheres to legal and ethical requirements for educators and is knowledgeable of the structure of education in Texas.*

63. What is the legal requirement for Ms. Cosgow to follow if she has reasonable suspicion that one of her eighth-grade girls is being sexually abused?

(A) Teachers should first confront parents when there is suspicion of abuse.

(B) Persons who have reasonable suspicion of abuse of any type are legally required to call the official state agency to report their suspicion.

(C) State law requires teachers to report suspected abuse to the campus leadership first (e.g., the principal, nurse, or counselor).

(D) Teachers are wise to discuss any reasonable suspicion of abuse with the student first, prior to making an issue of the suspicion by contacting the parents or the state.

64. Over lunch, Ms. Nagasaki indicates she plans to take a VCR home this weekend to record some videotapes. Mr. Brown immediately states that this is unethical, and he strongly encourages her to change her mind. Of course, everyone else at the table voices their opinion, and the general response is that it is completely permissible to take school equipment home under certain conditions. What is a situation where it is ethical to take school equipment home?

    (A) It is ethical to take school equipment home as long as the school knows you have it and its return is clearly scheduled so that others can use it for instructional purposes.

    (B) It is ethical to take school equipment home as long as you have permission and are willing to assume responsibility if it is lost, damaged, or stolen.

    (C) It is ethical to take school equipment home as long as it is removed from the building with permission and gone only when others will not need it.

    (D) It is ethical to take school equipment home as long as you have permission and the equipment is used only for authorized school business.

65. During lunch in the teachers' lounge, the staff talks about accepting outside consulting jobs. The chairperson of the science department has been hired to share with a school in a neighboring state the advanced physics curiculum she wrote last summer while under contract to the department. The ethics of accepting this contract are discussed. What would make this contract unethical?

    (A) The science department chairperson was the only author, and the curriculum was written during the summer without pay.

    (B) The curriculum was designed specifically for the physics department where it is now being used.

    (C) The preparation for the presentation was made after school based on responses from her students.

    (D) The curriculum was written on a school computer and was based on specific instructional resource materials from the department.

66. At the beginning of the school year a group of teachers are visiting over coffee to discuss preparing students for the administration of the TAKS in the spring. There are three first-year teachers present, and experienced teachers are giving them suggestions. Which actions would be unethical?

    (A) Giving content unit tests written in the style and format of the TAKS throughout the year to help students become familiar with it.

    (B) Giving teacher-made practice tests a few weeks before the TAKS and debriefing how to answer each question after completing the test.

    (C) Selecting to teach only content units that address specific objectives measured by the TAKS and giving unit tests in the TAKS format.

    (D) Answering student questions about what a word means or helping students with coding an answer during the TAKS.

67. Ms. Katherine, a seventh-grade teacher, has been working with the campus special education team to learn as much as she can about the protocol for referring students for special education services. As a first-year teacher, Ms. Katherine knows that she must follow certain regulations and guidelines prior to referring a student. One of the seventh-grade students is new to the campus and has shown signs of needing special services. What legal requirement must be met before Ms. Katherine makes an official referral?

(A) Prior to any special education referral, parents must be notified of the teacher's concern. Parents must provide written permission for testing before any testing for services may occur.

(B) Ms. Katherine should meet with the entire special education faculty to discuss her concerns with them prior to submitting her written referral for special education services.

(C) The special education team leader is the person responsible for arranging for testing, so the team leader should make the referral.

(D) Before she takes any steps, Ms. Katherine must keep anecdotal notes over a period of time to verify that her concerns are valid.

DECISION SET BEGINS HERE

Consuela Alvarez is a high school science teacher in her first year of teaching. Five weeks into the school year, another science teacher casually remarks to Ms. Alvarez, "I hear you have Liset Jordan in science this year. She was in my class last year and was a real challenge. She is so smart but not at all interested in school. So she is impossible to motivate and her grades suffer."

Ms. Alvarez is careful not to show her surprise because Liset has been a joy to have in class. She is one of a dozen students in her second-period class who seems especially motivated. She always completes her homework assignments, takes an active role in class discussions, and does well on quizzes. Ms. Alvarez had assumed that Liset and the other students had always enjoyed science and had been motivated to produce high-quality work because they were studying a subject they obviously enjoy. The comment by the other teacher prompts Ms. Alvarez to investigate the prior academic performance of Liset and the others in order to promote continuing high achievement and resiliency. Her first step is to examine their academic records.

Competency 010: *The teacher monitors student performance and achievement; provides students with timely, high-quality feedback; and responds flexibly to promote learning for all students.*

68. Ms. Alvarez determines from school records that Liset's grades have been good overall, with some slight variation. The greatest variation was in her science grades last year. As she interprets the grades in Liset's file, which of the following points should Ms. Alvarez always keep in mind?

   (A) High stress in the classroom is often indicated by minor fluctuations in a student's grades.

   (B) Grades based on a student's content work completed over a period of time tend to be inflated.

   (C) Science grades for females are expected to fluctuate because of the difficulty of the content.

   (D) Some variation is normal because of differences in teacher-student interactions and expectations.

As a result of talking with some of Liset's other teachers and examining her school records, Ms. Alvarez has concluded that Liset's academic performance was significantly weaker last year. She has also established that Hung and Steve, two other students from second period, are also performing better this year than last. Ms. Alvarez requests Liset, Hung, and Steve to meet with her after class. The following is a part of their discussion.

Ms. Alvarez:	I wanted to speak with you three students because you are doing so well in my science class but your performance in science last year was much weaker. You have all gone from barely passing science last year to earning an A in my class.
	The students glance at each other and the floor but not at Ms. Alvarez. No one speaks.
Ms. Alvarez:	Will you please tell me why your performances in science were so weak last year?
Hung:	I couldn't get my homework done. I always seemed to run out of time.
Ms. Alvarez:	What makes such a difference in your time from last year to this year?
Hung:	*Looking at the floor and seeming reluctant to speak, he mumbles.* I don't know.
Ms. Alvarez:	What was happening with you two? Liset? Steve? *She gets shrugs and they glance at each other again.* Fine. You can all leave now but think about what I have asked. I really want to know. I want to know how to help you continue to do well and avoid sliding back into last year's patterns.

Competency 005: *The teacher knows how to establish a classroom climate that fosters learning, equity, and excellence and uses this knowledge to create a physical and emotional environment that is safe and productive.*

69. What is a likely outcome of Ms. Alvarez's interaction with these three students?

(A) These students will feel confused about why Ms. Alvarez is asking about what happened before she taught here.

(B) These students will begin to think more about their academic efforts but be unsure why they are doing so.

(C) These students will generalize about more effort producing better results and apply themselves more.

(D) These students will acknowledge Ms. Alvarez's caring and begin to understand how to be more resilient.

Ms. Alvarez decides to meet with each student individually to see if he or she will be more forthcoming when alone with her. Liset tells Ms. Alvarez she didn't have time to do all her homework last year because she had to work two part-time jobs. When Ms. Alvarez says she is glad Liset was smart enough to cut down on her afterschool work this year, Liset reacts with frustration. She says her family needs her to work but that she has a full class load this year. Also, with her father unemployed since the local factory closed, she must have outstanding grades to get a scholarship for college. She feels torn in two directions. Ms. Alvarez sees that Liset is very stressed about her grades.

Competency 013: *The teacher understands and adheres to legal and ethical requirements for educators and is knowledgeable of the structure of education in Texas.*

70. How was Ms. Alvarez's behavior inappropriate during her meeting with these students?

(A) Ms. Alvarez indicated to these students that she was disappointed by their past performance and that it had impacted her opinion about them.

(B) Ms. Alvarez formed her opinion of the students based on others' ideas and past information rather than on her own observations.

(C) Ms. Alvarez violated student confidentiality for these three students when she discussed grades in a group setting.

(D) Ms. Alvarez embarrassed these students as she asked them to share prior experiences of which they probably were not proud.

Competency 004: *The teacher understands learning processes and factors that impact student learning and demonstrates this knowledge by planning effective, engaging instruction and appropriate assessments.*

71. What principle is best illustrated by this situation?

    (A) Teachers should get to know their students as individuals and be aware of home and community factors that affect student learning.

    (B) Teachers should ask about student family problems so that they can be sensitive to the learning challenges they can produce.

    (C) Teachers should make more of an effort to establish collaboration patterns between schools and families so that the school can help with problems.

    (D) Teachers should realize how strong an impact high and low teacher expectations can have on a student's academic performance.

Competency 011: *The teacher understands the importance of family involvement in children's education and knows how to interact and communicate effectively with families.*

72. The day following her second visit with Liset, Ms. Alvarez receives a call from Liset's mother. Ms. Jordan says Liset has discussed Ms. Alvarez's concerns with her and that she wants to talk about helping Liset maintain the grades she will need to be eligible for a scholarship while regaining her income from part-time work. What would be Ms. Alvarez's most appropriate response to Ms. Jordan?

    (A) Ms. Alvarez should direct Ms. Jordan to contact local agencies and organizations that assist families in need until one of the parents can find work.

    (B) Ms. Alvarez should arrange for Ms. Jordan and Liset to meet with her to discuss options for helping Liset continue to achieve well.

    (C) Ms. Alvarez should meet with Ms. Jordan to discuss Liset's grades and encourage Ms. Jordan to seek employment.

    (D) Ms. Alvarez should tell Ms. Jordan not to worry as other teachers think highly of Liset and will help ensure that her grades are good.

When Ms. Alvarez meets privately with Hung, he again states he is unsure why he could not complete his assignments or maintain his grades last year and says he is just glad that the problem has gone away. Ms. Alvarez assures him that the cause has not just disappeared never to return. She convinces him he must identify the problem to prevent it from occurring again when least expected. Through careful questioning, Ms. Alvarez helps Hung realize he was overextended with extracurricular activities last year. Ms. Alvarez asks Hung to

- Compare his key goals for last year to this year's goals.
- List choices he can make to ensure that he is not overextended again.
- Identify the benefits he sees of continuing to show strong achievement.

Competency 010: *The teacher monitors student performance and achievement; provides students with timely, high-quality feedback; and responds flexibly to promote learning for all students.*

73. What is a benefit of guiding Hung through this step-by-step analysis process?

(A) It models for Hung the many applications of problem-solving strategies in his daily life.

(B) It models an effective problem-solving strategy Hung can use in maintaining his resiliency.

(C) It models for Hung that lessons from class might have applications outside the school setting.

(D) It encourages Hung to be more self-reflective and open to taking risks in a safe environment.

By asking around, Ms. Alvarez discovers that in the past Steve had been a shy loner. During the summer he made friends with a group of academically gifted students, and his grades are reflecting his improved motivation. When Steve and Ms. Alvarez meet privately, Steve is aloof and unresponsive, responding to all her questions with uninformative brush-off statements. This especially concerns Ms. Alvarez because Steve's behaviors in class have altered during the week since their first conference. She has noticed that his participation is down and that he seems confused about directions and sleepy during class. She wonders if he may now be using drugs.

Competency 012: *The teacher enhances professional knowledge and skills by effectively interacting with other members of the educational community and participating in various types of professional activities.*

74. Based on her concerns about Steve, what would be the most effective strategy for Ms. Alvarez to try first?

(A) Ms. Alvarez should bluntly ask Steve why such a bright young man would waste his life by using drugs in an attempt to shock him into realizing that he is not fooling anyone and is only hurting himself with his recent bad choices.

(B) Ms. Alvarez should reiterate for Steve the expectations she and the school have for appropriate student behaviors and remind him that he is risking a bright future by poor choices he is now making.

(C) Ms. Alvarez should contact Steve's parents to discuss his sudden change in behavior and be sure they clearly understand the potential consequences of his continuing in this manner, especially if she is right that drugs are involved.

(D) While keeping in mind her concern about drugs, Ms. Alvarez should work with Steve and the appropriate school personnel to determine what has changed in Steve's life that might be responsible for the changes she is observing.

DECISION SET ENDS HERE

DECISION SET BEGINS HERE

Ms. Page's fifth-grade class is involved in a science unit that focuses on individual and societal responsibilities to the environment. A new topic in this series is water conservation. George comments on his experiences with saving water at his parents' farm. He states that his family has been installing water conservation catch basins and sprinklers in an effort to save water and to demonstrate their concern about potential water shortages. Other students indicate that they don't live on farms, so they can't do the same things that George and his family have done. One student asks if the teacher thinks that the actions taken by one family can make a difference. Another student tells about turning off the water while she is brushing her teeth. Another talks about using an off-on nozzle while she helps her dad wash their car. All the students have opinions that they want to share even though the time allotted to science class has ended. The teacher asks students to continue to consider other ways that they might help save water.

Competency 007: *The teacher understands and applies principles and strategies for communicating effectively in varied teaching and learning contexts.*

75. What purpose is best served by Ms. Page allowing students to engage in a problem-solving discussion such as this?

    (A) In-depth discussion of this topic allows students to think in appropriate directions to find the answer.
    (B) The extended discussion helps students clarify the problem so that they can continue to brainstorm possible solutions.
    (C) By allowing students to expand on George's experience, other students are encouraged to think about whether or not they could do the same things as George.
    (D) The discussion cues students about the teacher's view of what George has shared and the responses she expects from them.

Competency 004: *The teacher understands learning processes and factors that impact student learning and demonstrates this knowledge by planning effective, engaging instruction and appropriate assessments.*

76. What has been Ms. Page's primary instructional role in the discussion to this point?

    (A) She has encouraged students' higher-order thinking skills in a real-world context where problem-solving skills can be applied.
    (B) She has encouraged students to develop questions about issues that directly relate to the content unit being studied in class.
    (C) She has established a linkage between students' personal experiences and global events that they might encounter in the future.
    (D) She has provided students with factual information that they can use in future lessons about personal responsibility.

Competency 005: *The teacher knows how to establish a classroom climate that fosters learning, equity, and excellence and uses this knowledge to create a physical and emotional environment that is safe and productive.*

77. What important instructional event occurred because Ms. Page allowed the discussion initiated by George to continue?

(A) By allowing the discussion to continue, Ms. Page recognized students' interest and allowed them to take the topic further than what she might not have planned at this stage in the unit.

(B) By allowing the discussion to continue beyond a few minutes, she took time away from the next subject scheduled and thus reduced the students' learning of that content.

(C) By being an active participant in the discussion, Ms. Page helped students focus on this issue, implying that getting off task was permissible.

(D) By allowing the discussion to continue past the scheduled time, she deviated from her plan but can refocus the conservation unit tomorrow.

Competency 004: *The teacher understands learning processes and factors that impact student learning and demonstrates this knowledge by planning effective, engaging instruction and appropriate assessments.*

78. What is the main advantage of having students so highly engaged in suggesting ways to conserve water?

(A) Allowing students to be fully engaged in such a discussion relieves the teacher of some of the time needed for further planning of the science unit.

(B) Allowing students to brainstorm ways to conserve water plays to the strengths of individual students.

(C) Allowing students an empowered role in developing the unit increases students' sense of ownership of the lesson and increases their interest in the project.

(D) Allowing students to give strong input into the unit topic by discussing their experiences gives insight into individual student's background knowledge.

Competency 005: *The teacher knows how to establish a classroom climate that fosters learning, equity, and excellence and uses this knowledge to create a physical and emotional environment that is safe and productive.*

79. When the class next discusses water conservation, the question arises of an individual's impact on a global issue such as water conservation. Ms. Page asks students to consider the possible impact their ideas could have on the entire city or even the world. What is the most important outcome of this higher-level thinking activity?

    (A) Knowing the potential impact a fifth-grader can have on water conservation can help students recognize the value of discussing problems while waiting for guidance toward solutions from others.

    (B) Knowing the potential impact a fifth-grader can have on an environmental issue can help students develop a sense of purpose and place in addressing local and global problems.

    (C) Knowing the potential impact a fifth-grader can have on science-related problems can help students value clear research goals when attempting to answer a question.

    (D) Knowing the potential impact a fifth-grader can have on local and global problems can help students determine the importance of designing a clear question to research.

Competency 008: *The teacher provides appropriate instruction that actively engages students in the learning process.*

80. What is the most important aspect of students continuing to discuss conservation issues?

    (A) In discussion initiated by a student, all students learn to value group work for solving community problems.

    (B) The water conservation discussions will help students understand the critical value of listening to the opinions of classmates.

    (C) By discussing a local issue, students can learn how to find research related to a problem.

    (D) By listening to classmates and offering personal ideas, students gain motivation to find solutions for other problems by applying the same process.

DECISION SET ENDS HERE

DECISION SET BEGINS HERE

A new middle school has been built in a community where new housing has been added as the area's population has increased. Teachers at the new school want to clearly establish a collaboration between the school and the community as the school opens. They decide that one way to do this is to get parents/guardians and community businesses actively involved in school projects. This means the faculty must take an active role in recruiting volunteers and communicating information about school events.

Competency 005: *The teacher knows how to establish a classroom climate that fosters learning, equity, and excellence and uses this knowledge to create a physical and emotional environment that is safe and productive.*

81. Given that the area where the school is located is experiencing population increases, what would be the greatest benefit of having parents or citizens serve as volunteers in the classroom?

    (A) As community volunteers help with classroom duties, students learn more about other peoples' perspectives.
    (B) Having parental and citizen volunteers in the classrooms will foster a sense of community for students and will model for students how they might help others.
    (C) Volunteers in the classroom will relieve teachers of time-consuming routine tasks and may possibly give teachers a break at times.
    (D) Students are more likely to have better behavior when guests are in the classroom, especially if the volunteers are parents.

Competency 011: *The teacher understands the importance of family involvement in children's education and knows how to interact and communicate effectively with families.*

82. One of the experienced teachers now employed at the new school shares her experience with establishing a parent/guardian classroom volunteer cadre at a prior school. She explains that after a short time some of the parent/guardian volunteers stopped participating and indicated this was because they felt they were not truly welcome at the school. They also said that they did not feel that the time they spent on school volunteer work was useful, effective, or productive for either the school or themselves. What plans can the faculty make to ensure that these parent/guardian volunteers feel welcome and that they are making valuable contributions to the school?

   (A) Have a specific place at the school for parent/guardian volunteers to gather and work when they are not active in a classroom. Allow these adults to decide what role will most help the school and fulfill their own sense of worth and participation.

   (B) Have a specific place at the school for parent/guardian volunteers to gather and work. Allow teachers, as they need assistance, to draw from the pool of volunteers, which will keep a variety of tasks and opportunities available and reduce volunteer boredom.

   (C) Have a specific place at the school for parent/guardian volunteers to gather and work. Have a variety of tasks that need doing either during or outside school hours that clearly contribute to the smooth functioning of classrooms.

   (D) Have parent/guardian volunteers work only in classrooms where their child is present. This will allow them to see how their work contributes directly to an improved educational environment for their child.

83. A teacher with a background in both elementary and middle school teaching mentions that in her experience "it is easy to get elementary volunteers, but middle school is another story. Middle school students don't want their parents at school, and the parents aren't interested in being here." How can the teachers encourage parent/guardian interactions with the school if the attitude expressed by this teacher has some truth to it?

    (A) The school can set up communication pathways such as newsletters, phone trees, and e-mails to notify the community of school events such as sports events and musical programs where parents can interact in a non-threatening way.

    (B) The school can set the new school times to allow teachers to meet with all the parents to introduce them to the new school and ask them to get involved. Notices sent home and posters about the event displayed at local businesses can help spread the word.

    (C) Students can be motivated to help the school encourage their parents/guardians to visit by planning an open house where students give tours of the new building and earn bonus points if their parents attend.

    (D) Teachers can schedule individual conferences with the parents of each student to discuss the impact the school wants to make in the community and how their student can take an active role in this process.

    DECISION SET ENDS HERE

DECISION SET BEGINS HERE

Pam Landers is a first-year home-life skills teacher. A teacher with ten years' experience is mentoring her. As she begins to plan for her coed middle school classes, which are electives, she wants to ensure that students of both genders have a positive experience.

Competency 002: *The teacher understands student diversity and knows how to plan learning experiences and design assessments that are responsive to differences among students and that promote all students' learning.*

84. What is most important task for Ms. Landers to create the gender-equitable learning environment she wants?

   (A) She should explain to students that there are gender differences related to what they may be able to accomplish.

   (B) She should alternate class activities so that each gender finds some activities interesting while encouraging both genders to participate fully in each activity.

   (C) She should use gender-specific rubrics for evaluating each activity. Having separate rubrics accommodates gender differences in performance.

   (D) She should have the same expectations for all students, although she both acknowledges that gender differences exist and accommodates them.

Competency 006: *The teacher understands strategies for creating an organized and productive learning environment and for managing student behavior.*

85. Ms. Landers spends some time visiting with her mentor to discuss how she can allow students to work at the different pacing that will result from the varied backgrounds and skill levels of her students, while keeping them engaged in purposeful, on-task behaviors. Because the home skills class is an elective, she is worried that students will goof off rather than work independently as this type of class requires. What is the best advice Ms. Landers' mentor can share?

   (A) Select several students in the class who exhibit the type of purposeful, on-task behaviors you want and call the other students' attention to these excellent role models.

   (B) Set clear teacher expectations and ask for student self-evaluations of how effectively they think they are meeting these expectations for a weekly participation grade.

   (C) Establish routines and procedures for students to follow as they arrive in class, indicate attendance, collect the materials they will need for a project, and begin work.

   (D) Involve the students in designing the rules of classroom behavior, consequences for not following the rules, and grading scales used to determine student success.

Competency 008: *The teacher provides appropriate instruction that actively engages students in the learning process.*

86. What will be the most likely result of Ms. Landers following her mentor's advice to establish routines and procedures for students to follow as they arrive in class, indicate attendance, collect the materials they will need for a project, and begin work?

   (A) Students will reject any changes she tries to make from what they have come to expect.
   (B) Students will gain the skills needed to work independently and productively.
   (C) Students will learn to use problem-solving skills because Ms. Landers is not available.
   (D) Students will begin to arrive late to class because they are not under teacher supervision.

Competency 010: *The teacher monitors student performance and achievement; provides students with timely, high-quality feedback; and responds flexibly to promote learning for all students.*

87. After a teacher-directed lesson on a new skill, Ms. Landers plans for students to work in pairs and small groups as they practice new skills needed for a science project. This strategy encourages peers to offer classmates' suggestions without their having to wait until Ms. Landers has time to visit with each group. Which approach is most likely to produce constructive and positive interactions among her middle school students during peer feedback activities?

   (A) Teams are encouraged to determine performance criteria for the project to ensure that they are clear to all before starting.
   (B) Students will be given an option to work alone or in self-selected teams to complete the project.
   (C) Appropriate ways of giving their peers feedback for possible ways to improve are modeled for students as they work within their groups.
   (D) Students with widely ranging skill levels are placed together to assure a range of interactions and feedback suggestions.

DECISION SET ENDS HERE

DECISION SET BEGINS HERE

Ms. Reynolds takes her fourth-graders to the school's media center to teach them about the resources available as they do research on animal habitats. She wants all her students to learn to use the media center's computer stations and technology-based resources during their research. To this end, Ms. Reynolds demonstrates to her class how to use the available resources, which include books, journals and magazines, videotapes and CDs, interactive CD-ROMs, and the Internet.

Competency 002: *The teacher understands student diversity and knows how to plan learning experiences and design assessments that are responsive to differences among students and that promote all students' learning.*

88. What is the most important benefit of instructing these students in the use of these resources?

   (A) This instruction will assist these students in developing higher-level thinking skills.
   (B) This instruction will promote a sense of personal accomplishment in these students.
   (C) This instruction enables Ms. Reynolds to meet the needs of each individual student.
   (D) This instruction allows students to work in groups as they share resources.

Competency 009: *The teacher incorporates the effective use of technology to plan, organize, deliver, and evaluate instruction for all students.*

89. Because only a limited number of computers with Internet access are available, Ms. Reynolds schedules several days for online research to ensure that all who wish to use this resource have an opportunity. How can she best facilitate her students' work on these days?

   (A) Ms. Reynolds can make sure that each student knows how to bookmark useful URLs.
   (B) Ms. Reynolds can make sure that each student takes notes on the useful information they find.
   (C) Ms. Reynolds can make sure that each student prints all the pages from sites they find useful.
   (D) Ms. Reynolds can make sure that each student designs a web quest to share useful sites with others.

90. While using an Internet search engine to locate information on the prairie dog, Susan discovers there more than 3,000 entries on this topic. How can Ms. Reynolds best help her avoid tying up the computer as she searches through this huge number of entries?

(A) Ms. Reynolds can instruct Susan to use another search engine to see if it can reduce the number of entries.

(B) Ms. Reynolds can have Susan conduct a second search within the entries located by this search engine.

(C) Ms. Reynolds can conduct a second search for Susan to show her how to get a reasonable number of responses.

(D) Ms. Reynolds can instruct Susan on ways to narrow her search terms to get a reasonable number of responses.

DECISION SET ENDS HERE

Answer Key
SAMPLE TEST (GRADES EC–12)

Question Number	Correct Response	Competency	Question Number	Correct Response	Competency
1	C	001	26	B	006
2	A	001	27	C	006
3	D	001	28	C	006
4	A	001	29	A	006
5	B	002	30	A	006
6	D	002	31	B	007
7	A	002	32	C	007
8	B	002	33	D	007
9	C	002	34	D	007
10	B	002	35	B	007
11	D	002	36	C	007
12	C	003	37	B	008
13	B	003	38	A	008
14	C	003	39	A	008
15	C	003	40	B	008
16	D	003	41	A	008
17	A	003	42	C	008
18	A	004	43	C	009
19	D	004	44	D	009
20	A	004	45	A	009
21	A	005	46	A	009
22	C	005	47	D	010
23	D	005	48	A	010
24	C	005	49	B	010
25	D	006	50	A	010

Answer Key
SAMPLE TEST (GRADES EC–12)

Question Number	Correct Response	Competency	Question Number	Correct Response	Competency
51	B	011	71	A	004
52	C	011	72	B	011
53	C	011	73	B	010
54	A	011	74	D	012
55	B	011	75	B	007
56	B	011	76	A	004
57	B	011	77	A	005
58	B	012	78	C	004
59	A	012	79	B	005
60	C	012	80	D	008
61	C	012	81	B	005
62	D	012	82	C	011
63	B	013	83	A	011
64	D	013	84	D	002
65	D	013	85	C	006
66	D	013	86	B	008
67	A	013	87	C	010
68	D	010	88	C	002
69	A	005	89	A	009
70	C	013	90	D	009

CORRECT RESPONSES

1. **C** Lydia has not yet developed the ability to conserve substance and reverse liquid volume. (A) does not fit because the tea exists for Lydia whether it is visible (in the cups) or not (in the teapot), which would not be true if Lydia were at the sensorimotor stage of development. (B) is also an incorrect developmental stage for Lydia as children can reverse and conserve substances when at the concrete operational stage. (D) is unacceptable because there is no one-to-one correspondence present although one cup of tea per person could lead you to this answer if you are not clearly knowledgeable about Piagetian stages of development.

2. **A** The correct response is (A) as these two Piagetian levels of development best fit this student range. The sensorimotor stage begins at about 17 months and ends at about age 7 when students transition into the concrete operational stage. The age ranges for each stage are approximate and dependent on multiple factors such as experiences and maturation rates. (B) pairs two stages in the appropriate order but reaches beyond the expected developmental stages for this student range. Students at the concrete operational stage tend to transition into the formal operational stage beginning at age 11 if all conditions required have been met, which is not a given with any set of students. (C) pairs two developmental stages that do not occur together. Students transition from sensorimotor to preoperational rather than to concrete operational. (D) has the problem of being accurate for a very developmentally delayed group of students as the transition between these two stages can be expected to begin at 17 months.

3. **D** Response (D) allows for the range of student cognitive development present in the class. (A) groups students by their cognitive levels, and this is not supported by research on effective teaching and learning. It is effective to have students of different abilities work together to enrich the learning of all students, but the highly structured plan to use "study buddies" suggested in (B) is not as effective as using small groups of students with mixed abilities. It is not appropriate to make students at one ability level directly responsible for the success of students at another, which does not mean that students should not be supportive of the success of other students. (C) assumes there is a normal seventh-grade level of development and ample time to work with individuals. This strategy is more likely to overlook the needs of all groups when instructional levels don't match and time for individualization runs short.

4. **A** Unless the counselor can help this student focus on future consequences, she will not see beyond what is most important to her now, which seems to be leaving school and getting married. (B) has some validity because many students do not feel they fit. However, the counselor cannot provide this student a group. So although this might be part of her problem, it doesn't play much of a role in helping her decide whether to stay in school. Many high school and even middle school students are already planning for their futures so (C) is not valid. Students of this age may not want to acknowledge that adults have gone through many of the same experiences they have encountered, as indicated in (D). Yet

they know that this is true even when they decide not to accept the advice offered.

5. **B** Texas requires each teacher to address the grade level TEKS with each student at that grade level. With these limited English proficiency students, this must be done while also addressing their English fluency. (A) demands less of these students, which would result in putting them behind academically as well as behind in English. Expecting less will result in students learning less. These are not less able students but students that need intensive work with English. (C) again eliminates the TEKS dictated by the state. A plan to use TEKS that demand concrete materials first to strengthen English skills and save more abstract TEKS for later would be much wiser. (D) also leaves these students behind on the state-required TEKS while developing English skills. Both issues must be addressed at the same time to keep these students from falling behind. Research tells us that the further behind a student falls, the harder it is for that student to ever catch up.

6. **D** Feeling a part of the class is an important step toward student-student inter-actions and is important to language acquisition. It also allows students who do not show well on one style of assessment to shine on another. This gives a more accurate picture of the learning of all students. The self-assessment addressed in (A) is good, but it should not be restricted to the limited English proficiency students. Also, these students should not be singled out as being different from the rest of the class. The tutoring for any student who falls behind, as suggested in (B), is a good idea in general. Again, it should not be restricted to the limited English proficiency students nor should the assessment schedule label these students as different from the rest of the class. (C) is an appropriate way to gather some observational assessment data but should not be the only assessment used. The "study buddy" is also a second-grader and even with some training would not be able to provide the level of assessment needed.

7. **A** Instruction must be differentiated to meet the needs of students in ways that do not apply or reinforce labels that cause students to feel isolated or different. (B) is a form of grouping, which is neither supported by research nor accepted as a valid instructional strategy. (C) shifts responsibility for learning and success away from individuals and onto groups. Although group work is very impor-tant, all the members of a group must have a responsibility, not only to the group but also to themselves. (D) is appropriate as it enhances student motiva-tion. However, it is not the most important aspect to consider. Response (A) is more important to motivation and effective learning.

8. **B** Ms. Wong allows students opportunities to learn and apply the skills needed for this task in a step-by-step manner under direct teacher supervision. This allows for individual differences and, because of daily monitoring, prevents stu-dents from delaying or falling behind. The success this ensures can help with positive attitudes toward science. (A) depends on each student already having the skills needed to complete the science fair project. It does not monitor the

student's ability to apply these skills in a timely manner. Receiving a ribbon for participation will not help improve a negative attitude caused by frustration due to lack of information or skills. (C) can result in a negative attitude toward the project and toward science in general in students at all levels. The flexibility in participation and roles shifts more responsibility to grade-conscious students, and learning will be unequal. (D) implies that the skills for all scientific research are the same, which is untrue. It also allows for no individuals having a skill already, which can result in boredom because of the repetition. Students who feel they must endlessly repeat a lesson that is not clear to them, and so cannot be mastered, will develop a negative attitude and fall behind in working on the project.

9. **C** Response (C) encourages student participation in addressing the situation, which also increases student ownership of the solution. (A) would be more effective with much younger students who are still focused on pleasing an authority figure. It also attempts to deal with the tensions from an external rather than an internal focus when an internal reason is more powerful for students of this age. (B) will help defuse tension as students work together successfully, but it is not as effective a strategy as that suggested by (C). (D) is not effective, ethical, or legal. Student grades should only indicate progress toward learning. If this practice were used, it would have a potential for actually increasing tensions.

10. **B** It allows the teacher to guide students at all levels toward the successful completion of achievable steps. Each student is able to receive the assistance needed rather than having the teacher provide the same assistance to all students, which does not acknowledge individual differences in backgrounds and skills. (A) and (D) are valid strategies, but neither is as effective as (B) for guiding all students toward successful completion of the project. Some students will find that (A) allows too many choices or more freedom than they are comfortable with and will have the same difficulty as with (D). Partnering higher and lower achievers must be done with clear expectations that both members of the partnership bring strengths to the task and that each must play a clear role so that the higher-achieving student is not carrying the lower-achieving student. (C) is also a valid strategy, but again (B) is stronger. (C) is a way to provide the guidance some students will need.

11. **D** This choice allows for peer instruction in the different technologies available. Students in this age group are willing to explore and learn from peers more readily than from formal instruction, as suggested in (C). (A) allows access, but without peer support, and so it is not as effective. (B) allows students to continue to avoid or miss gaining technological skills rather than providing a supportive pathway to acquiring these needed skills. (C) is not the strongest answer as reading the instructions appeals to adults more than to high school students who readily check with peers before reading instructions. Many adults read the directions only when all else fails. Yet having access to instructions is useful when peers don't know and when trying what seems logical doesn't produce the desired results.

12. **C** None of Mr. Beaumont's goals can be met if students are not attentive during this time, and interest and familiarity are two good motivators for attentiveness. (A) indicates that the development of listening skills is not an appropriate instructional activity, which is not the case. Students are able to absorb content information without being alert to doing so, but counting on this is not a valid instructional strategy. (B) assumes that third-grade students are able to internalize new and unfamiliar information through abstract encounters such as reading and listening, although research indicates they need direct experiences instead. The word patterns in (D) are good for this age group, although fourth grade is when most students fall in love with puns. The calming effect is more a result of the quiet and stillness that comes with effective listening and will not be lost by choosing exciting books that are highly motivating.

13. **B** The response to his verbal questions will allow him to informally assess students' responses to both the affective and cognitive domains of his goals. Only the affective domain goal is assessed by (A), and even then he may not obtain accurate information. Students may calmly accept three days without listening to him read when they would strongly protest stopping completely. (C) again focuses on the affective domain goals without addressing the cognitive domain goals. Wanting to switch books does not mean listening skills have not improved. Adding a formal, written assessment as suggested in (D) will give data on each student's cognitive and affective domain growth in terms of goals but could be counterproductive for future growth as some students may be stressed about the resulting evaluation.

14. **C** This is the first step the team needs to take. Without knowing what is expected and without some common skills and topics, the task becomes overwhelming. This also keeps inappropriate material from being added to an overcrowded curriculum and important information from being lost as themes are selected and units planned. (A), (B), and (D) are all appropriate tasks for the team to address but not as a beginning or first step. A clear picture of the required curriculum needs to be the foundation of the planning efforts.

15. **C** Response (C) allows Ms. Lopez to work during the coming school year to strengthen weak areas while continuing to make adequate yearly progress with her students, which matches the state's expectations. This is harder and takes more planning than declining any responsibility for teaching knowledge and skills from earlier grade levels that a student might be lacking. The idea in (A) of being sure students have the test-taking skills for a particular format is appropriate but is not the best use of the assessment information. (B) has students being placed in ability groups, which is not appropriate. Nor is it appropriate to consider only one criterion when deciding on instructional practices for a school year. (D) seems to shift the remediation role for diagnosed weak areas to parents. Although it is not inappropriate to ask for parental assistance, the school should play the leadership role. It is not appropriate to begin a new year by focusing on problem areas rather than on positive ones. It can set a negative attitude in teacher, parents, and students that will impact the entire coming year.

16. **D** Teachers need a way to assess the learning of students and learning goals are the guide for assessment as well as instruction. This type of learning is not impossible to assess but needs some visible indication of appreciation such as "Students will choose to listen to music from other cultures during their free time" to indicate that the goal has been met. (A) presents a very narrow view of ninth graders. Music tends to be important to a large number of students at this age, but the types of music they value are very wide-ranging. Openness to new ideas presented in a nonthreatening manner is also typical of students of this age. Being told they are being "introduced to good music rather than that trash you have been listening to" will not get far with these students, but "See if you also like this music" will be more effective. (B) is just inaccurate. There are lessons on every conceivable topic available from the wide range of resources that teachers can draw on—plus teachers are creative individuals. (C) is also inaccurate. The prior knowledge needed for success must be considered as learning goals are selected but is not included in the goal. How the prior knowledge will be assessed to determine it is present is also part of a teacher's planning but not part of a learning goal.

17. **A** Staff development needs to be specific to the teachers and students of a specific campus to be most effective. No matter how carefully a staff development session is, there can be no guarantee of all teachers committing to it as suggested in (B). (C) is a good response. However, (A) is stronger because it meets the immediate needs of the school. (B) is also true but is also less of a rationale than is expressed in (A) for the same reason.

18. **A** Mr. Stewart knows a stressful situation such as a move can produce a regression to less advanced social skills and levels of play. There is a difference in educational standards across states, but (B) implies there is also a difference in developmental standards across states, which is not true. (C) assumes a great deal based on a limited observation time (one week) of one student and is guaranteed to get Paula's parents, the principal, and Paula's previous teacher and school upset with him. In (D) Mr. Stewart is making poor judgment calls in lowering his expectations after such a short time and in keeping information about Paula from her parents.

19. **D** The correct response is (D), although it would have been better for Paula if the student friends assigned to help her adjust had been implemented on the first day. Mr. Stewart is wise to allow both Paula and himself ample time before making a judgment about the accuracy of her label as socially advanced. It is also important that he not delay a conference about her adjustment or lack of adjustment too long. (A), (B), and (C) are guaranteed to be more stressful for Paula and cause her to regress even more. Her parents will probably be at school to visit with him before he is ready to conference with them. (B) also implies that Paula is choosing to regress, which is not the case. (C) also indicates her parents and her prior school were incorrect in their assessments.

20. **A** Jigsaw is a cooperative learning strategy in which subgroups are formed from the home groups. The subgroups learn about a specific topic and then return

to the home group to share the newly acquired expertise. Mr. Rivera formed the home groups and let the students form the expert subgroups. (B) lets students form their own groups, which is not a part of cooperative learning. (C) has students working in ability level groups, which are also not standard in cooperative learning. (D) uses strategies not part of cooperative learning by having students select topics for study and working in interest groups.

21. **A** We know research indicates that high teacher expectations are one of the most important variables for student success, but we also know all students do not learn in the same way and that differentiated instruction is important. (B) and (C) open Ms. Gonzales to making faulty instructional decisions based on educational myths about an identified group's ability to learn. Although we have some data suggesting that some groups face more learning challenges than others, we must be careful not to use this information as a rationale to expect less from students in these groups. Because all students were in the same school last year and are now in the same grade does not mean they learned at the same rate or will respond to the same instructional strategies this year. If this were so, as (D) implies, there would not be a distinct group of students with significant academic needs in second grade. (B), (C), and (D) are basically the same. If Ms. Gonzales or any teacher expects students to do less for whatever reason, they will. Each of these responses would result in lower teacher expectations of students.

22. **C** This allows the teacher to use more than the number of correct answers to establish progress. (A) is a good idea and will help with a positive and supportive learning environment, but peer feedback is not the same as assessing and assigning grades. (B) indicates that it is acceptable for some students to be and stay behind when this is not acceptable. (D) describes what any good test should do, which is to allow all students some success while distinguishing students who have mastered a concept from those who have not. Any teacher can develop a test that no one can pass or one where everyone can make a perfect score. Neither situation is effective in assessing student learning and indicating the next step for the teacher, which is the desired role of assessment.

23. **D** Having individual students working in different groups allows them to get to know students better they might know only slightly if they were not shifted. It is easier to stick to the familiar and easier to show rudeness or bias to those we do not know well. (A) allows students to stay in a comfort zone rather than meeting and establishing a working relationship with others in the class. (B) indicates that grouping like students will increase their comfort and reduce bias. This is not a valid assumption. Randomly assigning students, as in (C), does not solve the problem. Modeling a lack of bias is important. However, insisting that bias and harshness are unacceptable behaviors, and taking action each time they occur is more important.

24. **C** This selection is the correct answer as it is the only question she can clearly answer based on reading her students' learning journals. (A), (B), and (D) are

also good questions for a self-reflective teacher to ask, but pathways other than the learning journals are needed to answer them, such as a review of past plans.

25. **D** Your goal should be to model or guide students toward acceptable ways to reach a mutually agreeable settlement without having to involve an adult each time. (A) and (B) imply that ending discord now will keep it from reappearing the moment the teacher is no longer involved. Settled is very different than ended. Attempting to establish fault causes the settlement to be delayed. It is not necessary for the teacher to clearly understand the problem, as indicated in (C), as the teacher will not be issuing a settlement. The goal is for the involved students to establish a settlement they agree will be fair to all.

26. **B** Teacher proximity reminds students that the teacher is aware of and monitoring behaviors. The teacher is in a better position to observe a poor choice and take action if this continues. (A) ignores that a student is challenging the teacher for control of what happens in the room. (C) is not so much student discomfort with the teacher as an awareness of what the teacher observes as stated in (B). (D) will be true for some students who are still at a stage to please the authority figure or teacher, but (B) is the better answer.

27. **C)** The roles are not titles but important jobs that impact the completion or success of the task. Each student must perform responsibly in each role as the role rotates through the group. So peers depend on each other's performance. (A) has Ms. Sanderson nagging the groups, which is counterproductive to increasing the self-control of the students. (B) is also counterproductive. Students who are already not fully participating in their groups will probably not improve by being placed with other students needing more teacher attention. By placing them all together, it guarantees that they will achieve less and fall further and further behind. (D) allows everyone to have a job they can do successfully, assuming the students in the class have the right balance of skills. However, (D) does not make any provisions for growth in skills as other jobs are learned and performed. Grades are used as a motivation when other motivators could be more successful.

28. **C** The most time-efficient task that uses a spreadsheet program is given in (C)—using a weighted formula to compute students' grades. It draws on the strengths of spreadsheets to speed up a task. The task suggested in (A) would be better done using a word-processing program than a spreadsheet. The daily attendance records in (B) can easily be done on a spreadsheet, but limited computing is done on these records. The same is true of the parent-teacher communications paperwork in (D). A spreadsheet does not improve the efficiency of these two tasks as much as it does in calculating student averages using weighted grades.

29. **A** When students understand and follow classroom routines, the teacher has to spend less instructional time on getting the classroom to operate smoothly as that is what the routines achieve. (B) can also be a result of students understanding and following routines, but the increase in instructional and learning

time has a greater payoff. Although a sense of certainty will result, a positive attitude might not if a student strongly disagrees with a routine. (C) is true in that management demands such as maintaining discipline will decrease. However, (C) will increase a teacher's instructional time rather than planning time. (D) is accurate in that confusion will be reduced for both the teacher and the students. This may or may not allow for greater ease in student monitoring, but the increase in instructional and learning times in (A) has a greater value.

30. **A** A teacher's role in conflict resolution is to assist students in solving the problem in a manner acceptable to each rather than to solve the problem for them or allow it to continue. (B) is counter to the principles of conflict resolution because the teacher rather than the students provides the solution, which can result in a continuation of the problem if students dislike or disagree with the teacher's solution. Student buy-in is missing. (C) is again counter to the principles of conflict resolution where conflict is resolved without assigning blame. (D) describes the role a teacher can play in conflict resolution, but this is not the primary goal, which is students solving their own problems in an equitable and acceptable manner.

31. **B** Shorter wait time and restating questions for lower-achieving students are different behaviors and signal to all students of lower expectation levels for some students. This reinforces a feeling of inability to achieve in lower-achieving students because it seems that the teacher doesn't expect success. (A) does signal different levels of expectation but doesn't really cause resentment in either group unless it is directed toward the teacher who doesn't expect success from lower-achieving students. Students are aware that they must work to achieve success. (C) is inaccurate because the lower-achieving students actually feel that they are "on the spot" more as they fail to respond to a perceived greater number of questions with less success. Altering wait time for students at different levels of achievement is not an effective manner of instructional differentiation as stated in (D). Both groups need equal wait time and teachers need to allow effective wait time before restating a question or passing it to another student.

32. **C** Ms. Johnson should encourage her students to be creative and varied in their approaches to a problem. Many effective solutions are the desired outcome. (A), (B), and (D) all imply that there is only one correct solution or answer and one best method for finding it, which is counter to the problem-solving process.

33. **D** You should encourage students to think about what they already know, make connections with prior learning, and identify areas where they still have gaps in their understanding. (A) and (C) make inaccurate statements about the value of the information required in the log. Prior knowledge is activated but not altered, so students are not at a more uniform perspective as stated in (A). (C) is incorrect as the logs actually add to the time needed to complete the topic. (B) may be accurate in that logs will improve the scores on quizzes. However, that is not the most important reason to use logs in this situation.

34. **D** Response (D) needs to receive the greatest focus during the meeting with the mentor. The main reason for a class discussion is to determine the thoughts of the members of a group on a given topic, and this cannot occur without their listening to each other. (A) ignores the fact that the listening that is vital to an effective discussion must be nonjudgmental. After being told they are wrong, which is another way of indicating that their ideas are not valued, many students will refuse to share their ideas and the effectiveness of class discussions will be seriously curtailed. This is important but needs to be a secondary concern. (B) is not a problem in an effective class discussion, assuming the comments are on topic and the students are not speaking over each other. Directing all comments through the teacher can seriously limit a class discussion as students wait to be called on and are not selected in an appropriate order for the comments they wish to make to occur in a logical sequence, which addresses the problem with (C).

35. **B** Research on how students learn explains that students do not comprehend information until they can establish relationships. (B) is best because it is the only one that helps students focus on relationships. Being able to repeat the information is not the same as understanding and being able to use it during thinking or problem solving. (A), (C), and (D) do not guide students toward looking for or establishing relationships because (A) and (C) focus instead on renaming or repeating concepts without connecting them. (D) does a better job of asking students to connect information or establish relationships to them but does not fit this lecture conclusion.

36. **C** The strategy in (C) is the most concrete of those offered. It has a high level of student participation. It also allows a clear signal to the teacher about when enough examples needed for understanding have been presented. (A) and (B) are not incorrect strategies but are not as powerful as the strategy in (C) for the reasons mentioned above. (A) would be better if students were reviewing and repeating the major concepts rather than listening to the teacher do so as this would be a stronger engagement for students. (B) is a good strategy because it helps students activate prior knowledge; but it also assumes some prior knowledge, which may not be accurate. (C) is more effective as it points out specific examples of prior knowledge that students might have but not recognize as such because of the abstract nature of the concept. (D) is a fairly traditional way to introduce vocabulary in a study unit but is not as effective as introducing and defining a new term within context as it is needed.

37. **B** Ms. Swirczynski must determine why Pat is having difficulty before she can help. In (A), Pat will not feel ownership while dependent on Ms. Swirczynski. Ownership comes from independent success. (C) assumes a problem of focus or lack of attentiveness with no supporting evidence. (D) sounds good. However, reading with comprehension is a higher-order thinking skill. There is no evidence of why Pat is having difficulty.

38. **A** A variety of content topics and instructional methods are planned for the unit, which will allow students multiple learning opportunities. (B) addresses a

common misunderstanding about integrated units. Integration allows for greater instructional time per subject, but this does not always mean that less class time is required. Instead, integration means that the time is apportioned in different patterns to allow overlap between content areas. There is no information in the question to support the selection of either (C) or (D). The time allocated for the unit or pacing is neither mentioned nor indicated. Neither is individualized instruction.

39. **A** Ms. Koradji not only clearly states her expectations but also models them for her students. Research tells us that high expectations of students translate into higher student performances. This is especially so when the expectation is also modeled, and it is a case of "Do as I do" rather than "Do as I say." The effects described in (B), (C), and (D) also occur but are not as important as the effect in (A). Ms. Koradji also needs to monitor the success of students in understanding assignments as well as in completing them as stated in (C). Falling behind on comprehension is worse than falling behind on completion. Completion of an assignment does not ensure comprehension of an assignment. Although improved work habits are an excellent goal, students need this improvement for much more than success in high school. They need it in middle school as well as throughout their lives.

40. **B** Postponing the discussion of a highly emotional topic that students want to discuss ignores the strong motivation that occurs when a teacher takes advantage of a teachable moment. Connect it to curriculum to keep from losing instructional time needlessly. Responses (A), (C), and (D) assume that students can be redirected from such a highly emotional topic. Avoiding this discussion at school is not a reasonable expectation. It will occur as a subtopic while students ignore the teacher. They will also continue the discussion in the halls and the lunchroom. By allowing the discussion, the teacher can guide a balanced student discussion rather than allowing one student's perspective to overpower another. The teacher should also remind students that individuals can respond very differently on issues and encourage them to be respectful of the varied responses of others. Many possible responses are valid and must be treated with respect.

41. **A** Response (A) is the least emotional and has the broadest informational rather than emotional basis. Emotions run high following such an event and should be tempered rather than fanned. (B) could strengthen an emotional response when the debate forces a student to take a position counter to his or her own and others forget that this is not their actual opinion. (C) allows students to see where opinions lie, but this might not be good for students holding less popular points of view. They could become afraid to express their true opinions. (D) allows individuals to purge some of their emotion only if writing is an outlet for them. Students who do not readily write will find this task onerous. Asking for evidence to support an opinion will help keep emotions under control.

42. **C** Understanding why they are doing the experiment and how it is to be done guides student formation of a conceptual framework that helps them focus on the relationships required of true, long-term learning rather than on memoriza-

tion of information for short-term acquisition only. All students have performed the same opening activity for the experiment, but this does not give them all the same background on the topic of the experiment as implied in (A). (B) is true but is not as important as the conceptual framework discussed in (C). (D) is inaccurate as doing the preliminary writing actually extends the time needed to do the experiment although it probably increases accuracy by forcing students to be attentive to the entire experiment rather than approaching it one step at a time, as so often happens when an advance organizer is not used.

43. **C** Very young children are naturally curious and have been exposed to computers in multiple environments such as homes and businesses. They are ready to begin to explore the uses and capabilities of a computer. (A) and (B) focus on the lack of and need to develop fine motor skills in young children. Computers are motivating and can help with the practice needed to gain these skills but cannot and should not replace all the ways children developed fine motor skills before the invention of computers. Word processing with a computer is not an appropriate replacement for learning to write. We see the situation in (D) often as teachers attempt to teach a skill that is not developmentally appropriate because the students will need it next year. Instead, it should be learned in the future when it is both needed and developmentally appropriate.

44. **D** The best instructional strategy is learning and practicing computer skills within the context of other content lessons such as math and language arts. The drill and practice software in (A) will help with rote memory content such as math facts but is not the best way to acquire computer skills. As (B) states, motivation enhances learning, but student-selected software will result in a limited set of computer skills for his students. If all the students are allowed freedom of choice, there will be no consistency in the skills set they acquire. The direct instruction in (C) is important but should not occur in isolation from content knowledge—skill for the sake of a skill. Also, direct instruction should not be the purpose of each visit as learning is strengthened by practice and application.

45. **A** By establishing the rubric together, student input and ownership of the project are established while stating clear teacher expectations. Both groups know what is expected as the balance between content and presentation design. (B) gives much of the control of the final product to the teachers. Completing all the content work without considering any presentation components may block students from producing a creative product suggested by the content information but not on the suggested product list. (C) also keeps much of the control and creative process away from the students as they seek the teachers' approval for each component of the final product. The focus is on meeting the teachers' expectations more than on the creative use of media to produce an effective final presentation. The daily reminders from (D) will be considered nagging in a very short time. A written rubric, as suggested in (A), is much more effective.

46. **A** Citing the source of supportive material created by another is an ethical and legal obligation. None of us has to do everything alone with no assistance, but

we are obligated to acknowledge the assistance we receive. Responses (B), (C), and (D) are all true but are not the main reasons for citations being required for all work that is not original. Relocating information later is a reason for including citations. Failure to include a citation is to claim someone else's efforts as your own, which is plagiarism. Because an item is on the web does not mean it is in the public domain and does not eliminate the need to use citations.

47. **D** Observing students while they work will tell you if they are working together smoothly and making progress on the project. (A) will tell you how often students contribute to the project. However, it will not indicate if the contribution was appropriate or if learning is occurring. (B) will give a clear picture of the students' responses to the affective domain of group work but will not give information about cognitive learning. (C) will give information about the project's effectiveness from an adult's perspective and the adult's perceptions of the project's effectiveness with children.

48. **A** Response (A) gives Susan's mother real tasks to allow increased involvement, which is what she wants. It also provides Ms. Biggs with more prep time and information she does not have access to because she does not see Susan outside school. Inviting Susan's mother into the classroom, as in (B), is appropriate for some reasons, but she should not act as an untrained observer of all the students. This role opens the door to several potential problems. Susan's altered behaviors caused by her mom being in the room are just one example. (C) and (D) will offend Susan's mother as they both clearly indicate that she should go home and leave Susan's education to the professionals. This incorrectly indicates that parental assistance and involvement are not needed to effectively educate a child.

49. **B** Responses (A), (C), and (D) are appropriate for effective teacher-made tests. However, the alignment in (B) is the most important and therefore it is the best response. Testing what and how you have taught is imperative for an accurate assessment of learning.

50. **A** The student receives negative feedback ahead of positive feedback, with no concrete suggestions for improvement. The initial negative comment may be as far as the student reads. So the student may miss the positive comment about a sophisticated writing style or interpret this comment as being a negative one because of the initial negative tone. (B), (C), and (D) assume the initial negative comment about clarity will be outweighed by the comment about a sophisticated writing style. No clear suggested changes are given in either (B) or (C). So the student may have no idea how to improve. This is not a time for student freedom, as suggested in (D), but for clear modeling of a better style.

51. **B** Only (B) invites families to participate rather than demand that they do so. It will receive a much more positive reaction from parents/guardians for this reason. Because (A) is so demanding, it should not occur, but the ideas expressed in (C) and (D) are appropriate to increase parents/guardians' understanding of an idea the teacher feels is important for enhanced student learning and also to encourage greater family participation.

52. **C** To ensure a productive conference, (C) is the best response as it allows the parent to share why a conference was requested. This response allows the parent to express concerns or ask for clarification. Listening calmly and respectfully shows respect, but perhaps not agreement, with the parent's thoughts. It also allows time for the teacher to compose a thoughtful response. In (A), (B), and (D), the teacher assumes he or she knows or can guess the reason the parent wanted a conference. The assumed reason may be accurate or it may be completely off base and needlessly open another area of concern. Find out what is on the parent's mind so that you can work together in the student's best interests.

53. **C** Parents will become defensive if they feel that their student or their family is being judged. This defensiveness will interfere with finding a solution to the difficulties being experienced by the student. (A) shifts all responsibility to the parents, and (B) shifts all responsibility to the teacher when a solution needs to be a joint effort among teacher, parents, and student. (D) does not acknowledge the greater knowledge a parent has about a student and ignores information that might be vital to understanding the reasons for the difficulties in school.

54. **A** Although (B), (C), and (D) all have value, they are details that can help support the desired partnership. (A) is also the only response that mentions an interaction between teachers and families, yet this interaction is a required attribute of a partnership.

55. **B** Ms. Garcia can be reached by phone to schedule a conference but may not want to come to the school. So conference by phone. The value lost by not conferencing face to face is outweighed by the value of having a conference. In (A), Ms. Ming attempts to make Ms. Garcia feel guilty as a motivation to attend the conference, yet she probably already feels badly about being asked to do something that is uncomfortable for her. (D) attempts to use Carmen to guilt Mrs. Garcia into participating. There are many reasons parents are reluctant to attend school meetings. Clothing, language difficulties, lack of confidence, and intimidation are a few. To set a child against a parent is unprofessional. (C) makes a negative and unwarranted judgment.

56. **B** This choice involves Molly in improving her time management skills. This response also does not expect Molly to make the change alone. It also does not remove the responsibility for the behavioral change from Molly and shift it to the parents and teacher, as in (A), (C), and (D).

57. **B** This choice gives Molly the responsibility for recording her arrival time and establishing a predictable pattern for weekly parent-teacher communication. (A) is inappropriate as it draws attention to Molly in a negative manner. (C) removes responsibility from Molly. Instead, it assigns all the responsibility to Mr. Blackwell and Molly's parents. (D) addresses the situation with all Mr. Blackwell's students. However, it does not encourage communication with Molly's parents. So they are left out of the process although they have expressed a desire to help Molly.

58. **B** This has the information most needed by the technology coordinator as he assists Ms. Wolf in planning a project that makes effective use of her students' present technological skills and also allows for improvement in their skill levels. (A), (C), and (D) all contain suggestions for sharing information that might be interesting to the technology director but is not imperative to allow him to assist Ms. Wolf in planning an effective project. If all her students had strong technological skills, this information would be important to ensure that the planned project will require an appropriate level of skills, but we know that the range is broad and so the project must also require a broad range of skills. The gaps in Ms. Wolf's technological skills can be addressed as she improves while helping her students with the project, but this is not a significant goal. Very likely, students with strong skills will help those who need assistance, and the technology director will be asked for help in solving major technological challenges that arise as the project progresses. The grouping of students is a minor consideration based on available technology and should be a joint decision.

59. **A** Mr. Grant needs to allow himself time to become a member of the community rather than act as an outside crusader who has arrived to solve problems the community has been unaware of or ignoring, which is the scenario depicted in (B), (C), and (D).

60. **C** Matt and his students will benefit from his staying up-to-date on research, trends, and issues. (A) and (B) are also true but are not as significant and as far-reaching as (C). (D) is also true, and Matt will find it time-saving, but the significance to his students falls behind that of (A) and (C).

61. **C** Only (C) addresses the remaining state standards for his content area as is required by state law. (A) and (B) are ways Mr. Jeremy might do this. However, staying focused, as in (C), is needed even to blend the lessons or team with his mentor. The group work suggested in (D) is another way Mr. Jeremy can address state standards with his class. However, his groups will function better if they are not ability groups.

62. **D** This selection directly responds to the required IEP for students with disabilities. It also creates a partnership between the classroom teacher and the special education resource team leader to best meet the learning and disability needs of Miranda. (A) and (C) are inappropriate because they ask the special education teacher to be involved with the mathematics content rather than with addressing the special needs of the student. (B) is incorrect. Although it does involve the special education teacher in suggesting physical space changes, it does not address Miranda's IEP requirements.

63. **B** State law requires that persons who have reasonable suspicion of child abuse are to report, within 48 hours of the reasonable suspicion, to the official state authorities. (A), (C), and (D) all suggest actions other than the official legal requirement.

64. **D** School equipment is purchased with school funds to be used to conduct school business. It does not matter if the school business is conducted on or off

campus or during school hours or outside school hours. The ethical and legal position is that school equipment should be used only for school business, which eliminates (A), (B), and (C).

65. **D** This choice describes a situation where it is unethical to perform a consulting job because a school laptop was used to write the curriculum for the school at the school's request. This means the curriculum belongs to the district and cannot be used for personal gain such as the consulting fee. This is true whether or not the chair was paid by the district. Nothing in (A), (B), and (C) is unethical. They each give information on the development. The department chairperson worked alone and did the planning work for a specific population of students. Basing a presentation on the responses of these students that can be ethically given is also acceptable.

66. **D** Assisting students with questions about vocabulary during the TAKS is unethical. Teachers may not read the TAKS questions during testing nor prompt students on how to answer a question or code an answer. (A), (B), and (C) are all appropriate ways to help students learn how to succeed on the TAKS before the exam. All assessments should not model the TAKS format, but there should be sufficient practice with it for students to be comfortable.

67. **A** Parents/guardians must give written permission before a teacher or school can seek testing or an evaluation for special education services. (B), (C), and (D) all give steps and procedures that must be taken before evaluating a student. However, these steps need to come after contacting parents and gaining their written permission.

68. **D** Students can interact very differently with individual teachers based on many factors such as respect, classroom control, and an endless variety of other reasons such as students feeling confident or defeated. Also, individual teachers have differing expectations and set different standards for grades. (A) may be true also, but there are other reasons for minor fluctuations, as noted in (D). Rather than being inflated, as indicated in (B), grades collected over an extended period of time can be very stable although individual assignment grades might fluctuate widely based on outside events impacting a student's efforts and participation. The more assignments used to assign a grade, the less impact a few wide variations will have. (C) states the myth that males and females vary in their abilities to learn science. The variation sometimes seen is more dependent on interest, effort, and societal expectations than on gender.

69. **A** The reaction most likely to be produced by this interaction is (A). Ms. Alvarez questioned the students in a group with a limited explanation of why she was doing so. They are doing well now and wonder about her interest in their past. They were embarrassed in front of their peers. If the students do give philosophical thought to their academic efforts, as in (B), they will know exactly who planted the idea because in her last statement Ms. Alvarez asked them to continue to think about this issue. Ms. Alvarez was trying to produce the results in (C) and (D) but was not successful.

70. **C** Very specific criteria are in place regarding student confidentiality. (A), (B), and (D) may have occurred during this conference. These results were unwise and unnecessary but not unexpected because of the way the meeting was structured. Violating student confidentiality is Ms. Alvarez's biggest problem although there could be negative repercussions from these students as a result of her thoughtlessness.

71. **A** Although Ms. Alvarez may not live in the school's neighborhood, a factory closing will have a financial impact on many of the local families and this will be seen at school. This information should come from the news and from awareness of the community in which you teach rather than from questioning students as suggested in (B), which would be perceived as nosiness and intrusiveness. (C) is good, but there are many problems families face that the school cannot help with. Liset can be guided toward effective ways to locate possible scholarships and how to apply for them, but the school has no money to assist any of the families facing financial problems. (D) is true but is not directly related to the second meeting with Liset.

72. **B** This choice includes both Liset and her mother in the planning discussion. (C) leaves Liset, who is most affected, out of the process. Suggesting that Ms. Jordan seek employment is also out of line. There are many reasons why this may not be desirable or possible for her. The suggestion in (A) must be handled very tactfully so that pride is not injured or offense taken. At this point Ms. Alvarez's record for being tactful is not strong. (D) offers Liset either a platitude or a gift of grades, which are inappropriate and possibly undeliverable, rather than constructive assistance.

73. **B** This is the greatest benefit for Hung. (A) indicates that this encounter has given Hung multiple problem-solving skills rather than just one. Yet using one successfully does much for Hung's resiliency. Hopefully this is not the first connection he has seen between information learned in school and daily life, as indicated in (C). The self-reflection mentioned in (D) is accurate, but the risk taking is not. And the first time Hung met with Ms. Alvarez didn't sound like a safe environment.

74. **D** The first strategy Ms. Alvarez should try is working with Steve and other school personnel to diagnose and solve whatever problem is causing the new behaviors. This needs to occur before she involves Steve's parents, as in (C). Telling Steve's family he is using drugs with no supporting documentation is sure to destroy any trust in or respect for her that either Steve or his family has ever had. He may have been spending time with a hospitalized relative after school, which would also account for her observations. The accusation in (A) might shock Steve, but shock is not an especially helpful approach to problem solving. The hectoring and judgmental tone of (B) is also sure to irritate Steve rather than invite his confiding in her. Again, she is not using good judgment in her student interactions.

75. **B** Ms. Page expanded on George's example to help students focus on exactly what the problem is so they will be ready to brainstorm possible solutions. (A)

and (D) imply there is a correct answer or solution, which is not the case. Students do need to stay focused on a problem and not be distracted by parallel or divergent situations. (C) suggests that George has a solution and that they should try to duplicate this.

76. **A** Ms. Page has encouraged her students to tackle the impact of one or more fifth graders on water conservation. The issue is real. Possible solutions will be varied and will require the students to apply problem-solving skills. (B) focuses the discussion on student-initiated questions related to school content. Although this is important, it is not as important as (A). (C) will be a result of the discussion and follow-up tasks. The learning is moved out of the traditional classroom instructional style. The students have some knowledge of water conservation from prior experiences. (D) is inaccurate. Ms. Page did not provide factual information, and nothing indicates she plans a future unit on personal responsibilities.

77. **A** If Ms. Page had been unwilling to allow the discussion to continue and had not been open to student-initiated directions, she would have lost a teachable moment. That teachable moment could result in a more powerful learning experience for her students than originally planned. (B) is not an accurate statement. Ms. Page could adjust for the shift in the time allocation in several ways. She could "return" time to the next subject tomorrow by using some science time or could integrate the two subjects in the direction students want. (C) implies that the students and Ms. Page have collaborated in distracting or off-task behaviors that block learning, which is not accurate. Ms. Page actually hopes that in the future, students will be so interested and excited by a lesson that they will again take an active role in directing the instructional goal. (D) indicates that although Ms. Page allowed and encouraged the discussion today, she has no plans to follow through on shifting the direction of the unit's focus. It suggests that science class will again be teacher-directed tomorrow, which might close the door on a wonderful teachable moment.

78. **C** Decision making increases student ownership and retention. (A) might be a result of student involvement in discussions, designing, and planning but should not be the reason for student involvement. (B) and (D) could also be a result of student participation in discussions and planning. However, they more likely result from successful completion of the water conservation project.

79. **B** Although (B), (C), and (D) will all be outcomes of this class project, (B) is the most important outcome. A sense of purpose and place to impact global problems, as described in (B), will encourage students to attack a future problem using the skills identified in (C) and (D). (A) is an abdication of responsibility, as students are waiting for others to guide them through the steps to a single answer.

80. **D** The knowledge and skills students gain are the most important outcome. Students can use these skills in the future. (A), (B), and (C) all involve attitudes and skills students may gain while exploring the conservation issue. However,

the motivation to apply these attitudes and skills will be more important to the students in the future.

81. **B** Community volunteers will increase the sense of the school as a part of the community. Modeling behaviors we want students to replicate is also important. (A), (C), and (D) can result from having community volunteers in the classroom. However, there is no guarantee that any of these responses will occur. Some new perspectives might be shared, as in (A). However, the volunteers might restrict their interactions with students and work in the office or workroom most of the time. Some teachers will achieve more work given assistance, as indicated in (C), rather than working less or taking breaks. Some students may choose to act out more when a guest is present rather than act better, as indicated in (D).

82. **C** Parent/guardian volunteers need a place at the school where they feel comfortable as they do their tasks. It does not have to be exclusive to the volunteers but must be a place where they do not feel they are in the way or are intruding. The tasks they do need to clearly make a contribution, and it should be possible to perform some of the tasks outside school hours so that volunteers are not limited to those who do not work during the school day. Phone calls to arrange a field trip can be made from an office as easily as from the school. Preparing math manipulatives can be done in the evening after work and school. (A) provides the welcoming environment parent/guardian volunteers need but does not give them the guidance they require to be most helpful. A task a volunteer may see as needed may have a very low priority for the teachers. Teachers may have a greater need but hesitate to ask because they do not want to appear to be bossing the volunteer. (B) sounds like a room of volunteers sitting around waiting to be given a task, which is not a situation that would encourage volunteers to show up. Tasks need to be clearly thought out and communicated to the volunteers. Both teachers and volunteers need to know when the volunteers will be available and what they will be doing. The volunteers need to know and feel comfortable with the teachers they will be assisting, which does not mean that they will work with only one person or only in one classroom or only in the classrooms where their children are students as indicated in (D). Volunteers should always know how the tasks they are performing will benefit students.

83. **A** This choice gives all community members, not just parents/guardians, a valid reason to visit the school, which they will be curious about because it is new. It does not focus on which students have parents/guardians who participate and which do not. If the community members have a positive experience, they are much more likely to visit again. It also establishes communication pathways the community can watch for future announcements. (B) and (C) are more traditional and will draw the more active and confident parents/guardians to the school but not those who are shy or hesitant. A student whose parent/guardian falls into this reluctant group will not be able to earn bonus points and so will be penalized, which is not appropriate. (D) is the most traditional and is the hardest to do successfully. It is extremely time-consuming and should be used when there is a problem that must be addressed. When an individual conference

is called, the parents/guardians' schedule must be considered rather than demanding that the conference occur only during teacher planning times or during the school day, which might not match the parents/guardians' work day.

84. **D** Most public school and many private school classes are coed. Activities must be selected that appeal to both genders to motive all. (A) encourages and increases gender differences fostered by society and culture at a time when education is trying to decrease differentiated educational opportunities based on gender. (B) is guaranteed to cause management and discipline problems during classes. Planning for part of the student population to have a lower participation rate because of lower interest is poor planning and will produce negative consequences. The different rubrics for each gender mentioned in (C) are not a good idea as again it sets different expectations for performance based on gender. Performance should be evaluated based on effort and achievement.

85. **C** Establishing these routines and procedures early sets clear teacher expectations that students will follow them and be able to work independently. They also set clear standards regarding how this will happen without the teacher having to remind students of the same information daily. Students will know what is expected of them. This will free Ms. Landers to work with students who need assistance rather than having to constantly address behaviors with the entire class. This is the best of some good advice. (A), (B), and (D) each have a value and a flaw. Extreme care must be taken if (A) is used. It is a clear example of a teacher manipulating students and can backfire. Recognizing students who follow the routines is not the problem because students deserve praise for good behavior. Using them to encourage misbehaving students to improve their behaviors is effective with young students who have a strong interest in gaining the approval of an authority figure, but this effectiveness declines when dealing with adolescents who are more interested in gaining the approval of their peers. It is unlikely that adolescents will give an accurate weekly self-assessment, as indicated in (B). Self-assessments and peer assessments are both valuable, but weekly use can change this practice from a valuable strategy to a rubber-stamping of actions through overuse. (D) includes some strategies where student input is invaluable to help empower students; however, teachers, schools, and school districts set the grading scale. This is different than setting criteria for evaluation in a rubric, which is another area that can benefit from student input.

86. **B** As Ms. Landers empowers students, they will respond positively. Knowing what to expect and that individual teacher assistance is available is the opposite of (A). Changes made arbitrarily and regularly will be counterproductive. However, adolescents respond to changes in routines made for a valid reason and that are explained to them. (C) and (D) imply that the students are without teacher supervision or interaction, which is not the case, but instruction does not occur at the same pace for all students daily, which should be a motivator for students of this age who sometimes feel they have no control.

87. **C** This choice will most likely produce constructive and positive interactions. If students are not sure what is expected, they will be confused and unable to

provide effective feedback for their peers. Modeling is an effective way to increase clarity of a new skill. Seeing appropriate techniques modeled will be much more effective than hearing them explained or reading about them. Role playing is also effective. (A) is inappropriate. Students should not be setting the criteria unless it is done by the entire class with teacher guidance. (B) is counterproductive to having students working together. Peer supervision and support can ensure a greater chance of learning a skill correctly. (D) will not be as productive as (C), although mixed-ability groups are desirable.

88. **C** The most important benefit, meeting the instructional needs of individual students, is given in (C). The wide range of resources allows individual students to select resources that are of high interest, which is a motivator and also allows them to work using their preferred learning styles. (A) assumes that a variety of resources ensures that students are thinking at a higher level, which is not a valid assumption. Many young students simply copy from a source as they begin to learn research skills. There is no indication of how these students use these resources. They may be operating at a higher level but can just as easily still be functioning at a lower level. Altering the resources does not automatically alter the level of thinking. (B) is correct but is less important and is a by-product of (C). The sense of accomplishment that individual students feel from successfully using these varied resources to complete their research results from successfully meeting individual student needs. (D) may or may not be true. Some students might work as a group by sharing resources. However, group work was not indicated. Additionally, many resources are available that students could use individually.

89. **A** This is the best way for Ms. Reynolds to facilitate her students' work during these days. Creating bookmarks allows students to move on and off computers without fear of losing information. Having to take notes from each site, as indicated by (B), keeps a computer tied up with one student while another waits. The printing suggested by (C) uses a lot of paper and ink for information a student may or may not need later as they locate other helpful sites. (D) does not fit the task Ms. Reynolds has set for the class. She might later want the students to design a web quest as a way of sharing their research, but at this time her goal is to have students learn to use varied resources to conduct research.

90. **D** It is very similar to (C) but is stronger because it has Ms. Reynolds instructing Susan rather than doing the task for her. It would be faster for Ms. Reynolds to show Susan what to do in this situation, but by doing rather than teaching, she establishes a pattern where she will again have to show her what to do the next time this problem occurs. Fourth-grade students learn better by doing rather than by watching, as they are concrete learners. (A) will not be helpful as changing search engines without changing search terms is as likely to increase as to reduce the number of hits. (B) is also a problem. If Susan conducts a search within a search without narrowing her search terms she is likely to get the same results.

Suggested Websites for Studying the PPR Competencies

The following websites are suggested for your further study. This list is in no way intended to be exhaustive. A simple search engine review of particular topics would yield a wealth of sites. This list is to get you started on searching the Internet for additional information. Every effort has been made to provide accurate and current Internet information. However, one of the benefits of the Internet is the ease with which it changes. Some of these Internet addresses will inevitably change and therefore may not be available when you attempt to access them.

Texas Education Law & Rules
   http://ritter.tea.state.tx.us/educationlaw.html

Effective Teaching Strategies
   http://www.teachervision.fen.com/teaching-methods/pro-dev/2936.html

Texas Education Network
   (For useful, current resources for the Texas education community)
   http://www.tenet.edu/

Texas Education Agency
   http://www.tea.state.tx.us/

Texas Essential Knowledge and Skills (TEKS)
   http://list.tetn.net/teks/

State Board for Educator Certification (SBEC)
   http://www.sbec.state.tx.us

Special Education in Texas
   http://www.tea.state.tx.us/special.ed/

Links to summaries of 50 major educational theories about learning and instruction
   http://tip.psychology.org/theories.html

St. John's University and Its Center for the Study of Learning and Teaching Styles
   http://www.learningstyles.net/

Information on learning styles, style inventories, and resources for teachers
http://www.ldrc.ca/projects/projects.php?id=26

Gardner's theory of multiple intelligences
http://www.edwebproject.org/edref.mi.intro.html

Research, practices, and activities for moral development and character education
http://tigger.uic.edu/~lnucci/MoralEd/

Links for information on critical thinking
http://www.middleweb.com/crithinklnks.html

Links to how-to guides on classroom management
http://www.teachnet.com/how-to/index.html#Classroom

Code of Ethics and Standard Practices for Texas Educators
www.tcta.org/capital/sbec/codeapproved.htm

Suggested Printed Resources and References

Bandura, A. (1986). *Social foundations of thought and action: A social cognitive theory.* Englewood Cliffs, NJ: Prentice Hall.

Burden, P. R. (2003). *Classroom management: Creating a successful learning community* (2nd ed.). New York: John Wiley & Sons.

Caine, R., and G. Caine. (1997). *Education on the edge of possibility.* Alexandria, VA: Association for Supervision and Curriculum Development.

Cairn, R., and S. Cairn. (1999). Service learning makes the grade. *Educational Leadership* 56(6):66–68.

Campbell, L., B. Campbell, and D. Dickinson. (1996) *Teaching and learning through multiple intelligences.* Needham Heights, MA: Allyn & Bacon.

Cangelosi, J. S. (2004). *Classroom management strategies: Gaining and maintaining students' cooperation.* Hoboken, NJ: John Wiley & Sons.

Charles, C. M. (2000). *Synergetic classroom: Joyful teaching and gentle discipline.* Reading, MA: Addison Wesley Longman.

Druin, A., and C. Solomon. (1996). *Designing multimedia environments for children.* New York: John Wiley & Sons.

Emmer, E. G., et al. (1999). *Classroom management for elementary teachers* (5th ed.). Needham Heights, MA: Allyn & Bacon.

Emmer, T. E., et al. (1999). *Classroom management for secondary teachers* (5th ed.). Needham Heights, MA: Allyn & Bacon.

Gardner, H. (1993). *Multiple intelligences: The theory in practice.* New York: Basic Books.

Good, T. L., and J. E. Brophy. (2000). *Looking in classrooms* (8th ed.). Needham Heights, MA: Allyn & Bacon.

Jensen, E. (1998). *Teaching with the brain in mind.* Alexandria, VA: Association for Supervision and Curriculum Development.

Johnson, D. W., R. T. Johnson, and E. J. Holubec. (1994). *The new circles of learning: Cooperation in the classroom.* Edina, MN: Interaction Book Company.

Jones, V. F., and L. S. Jones. (2001). *Comprehensive classroom management: Creating communities of support and solving problems* (6th ed.). Needham Heights, MA: Allyn & Bacon.

Payne, R. (2005). *A Framework for Understanding Poverty*, (4th ed.). Highlands, TX: aha! Process, Inc.

Wiggins, G. and McTighe, J. (2006). *Understanding by Design* (expanded 2nd ed.). Upper Saddle River, NJ: Pearson Education.

Wright, J. L., and D. Shade. (1994). *Young children: Active learners in a technological age*. Washington, DC: National Association for the Education of Young Children.

Code of Ethics and Standard Practices for Texas Educators

TEXAS ADMINISTRATIVE CODE

TITLE 19	EDUCATION
PART 7	STATE BOARD FOR EDUCATOR CERTIFICATION
CHAPTER 247	EDUCATORS' CODE OF ETHICS
RULE §247.2	**Code of Ethics and Standard Practices for Texas Educators**

(a) Statement of Purpose. The Texas educator shall comply with standard practices and ethical conduct toward students, professional colleagues, school officials, parents, and members of the community and shall safeguard academic freedom. The Texas educator, in maintaining the dignity of the profession, shall respect and obey the law, demonstrate personal integrity, and exemplify honesty. The Texas educator, in exemplifying ethical relations with colleagues, shall extend just and equitable treatment to all members of the profession. The Texas educator, in accepting a position of public trust, shall measure success by the progress of each student toward realization of his or her potential as an effective citizen. The Texas educator, in fulfilling responsibilities in the community, shall cooperate with parents and others to improve the public schools of the community.

(b) Enforceable Standards.

(1) Professional Ethical Conduct, Practices and Performance.
- (A) Standard 1.1. The educator shall not knowingly engage in deceptive practices regarding official policies of the school district or educational institution.
- (B) Standard 1.2. The educator shall not knowingly misappropriate, divert, or use monies, personnel, property, or equipment committed to his or her charge for personal gain or advantage.
- (C) Standard 1.3. The educator shall not submit fraudulent requests for reimbursement, expenses, or pay.

    (D) Standard 1.4. The educator shall not use institutional or professional privileges for personal or partisan advantage.

    (E) Standard 1.5. The educator shall neither accept nor offer gratuities, gifts, or favors that impair professional judgment or to obtain special advantage. This standard shall not restrict the acceptance of gifts or tokens offered and accepted openly from students, parents, or other persons or organizations in recognition or appreciation of service.

    (F) Standard 1.6. The educator shall not falsify records, or direct or coerce others to do so.

    (G) Standard 1.7. The educator shall comply with state regulations, written local school board policies, and other applicable state and federal laws.

    (H) Standard 1.8. The educator shall apply for, accept, offer, or assign a position or a responsibility on the basis of professional qualifications.

(2) Ethical Conduct Toward Professional Colleagues.

    (A) Standard 2.1. The educator shall not reveal confidential health or personnel information concerning colleagues unless disclosure serves lawful professional purposes or is required by law.

    (B) Standard 2.2. The educator shall not harm others by knowingly making false statements about a colleague or the school system.

    (C) Standard 2.3. The educator shall adhere to written local school board policies and state and federal laws regarding the hiring, evaluation, and dismissal of personnel.

    (D) Standard 2.4. The educator shall not interfere with a colleague's exercise of political, professional, or citizenship rights and responsibilities.

    (E) Standard 2.5. The educator shall not discriminate against or coerce a colleague on the basis of race, color, religion, national origin, age, sex, disability, or family status.

    (F) Standard 2.6. The educator shall not use coercive means or promise of special treatment in order to influence professional decisions or colleagues.

    (G) Standard 2.7. The educator shall not retaliate against any individual who has filed a complaint with the SBEC under this chapter.

(3) Ethical Conduct Toward Students.

    (A) Standard 3.1. The educator shall not reveal confidential information concerning students unless disclosure serves lawful professional purposes or is required by law.

    (B) Standard 3.2. The educator shall not knowingly treat a student in a manner that adversely affects the student's learning, physical health, mental health, or safety.

    (C) Standard 3.3. The educator shall not deliberately or knowingly misrepresent facts regarding a student.

    (D) Standard 3.4. The educator shall not exclude a student from participation in a program, deny benefits to a student, or grant an advantage to a student on the basis of race, color, sex, disability, national origin, religion, or family status.

(E) Standard 3.5. The educator shall not engage in physical mistreatment of a student.

(F) Standard 3.6. The educator shall not solicit or engage in sexual conduct or a romantic relationship with a student.

(G) Standard 3.7. The educator shall not furnish alcohol or illegal/unauthorized drugs to any student or knowingly allow any student to consume alcohol or illegal/unauthorized drugs in the presence of the educator.

Source Note: The provisions of this §247.2 adopted to be effective March 1, 1998, 23 Tex. Reg. 1022; amended to be effective August 22, 2002, 27 Tex. Reg. 7530

Texas Professional Standards for Teachers

TEXAS TEACHER PROFICIENCIES

These proficiencies guide preservice preparation, professional development, and teacher appraisal practices for teachers in Texas. **Source:** *State Board for Educator Certification, Revised 1997* (www.sbec.state.tx.us)

LEARNER-CENTERED KNOWLEDGE

The teacher possesses and draws on a rich knowledge base of content, pedagogy, and technology to provide relevant and meaningful learning experiences for all students.

The teacher exhibits a strong working knowledge of subject matter and enables students to better understand patterns of thinking specific to a discipline. The teacher stays abreast of current knowledge and practice within the content areas, related disciplines, and technology; participates in professional developmental activities; and collaborates with other professionals. Moreover, the teacher contributes to the knowledge base and understands the pedagogy of the discipline.

As the teacher guides learners to construct knowledge through experiences, they learn about relationships among and within the central themes of various disciplines while also learning how to learn. Recognizing the dynamic nature of knowledge, the teacher selects and organizes topics so students make clear connections between what is taught in the classroom and what they experience outside the classroom. As students probe these relationships, the teacher encourages discussion in which both the teacher's and the students' opinions are valued. To further develop multiple perspectives, the teacher integrates other disciplines, learners' interests, and technological resources so that learners consider the central themes of the subject matter from as many different cultural and intellectual viewpoints as possible.

LEARNER-CENTERED INSTRUCTION

To create a learner-centered community, the teacher collaboratively identifies needs; and plans, implements, and assesses instruction using technology and other resources.

The teacher is a leader of a learner-centered community, in which an atmosphere of trust and openness produces a stimulating exchange of ideas and mutual respect.

The teacher is a critical thinker and problem solver who plays a variety of roles when teaching. As a coach, the teacher observes, evaluates, and changes directions and strategies whenever necessary. As a facilitator, the teacher helps students link ideas in the content area to familiar ideas, to prior experiences, and to relevant problems. As a manager, the teacher effectively acquires, allocates, and conserves resources. By encouraging self-directed learning and by modeling respectful behavior, the teacher effectively manages the learning environment so that optimal learning occurs.

Assessment is used to guide the learner community. By using assessment as an integral part of instruction, the teacher responds to the needs of all learners. In addition, the teacher guides learners to develop personally meaningful forms of self-assessment.

The teacher selects materials, technology, activities, and space that are developmentally appropriate and designed to engage interest in learning. As a result, learners work independently and cooperatively in a positive and stimulating learning climate fueled by self-discipline and motivation.

Although the teacher has a vision for the destination of learning, students set individual goals and plan how to reach the destination. As a result, they take responsibility for their own learning, develop a sense of the importance of learning for understanding, and begin to understand themselves as learners. The teacher's plans integrate learning experiences and various forms of assessment that take into consideration the unique characteristics of the learner community. The teacher shares responsibility for the result of this process with all members of the learning community.

Together, learners and teachers take risks in trying out innovative ideas for learning. To facilitate learning, the teacher encourages various types of learners to shape their own learning through active engagement, manipulation, and examination of ideas and materials. Critical thinking, creativity, and problem solving spark further learning. Consequently, there is an appreciation of learning as a life-long process that builds a greater understanding of the world and a feeling of responsibility toward it.

EQUITY IN EXCELLENCE FOR ALL LEARNERS

The teacher responds appropriately to diverse groups of learners.

The teacher not only respects and is sensitive to all learners but also encourages the use of all their skills and talents. As the facilitator of learning, the teacher models and encourages appreciation for students' cultural heritage, unique endowments, learning styles, interest, and needs. The teacher also designs learning experiences that show consideration for these student characteristics.

Because the teacher views differences as opportunities for learning, cross-cultural experiences are an integral part of the learner-centered community. In addition, the teacher establishes a relationship between the curriculum and community cultures. While making this connection, the teacher and students explore attitudes that foster unity. As a result, the teacher creates an environment in which learners work cooperatively and purposefully using a variety of resources to understand themselves, their immediate community, and the global society in which they live.

LEARNER-CENTERED COMMUNICATION

While acting as an advocate for all students and the school, the teacher demonstrates effective professional and interpersonal communication skills.

As a leader, the teacher communicates the mission of the school with learners, professionals, families, and community members. With colleagues, the teacher works to create an environment in which taking risks, sharing new ideas, and innovative problem solving are supported and encouraged. With citizens, the teacher works to establish strong and positive ties between the school and the community.

Because the teacher is a compelling communicator, students begin to appreciate the importance of expressing their views clearly. The teacher uses verbal, nonverbal, and media techniques so that students explore ideas collaboratively, pose questions, and support one another in their learning. The teacher and students listen, speak, read, and write in a variety of contexts; give multimedia and artistic presentation; and use technology as a resource for building communication skills. The teacher incorporates techniques of inquiry that enable students to use different levels of thinking.

The teacher also communicates effectively as an advocate for each learner. The teacher is sensitive to concerns that affect learners and takes advantage of community strengths and resources for learners' welfare.

LEARNER-CENTERED PROFESSIONAL DEVELOPMENT

The teacher, as a reflective practitioner dedicated to all students' success, demonstrates a commitment to learn, to improve the profession, and to maintain professional ethics and personal integrity.

As a learner, the teacher works within a framework of clearly defined professional goals to plan for and profit from a wide variety of relevant learning opportunities. The teacher develops an identity as a professional, interacts effectively with colleagues, and takes a role in setting standards for teacher accountability. In addition, the teacher uses technological and other resources to facilitate continual professional growth.

To strengthen the effectiveness and quality of teaching, the teacher actively engages in an exchange of ideas with colleagues, observes peers, and encourages feedback from learners to establish a successful learning community. As a member of a collaborative team, the teacher identifies and uses group processes to make decisions and solve problems.

The teacher exhibits the highest standard of professionalism and bases daily decisions on ethical principles. To support the needs of learners, the teacher knows and uses community resources, school services, and laws relating to teacher responsibilities and student rights. Through these activities, the teacher contributes to the improvement of comprehensive educational programs as well as programs within specific disciplines.

Legislative Mandates and Education Codes

APPENDIX

Teaching in Texas requires that you know the education codes that direct teacher behaviors. The following items are certainly not all-inclusive of the federal and state legislative mandates or the Texas education codes but are presented here solely to help you recognize that there are many regulations governing the educational process. You are encouraged to access a Texas law book that has a section on school law and to search the Internet for more information about the education codes and state regulations related to education. The following general comments can be made.

- The local school board has the responsibility and authority for ensuring that the district conforms to the state guidelines and regulations.
- The board has the authority to hire and dismiss teachers and administrators.
- The state delegates power to the board to see that the district is properly run.
- The board appoints the superintendent, and the superintendent is the executive officer.
- The district may search students' lockers with probable cause. Lockers, desks, and all other equipment in the school are the property of the school; therefore, they do not carry privacy rules that might apply to students' personal property.
- Campuses have the right to what is called site-based decision making. This allows the principal and the teachers to make decisions about textbooks, hiring of new teachers, scheduling of professional development (in some cases), and other elements that have to do with the efficient and effective running of the school.
- All students and all teachers have the right to due process. This ensures that there are required procedures in place that safeguard people against arbitrary, capricious, or unreasonable policies, practices, or actions.
- The federal Family Rights and Privacy Act provides parents the right to view their child's educational records. Students older than 18 years of age may execute this same right.
- The State Board for Educator Certification (SBEC) can suspend or cancel a teacher's certificate for violation of state laws or for the violation of the Code of Ethics, being unworthy to teach, or for abandonment of the contract.
- Teachers can be dismissed for cause for immorality, incompetence, or insubordination. Due process must be followed in such cases.
- Each district must have in place a discipline management plan. This plan must be received and signed by parents. Included in this plan are the strategies that will be used for addressing inappropriate behaviors.

- Districts must provide an identified number of days for instruction plus an identified number of days for staff development and teacher planning.
- Teachers must follow all the rules of administering state-mandated standardized tests. Careful adherence to the protocol for the standardization must be assured. Teachers must not guide students to correct answers in any way during the administration of the state exams.
- A teacher must report reasonable suspicion of child abuse to the appropriate law enforcement agency within 48 hours of the reasonable suspicion. Knowing of such abuse and failing to report it constitute a Class B misdemeanor. Simply reporting to a school authority is not sufficient. As soon as possible after making the report to the official state authority, let your school administrator(s) know.
- Public Law 94-553 is the copyright law that must be followed. Be sure to stay current with rules regarding electronic information. Teachers are allowed some copying privileges solely for the purpose of instruction; however, you must know what the limitations of those permissions are. Copyright laws also apply to computer technology, as in the case of copying or sharing software. Any public library can provide you a copy of the latest version of copyright laws as they apply to educational purposes.

Glossary of Terms

The following terms are defined for your study to ensure that you know the language of the education profession. Terms can be used within the text of this study guide or are presented here because of their application to the Texas PPR examinations. Review these terms until you have a working knowledge of their meaning and can use them in the context of a classroom setting.

academic year – the time between the start and end of the official school calendar

accommodation – an adaptation or adjustment made to address needs; in Piagetian terms, when learners do not have sufficient prior knowledge for ease of learning, schema accommodations must be made for the new concepts to be understood

accountability – being held responsible for what does or does not happen; on a high-stakes test like the TAKS, teachers are held accountable for student learning

administrator – any state-certified person who leads the school, such as the principal or assistant principal

admission, review, dismissal committee (ARD) – (1) a committee of teachers and experts who design and oversee an inclusion student's IEP; (2) a university committee that oversees and guides preservice teachers through challenges and problems that potentially impact their future success as teachers

alternative certification – accepted and approved alternative pathway to state certification; it may be offered by universities, school districts, region service centers, or private entrepreneurs and is designed to prepare for certification any person who earned a bachelor's degree in an area other than teacher education

assimilation – new information is taken in or absorbed and blended with existing schema/prior knowledge in a way that makes sense of the new

basic human needs – required for survival and development; physiological (food, shelter, temperature regulation), safety (sociable, predictability, environmental security), belonging (affection, attention, relationships), self-esteem (power, freedom, acceptance)

beginning teacher – in Texas, any person in a first-year teaching assignment or any teacher who has less than three years of teaching experience; such persons must be provided a mentor teacher, especially during their first year

behavioral objectives – state the nature and degree of a measurable performance expected for a specified instructional outcome

bilingual education – teaching strategies and approaches used to educate students who speak a primary language other than English; targeted programs for English language learners who have limited English proficiency

concrete operational – Piagetian developmental level occurring from about age 7 to age 11; first organized system of logical thought in mental development; requires the use of models or manipulatives for ease of learning

cooperative learning – students working together in groups to support each other as they achieve learning goals; several formats exist such as jigsaw, student teams, and achievement division

creative thinking – thought processes showing unique problem identification, hypothesis formation, and/or solution evaluation patterns; brings new perspectives and approaches to a situation

criterion-referenced test – assessment of performance in terms of behaviors expected with a given score

critical thinking – an instructional approach intended to assist students in evaluating the worth of ideas, opinions, or evidence before making a decision or judgment

culture – characteristic features or behaviors typical of a group

deductive logic – flows from the general/whole to the specific/parts; the conclusion follows from the stated premise or known element

disequilibrium – to unbalance; to cause a questioning of prior beliefs; according to Piaget, learning occurs at the point of disequilibrium

diversity – having differences, especially differences that can impact the ability to learn such as low socioeconomic status or gifted cognitive ability; also cultural variances that indicate diverse ways of knowing, unique ways of perceiving, or particular ways of communicating

due process – procedural steps to protect a person's constitutional right to receive fair and equitable treatment and protection under the law

egocentric – self-centered; indifferent to or unaware of others; a young child's *inability* to shift into or see another's point of view

English as a second language (ESL) – students whose native language is other than English; initially, ESL learners may have difficulty understanding or using English in the classroom setting

ethnicity – sharing common and distinctive traits with a large group of people based on culture, religion, language, customs, background, allegiance

formative evaluation – assessments or checks for understanding that occur during the teaching and learning process; assists with planning decisions such as whether to continue forward or to regroup and reteach

hidden curriculum – components of teaching and learning that occur in schools, which are not a part of the explicit or formal curriculum; also called the *implicit* or *informal* curriculum

hierarchy of human needs – ordering of *basic human needs*; higher needs will be met only after lower ones are satisfied

highly qualified – a teacher who holds a baccalaureate degree, has achieved full state certification, and has demonstrated competency in the content areas that individual teaches

inclusion – a commitment to educate all children to the maximum extent appropriate within the regular school and classroom environment rather than in separate classes or institutions

individualized education plan (IEP) – an educational program management tool required by the Individuals with Disabilities Act; must indicate (1) current level of performance, (2) short- and long-term instructional objectives, (3) services to be provided, and (4) schedules and criteria for evaluation of progress

inductive logic – flows from the specific to the general

industry versus inferiority – Erickson's fourth level of psychosocial development of children; generally during 6–11 years of age; at this stage, children need to experience activities that result in their feeling that they are industrious, productive, and capable of performing up to expectations; if such experiences are not offered, children often develop attitudes and beliefs that they are inferior to others

integrated curriculum – curriculum that includes two or more content disciplines such as science and math through themes to coordinate timing of the overlap of instruction appropriate to both disciplines

interdisciplinary studies – also called *integrated curriculum*; curriculum that crosses at least two subject areas

internship – the period of time when a beginning teacher gains initial experience under the guidance and supervision of a mentor teacher; typically the first year of teaching

intradisciplinary studies – curriculum that includes two or more overlapping areas or connections within a content discipline such as subtraction and division in mathematics or biology and chemistry in science to establish relationships by coordinating instructional timing

learning disability – a condition that prevents students from learning to the potential indicated by their IQ; a mismatch between intelligence and performance

least restrictive environment (LRE) – a component of the Education for All Handicapped Children Act that requires that students with disabilities be provided opportunities to participate in regular education programs to the greatest extent appropriate

mainstreaming – attendance of special education students in regular education classes for at least part of the day while they continue to have access to additional programs, services, or classes as needed

manipulatives – concrete items used to assist students as they develop or learn a concept

mentoring – guiding a novice both professionally and personally; students may have mentors in upper grades—adults from the community or family members; beginning teachers are required by state law to have an assigned mentor to guide them and scaffold their initial teaching experience

metacognition – knowing about knowing; ways of organizing knowledge to make it easier to learn and remember based on our own learning and organization patterns; understanding how you think; monitoring your thinking processes

moral development – Kohlberg's six stages of children's moral beliefs and behaviors; stages range from no sense of right or wrong, to a "good girl/good boy" attitude, to following state rules, to considering the wants and needs of others, to taking a risk to change laws or rules that are not equitable to all people

multiple intelligences – theory of cognition developed by Howard Gardner that identifies at least eight dimensions of intellectual capacity used to approach problems and create products

multitasking – attending to more than one event at a time

norm-referenced test – assessment of performance in relation to the group used to establish the expected level of performance or *norm*; used in standardized testing; compares one student or group to another

performance assessment – assessment or evaluation based on a process or product rather than a test; focuses on what students can do; also called *authentic assessment*

portfolio – a collection of a person's work; samples used to indicate levels of performance on a task; useful in *authentic assessment*

preoperational stage – Piagetian stage of development from about age 2 to age 7; representational rather than logical thought characterized by egocentrism, lack of reversibility, lack of concern with proof or evidence

prior knowledge – knowing because of previous experiences

professional development – efforts made to improve the professional skills and competencies of faculty/staff; also *staff development* and *in-service development*

psychosocial development – Erikson's work on the developmental stages of children based on ability and style of resolving a problem besetting a child

reasonable suspicion – usually not "It crossed my mind to wonder" but rather sufficient indicators to prevent a questioning or concern from being laid to rest; in issues of child abuse, teachers must have reasonable suspicion that abuse is occurring before reporting the suspicion to legal authorities

reflective thinking – a habit of thoughtful and regular self-analysis; evaluating and examining the impact of self on others

ripple effect – an outbreak of contagious misbehavior often triggered by a teacher behavior, such as embarrassing a student, to which the others respond; may also be used for positive purposes, such as praising the choices of one student in a group in order to motivate other group members to behave in the same positive manner

scaffolding – providing assistance through structure, clue, or cues to remember or apply knowledge appropriately; a learner is near solving a problem, but needs help to complete the process

schema/schemata – an individual's knowledge structure; how information is stored and processed in memory; comprehension depends on integrating new knowledge with a network of prior knowledge

self-fulfilling prophecy – perceived expectation of behavior that results in that behavior; strongly connected to teacher expectations

self-monitoring – the conscious awareness of the progress of the individual on the task, whether that is the brain (thinking about thinking and learning or metacognition) or the body, within an environment

simulations – produces conditions and phenomena under test conditions, such as role-play, that are equivalent to actual events; may be used effectively to help learners understand others' points of view; also used in technology for examining "what if" situations

spiral curriculum – major themes or principles are first introduced and then reappear at another time and at a greater complexity or depth

strategic planning – developing an overall plan, such as school improvement, paired with action steps for moving the plan forward

summative evaluation – assessment that occurs at the end of an activity or instructional unit rather than during the lesson; can indicate a need to reteach rather than moving forward

tenure contract – protects from dismissal without probable cause; veteran teachers typically receive tenure contracts and are thus not dismissed unless with cause

term contract – may be dismissed without cause being indicated; a beginning teacher will be given a term contract

test bias – the ability/inability of a test to measure what is being measured in all populations—e.g., a test that is biased against one gender has test bias

test reliability – the ability of a test to measure consistently what it purports to measure at the same level of accuracy

test validity – the ability of the test to measure what it was intended to measure

withitness – the ability of a teacher to be aware of what is going on throughout the learning environment and to communicate this awareness nonverbally to students; useful in behavior management

Index